Passschendaele 1917

Passschendaele 1917

THE STORY OF THE FALLEN AND TYNE COT CEMETERY

Franky Bostyn

Kristof Blieck • Freddy Declerck • Frans Descamps • Jan Van der Fraenen

Pen & Sword
MILITARY

Introduction

On 12 July 2007 various heads of state and government leaders will be paying their respects at Tyne Cot Cemetery in Passchendaele, where they will be attending the official commemoration ceremony on the occasion of the 90th anniversary of an infamous battle which is officially known as the Third Battle of Ypres, but is mostly referred to as 'Passchendaele'. Passchendaele was one in a long series of abortive attempts to break through the stalemated Western Front in Flanders. After a hundred days of bloody fighting the offensive finally came to an end on 10 November 1917 atop the Mid West Flanders Ridge. The human toll in terms of killed, wounded and missing was enormous: 245,000 men of the British Imperial forces and 215,000 Germans in exchange for pushing the line forward barely eight kilometres. 'Passchendaele 1917' thus joined Verdun and the Somme in 1916 as bywords for slaughter in the history of the First World War on the Western Front.

On Anzac day 2004 a new military history museum was opened, in the Zonnebeke Chateau, devoted to the Battle of Passchendaele, which has since received over 135,000 visitors. In 2006 a second venue was added in the form of a new visitors centre located behind the famous Tyne Cot Cemetery. It was formally opened by Queen Elisabeth II and King Albert II of Belgium on 12 July 2007. The two sites are linked by the restored Ypres-Roulers railway, across which visitors can retrace the attack of 4 October 1917. These three projects were made possible thanks to the financial support received from Zonnebeke Town Council; the Province of West Flanders (Westtoer & the War and Peace in the Westhoek project); the Flemish Community (Toerisme Vlaanderen); the Europe Community (5B Phasing Out); and a private partner.

Passchendaele is a subject which has been repeatedly covered (and at great length) in the English-language historiography in the form of large-scale military analysis and in personal accounts. Yet surprisingly little has been written to date about the tens of thousands of men who died in the battle. How was it possible that so many men were killed? How were they buried and how have they been remembered up to the present day at Tyne Cot Cemetery? These two fundamental research questions have resulted in a two part book, which is based on two innovative projects in the area of biographical research: the Passchendaele Archives and the Tyne Cot Cemetery Inventarisation Project. In order to be as thorough as possible we were obliged to limit ourselves from the outset to the dead of what was then the British Empire: the United Kingdom itself (which at the time still included the present day Republic of Ireland), Canada, Australia, New Zealand and South Africa. We hope that, in the future, a similar research project can be set up to study the German dead and the specific problematics of the vanished cemeteries.

The Passchendaele Archives represent a unique memorial concept which sets out to restore faces to the names of the those killed at Passchendaele. For this reason we specifically concentrated on military personnel from the present Commonwealth countries who died in Flanders during – or due to the consequences of – the Battle of Passchendaele (July-November 1917) and of whom a photograph has been preserved. These photographs were located via three main channels. First of all, we began by going through several hundred hard to find 'Rolls of Honour', which were mostly published shortly after the war by town and village councils, companies and schools which included information (often accompanied by photographs) about 'their' war dead. We then went on to contact dozens of national and regimental museums. The most extensive collections of photographs of the fallen are those held by the Australian War Memorial and the Auckland Cenotaph, but among the other museums contacted we are very grateful to: the Military Intelligence Museum (Helen O'Hara); the Museum of Army Chaplaincy (David Blake); the Royal Irish Fusiliers Museum (Amanda Moreno); the Sherwood Foresters Collection (Cliff Housley); the Bedfordshire & Hertfordshire Regimental Association (Nigel Lutt); the Black Watch Regimental Museum; the Princess of Wales Own Regiment Military Museum (Al Lloyd); the Canadian Letters and Images Project (Stephen Davies); the Canadian Expeditionary Force Study Group; the 48th Highlanders Association (Tom Thompson); the Princess Patricia's Canadian Light Infantry Regimental Museum and Archives (Lynn Bullock); and the Saskatchewan Dragoons (Gerry Carline). The third – and certainly the most interesting – source of visual images came from the families of the war dead themselves, who were located by means of an extensive media campaign; questions put to visitors at the Memorial Museum reception desk; and via Internet. Our heartfelt thanks also go to Keith Perry, who very generously put all the photographic material he had collected for his book *With a Poppy and a Prayer: Officers died at Passchendaele* at our disposal. Marika Pirie, Dennis Otter and Avalon Eastman also did a magnificent job in researching dozens of photographs, often in old newspapers.This extensive gathering operation finally resulted in the creation of over 3,000 personal files, which were then supplemented with information from military service and red cross files of the men concerned; regimental accounts and war diaries; and data maintained by the Commonwealth War Graves Commission. For the practical implementation of this pictorial research we were able to take on an additional temporary member of staff thanks to a 'Cultural Heritage' project subsidy provided by the Flemish Minister of Culture.

The first part of the book follows the chronology of the Battle of Passchendaele itself. Each section begins with a brief historical overview of the stage of the campaign to be covered and then goes on to focus in detail on the experiences of one or two divisions. Telling all 3,000 personal stories of the combatants in context is an impossible task. We thus opted to tell some twenty stories for each stage of the battle as part of a single episode to be examined in depth. Project assistant Jan Van der Fraenen prepared the biographical files and sketched out the broad lines to be followed for each chapter. Assistance in photographing hundreds of service files at the National Archives in Kew was given by Geoff Baxter, Hans and Arnold Van der Fraenen, Johan Strobbe and Roger Hermans. The Society Passchendaele 1917 took charge of working up all the research into a finished text. Franky Bostyn was responsible for overall revision of the Dutch version with a lot of help from Freddy Declerck, who also wrote the section on the New Zealanders. Erwin Ureel did the chapter dealing with the Irish troops, Frans Descamps focused on the war in the air and Charlotte Cardoen chronicled the part played by the Royal Naval Division. Lieve Deprez, Dirk Ooghe, Jan Vancoillie, Ian Mac Henry and, above all, Bert Heyvaert made an important contribution in correcting the texts.

In the second part of the book, general editor Franky Bostyn, investigates what happened to the fallen of Passchendaele after the battle. This in fact became an extensive study of the largest and most visited cemetery on the Western Front: Tyne Cot Cemetery. New historical research was combined with an innovative project conducted by Frans Descamps, assisted by a number of volunteers. All the 12,000 graves were placed onto a series of manually created files, which Dany Titeca and Jeannine Desender then entered into a database, especially created for this purpose. This information was then combined with that obtained from the 'Burial Return Sheets' kept in Maidenhead, which indicate, for each of the graves concerned, where the mortal remains came from and how they were identified or proved unidentifiable. This is the first time that the Commonwealth War Graves Commission has made these exceptional documents available for the conduct of such a comprehensive study. We are very grateful for the help and cooperation received in Maidenhead from PR manager Peter Francis, archivist Roy Hemington and historian Julie Summers. Moreover, we were always able to put our numerous questions to the Northern Europe Office in Ypres and our thanks go to director Philip Noakes, staff workers Chris Farrell, Regine Huyghe, Christine Ketels and senior head gardener Callum Leggatt. We are also indebted to Commander Rob Troubleyn of the Belgian War

photo page 2: unburied body during the battle of Passchendaele , 1918 (Deraeve)

photo page 4: The Menin Road or Ypernstrasse at Gheluvelt, October 1917 (Deraeve)

Graves Bureau and Major-General Paul Stevens of the Office of Australian War Graves, and their respective staff for the large quantities of information they provided.

All the pictorial material collected was processed and described in the Memorial Museum itself by Kristof Blieck. Various maps were drawn by Jan De Leersnyder. Many of the illustrations used in this book came directly from family members of the Passchendaele war dead. Although they were not asked to send the originals, many of them did, as they felt it was more appropriate that their authentic memorabilia should be entrusted to the museum. A selection of the items thus donated are now on permanent display in the Tyne Cot Cemetery Visitors Centre. In addition to personal photographs of the fallen themselves, we also used photographic material from the Imperial War Museum (IWM, London); the Australian War Memorial (AWM, Canberra); the Canadian War Museum (CWM, Ottawa); the New Zealand Army Museum (NZAM, Caiouru); and the Commonwealth War Graves Commission (CWGC, Maidenhead).
We were also able to make use of the rich German photographic collection of Wilfried Deraeve (Oostnieuwkerke); Walter Lynneel's unique collection of obituary cards (Leffinge); and, with regard to post-war commemorations, the documentation held by Raoul Blanckaert-Carrein (Passchendaele).

We would also like to thank Emanuel David, Evelyne Osaer and Debbie Manhaeve, all members of the museum staff, for the extra work they took on during the editing phase. The English translation and revision of the first part of the book was provided by Accolade b.v.b.a (Richard Turner, Nuria Alvarez and Annie Goddaer) and for the second part of the book by Martin O'Connor. Thanks are also due to Jan Ingelbeen and his team at Roularta Book for the professional design, promotion and publication of this book. Finally, we owe a particular debt of gratitude to the commissioners of this book, Zonnebeke Town Council and, in particular, Mayor Dirk Cardoen, Alderman Franky Bryon and Secretary Francis Claeys who have been the driving forces behind this project. Their unconditional support for the Memorial Museum Passchendaele 1917 and their efforts on its behalf have been a determining factor in every aspect of the success of the past four years. Together with the museum team and the volunteers from the Society Passchendaele 1917 they have been the pillars of the commemoration programme 'Passchendaele, 90 years on'.

With this book, Zonnebeke Town Council, the Memorial Museum Passchendaele 1917 and Roularta Books hope, at all events, to have given an important impetus to the commemorations to be held from 12 July to 11 November 2007. We also hope to have made a lasting contribution to our understanding of the First World War in general and of the tragic fate of the fallen of Passchendaele, in particular.

FRANKY BOSTYN, *Curator Memorial Museum Passchendaele 1917*
12 July 2007

Summary

PART I The fallen of 1917

1917 was the bloodiest year of the First World War in Flanders. After the Somme in 1916, Passchendaele 1917 was to be yet another disaster for the troops of the British Empire. In one hundred days the armed forces of the present day Commonwealth countries sustained 245,000 casualties. One out of three were killed or died later of their wounds. How was it possible that so many lives were lost in so short a time? Based on the study of more than 3,000 individual cases, the 'Passchendaele Archives' project has arrived at new insights as to how a whole generation was lost. In the first part of the book we follow the chronology of the Battle of Passchendaele from July to November 1917. Each section begins with a brief historical overview and then goes on to focus in detail on the experiences of one or two divisions. Telling all 3,000 personal stories of the combatants, in context, is an impossible task, thus some twenty stories are told for each stage of the battle, as part of a single episode to be examined in depth. Seeing the battle from the perspective of the individual men who fought in it makes it possible, for the first time, to really understand what the Great War meant, here in Flanders, in terms of human suffering.

‹ *Dead Highlanders of the 9th Division before Zonnebeke, September 1917 (IWM Q11657)*

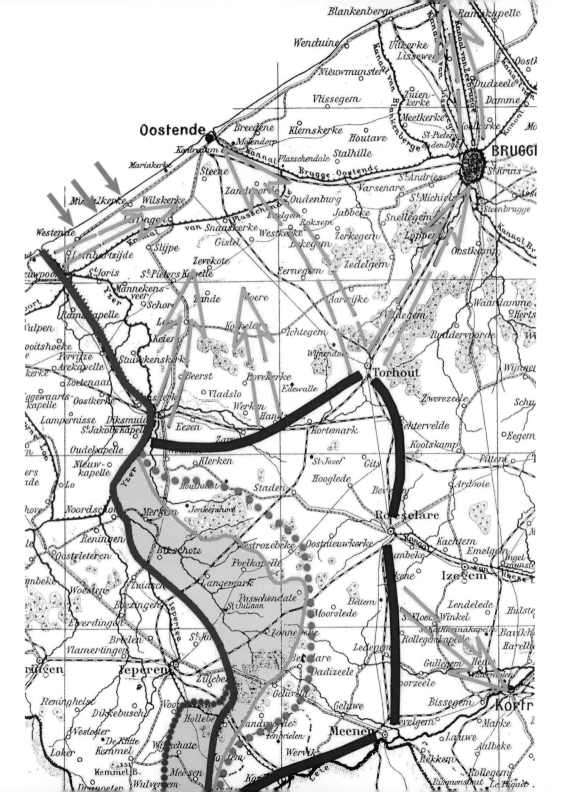

Map showing the plan of the offensive

- British front line prior to 7 June 1917
- British front line after 31 July 1917
- Phase 1 of the plan
- Phase 2 of the plan
- Phase 3 of the plan
- Landings during phase 3
- British front line November 1917

Haig's Flanders Offensive

In terms of strategy the fundamental problem of the First World War was the stagnated front in the west and the impossibility of achieving a breakthrough. The British Commander-in-Chief, Sir Douglas Haig, was firmly convinced that the deadlock on the Western Front could only be broken in Flanders. However, his plans for a major offensive on Flemish soil had to be shelved in the summer of 1916, when it became clear that the Germans were gradually exhausting the French at Verdun. The only alternative for the British was to relieve the pressure on their ally at Verdun by launching their own attack on the Somme. The Battle of the Somme ended without significant results and with the British Imperial Forces alone sustaining losses amounting to 420,000 killed, wounded and missing. In the spring of 1917 the French General Nivelle also became convinced that he could break the back of German resistance single-handedly by a major offensive that would, in only 24 hours, deal a decisive blow capable of turning the tables in favour of the allies for once and for all. Yet Nivelle's attack on the Chemin des Dames (April 1917) ended in yet another bloody débâcle. Nor had the war-weary French poilus forgotten the hell of Verdun, which was still all too fresh in their memory and a spate of mutinies shattered the morale of the French army. The French defence was at breaking point and it was only a matter of weeks before the Germans also realized this.

A second motivation behind Haig's plan for a major offensive in Flanders was that German U-boats – operating from bases on the German occupied Belgian coast – were playing havoc with British merchant shipping. By June 1917 enemy submarines were sinking one out of every four merchant ships headed for Britain and – in that month alone – the Merchant Navy's losses came to nearly half a million tons of shipping. Admiral Jellicoe, the British First Sea Lord, warned that if nothing was done to stop this, Britain would not have the supplies to go on fighting. Haig's plan thus also envisaged that a breakthrough on the Ypres front would be accompanied by an attack along the coast and amphibious landing operations at Ostend and Zeebruges to be carried out by the Royal Navy, thereby attacking the U-boat bases in these ports on three sides.

The most difficult operation in Haig's grand design was breaking through on the Ypres front and Haig entrusted this task to General Hubert Gough's Fifth Army. The most important obstacle was the Mid West Flanders Ridge, a line of low hills of between forty and sixty metres in height, running from Westrozebeke through Passchendaele, Broodseinde, Polygon and Gheluvelt, skirting around the villages of Zillebeke and Hollebeke, and on to Wytschaete and Messines, with a spur projecting in a southwesterly direction towards the 'mounts' of West Flanders. The line of this ridge determined the shape of the frontline from 1915 to 1917, which took on the form of an inverted letter 'S' with the Ypres Salient in the north and the Messines Ridge in the south.

Before any attack could be made on the Ypres front towards Roulers, the Salient to the south of it would first have to be straightened. For this purpose, from late 1915 onwards, special Tunnelling Companies had placed 24 powerful underground explosive mines under almost all the German forward positions in the Salient. 19 of these were eventually exploded on 7 June 1917. Almost half a million kilos of high explosive, mostly ammonal, created the largest man-made earthquake that the world had hitherto known. The confusion caused was so great that the Germans were driven out of Wytschaete and Messines in a matter of a few hours by Irish and New Zealand troops, respectively. A week later General Plumer's Second Army had completely straightened the British front line and the Germans had withdrawn to their third (Oosttaverne) line. The Battle of Messines-Wytschaete is generally regarded as one of the greatest military successes of the entire war. However, the fighting was over so quickly that the troops in the north were still not quite ready. This was a crucial mistake, as would become apparent later, as in the six full weeks which followed the Germans were able to completely reorganize themselves for the great *Abwehrschlacht* (defensive battle).

By September 1916 the German commanders in Flanders had firmly decided to adopt a system of defence in depth based on six lines of defence: the frontline; the *Albrecht-Stellung* (2nd line); the *Wilhelm-Stellung* (3rd line); *Flandern I* (4th line); *Flandern II* (5th line); and *Flandern III* (6th line). Interlaced between these six lines were various *Riegels*, connecting lines between the main defence lines from which, from which – in the event of an allied breakthrough – the allied assault troops could be attacked on their flanks. All these positions followed the heights of the Mid West Flanders Ridge. Scattered in between were hundreds of pillboxes, which were often built into pre-war constructions. In the *Flandern I-Stellung* the heavily-manned trenches were almost entirely replaced by strong concrete bunkers, most of which were proof against even the heaviest of artillery bombardments. So when the British artillery stopped their shelling and the infantry went over the top, the Germans merely clambered out of their bunkers, set up their machine guns and unleashed a murderous rain of bullets onto the advancing troops. The German defences were mainly concentrated on the *Wilhelm-Stellung* and *Flandern I*. The Allies never reached *Flandern II* while *Flandern III* was actually still under construction. In the spring of 1917 the Germans had plans

to build 1,540 additional concrete constructions around Gheluvelt alone.

On 13 June 1917 the Germans put Von Lossberg, their best defence specialist, to work on organizing the defence of the Fourth Army, reporting directly to Rupprecht von Bayern and the German Commander-in-Chief Erich Ludendorf. Every line had to be able to defend itself autonomously. In the event of an allied breakthrough the infantry could withdraw to the next line, from which an organized counter-attack should then be launched immediately in order to recapture the terrain ceded. In addition to a system which rotated first line troops and reserves, special *Eingreifdivisionen* (counter-attack divisions) were also created. In theory, these were supposed to be held out of range of the British field artillery, but had to be able to move up to their assembly points in the forward area within a few hours in order to launch counter-attacks.

Herbert Plumer and Hubert Gough, the commanders of the British Second and Fifth Armies respectively, had fundamentally different views on how a breakthrough could be achieved on the Ypres front. Plumer wanted a series of step-by-step attacks, each with a limited objective, while Gough favoured an attack en masse across the entire width of the front. Haig preferred Gough's grand schemes to Plumer's more cautious approach and chose Gough and his Fifth Army to spearhead the offensive. Haig and Gough were both cavalry officers and once the infantry had broken through on the ridge they intended to deploy the cavalry in order to push on to the Roulers-Torhout line. Further south, Plumer was told to be ready to take Menin and Kortrijk in the event of Gough's men penetrating the German lines. After a massive artillery bombardment, which was supposed to completely destroy the German defences, tens of thousands of infantrymen would immediately advance as far as the *Wilhelm-Stellung* and – with luck – perhaps even to just short of

Flandern I, where they expected to encounter the first genuine resistance. Of vital importance, at all events, was the capture of the high ground around Gheluvelt (known as the Gheluvelt Plateau), which jutted out towards the British line. This had to be taken before any advance could be made towards Passchendaele Ridge itself.

On 6 July the German commander Rupprecht von Bayern indicated that he was now ready for the impending British offensive. Due to a variety of problems the start date for the attack was repeatedly postponed until it was eventually set for 31 July 1917. This gave the Germans even more time to prepare their Abwehrschlacht. The British Engineers and Pioneers worked flat out to get all the materials that would later be needed in place. Everywhere the finishing touches were put to headquarters; tracks and narrow gauge railways were laid; bridges were built and supply dumps prepared. Of course, the Germans did not let them make all these preparations unhindered, of course. On 10 July they experimented for the first time with shells filled with mustard gas, known in German as *Gelbkreuz* ('yellow cross'). Two days later bombarded Ypres with mustard gas shells, giving rise to the other British name for mustard gas 'Yperite'. It was to be one of the most notorious weapons of the *Flandernschlacht* (Battle of Flanders). In all, the battle claimed 2,014 casualties – a great many of those from the 15th Division. Various sources thus rightly claim the 12 July 1917 as the unofficial starting date of the Battle of Passchendaele. Between 12 and 27 July 1917 Gough's Fifth Army lost 13,284 killed, wounded and missing, principally due to gas, airborne and artillery bombardments. For the attack itself Gough had eighteen divisions at his disposal, supported by three brigades of seventy-two tanks each. The right flank was covered by Plumer's Second Army with a further 12 divisions and four French divisions took charge of the left flank.

For their preparatory bombardments the British had put together the biggest collection of artillery batteries ever combined. The Fifth Army alone had over 2,229 artillery pieces, including: 752 heavy guns, 324 4.5 inch howitzers and 1,098 18 pounders. Together, in the two weeks prior to the attack of 31 July, they fired more than 4,200,000 projectiles onto the German positions – more than two and a half times as many as had been fired on the Somme the year before. These gargantuan bombardments destroyed the entire drainage system of the area causing some streams to overflow their banks by often as much as over 100 metres. Every house, tree or street was blown to pieces – nothing was left standing. In the space of two weeks the entire terrain between Ypres and Zonnebeke was converted into a pitiless, cratered landscape in which men, animals and machines were sucked into the earth and drowned. In the end the British bombardments were so destructive that they made the advance of their own troops across this totally devastated terrain almost impossible, while at the same time they were not precise enough to take out the Germans' concrete bunkers. When, on top of all this, it also began to rain, a human tragedy of epic proportions was almost unavoidable.

4 July 1917:
Lieutenant Lord Basil Temple-Blackwood
2nd Grenadier Guards

Lord Basil Blackwood was born in December 1870 on his family's estate at Clandeboye, near Bangor in County Down, in what is now Northern Ireland. He grew up in a family with a military tradition. His great uncle, who held the rank of Major, was killed at Waterloo and his father had served with the 9th Lancers before becoming a top British diplomat occupying, in the course of his career, a wide variety of posts including Governor General of Canada, Head of Administration in India and British ambassador in Paris. Blackwood's older brother Archibald was killed in 1900 during the South African war, in which one of his younger brothers, Frederick, was wounded. Blackwood was educated at Harrow Public School and went on to Balliol College, Oxford, where he was an active member of the Rhodes-Milner Group, an influential society to which John Buchan and Rudyard Kipling also belonged. After coming down from Oxford Blackwood worked as a barrister. In 1897 he was given a senior post in the British administration in South Africa through Lord Milner's connections. Among other posts held he was Assistant Colonial Secretary in the Orange River Colony. Blackwood had a talent for drawing and was always cheerful. *'His serene good temper was unshakeable'* (...) *'and I do not think he was ever bored in his life.'* After two years as Colonial Secretary in Barbados Blackwood returned to England in 1910.

Intelligence Corps
'The first hint of war was, of course, to him what the first waft of scent is to a pack of hounds. He was off like an arrow on the old search for adventure. To most of us the war was the wrecking of cherished shelters; to Basil it was the breaking down of barriers.' Blackwood secured a commission with the Intelligence Corps and was attached to the 9th Lancers, his father's old cavalry regiment and left for France. *'I am sure that in those days he was perfectly happy, for he had his friends around him, a horse between his legs, and before him all the unmapped possibilities of war.'* Blackwood and his unit ended up at Messines in October 1914, where he was

seriously wounded in the left shoulder and taken to a field hospital. He went back to England two days later, but his convalescence was to take a long time. When he was fit again for light duties he was appointed Private Secretary to the Lord Lieutenant of Ireland in Dublin Castle, *'in which capacity he had many curious adventures during the Sinn Fein rebellion of Easter 1916.'*

Grenadier Guards
By mid-June 1916 Blackwood was again fit for active service and was made a Lieutenant with the Grenadier Guards. On 2 July 1917 he was with the 2nd Battalion in the trenches at Boezinge. Along the whole front the British army was busy preparing for the big offensive and small teams carried out trench raids at different points along the German line. The high command hoped that this would provide them with additional intelligence about enemy positions and strengths. The following night, at around 11.30 p.m., Blackwood was ordered to reconnoitre a nearby German trench with a group of five men. It was a pitch-black night, making the operation more difficult, but even so they managed to cross the canal at Boezinge quite easily. *'After going a considerable distance over rough and broken ground, rifle-fire was suddenly opened on them from a dug-out. Lord Basil Blackwood's orderly was wounded, while a sapper (...) was killed. The remainder at once lay down in shell-holes, and as they waited bombs were thrown at them from the same direction. Owing to the two men who originally followed him having become casualties, the party became scattered. Beyond this point little is known. A corporal (...) said that he saw Lord Basil Blackwood crawl forward after the shots were fired, but subsequently lost sight of him.'* Blackwood must have been wounded at the very least and he was listed as missing. His rich and influential family immediately used all its foreign connections to find out more about what had happened to him. In September they received the tragic news from the German Red Cross via the Queen Victoria Jubilee Fund Association. The German government notified the War Office that Lord Basil Blackwood had died on 4 July 1917. He is remembered today on the Menin Gate in Ypres.

Basil Temple-Blackwood at his desk
(These for Remembrance)

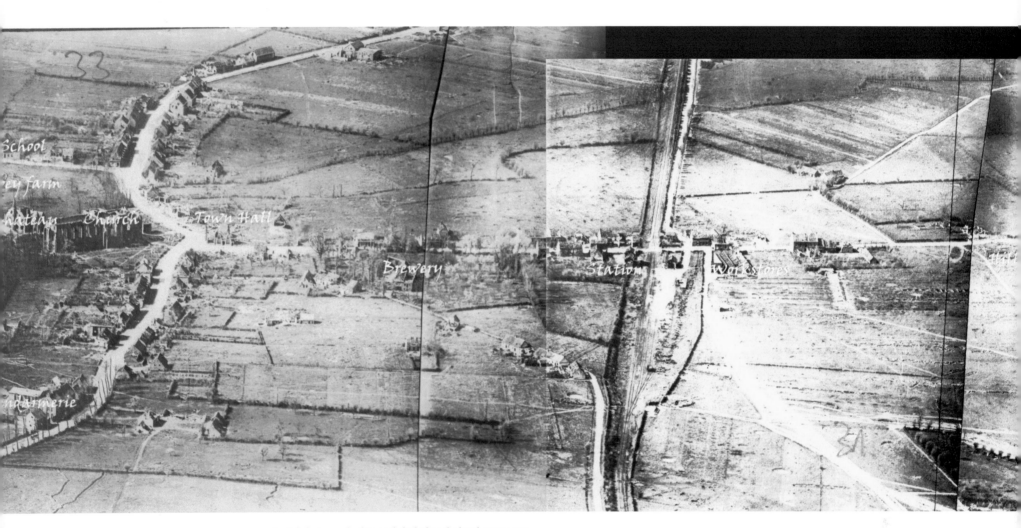

Aerial photograph of Zonnebeke before the battle (Deraeve)

1 The Battle of Pilkem Ridge: 31 July–2 August 1917
15th & 8th Divisions

SITUATION: All the final preparations for the British attack had been completed. In the weeks immediately prior to the offensive specially-selected raiding parties had carried out a series of small sorties with the aim of seizing prisoners of war and thus obtaining up-to-date intelligence so that the planners could make last-minute adjustments to the plans of attack.

Ground conditions were still good. *'On the 31st July, No Man's Land was green with grass and weeds; few woods remained, but the landscape was by no means the uniform brown it later assumed.'*[1] That said, however, it was already on its way to being converted into the desolate lunar landscape it was later so infamously to become. Thousands of artillery pieces were brought to bear on the German lines with the intention of pulverizing their defences. The men had been well-trained, especially in the capture of pillboxes and the weather on the morning of 31 July was misty and overcast, but dry.

OBJECTIVES: The Fifth Army had been given at least four objectives for the initial phase of the offensive. First and foremost, the German frontline and the support area immediately behind it had to be taken. Once this has been achieved the plan dictated that the attackers advance towards Pilkem, which was part of the Frezenberg Ridge and Westhoek, which meant breaking through the *Albrecht-Stellung*. In order to reach their third objective the infantry were to advance until just before Langemarck and St. Julien, and take part of Polygon Wood and Tower Hamlets, which would give the British control of the *Wilhelm-Stellung*. As a fourth and final objective it was hoped that the *Flandern I-Stellung* could be breached at various points, which in turn would mean that Langemarck, 's Graventafel and Broodseinde would fall into British hands. The centre of the attack was the most important objective. This was where the high ground in front of Gheluvelt would have to be captured, which was regarded as a key position for the rest of the campaign.

The Second Army, which manned the frontline from Klein Zillebeke to just south of La Basse Ville, was given more limited objectives and its divisions had only flanking functions.

COURSE OF THE BATTLE: The Second Army's attack was a resounding success. Basse Ville was taken by the New Zealanders, while the Australians captured a number of strong points. Hollebeke was also taken. The 24th Division attacked from Shrewsbury Forest, although they soon came under heavy fire from a strongly defended German position at Lower Star Post just before reaching their second objective, making further advance impossible. At Sanctuary Wood the 30th Division had difficulties from the outset. The entire area came under very heavy shelling from German artillery, with the result that the men of the 21st Brigade immediately lost the cover afforded them by their own protective barrage. In the confused fighting which ensued the 90th Brigade got lost and ended up advancing towards Chateau Wood instead of Glencorse Wood. In the end, the division had to halt its attack just before its first objective.

The 8th Division attacked at Chateau Wood. The brigade on the left advanced with relative ease and successfully achieved its second objective, but then came under heavy machine gun fire. As the 90th Brigade was not where it was supposed to be, the right hand brigade of the 8th Division could not do as much as had been hoped. Without the necessary support on their right flank further advance was impossible. Various tanks tried to break through at the Menin Road, but they moved so slowly and with such difficulty that the Germans

< *New Zealanders inspecting a captured anti-tank gun near Stirling Castle, 15 January 1918 (NZAM NZH344)*

merely picked them off one by one.

North of the Ypres-Roulers railway the 15th Scottish Division managed to stay in contact with the 8th Division and was able to push its way through to its second objective. Some units even got past the Zonnebeke-Langemarck Road as far as the German *Wilhelm-Stellung*. Despite heavy fighting the 55th Division was also able to take the second objective and eventually – despite heavy losses – even pushed forward towards the third objective. St. Julien was taken by the 39th Division and the 51st and 38th Divisions advanced as far as the Steenbeek. The Guards Division managed to capture and hold the third objective and the entire support area behind it. The French units, who were responsible for the northernmost wing of attack, managed to do the same.

By the afternoon most of the divisions had reached their objectives. However, the 8th, 30th and 24th Divisions, on whose progress the overall success of the offensive depended, had not managed to advance anything like as far as the plan required. Moreover, the German reaction was – predictably – not long in coming and the British troops soon came under heavy pressure. The Germans launched counter-attacks in considerable strength on both 31 July and 1 August and were able to recapture a large part of the ground they had lost.

RESULT: Losses were heavy, but – compared to the first day of the Battle of the Somme, only a year before – not as bad as they might have been. So in that sense Haig had reason to be pleased with how things had gone. However, the first phase of the offensive was crucial to the future success or failure of the campaign as a whole. Yet the advance had ground to a halt on half of the objectives and the effective strength of most of the divisions had been more than halved. The men who had come out unscathed from the first day were exhausted and in urgent need of being relieved.

Starting from the Ypres-Roulers railway and the line between Warwick Farm, Iberian Farm and Hill 37, the 15th Division was required to take three objectives in three phases and – if possible – to push on to a fourth objective. First, they were to advance to what British planners had called 'the Blue Line', which corresponded to the German frontline and the support lines immediately to the rear of this.

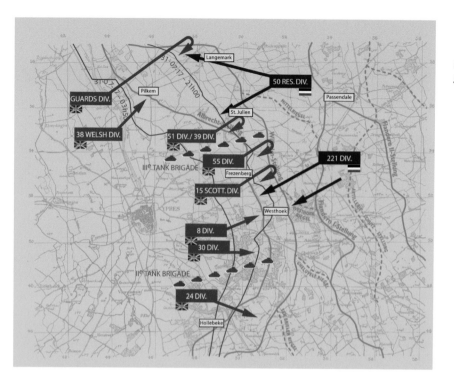

31 July 1917: general situation (MMP)

The 15th Division and 8th Division on 31 July 1917

15th Division
  44th Brigade
    8th/10th Gordon Highlanders, 9th Black Watch, 8th Seaforth Highlanders
  45th Brigade
    6th/7th Royal Scottish Fusiliers, 6th Cameron Highlanders, 11th Argyll & Sutherland Highlanders, 13th Royal Scots
  46th Brigade
    7th/8th King's Own Scottish Borderers, 10th/11th Highland Light Infantry, 10th Scottish Rifles, 12th Highland Light Infantry
8th Division
  23rd Brigade
    2nd West Yorkshire Regiment, 2nd Devonshire Regiment, 2nd Scottish Rifles, 2nd Middlesex Regiment
  24th Brigade
    1st Worcestershire Regiment, 2nd Northamptonshire Regiment, 2nd East Lancashire Regiment, 1st Sherwood Foresters
  25th Brigade
    2nd Lincolnshire Regiment, 1st Royal Irish Rifles, 2nd Rifle Brigade, 2nd Royal Berkshire Regiment

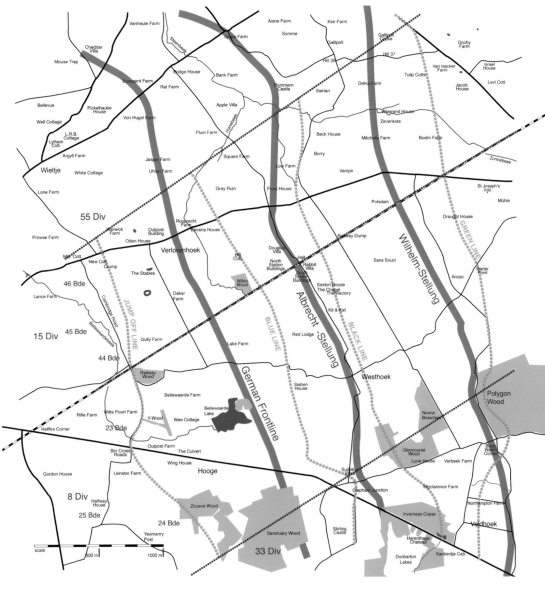

31 July 1917: 15th and 8th Divisions (MMP)

Their second objective, referred to in the plan as the 'Black Line', was the German second line, the so-called *Albrecht-Stellung*. The plan required the 44th and 46th Brigades to advance side by side and to capture and consolidate both lines. As soon as they had done so, the 45th Brigade would then take over the attack and push on towards the Green Line, which constituted the third objective. This was the infamous *'system of trenches and concrete defensive positions some 1500 yards further back.'*[2] If they managed to reach this line, the 44th Brigade was to attack again and forge ahead to the Zonnebeke-Langemarck Road. Two tank companies were on hand to provide support.

The 8th Division's plan of attack was more or less the same. The 23rd Brigade was to advance to the first two objectives, while on their flank (which was parallel to the railway) the 24th Brigade had to advance along an imaginary line running from Zouave Wood across the Menin Road to the north side of Glencorse Wood. As soon as the first two objectives had been taken, it was up to the 25th Brigade to push on to the third German line (designated the Green Line). If they managed to reach this, another battalion would advance to the Red Line. Here, too, tank support was provided.

Preparations

In the days before the offensive, British parties made several daring raids into No Man's Land and the German frontlines in order to gather intelligence about German troop dispositions and defences. Despite the fact that several of these raids were carried out in broad daylight, they were – by and large – fairly successful and casualties were low. A typical example was a raid carried out on 24 July involving some 200 men of the 12th Highland Light Infantry. They took eighty prisoners with very few losses: one man killed, three missing and seventeen lightly wounded.[3]

Inevitably, the heavy British artillery bombardment provoked a German response, making the British frontline and the area immediately behind it a very dangerous place to be and killing British soldiers with clockwork regularity.

On 27 July 1917 the 2nd Battalion Northamptonshire Regiment's battalion HQ was hit by a German shell. The battalion was making its last minute preparations for the coming attack and Battalion Headquarters itself – the centre of all these activities – and the area immediately around it was crowded with officers and men engaged in various duties. Casualties were thus correspondingly high. A number of men were wounded and Second Lieutenant **Frederick Menyn Hills** was killed. The 35-year-old Hills had at least six brothers, three of whom saw active service during the war. He was born in Maidstone in February 1883 and attended Tonbridge School from 1897 to 1901, before moving to Dublin, where he found work. Hills soon got tired of this and went to the United States to study civil engineering. He helped in the laying of a subway line under the Hudson river in New York and – after a brief period in Cuba – worked in Canada where he supervised the laying of numerous railway lines. He returned to England for a holiday in the spring of 1914 and in September of that year joined the Royal Fusiliers Regiment as an ordinary soldier. He was promoted to Second Lieutenant with the Northamptonshire Regiment in early May 1915. In May of the following year he returned to England to recover from a severe bout of pneumonia and was not able to return to his unit till December. He spent his last leave at home in July 1917. The battalion commander later wrote to Hills' family: 'We all feel his loss very much'.[4] Second Lieutenant Frederick Hills was buried in Perth Cemetery (China Wall), not far from where he was killed.

During the night of 30 to 31 July the assault battalions took up their positions at the front. The men of the 15th Division installed themselves in Cambridge Road, just behind the British lines, while the 8th Division took up its positions between Railway Wood, Birr Cross Roads and Zouave Wood.

The 8th Division's attack

At exactly 3.50 a.m. the men of the 8th Division clambered out of their trenches: 'The morning was very dark – faint streaks of light in the East served but to show where the dawn would come – and companies had to move by compass bearings.'[5] The 1st Battalion Worcestershire Regiment, which made up the 24th Brigade's right flank, was protected by the 30th Division. The attack on the left side of the brigade

was carried out by the 2nd Battalion Northamptonshire Regiment. The Worcestershires over-ran what was left of the German trenches and pushed on towards the Blue Line, quickly disposing of any resistance they encountered. A German pillbox in a tunnel under the Menin Road which was expected to cause heavy casualties in the end offered scarcely any resistance at all and the Worcestershires quickly took the German frontline. Likewise, 'Ignorance Support' – the immediate support trenches behind the firing line – proved no obstacle either. The troops forged ahead, but gradually met increasing resistance when various machine guns opened up on them.[6] Among those killed was Second Lieutenant **Ronald Anderson Budden**, who was shot in the head. He was not yet twenty. Budden went to school in Bournemouth from 1910, before going on to Sandhurst and in early April 1916 he was commissioned as a Second Lieutenant. During a raid at the end of July 1917 Budden handled himself, 'with skill, judgement and determination'. His death was mourned by men and fellow officers alike. Captain Urwick wrote to the young lieutenant's parents: 'He met his death in the most gallant fashion. The company of which his platoon formed part, already attacked and captured the front and second lines of the front trench system held by the enemy. While attacking a third line they were checked for a moment by Machine Gun fire. Your son very promptly organized a small party from his platoon, and led them forward from shell-hole to shell-hole, with a view to attacking and silencing the nearest of these Machine Guns. While within point-blank range of the gun, he raised himself on the lip of the crater to throw a bomb, and was shot at that instant. The men with him immediately rushed the gun and bayoneted the crew, including the man who sniped your son.' Budden's body could not be found, which proved devastating for his mother. In a letter to the army in connection with her son's back pay she wrote. 'It is 18 weeks today since my dear son gave his dear life for his country and broke his mother's heart. Not only his life, but his dear body could not be taken back and I now have given up all hope. This terrible War seems going on which means more dear lads are murdered and more parents to go through this terrible agony.'[7] The bodies of many of those who went missing on that day were subsequently found after the war, but Second Lieutenant Budden's body was never recovered. He is remembered today on the Menin Gate. Despite German resistance they were able to continue their attack

Second Lieutenant Frederick Menyn Hills (Tonbridge School)

Second Lieutenant Ronald Anderson Budden (Perry)

Captain Thomas Riverdale Colyer-Fergusson (Snelling)

The ruins of 'Hooge Chateau' (Deraeve) >

and the battalion reached the Blue Line without any further problems and began consolidating the captured positions.

The men of the 2nd Northamptonshire Regiment, on the other hand, were facing a much more difficult task. The terrain was treacherous and difficult to negotiate. Not only had the Battalion been split in two by their having to skirt round Bellewaerde Lake, but the entire area was also covered in exploded trees which were perfect hiding places for machine gun nests and pillboxes. *'The whole formed an extraordinary difficult piece of country, and that the Northamptonshire took it all and gained their objectives speaks volumes for the spirit of the men and the leading of the junior commanders.'*[8] Despite this the battalion took the German frontline and the area immediately behind it with ease. Bellewaerde Lake also proved not to be the obstacle they had expected it to be and the men now tried to move on towards the Blue Line. However, this last piece of ground immediately in front of the Blue Line proved problematic and a heavily-armed and well-defended pillbox in Jacob Trench held up their advance.

Captain **Thomas Riversdale Colyer-Fergusson** took ten men and captured the trench. Once inside they saw a company of German infantrymen coming towards them at a distance of only a hundred metres. They took out twenty of them with rifle fire, after which the remainder surrendered. Further ahead they came under fire from a German machine gun. Colyer-Fergusson and one of the men stormed the position and succeeded in capturing the machine gun, which they immediately turned round and used on the Germans. A little while later the 21-year-old Captain captured a second machine gun, after which the battalion commander appeared on the scene: *'He had now been joined by the rest of his company and had begun to consolidate his position when, hearing that Colonel Buckle had arrived, he went to him to report.'* He was then given new instructions for the consolidation of the positions and it was while he was conveying these orders to his company, that he was killed by an enemy sniper. Colyer-Fergusson was born into an upper class family and excelled at country sports such as hunting and riding. He joined up as soon as war broke out, was commissioned in February 1915 and was sent to France at the end of that year. He was wounded in July 1916 during the battle of the Somme, but returned to his unit after a period of convalescence. His promotion to the rank of Acting Captain came

through in January 1917 and in the following month he distinguished himself at the front in Bouchavesnes.[9] For his bravery on 31 July 1917 Colyer-Fergusson was awarded a posthumous Victoria Cross, the highest British military decoration. Captain Colyer-Fergusson was buried in the Menin Road South Military Cemetery.

The men of the battalion reached the Blue Line and began consolidating their positions. The 24th Brigade had reached its first objective.

The 23rd Brigade, which attacked between the 24th Brigade and the Ypres-Roulers railway, was able to reach all its objectives. On the right flank the 2nd West Yorkshire Regiment managed to break through without difficulty to the Blue Line with only minor losses. The 2nd Battalion Devonshire Regiment encountered more resistance, but was also ultimately able to reach the Blue Line, meaning that the entire 8th Division was now on the Blue Line. The attack had gone as planned.

Behind the Devonshires was the 2nd Battalion Middlesex Regiment

which pushed on via the Blue Line to the Black Line, just short of the German *Albrecht-Stellung.* Like the Devonshires, they also encountered very little resistance and were able to reach their objective easily. The 2nd Battalion Scottish Rifles was supposed to advance through the West Yorkshires to the Black Line, but had a much more difficult time of it. Machine gun fire and German snipers hampered their advance from the outset. They succeeded in reaching the objective, but then came under fire from a German position known as 'Kit and Kat', just north of Westhoek, although the battalion was soon able to put paid to this.

The 1st Battalion Sherwood Foresters, as part of the 23rd Brigade, attacked on the 8th Divisions left flank. They were required to advance from Bellewaerde ridge to the Black Line. However, they came under heavy fire from Surbiton Villas and Clapham Junction on the Menin Road. The attack was held up, which risked their losing the protection of the artillery barrage. In the end they were able to press on and took out the remaining pockets of resistance as they did so. The battalion reached the Black Line, albeit somewhat behind schedule and not without losses. One of these was Private **Robert William Thornber**, from Bolton-by-Bowland, a small village near Clitheroe, in the north of England, who had only just turned nineteen when he was killed near Bellewaerde. Private Thornber is remembered today on the Menin Gate, which means that his body was never found.

Private **Walter Lee** lost his life in the same action. He was from Clapton, near London and had a wife and son. He joined the Sherwood Foresters as a volunteer on 15 September 1916 and was sent to the front in May 1917. He was badly wounded during the attack on 31 July and was taken to the Casualty Clearing Station at Mendinghem in Proven, where he died the following day. The 33-year-old Private Lee was buried in the cemetery nearby.

As evening fell the fighting had largely died down. Even so, shots were regularly exchanged and lives were still being lost, one of whom was Private **Ernest Meadows.** He came from Castle Gresley near Burton on Trents and worked as a Oddman at Cadley Hill Colliery, a large local coal mine. He joined up at the beginning of 1915, serving initially with the 3rd Battalion and later, from April 1916, with the 1st Battalion Sherwood Foresters. He was wounded at the end

Private Robert William Thornber (Craven's Part in the Great War)

Private Walter Lee (de Ruvigny)

Private Ernest Meadows (Sherwood Foresters)

of October 1916 and spent a month and a half convalescing. Private Meadows was killed by an artillery shell on 31 July on his way up to the old British lines.[10] He was listed as missing for a long time, but his body was eventually found after the war and reburied in Hooge Crater Cemetery.

To the right of the Sherwood Foresters the 2nd Battalion East Lancashire Regiment tried to push through to the Black Line, but came under heavy fire on their right flank. The 30th Division had been held up and was thus not able to protect their flank as the plan required. Clapham Junction and Glencorse Wood were therefore still in German hands and the German machine gunners had a perfect view of the attacking troops. The men of the East Lancashire Regiment tried to advance further, but the flanking fire was decimating their ranks. It was here that Private **Benjamin Ellison** was killed. Born in early December 1882 in Crawshawbooth, a small village in Lancashire, he joined the army and was posted to the 2nd Battalion of the East Lancashire Regiment. His death did not go unnoticed on the home front and his family still have a collection of newspaper cuttings relating to his death. They also had a special silk bookmark made in remembrance of him with a photograph and the inscription: '*In Loving Memory of Private Benjn. Ellison (...), Aged 34 Years, Who was Killed in Action at Ypres, Belgium, July 31st, 1917, in the Great European War'.* Private Ellison's body could not be found, however,

Private William Henry Woods (Rutter)

Private Benjamin Ellison (Fischer)

and he is now remembered on the Menin Gate.

Among other members of the battalion killed on 31 July was Private **William Henry Woods**, who was twenty-nine years old. He was born in Oswaldtwistle and lived with his wife in Great Harwood, North East Lancashire. Private Woods is also remembered on the Menin Gate.

Two battalions of the 18th Division were sent forward and made a brave attempt to bring the 30th Division up to the same line as the men of the 8th Division, but their advance was cut short by the action of German machine gunners. This left the 8th Division's right flank completely exposed, resulting in the deaths of a large number of men. The plan of attack stipulated that as soon as the Black Line was taken the 25th Brigade were to push on to the Green Line, an objective which lay just in front of the *Wilhelm-Stellung*. Three battalions were to lead the attack.

The 2nd Battalion of the Rifle Brigade was the furthest removed from the chaos on the right flank and pushed on towards their objective along the Ypres-Roulers railway. They were able to advance a good distance and managed to set up a defensive position at Hanebeke Wood.

Among the many men killed in this part of the battle was Sergeant **Alfred James Cross**, the 21-year-old son of a gamekeeper from Spelsbury, Oxfordshire. He had three brothers and four sisters who, like him, attended the local school. Cross probably joined the army after leaving school as, when war broke out, he was already serving as a soldier. He was quickly promoted to the rank of Sergeant and was widely regarded as a good soldier. In early April 1917 he was awarded the Distinguished Conduct Medal for his *'courage and initiative'* during a patrol. After his death the battalion chaplain Kitson wrote in a letter to his mother: *'I know that at times like these words are of very little use, but I am writing because I should like you to know that your loss is shared by the whole battalion and that he was immensely respected and admired by every officer and man in it.'*[11] Sergeant Cross's name is inscribed on the Menin Gate.

On the Rifle Brigade's right flank the men of the 1st Battalion Royal Irish Rifles had great difficulties in advancing towards the Green Line, which meant that an opening was created between the two battalions, forcing the Rifle Brigade to withdraw from the copse at Hanebeek to a position just in front of the Black Line. This line proved difficult to hold, however, and the surviving officers decided to fall back to the Black Line. While this was going on, the Irish were under continual heavy machine gun fire from Glencorse Wood and Nun's Wood. Their commander, Lieutenant Colonel **Alexander Daniel Reid**, was among those killed. Reid was originally with the 7th Royal Inniskilling Fusiliers, but was given command of the 1st Battalion Royal Irish Rifles on 5 June 1917. The men of the Inniskilling Fusiliers were sad to lose him: *'For three years he served with 'The Seventh', during which time he worked indefatigably for the good of the battalion, and in return had won the respect of all with whom he had come in contact.'*[12] Not only were the Inniskilling Fusiliers saddened by his death, it was also a bitter pill for the Royal Irish Rifles as Reid *'had already won the affection and confidence of all ranks.'*[13] The 35-year-old Reid was the son of a former army captain and his parents lived in Vancouver, Canada. Lieutenant Colonel Reid's name is now inscribed on the Menin Gate. Part of his battalion was able to advance further to just beyond the Hanebeek, but was eventually forced to pull back under heavy pressure from the German defenders. The

rest of the unit was pinned down by German machine gun fire from Glencorse Wood. They consolidated the line which had been won and managed to beat off several localized counter-attacks. Shortly afterwards, however, they found themselves taking the brunt of the enemy fire and suffered extremely heavy losses.

The 2nd Battalion Lincolnshire Regiment which attacked on the Irish right heading towards the *Wilhem-Stellung*, suffered the heaviest losses: *'All companies, however, reported casualties from Machine Gun fire, whilst passing through Chateau Wood and from shell fire between the Wood and Westhoek.'* [14] Without the protection of the 30th Division on the right flank it was not difficult for the German machine guns to shoot the entire attacking force to pieces without any hindrance at all. *'To make matters worse, our barrage fell beyond the German Machine Guns, which left the latter free to pour a destructive fire upon the gallant troops of the 25th Brigade.'* Further advance was impossible and the men set about consolidating the ground they had won, meagre as it was.

Battalion losses were heavy, amounting to more than 40 killed and 180 wounded. Among the wounded was the 31-year-old Lieutenant **Arnold Grayson Bloomer**. A bank clerk from Stratford-on-Avon when war broke out, he enlisted as a volunteer in the Royal

Sergeant Alfred James Cross (Cross)

left: Memorabilia of Sergeant Cross (Cross)

Lieutenant Colonel Alexander Daniel Reid (7th Royal Inniskilling Fusiliers)

Lieutenant Arnold Grayson Bloomer (Perry)

*Lance Corporal Foster Yerkiss
(Craven's Part in the Great War)*

*Second Lieutenant Archibald Charles Spark
(Perry)*

Warwickshire Regiment at the beginning of September 1914. Bloomer was made an officer and was posted to the Lincolnshire Regiment in March 1915. He became seriously ill in late December and was sent to a hospital in England. After more than seventeen months on active service at the front he was physically and mentally exhausted. He was granted a few months to convalesce, after which he returned to his unit. On 31 July he was wounded at Jabber Trench, just south of Westhoek and was taken to an aid post, where a medical officer sent him to the rear. He was moved to Ypres and finally ended up in a hospital in Vlamertinghe, where he died of his wounds on 3 August. Lieutenant Bloomer was buried in Brandhoek New Military Cemetery.

The 2nd Battalion of the Royal Berkshire Regiment sent one company forward to do what they could to protect the Lincolnshires' right flank. 21-year-old Lance Corporal **Foster Yerkiss** from Earby, Lancashire, was mortally wounded during this action. He was taken to an aid post and from there, via a field hospital, to a hospital in France, where he died of his wounds on 11 August. Lance Corporal Yerkiss was buried in Etaples Military Cemetery.

At various points along the new British line the Germans tried to mount small counter-attacks, but they were not able to break through and had to abandon their attempts with heavy losses.

Difficult progress north of the railway

The 15th Division attacked north of the Ypres-Roulers railway. As in the case of the 8th Division, two brigades were supposed to reach the Blue and Black Lines. Once these were taken, a new brigade was to push on to the Green Line. The 44th Brigade was in contact with the 8th Division on the right flank and the 46th Brigade with the 55th Division on its left flank.

The battalions of the 44th Brigade set off from Cambridge Road heading towards the Blue Line. The 8th/10th Battalion Gordon Highlanders advanced through a desolate and *'remorselessly bombarded country such as landmarks as existed were at first unrecognisable.'*[15] They made good progress and 'apart from the usual Machine

Gun fire' there was sporadic hand-to-hand combat in which the Scots made short work of the enemy. *'Amid the stumps of a copse known as Wild Wood, the fighting was very sharp.'*[16] The Blue Line lay just beyond it.

During the heavy fighting in the remnants of the wood Second Lieutenant **Archibald Charles Spark** was killed by machine gun fire. Spark, the oldest son of a Scottish minister, was a student of humanities at the University of Aberdeen. He joined the British army in May 1916 and was promoted to Lance Corporal a month later. In mid-August 1916 Spark put in a request to be sent on an officer training course. His request was approved and after additional training he was made Second Lieutenant with the Gordon Highlanders. Spark left for the front in May 1917 and was killed on 31 July. A fellow officer who survived the engagement later wrote to Spark's parents: *'We were all very sorry to lose your son on the 31st of last month during the advance. Unfortunately I was wounded early in the action, but when I last saw him, he was leading his men in a very gallant manner.'* The 21-year-old Second Lieutenant Spark was buried in the wood itself.[17] His grave and that of sixteen others, including a number of other Gordon Highlanders who had also been killed on 31 July 1917, was found after the war. Their mortal remains were taken to White House Cemetery, where they were subsequently reburied.

The Gordon Highlanders were able to reach the Blue Line without difficulties. They then pushed on further and managed to reach the Black Line despite heavy resistance. The 9th Battalion Black Watch attacked on the left of the Gordon Highlanders and also succeeded in reaching the Blue Line and – later on – the Black Line. A and D companies of the 8th Battalion Seaforth Highlanders, who were following immediately behind the Gordon Highlanders and the Black Watch, ended up getting mixed up with the men of the two other battalions. They proved a welcome reinforcement for the two attacking battalions, however, and suffered few casualties. *'While crossing through No Man's land owing to the darkness, it is difficult to estimate casualties but except for 'B' Coy. who report about 20, almost entirely from shell fire, the remaining Coys. suffered very slightly.'*[18]

One of the men of the Seaforth B company killed was Private **James Collie Davidson**, the son of a shoe salesman from Glasgow.

When Davidson joined up he was originally posted to the Argyll & Sutherland Highlanders. His older brother, John, was Company Quartermaster Sergeant with the 7th Battalion Seaforth Highlanders and another brother had also enlisted and survived the war. Davidson ended up in the Seaforths and went into action with them on 31 July 1917 in the attack between Cambridge Road and the German frontline trenches. It was in this barren piece of No Man's Land that Davidson was killed by an artillery shell. The body of 21-year-old Private Davidson was never found and his name is, therefore, inscribed on the Menin Gate.

The 46th Brigade, which was responsible for the left flank of the 15th Division's front, encountered greater difficulties. The 7th/8th King's Own Scottish Borderers lost all their company commanders soon after the attack began and the men became disorientated. They still managed to reach the Blue Line without undue problems, however. Some of the platoon commanders then took control and reorganized the battalion. The advance to the Black Line progressed very slowly, however. Machine gun and artillery fire made life very difficult for the advancing troops and they sustained numerous casualties, particularly at the Frezenberg Redoubt – a strengthened position on the Ypres-Zonnebeke Road, that was part of the *Albrecht-Stellung*: '*This work lay just behind the crest-line and directly they reached it, the leading waves of the K.O.S.B. were met with Machine Gun fire from concrete emplacements on either side of the road, suffering heavy casualties.*'[19]

One of those killed was Second Lieutenant **Samuel Eric Ditchfield**, the only son of Percy and Alice Barlow. He was born in July 1895 and went to school in Ilkley, a small village northwest of Leeds. Ditchfield was a an engineer and sat on the board of directors of the Scottish Widows' Fund Assurance Society in Leeds. In early November 1916 he joined the Inns of Court Officers' Training Corps where he underwent officer training. He was commissioned as a Second Lieutenant in early May. After a few weeks of additional training the young Ditchfield was able to join his unit at the front. The 31 July 1917 was his first attack and he was killed almost immediately: '*he got killed by a sniper, shot through the heart, and his death was instantaneous.*'[20]

The 36-year-old Lance Corporal **William Gordon** from Glasgow was wounded on the same day. He was taken to a dressing station

Private James Collie Davidson (Fielding)

British position shortly after being captured by the Germans. The dead have been stripped of their shoes, August 1917 (Deraeve)

left: Second Lieutenant Samuel Eric Ditchfield (Perry)
right: Lance Corporal William Gordon (Perry)

Lieutenant Albert Edward Keppel (Perry)

and from there was transferred to a Casualty Clearing Station in Vlamertinghe, where he died from his wounds the following day. Before the war Gordon worked for McCorquodale, a big printing firm and paper manufacturer in Liverpool. He gave up his job in early September 1914 and joined the 16th Battalion Highland Light Infantry, but was later transferred to the King's Own Scottish Borderers. Lance Corporal Gordon was buried at Brandhoek New Military Cemetery. The unexpectedly strong resistance at the Frezenberg Redoubt could only be overcome at the cost of very high casualties. The men dug in just short of the Black Line and tried to consolidate the positions they had won. The attack did not go as hoped for the 10th/11th Battalion Highland Light Infantry, either. Everything went according to plan until they reached the Blue Line, but the advancing Scots then came under heavy fire from Square Farm and Frost House. German resistance was eventually overcome in both locations and the Germans Low Farm were also forced to surrender. Later on, however, the battalion's advance was brought to a standstill at Pommern Castle by various enemy machine guns and they did not reach the Black Line until 10.00 a.m.

While this was going on the 45th Brigade had already begun its advance towards the Green Line. The 6th/7th Battalion Royal Scots Fusiliers were on the left flank, while the 6th Battalion Cameron Highlanders took care of the brigade's right. The positions of the 44th and 46th Brigade had not been fully consolidated, however, and before they could begin their own advance towards the Green Line, the Cameron Highlanders had to deal with a few remaining pockets of resistance. Just beyond the Black Line the German machine guns rained their deadly fire from Beck House and Iberian Farm onto the advancing Scots. Despite heavy losses the Scots still tried to find a way through the thick rows of barbed wire to the east of Beck House and reached the Green Line at around 11.30 a.m. The Royal Scots Fusiliers had even worse luck. The men of the 8th Division had not yet taken the Black Line in its entirety and the German troops who were still holding the line, trained their fire onto the advancing Scots. In the end the Scots were not able to get further than Bremen Redoubt, just short of the Green Line.

The German counter-attack

'Between noon and 1 p.m. three enemy planes flew very low over the Division front, carrying out a thorough reconnaissance of the position without receiving any attention on the part of the R.F.C. The result was soon apparent.'[21] The Germans had already launched several unsuccessful local counter-attacks in the course of the morning, but the attack which now came was on quite a different scale. On the 8th Division's section of the frontline the Lincolnshires and the Irish Rifles were subjected to a merciless artillery barrage, which was immediately followed by the first wave of German infantry. The Lincolnshires were forced to give up some of the ground they had captured earlier in the morning, but – with the help of the Irish Rifles – they were later able to win this back. The Germans were driven off with heavy losses. Around 5.00 p.m. the Germans made another attempt at dislodging the division. This time they came up against the Rifle Brigade and here too they were again pushed back.

Among the officers killed during this counter-attack was Lieutenant The Honourable **Albert Edward Keppel**, who was the fourth son of the Earl of Albemarle. He attended Eton College, going on later to Sandhurst and on 20 October 1915 he was commissioned as a Second Lieutenant. On 31 July 1917 *'when leading his platoon during a counter-attack, before which the enemy were retiring, Lieutenant Keppel ran forward through the scrub with a Lewis gun in pursuit of some Germans and was shot dead.'* It was not until the end of November that notification came that his body had been buried, after Australian troops had come across his remains south of the Ypres-Roulers railway, close to what is now a motorway slip road. The 19-year-old Lieutenant Keppel was buried by men of the 2nd Australian Pioneer Battalion in Aeroplane Cemetery.[22]

The 15th Division also had to deal with a fierce German counter-attack. The Cameron Highlanders were fighting with open flanks and were short of ammunition. The sheer weight of the German counter-attack left them no choice but to pull back from the Green Line. The 13th Battalion Royal Scots came to their assistance but were also unable to turn the tide and the remnants of the two battalions were forced to move back even further. Additional reinforcements were hastily brought forward from the 45th Brigade and several machine gun units managed to halt the German attack. The entire frontline was now in chaos, but order was restored as evening fell.

When their aerial observers spotted an opening in the British frontline, the Germans decided to try again the next day. There was a large gap in the line between the Royal Scots and Seaforth Highlanders of almost 500 metres and the German infantry eagerly tried to exploit this. '*At 2.30 p.m. the observers were surprised to see hordes of field-grey figures advancing on the right, and at the same hour hostile guns began to shell the Frezenberg Ridge with terrific violence.*'[23] Part of the frontline which the Royal Scots were holding was surrounded and a great many of them were killed or taken prisoner.

Second Lieutenant **Charles Wilfrid Guthrie** from Lanark was among the killed. He had been a pupil at Loretto, a prestigious Scottish boarding school from 1914 to 1916 and joined up in 1916, receiving commission in the 13th Royal Scots in May 1917. Second Lieutenant Guthrie was killed on 1 August 1917 during the German counter-attack not far from Frost House, where his body was found in late September 1919. The 19-year-old officer was then reburied at Tyne Cot Cemetery in Passendale.[24]

The Scots were obliged to relinquish Beck House and Borry Farm to the Germans again and Square Farm was also under threat for quite a while, although the rest of the counter-attack was successfully repulsed with efficient machine gun fire. The Gordon Highlanders were also pushed back by the advancing Germans and a new line of defence was quickly organized at North Station Buildings. '*In the meantime the left of the Gordons and the right of the Seaforths stood firm, and, with the help of two Vickers-guns of the 44th Machine Gun Company, poured a devastating fire into the rear lines of the attacking Germans. Their casualties from this fire must have been exceptionally heavy, but alas! so were those of the Gordons.*'[25] The Germans continued to advance, however, which eventually allowed the Scots to launch two devastating attacks on their exposed flanks. A brief fight ensued and after a few minutes most of the German attackers decided to take to their heels, allowing the Scots to restore their original line. There was still some minor skirmishing in different parts of the line the following day, but the 8th and 15th Divisions held on doggedly to the ground they had captured.

Destructive effects of shelling in the grounds of 'Hooge Chateau' (Deraeve)

Relief

'*The importance of the feat which the 8th Division had accomplished was accentuated by circumstances over which neither combatant had control. From the opening of the battle rain had been threatening, and in the course of the afternoon there began a downfall which for four days and nights continued without appreciable intermission. The effect upon the shell-tormented battle ground is known only to those who saw it with their own eyes, for it cannot be described in words. It was to prove the decisive factor in the offensive.*'[26] The exhausted and decimated troops of both divisions were in urgent need of being relieved. On the night of 31 July to 1 August the bulk of the 25th Brigade was taken out of the frontline, with only the Royal Berkshires staying in position until the following day. They and the 24th and 23rd Brigades were then relieved by the 25th Division.

The losses suffered by the 8th Division were considerable: more than 3,160 officers and men killed, wounded or missing.[27] The Royal Irish Rifles lost 13 officers and 193 men, including 36 killed and 18 missing.[28] Casualties among the Lincolnshires came to 51 killed, 182 wounded and 77 missing.[29]

The exhausted men of the 15th Division were also relieved. On the afternoon of 2 August the 46th Brigade came down from the front-line and the 45th Brigade was relieved that night by a brigade of the 16th Division. The 44th Brigade could not be pulled back until the following night, however. The 15th Division had lost 3,580 killed, wounded and missing. The 13th Royal Scots paid the highest price, with only 50 officially killed, but 197 missing.[30] Most of these were the result of the German counter-attack on 1 August.

The 8th Division's divisional historian was also well aware of the damage that the German fire could do: '*Apart from the heavy shelling, the factor which contributed most to the losses suffered was the deadly enfilade fire from beyond the southern flank of the division, a fire made possible by the fact that the critical positions on the high ground around Stirling Castle could not been taken.*'[31] The British were to attack these positions again on 10 August.

*Bellewaerde farm just before the battle
(Deraeve)*

*Second Lieutenant Charles
Wilfrid Guthrie (Perry)*

31 July 1917:
Lieutenant Colonel Edgar Mobbs
7th Northamptonshire Regiment

Rugby

Edgar Robert Mobbs was born on 29 June 1882 as the son of Oliver and Elizabeth Mobbs. He grew up in Northampton, some 100 kilometres northwest of London and attended Bedford Modern School from 1892 to 1898. Not only was Mobbs a good student, but he also excelled at football, cricket and rugby. At the age of 16 he went to work for the Pytchley Autocar Company, which belonged to his older brother Noel. Around the turn of the century the family moved to Olney, a small market town near Northampton. Mobbs was 1m 85 and weighed more than 90 kilos and thus possessed the ideal physique for rugby. He joined a local club in 1903, playing the following year for the Weston Turks and joined the Saints, the Northampton Rugby Club, in 1905. He stayed with the Saints for a long time and was their captain from 1907 to 1913. The following season he played for the English national team against Australia, France, Ireland, Wales and Scotland, among others. He gave up rugby in 1913. By that time he was managing one of the Pytchley Autocar Company's branches in Market Harborough, a small town which was linked to Northampton by rail.

From Private to Lieutenant Colonel

At the outbreak of war Mobbs immediately wanted to serve as an officer. He was too old, however and on 14 September 1914, at the recruiting office of Little Bowden, a district of Northampton, he enlisted as a private. Mobbs was posted to D company of the 7th Battalion the Northamptonshire Regiment and was immediately made a sergeant. A week later he managed to get more than 400 other men to join the regiment with him. He submitted a request for a temporary commission before the end of the month and he was made a Lieutenant with the 7th Battalion a month after that. The unit became part of the 73rd Brigade of the 24th Division of the British army. After months of training, the division was sent to

France in late August/early September 1915. Mobbs had been promoted to Captain at the beginning of July 1915 and was given the rank of Major after arriving in France. The division went on active service immediately and Mobbs saw action at Loos, just behind the front line, on 25 September 1915. The British army attacked that day but was not able to force a breakthrough. The following day the raw and inexperienced men of the division, including the 7th Battalion in which Mobbs served, were thrown into the battle. The battalion lost 377 men, including 11 officers. Their commanding officer, Lieutenant Colonel Arthur Parkin, was also killed and *'Mobbs took charge in a very difficult and trying position.'* A few months later he was made the battalion's new commander. In August 1916 the battalion again found itself in the thick of things during the Battle of the Somme, where Mobbs was hit by a piece of shrapnel. He was taken out of the line via the medical evacuation route and was treated for his wounds in Rouen. A few days later his family received the following notification: *'Beg to inform you Lt-Col E. R. Mobbs (...) was admitted 2 Red X Hospital Rouen Aug 20th with gunshot wound shoulder slight.'* On 22 August he boarded a hospital ship in Le Havre which took him to Southampton, from where he was taken to a hospital in Northampton. He was fit again at the beginning of October and was able to return to his unit. For his actions on the Somme he was awarded the Distinguished Service Order in early January 1917. In July of that year the 24th Division was transferred to Ypres, where they were to take part in the long-awaited breakthrough on the Flanders front. On the night of 29 to 30 July the battalion took up their positions in the front line. The 24th Division was in Armagh Wood in Zillebeke and constituted the protective flank of the 30th Division, which was due to attack south of the Menin Road. The 7th Battalion Northamptonshire Regiment, which had now acquired the nickname 'Mobbs' Own' were just in front of Mount Sorrel. In the early morning the men clambered out of the

Lieutenant Colonel Edgar Mobbs
(www.world-rugby-museum.com)

trenches and made their way through No Man's Land towards the German positions. Halfway to Shrewsbury Forest they came under heavy fire on both flanks. The German fire from Lower Star Post was particularly savage and tore the advancing ranks to shreds. Most of the company officers were either killed or wounded and the men became disorientated. The reports coming back to battalion headquarters were contradictory and a clear picture of the situation could not be obtained. Mobbs decided to take a look for himself in order to organize the consolidation of the ground which had been taken. *'It was then that the Commanding Officer (Lt. Col. E.R. Mobbs D.S.O. and 2/Lt Berridge M.C.) arrived in the front line. The former with a handful of men charged an enemy Machine gun post, and was seriously wounded.'* He received a bullet in the neck and fell, mortally wounded, into a shell hole, although he still managed to indicate the position of the pockets of resistance on a map. He sent a runner back to battalion headquarters with the map and orders to bring up the reserve troops. The message never reached the battalion HQ but it did come into the hands of another officer in the firing line. Lower Star Post could not be taken that day, however. The body of the 35-year-old Lieutenant Colonel Mobbs was never recovered and his name is inscribed on the Menin Gate.

Mobbs Memorials

Edgar Roberts Mobbs was very popular and both his successful international rugby career and his immediate enlistment in the army secured him lasting fame. As Lord Downe expressed it, in an address: *'That was a gallant man. Shall we ever be able to forget him? (Cries of NO!)'* On Thursday 10 February 1921 the first Mobbs Memorial Match was played in his honour and the two teams taking part were certainly not minor clubs: the East Midlands against the Barbarians. The match became an annual tradition and it is still played today. Yet the Memorial Match was not the only step taken to ensure Mobbs's immortality. A monument was also erected in his honour: *'TO THE MEMORY OF A GREAT AND GALLANT SOLDIER SPORTSMAN',* the sponsorship campaign for which started immediately after his death. The memorial, which was unveiled in July 1921, originally stood on market square in Northampton, but

in 1937 the borough council decided to move it to the Memorial Garden, where it still stands today. Bedford Modern School also made their own contribution to preserving Mobbs's memory and in 1925 they re-named one of the rooms in the school building the 'Memorial Hall', featuring a photograph and a life-size portrait of their illustrious alumnus. In the 1950's the school moved to a new site, where the portrait was again given a prominent place. Finally, Northampton borough council has named a new road after its former sporting and war hero: Edgar Mobbs Way. The road is close to the rugby pitch where Mobbs scored many a try for Northampton Saints Rugby Club and many fans now drive along the new link road to watch their favourite club play. Edgar Mobbs Way was officially opened in late November 2006.

top: Programme booklet for the Mobbs Memorial Match, March 1993 (www.world-rugby-museum.com) bottom: The Edgar Mobbs Memorial on market square, Northampton. It was moved to the Memorial Garden in 1937 (www.roll-of-honour.com)

2 Westhoek and the Battle of Langemarck: 10/16–18 August 1917
16th & 36th Divisions

The heavy rainfall continued unabated on the day after 31 July, converting the entire area of operations into a hideous quagmire and the devastated landscape was covered in water-filled shell holes. No Man's Land was strewn with ruined buildings which had been blasted to smithereens and the small number of viable routes across the terrain were perfect targets for the German artillery, which eagerly brought their firepower to bear on these bottlenecks. Stepping off the 'duckboards' (wooden plankways laid over the mud) was to risk almost certain death. Any soldier who lost his balance and fell into the quicksand-like mud could only be pulled out with an almost superhuman effort and attempts to do so did not always succeed. Numerous soldiers drowned in the mud while their friends looked on impotently, unable to save them.

The tracks and pathways had to be continually repaired as a result of the continuous enemy bombardment. Not only was bringing fresh troops up to the line a hazardous undertaking, but the enormous stock-piles of materials and munitions which would be necessary to keep the attack going also had to be brought forwards across the same impassable terrain. Tanks, which at this early stage in their evolution, were slow, clumsy machines, could not be deployed in such conditions and in the few instances where the British did try to do so, this often ended in fiasco.

With the ground conditions as they were, an attack was out of the question. British planners thus had no option but to postpone the resumption of fighting scheduled for 2 August 1917. The new date for the attack on the Gheluvelt plateau was set for 9 August. The re-opening of the offensive would then follow on 13 August. However, the atrocious weather put a spanner in the works once more and the date had to be put back yet again. It finally went ahead on 10 August

10 August, general situation (MMP) >

< Transporting 4 inch Stokes mortars at Westhoek, 11 August 1917 (IWM Q5853)

and the Battle of Gheluvelt, the second great offensive in the struggle to control the strategic hills, began.

Just after half past four in the morning the British launched an attack across the whole front, deploying (from north to south): the 25th, 18th and 24th Divisions. The 25th Division lay directly opposite Westhoek, with its left flank against the Ypres-Roulers railway. The 18th Division was in the middle. A crucial point in this sector was Inverness Copse, left and right of the Menin Road. The 24th Division was south of them, but would not take part in the fighting.

The 18th Division played a central role in the attack. The plan stipulated the formation of a defensive flank around Inverness Copse. This line would then be extended through Glencorse Wood up to the railway. The northernmost section of this line, including Westhoek, was allocated to the 25th Division. It is interesting to note that the 18th Division deployed two brigades: the 54th and 55th, while the 25th Division used only one brigade (the 74th Brigade), even though its sector was considerably bigger, which underlines the very flexible composition of the units to be used in the attack in the light of the conditions expected. The attack was to be carried out in one movement without interruption and for that reason the 25th Division was given a protective artillery barrage of scarcely half an hour, whereas the barrage provided for the 18th Division lasted a good three quarters of an hour. Yet it was precisely in this sector where things went seriously wrong.

On the northern front the attack went more or less according to plan. Four battalions of the 74th Brigade, the 13th Cheshire, 2nd Royal Irish Rifles, 8th and 11th Loyal North Lancashire, stormed a line which was approximately one and a half kilometres wide. The Irish captured Westhoek and shortly afterwards dug themselves in at or near their objective, a few hundred metres east of Westhoek. The muddy condition of the terrain around the Hanebeek made a German counter-attack difficult to get off the ground, which allowed the British to consolidate the positions they had seized despite heavy artillery bombardments. Private **Edwin Tidey** was one of the men who took part in the fighting in this part of the battle. His father had been a labourer in a brickworks in Ware, Hertfordshire, but later became a policeman. Edwin had four sisters and a brother. Before he enlisted in the British army and was posted to the Bedfordshire Regiment, he also worked in the same brickworks. Private Tidey was killed at the age of 36 in fighting at Glencorse Wood on 10 August. He is remembered today on the Menin Gate.

In their sector, the men of the 18th Division came up against even greater problems. Three battalions were deployed: the 7th Queens, the 11th Royal Fusiliers and the 7th Bedfordshire Regiment. The 7th Queens Battalion tried to reach a point east of Inverness Copse with an approximately 350 metre wide front. Unfortunately, the company on their extreme right did not manage to establish a defensive flank on the south side of the wood. The Germans had spotted them as they took up their start positions and immediately began raining artillery and machine gun fire on to them, causing heavy losses even before the men went over. Under threat of encirclement the 7th Queens were forced to withdraw.

Subsequent attempts to break through also failed, which had serious consequences for the centre of the British attack. The 11th Royal Fusiliers and the 7th Battalion Bedfordshire Regiment, however, did succeed in reaching their objective and captured various German pillboxes at Fitzclarence Farm and Glencorse Wood and, despite heavy losses, they were able to fight off the inevitable German counter-attacks. The 11th Battalion Royal Fusiliers lost all its officers, however. One of them was Second Lieutenant **Vernon Haddon** of B company, although he was not officially listed as killed until 1918. Haddon was the son of Benjamin Percy Haddon, heir to a one hundred-year-old company *John Haddon & Co. Indian and Colonial Exporters and Importers.* In September 1914 the 16-year-old Haddon joined the Officers Training Corps at Dulwich College school and later continued his preparation in the Officer's Cadet School at Trinity College, Cambridge, which he joined in November 1916. At the end of April 1917 Haddon was commissioned as a Second Lieutenant with the Royal Fusiliers. He was killed on 10 August: *'I did not personally see Lt Haddon on the 10th August. But one of the men in his Coy (B Coy) said that a tall officer in B Coy had been sniped and killed just near him. The officer, he said, was not the Coy Commander and as Haddon was the only tall subaltern in B Coy I presume he must have been the officer killed'.* The body of the 19-year-old Second Lieutenant Haddon was never recovered.

The attacking battalions quickly ran into problems of supply, leading to shortages of just about everything, not least of fresh troops. They had already made such heavy use of the brigade reserve during the previous day that even these men could not be deployed and additional reserves were not immediately available. The Germans were not slow in exploiting the opportunity and launched a heavy attack against the 18th Division's vulnerable right flank just after 7.00 p.m.

Private Edwin Tidey (Wilkes)

Second Lieutenant Vernon Haddon (Perry)

In most places the British could do nothing other than fall back to the start line, where they consolidated their position and prepared for a new attack. In the end, however, this was postponed and then, shortly afterwards, cancelled.

The Battle of Westhoek had been everything but a success. For the second time in a row the British attack had not gone as expected. It was later to go from bad to worse, however.

16 August: General course of the battle

SITUATION: The strong German counter-attack of 10 August meant that the British did not hold the high ground around Gheluvelt. Yet this was an absolute sine qua non if they were to have any chance at all of breaking out in the direction of Zonnebeke and Passchendaele. Even so, the British high command stuck to their plan to force a decisive breakthrough.

After an initial postponement from 13 to 14 August, heavy rain again caused a new delay, so that the date was ultimately fixed for 16 August 1917. The poor weather conditions and the almost impassable terrain meant that it was extremely difficult to bring troops up to the frontline in readiness for the attack. The rain finally abated and in the early morning of 16 August the sun even came out. However, most of the battalions had been exhausted by the raids and reconnaissance missions, repair work carried out on tracks and other heavy fatigue duties which went on day in, day out and which had damaged their effectiveness. In combination with pre-existing manpower shortages most of the battalions were at only 60 to 70% of their supposed strength, and in some cases even less. The prospects were thus not overly rosy: tiredness, understrength, an almost inaccessible terrain and a strong German defence with pillboxes and machine guns.

OBJECTIVE: The plan was to take the German *Wilhelm-Stellung* from the Menin Road to Langemarck. Specific objectives included part of Polygon Wood, part of Zonnebeke, St. Julien and Langemarck.

COURSE OF THE BATTLE: The 56th Division attacked at the Menin Road with three brigades. The men had to contend with a heavy German bombardment and it proved difficult to make headway. Only a few small groups managed to reach the objective and even they

16 August 1917: general situation (MMP) >

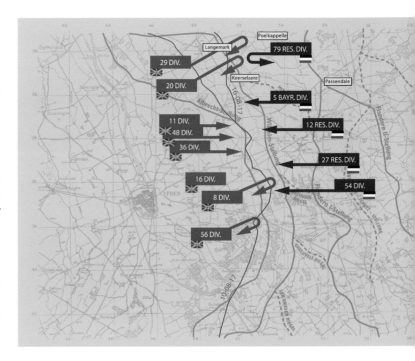

were subsequently pushed back almost to the start line by a German counter-attack. However, the men of the 8th Division, who went into action just south of the Ypres-Roulers railway, reached their objective without undue problems. Only the brigade on the left encountered heavy resistance. But here too, a German counter-attack put paid to their success and the whole division was forced to fall back to its start positions. The 16th Division, just north of the railway line, went over with two brigades. The 48th Brigade was absolutely decimated by hidden machine guns in fortified farmhouses. The 49th Brigade also came upon heavy resistance and was not able to advance any significant distance. The same happened to the 36th Division, whose attack also failed. The 48th and 11th Divisions attacked between St. Julien and Langemarck. The 48th Division did not advance very far, but the 11th Division was able to reach its final objective. The 20th Division took Langemarck and the 29th Division also achieved what the plan had stipulated. The French also made good progress at Bikschote.

Ruined buildings on Frezenberg Ridge, just before the battle (Deraeve)

16th and 36th Divisions on 16 August 1917

16th Division

48th Brigade

7th Royal Irish Rifles, 1st Munster Fusiliers, 9th Royal Dublin Fusiliers, 2nd and 8th Royal Dublin Fusiliers

49th Brigade

7th and 8th Royal Inniskilling Fusiliers,

7th/8th Royal Irish Fusiliers, 6th Royal Irish Regiment.

47th Brigade (reserve)

36th Division

108th Brigade

9th Royal Irish Fusiliers, 13th Royal Irish Rifles,

11th Royal Irish Rifles, 12th Royal Irish Rifles

109th Brigade

14th Royal Irish Rifles, 11th Royal Inniskilling Fusiliers,

9th Royal Inniskilling Fusiliers,

10th Royal Inniskilling Fusiliers

107th Brigade (reserve)

RESULT: The best results were obtained by the 11th, 20th and 29th Divisions around St. Julien and Langemarck. Yet the ground gained here was not enough to disguise the failure of the offensive as a whole. It was precisely due to the limited success of the operation of 16 August that it eventually received the official name: 'Battle of Langemarck', even though the area around Langemarck was, in point of fact, tangential to the original attack. Thus, the poor result of the third major attack since the start of 'The Third Battle of Ypres' was papered over. This was, above all, intended to distract attention from the drama of which, *inter alia*, the two Irish divisions were to be the protagonists.

The Irish divisions on the Western Front: the odd men out in the British army

At the start of the First World War, Ireland, which was still an integral part of the United Kingdom, was on the brink of civil war. Moderate Irish nationalists were asking for Home Rule by parliamentary means, while at the other extreme of the political spectrum radical nationalists sought an approach to Germany with an eye to organizing a rebellion against the British. The Loyalists on the other hand, most of whom were Protestants, would hear nothing of Home Rule and were rapidly arming themselves. Each political tendency had its own militia, which in some cases numbered more that 100,000 members. The eventual decision of the British parliament to grant home rule led to enormous tensions and only its postponement until after the war succeeded in calming tempers somewhat. The pro-British loyalists were reassured and were quickly found to be prepared to convert their Ulster Volunteer Force (UVF) into a regular volunteer unit: the 36th (Ulster) Division. The composition of the UVF was one of the most explicit examples of local recruiting, implemented as it was on a neighbourhood and even a street basis.

For the moderate nationalists taking part in the war was a much thornier issue and their leader, John Redmond, had to square a particularly difficult circle. On the one hand he had the anti-British radicals breathing down his neck, while on the other hand he did not wish to squander the promised Home Rule by being disloyal to the British Empire. After some hesitation he finally took the bull by the horns and called for the formation of an 'Irish Brigade' which

The Menin Road seen from Frezenberg Ridge, looking towards Hanebeek, 20 September 1917 (IWM Q2868)

would eventually become the 16th (Irish) Division. John Redmond's brother William, an M.P. in Westminster, was a prominent supporter of this decision and despite his unsoldierly age (he was 53) joined up himself, but was killed very early on, during the mine attack of 7 June 1917. Many moderate Irish nationalists were to follow his example in the first years of the war and volunteered to fight.

Harp and crown: the Irish bloodbath on the Frezenberg Ridge
The central sectors north of the Ypres–Roulers railway were assigned to Irish units. The 16th Division was responsible for the area between the railway and the Zonnebeek, while the 36th Division was placed on the left, on the other side of the stream.

Until 4 August 1917 the 16th Division was kept in army corps reserve, yet the need for reinforcements was so great that several of its battalions had to be moved up to the frontline in any case. The rest were used for supply, digging trenches, repairing tracks and burying telephone cables. This mostly took place in full view of the German artillery and by 15 August the Division had already lost a third of its fighting strength. Weather conditions also remained very poor. An artillery officer wrote that: '*No decent language can express this weather. The country is a marsh: horses up to the breasts in mud. Wagons can only move on proper metalled roads. My clothes are a mass of mud, one pair of putties has simply rotten on my legs*'.[32] Some trenches – or what passed for trenches – were completely underwater. Weapons regularly refused to fire due to their being clogged up with mud and many of the troops were suffering from 'trench feet', essentially foot rot caused by standing too long in water, for which amputation was sometimes the only remedy. The area around the frontline was strewn with the bodies of men and animals. The Irish chaplain and Jesuit Father Doyle describes how he found '*a young soldier lying on his back, his hands and face a mass of blue phosphorus flame smoking horribly in the darkness*'.[33]

The night before the start of the attack it seemed as if all the German firepower had been trained on the 36th Division. Large numbers of casualties were suffered, especially by the 12th Battalion Royal Irish Rifles, of whom one was Rifleman Adam Craig[34]. Craig was from

Rifleman Adam Craig (Thompson)

16 August 1917: 16th and 36th Divisions (MMP)

Galgorm, a small village near Ballymena in Country Antrim, in what is now Northern Ireland. Before the war he had worked at Lisnafillan Bleaching Works and belonged to the Ulster Volunteer Force, which meant that he was automatically posted to the 36th Division. Craig came through the Battle of the Somme unscathed. He sent a sprig from a tree he had found at the front to his wife Jane Anderson and their five children. She planted it in their garden, where it later grew to be a full-sized tree which is still maintained by the family. The body of the 35-year-old Craig, who was probably killed by German artillery, was never recovered and his name is inscribed on the Men-in Gate in Ypres.

'*Between midnight and 2.30 a.m. the four leading battalions must have suffered on an average fifty casualties apiece*'.[35] The 16th Division also came under heavy artillery fire and likewise sustained considerable losses. Among those killed was Private **Luke Joseph Hartigan** of the 1st Battalion Royal Munster Fusiliers of the 48th Brigade. Hartigan, born in New York in 1894, and his brother Edward, enlisted as volunteers in the British army in August 1915. Both of them lived with their parents on a farm in Ardagh, County Limerick in Ireland and were posted to the 8th Battalion Royal Munster Fusiliers. Edward was made a Second Lieutenant and was subsequently transferred to No 57 Squadron of the Royal Flying Corps. Luke stayed with the 8th Battalion Royal Munster Fusiliers, which was amalgamated with the 1st Battalion after the Battle of the Somme. The 23-year-old Private Hartigan was probably also killed by German artillery and his name is inscribed on the Menin Gate. His brother, Second Lieutenant Hartigan, flew various missions over the front in Flanders as an observer and he and his pilot managed to shoot down five German machines. They were killed a few months later when their plane crashed near Cambrai.

It was thus a rather shaken 16th Division which finally went into action on 16 August. Nor did the 36th Division have it any easier. '*The story of the attack, alas! is not a long one*' [36] As soon as the men went over the top at 4.45 a.m. the German guns again opened fire. Lieutenant Colonel **Audley Charles Pratt**, who was just outside the entrance to Wieltje dug-out, was one of those hit. Pratt, who was commander of the 11th Battalion Royal Inniskilling Fusiliers, died

from his wounds shortly afterwards. He had served as a Second Lieutenant with the Royal Scots during the Boer War and came from Crossmolina, County Mayo in the west of what is now The Republic of Ireland. Lieutenant Colonel Pratt was buried in Ypres Reservoir Cemetery.

The objective of the Ulstermen was a line which ran from Aviatik Farm to Gallipoli Copse along the Zonnebeke–Langemarck road, an area that was riddled with German pillboxes. Against all expectations most of these pillboxes had survived the weeks of artillery bombardment which preceded the attack more or less intact and they were protected by thick rows of barbed wire, which were also intact. In the absence of special units detailed to capture pillboxes, it was often necessary to skirt around these in order to reach the final objective on time, an expedient for which the attackers were to pay a very heavy price. Yet there was little choice: if they took too long over capturing a pillbox, they would lose the protection of the artillery barrage. The Irish battalions, which were already significantly under strength at the outset, suffered enormous losses, making the attack even more difficult. Nevertheless, both the 36th Division and the 16th Division initially managed to advance a considerable distance, inter alia, in the direction of Hill 35 and Potsdam. Once there, however, the attack ground to a complete standstill. When the men tried to push on further, they came up against thick rows of barbed wire, south and east of Gallipoli Farm, which again halted the Irish advance. In the meantime the covering barrage had moved on a lot further and a large number of German strong points such as Aisne Farm, Martha House and Hill 37 could now fire on the advancing Irish without hindrance. The War Diary of the 9th Battalion Royal Irish Fusiliers records that: '*Casualties were very heavy now (...) it was found impossible to push on.*'[37] One of those killed at Gallipoli Farm was Lieutenant **William Graham Boyd**. A soldier from his unit later wrote to Boyd's mother: '*I regret to state that a shell burst just above our heads and several of us were wounded. I went to where I saw Lt Boyd laying and found that he was mortally wounded and he died soon after*'. In the absence of a body, Boyd's mother Sarah found it very difficult to accept that her son was actually dead. '*Would it not be possible the Germans made him prisoner and he is on one of there [sic] hospitals?*'

Private Luke Joseph Hartigan (Johnson)

Lieutenant Colonel Audley Charles Pratt (Perry)

Lieutenant William Graham Boyd (Shaw)

Captain Thomas Graham Shillington
(Royal Irish Fusiliers)

Private Ambrose William Church
(Basey)

Lance Corporal John Thomas Robinson
(Hamill-Keays)

Private William Bradbury
(de Ruvigny)

The body of the 21-year-old Lieutenant Boyd from Carrickfergus, County Antrim was never recovered, however.[38] In the same attack Captain **Thomas Graham Shillington** was also wounded, in his case for the second time. He had received bullet wounds to the thigh and calf in July 1916 which had landed him in hospital. Now he was taken to a Casualty Clearing Station at Brandhoek with a serious bullet wound to the throat, from which he died two days later.[39] Captain Shillington was from Portadown, County Armagh.

The operational order anticipated a gain in ground of approximately one and a half kilometres. In some places about half of this distance was reached. Even this limited success was short-lived, however. At Borry Farm things went very wrong indeed. The various stalwart attempts of the 8th Battalion Inniskilling Fusiliers to take this heavily defended position each ended in a blood-soaked fiasco. Among those killed was 19-year-old Private **Ambrose William Church**. He was the son of a corn merchant from Acle, Norfolk, in England and had enlisted as a volunteer in the Norfolk Regiment, but eventually ended up with the 8th Battalion Royal Inniskilling Fusiliers.[40] Private

Church's name is inscribed on the Tyne Cot Memorial. Private **William Bradbury** was seriously wounded in the attempt to take Borry Farm. Bradbury, who was also only nineteen years old, was a barber from Wallasey, Cheshire who had only joined the Cheshire Regiment in April 1917, although he was immediately transferred to the Royal Inniskilling Fusiliers. He joined his battalion at the front at the end of June 1917. After being wounded on 16 August, he was taken to a Casualty Clearing Station, where he died the following day. Private Bradbury is buried in Brandhoek New Military Cemetery No. 3. His brother George, who served with the Royal Garrison Artillery, died a few days before the armistice in November 1918 as a result of an illness.[41]

The failure of the attack on Borry Farm was attributed to poor communication on the battlefield. The battalion headquarters at Low Farm was subjected to continuous German artillery fire. Messages between the frontline and headquarters had to be carried by runners who were exposed to sniping and artillery fire.[42] One of these runners was Lance Corporal **John Thomas Robinson**, a signaller with the 8th Battalion Royal Inniskilling Fusiliers who was shot by a German sniper. Robinson was a 27-year-old tram driver from Belfast who had volunteered for the Army Cyclist Corps when war broke out. He was married to Mary Elizabeth Wood and had two small children, Stella and Zoe, both of whom where born during the war.[43] Lance Corporal Robinson's mortal remains were never recovered and he is therefore remembered today on the Tyne Cot Memorial. Even the additional support provided by a company of the 7th Battalion Royal Irish Fusiliers was not enough to make a significant difference. The company was commanded by Second Lieutenant **Charles Lennox Henry**. He was a bank clerk from Dublin who had joined up in September 1914. He fought as a private at Gallipoli, the Balkans and in the Middle East and was trained as an officer in July 1916, being commissioned as a Second Lieutenant with the Royal Irish Fusiliers in January 1917. Nothing more was heard of him or anyone else from his company during the rest of the offensive.[44] They were probably all killed at Borry Farm. Second Lieutenant Henry's name is also inscribed on the Tyne Cot Memorial.

At 3.30 p.m. the Germans launched a powerful counter-attack from Zonnebeke. The attacking Irish had failed to mop up the remaining pockets of resistance in the terrain they had conquered and this was now to cost them dear. During the withdrawal they were exposed to continual fire from the Germans who had held on and now opened up on their backs as they withdrew. To make matters worse, the position which the Irish had taken at Gallipoli now appeared no longer to be tenable. It was here that Second Lieutenant **Richard Douglas Miles** of the 9th Battalion Royal Irish Fusiliers was severely wounded. Miles was the son of the head of customs and excise on the British island of Jamaica in the British West Indies. He was born there in 1888 but went to school in Bedford, England. After leaving school he set out for Canada where he worked from July 1908 until his voluntary enlistment in the Canadian army in November 1914, where he was given the rank of Lance-Sergeant. In August 1915 Miles requested to be sent on an officer training course for a commission in a British regiment and was commissioned as a Second Lieutenant in the Royal Irish Fusiliers at the beginning of October 1915. The 28-year-old bank clerk was slightly wounded a year later, but remained

on active duty and was awarded the Military Cross in June 1917. On 16 August Second Lieutenant Miles was sent to a Casualty Clearing Station at Brandhoek, Vlamertinge, where he died the next day as a result of *'a bullet wound which penetrated the abdomen.'*[45] Despite its enormous losses the battalion was ordered to make another counter-attack, but there were not enough men left to carry out this order effectively.

Captain **James Owen William Shine** came from a military family. His father was a Lieutenant Colonel with the Royal Army Medical Corps and his two younger brothers also served as regular officers in the British army. Shine was born in Allahabad, India, and attended Downside School in England from September 1902 to July 1909 before entering the Royal Military College in Sandhurst. On passing out he was given a commission with the 1st Battalion Royal Dublin Fusiliers which was stationed in India at the time. When the war broke out Shine's unit was transferred to the Western Front. His brother John Dennis, a Second Lieutenant with the Royal Irish Regiment, was killed at Mons in August 1914 and less than a year later, the family's second son, Second Lieutenant Hugh Patrick Shine, was listed as missing in action at Ypres on 24 May 1915. On 1 July 1916 Captain Shine himself received a bullet in the leg at Beaumont Hamel on the Somme and was taken to England for convalesce. He was able to join his unit again in 1917 and was killed near Potsdam on 16 August.[46] His name is inscribed on the Tyne Cot Memorial.

Chaplain 4th Class the Reverend **William Joseph Doyle** spent the whole day administering the last sacrament to the seriously wounded in No Man's Land and bringing the lightly wounded back to their own lines. This was not the first time that Doyle, an Irish Jesuit from Dublin, had done this. In 1916, during the Battle of the Somme, he was awarded the Military Cross for a similar act of bravery. Father Doyle had also distinguished himself at Wytschaete in June 1917. In fact, many of the men believed him to be immortal. Time after time he had risked certain death and come out without so much as a scratch. Doyle describes one such incident in the final entry in his diary, dated 11 August 1917. He was on his way to bury some soldiers in a trench: *'I had reached a sheltered corner, when I heard the scream*

Second Lieutenant Charles Lennox Henry (Bank of Ireland)

Second Lieutenant Richard Douglas Miles (Letters from the Front)

Captain James Owen William Shine
(Downside & the War)

William Doyle in the uniform of a Chaplain 4th Class (O'Rahilly)

‹ *Father William Joseph Doyle dressed as a Jesuit priest (O'Rahilly)*

of a shell coming towards me rapidly, and judging by the sound, straight for the spot where I stood. Instinctively I crouched down, and well I did so, for the shell whizzed past my head – I felt my hair blown about by the hot air – and burst in front of me with a deafening crash. It seemed to me as if a heavy wooden hammer had hit me on the top of the head, and I reeled like a drunken man, my ears ringing with the explosion. For a moment I stood wondering how many pieces of shrapnel had hit me, or how many legs and arms I had left, and then dashed through the thick smoke to save myself from being buried alive by the shower of falling clay which was rapidly covering me. (...) My escape last year at Loos was wonderful, but then I was some yards away and partly protected by a bend in the trench. Here the shell fell, I might say at my very feet; there was no bank, no protection except the wall of your good prayers and the protecting arm of God'.* However, Doyle's luck ran out a few days later and he was killed by an artillery shell while comforting the wounded on the battlefield. The precise date of his death is not known. Conflicting sources give 16, 17 and 18 August as possible dates, but Doyle was probably killed in the late evening of 16 August. While he was tending to a wounded soldier, the German artillery increased its pressure on the British positions. Doyle and three other officers tried to reach the safety of a pillbox, but he was killed by a shell just as he was going inside. Three senior officers put his name forward for a posthumous Victoria Cross, but in the end he received nothing. *'Though Father Doyle cared nothing for human decorations (...) it seems right to chronicle this judgement of others and to record the fact that he was recommended for the D.S.O. at Wytschaete and the V.C. at Frezenberg Ridge (...). However the simple disqualification of being an Irishman, a Catholic and a Jesuit, proved insuperable'.*[47] Some soldiers claimed to have buried Doyle shortly thereafter and Doyle's service record also mentions a grave at the crossroads east of the Frezenberg Ridge, just beyond the British lines, but his mortal remains could not be found after the war. The 44-year-old Reverend Doyle is thus remembered today on the Tyne Cot Memorial.

After the battle
The men in the frontline were relieved by the reserve brigade of the 36th Division that same night, but the whole division was not able to come down from the line until the following night. A start was

also made on relieving the 16th Division.

Between 2 and 18 August 1917 the 36th Division lost 144 officers and 3,441 men.[48] Losses of more than sixty per cent per battalion were not unusual. The 7th Battalion Royal Inniskilling Fusiliers of the 16th Division lost 16 of their 20 officers and 368 out of their 472 men.[49] The 36th was the only division which had managed to take even a few metres of ground, but compared to the objectives this was negligible. The entire attack had ended in a blood-soaked fiasco and at a huge cost in human lives. After the fighting on the Frezenberg Ridge both Irish divisions lost their specific character as volunteer units and this was also the beginning of the end for the 16th Division. Recruiting problems, which were acute even before the battle, now became much worse. Following a further battering during the German spring offensive of 1918, the division was completely deprived of its Irish identity as almost all the battalions were replaced by English, Scottish and Welsh units.

The Battle of Langemarck was yet another confirmation of the careless preparation and unrealistic expectations which was so typical of the staff of the 5th Army. General Gough tried to blame the failure of 16 August on the 16th Division. In his later correspondence he wrote: *'I was aware that the Division was not of the highest standard'*. He also says that an army corps commander had told him that *'he thought the Division no longer "politically reliable"'*.[50] Gough was unable to provide any valid argument to support this statement, however. His assertion must also be seen in the light of the Irish political situation. Gough was the son of a wealthy Irish family of loyalist pro-British sympathies and had a deep-rooted mistrust of the 16th Division, which mostly consisted of Catholics.

The major supply routes for keeping the battle going ran through Westhoek. Men and pack animals at Idiot Corner, 5 November 1917 (AWM E1480)

Unique photograph of a German officer with his dead comrades, Frezenberg Ridge, August 1917 (Deraeve) >

16 August 1917:

Private Jesse Marston

6th King's Shropshire Light Infantry

To Ypres

Jesse Marston was from the village of Stanton Long, south of Shrewsbury. He was a genuine country lad who had spent his youth on a farm and was an accomplished horseman. In early October 1914 the 17-year-old Marston, who had previously belonged to the local militia, joined the Shropshire Yeomanry, a cavalry regiment. Like a number of other troopers he was later transferred to the 6th Battalion King's Shropshire Light Infantry. He was slightly wounded during fighting on the Somme at the beginning of November 1916 and was treated in a hospital in Rouen. From his arrival in France Marston kept a diary in which, in addition to a few longer passages, he recorded brief notes about his daily activities. One such entry is the following description of an attack dated 22 April 1917. *'We had orders to go over the top to take about 1500 yds. (...) of ground. We started at 8 o/c P.M. the lads went with a good heart. Fritz had several machine guns turned on us, but it was marvellous what slight damage he did with them. We passed our first objective & went on too fast & got held up in our own barrage fire, & I am sorry to say had several casualties. My No. 2 F. Williams was hit through the leg, & a piece of shrapnel temporaly [sic] put my gun out of action, but not before 2 magazines were let go at one of his machine guns. We gained our objectives easily & dug ourselves in. We were up at it, all night, so were jolly tired. We were relieved by the 'C & D' Coy on the night of the 23rd. The Captain told me I had done good work & had put my name to the Colonel. I was never more surprised in my life.'* Marston regularly received letters and parcels from home, which he was always pleased to get, especially when it meant a welcome change from his monotonous diet as a soldier: *'May 14th: (...) I had a parcel from Home of lovely Bread & roast Beef – Only biscuits in the rations!!"* On 30 May 1917 one of his friends, Charlie Lewis, was admitted to hospital with a brain tumour, about which he made the following annotation on 9 June: *'We received news of poor Charlie Lewis' death, he died on the 31st May. I wrote to his home, We do miss him.'* At the end of July, Marston left for Flanders with his battalion. With his countryman's eye he observed on 21 May: *'(...) entrained 12 noon for Poperhinge – We are in Belgiun [sic], rather flat country, but much more fertile than France – Crops looked well, including Hops, Maize & Tobacco – We camped near a place called Proven about 6 or 7 miles from Poperhinge."* His last diary entry was dated 29 July 1917: *'Sunday. Very heavy thunderstorm – We are in the Ypres Sector and are getting ready to give him something to go with – Thousands of men & guns & aeroplanes. It is really wonderful how it is all organised on the Ypres Front.'* Marston later entrusted the diary to a friend due to go on leave in England, who in turn gave it to Marston's mother. Marston had written another long entry in which he said that he would soon have to go into action. He finished with a long valedictory section and hoped to be home soon...

Langemarck 1917

On the night of 15 to 16 August the men made themselves ready. The 6th Shropshires were part of the 60th Brigade of the 20th Light Division, which was at Langemarck, south of the Ypres-Staden railway line. At 4.45 a.m. the following morning the British artillery commenced their barrage and the men began their advance. Marston was in command of a group of Lewis Gunners, who were to support the attack with machine gun fire. Despite the poor state of the ground, the battalion made rapid progress and took 50 prisoners of war at Au Bon Gite, one of the many fortified farm houses. They also captured the village church of Langemarck, which by then had already been shot to pieces, and Aloutte, a very well defended farm house. Around 7.20 a.m. the men tried to push on to the last objective, south of Schreiboom. However, on their way across they came under heavy fire from White House and Rat House. Their losses were high, but the

Private Jesse Marston with Imperial Service Badge (Ryan)

Jesse Marston, standing second from the right, with Pattern '03 equipment and Long Lee Enfield (Ryan)

Langemarck 1924

In September 1924 Marston's sister, Olive, made the crossing to Flanders to visit the grave of her dead brother. Just as he had done, she also kept a diary in which she made a daily record of her short tour of the battlefields. *'First went to the I.W.G.C. & they are very kind & have walked over the ground where Jesse went & have walked round Langemarck Church which was raised to the ground, now half finished rebuilding (...)'* The following day she visited Langemarck again: *'I went by the 12-30 train to Lange-marck & walked all round there, by the Cement House Cemetery, Minty House, La Belle Alliance Divisional Collecting Post etc, but round here, there are many cemeteries all beautifully kept & many many 'unknow [sic] Soldiers, but known unto God' buried in all of them. Near Langemarck I went round some of the pill-boxes, 6ft; cement with steel girders through it crossed by wires, almost impossible to break through these are dotted round, 2 or three close together 1 or 5 + 20 on sometimes 20 or 40 yds apart, but these part would often be no mans land (...).'* Olive Marston also visited Hill 60, the ramparts of Ypres, various cemeteries and the tank graveyard on the Menin Road. She was unable, however, to find her brother's grave and he may be one of the many unknown soldiers buried in the cemetery at Langemarck. Marston's name is inscribed on the Tyne Cot Memorial.

Shropshires were able to reach their final objective shortly afterwards, where they consolidated the line and stopped the German counter-attacks with artillery fire. The battalion had suffered many casualties, but in comparison to other units which also attacked on 16 August, the number was not particularly high: 39 dead – one of whom was Marston – and 147 wounded. Five of the casualties drowned in the mud. The commander of Marston's platoon wrote, in a letter to Marston's parents: *'We attacked the Boche at 4-45 a.m. on August 16th, and at 6 a.m. your son and his Gun Team went forward to occupy a trench which our first wave had captured. He was shot through the head by a sniper and died instantly.'* Private Marston was buried where he was killed, probably near the church at Langemarck.

3 Preparations for a new Offensive: August–September 1917

< Two Australians in a dugout at Westhoek, 6 November 1917

Private Ernest Leonard Gays
(At the going down of the Sun)

After the bloodbath of 16 August

On 16 August the British offensive had came to a bloody end. The exhausted men were not able to advance very far and the German machine guns had decimated their ranks. The remnants of the divisions which had attacked on 16 August were, therefore, quickly relieved. On 17 August the 46th Brigade of the 15th Division took over the front from the 16th Division and the 61st Division replaced the 36th Division. That same day Gough decided that those objectives which had not been reached on 16 August would be set as objectives for another attack to be carried out on 25 August, but first a series of local attacks on 22 August would have to make a considerable improvement to the British jumping-off positions.

In the meantime, thousands of British troops all over the Salient were engaged in extending the trenches, bringing up supplies, laying communication lines, and other preparations. Engineers, Pioneers and Labour Battalions could no longer cope with the increasing volume of work and other units had to be called in to help them, which is how, on 18 August, the men of the Cyclist Battalion of the Xth Corps found themselves carrying out fatigue duties at Hill 60. *'We were up at Hill 60 digging cables trenches for the Royal Engineers - and the Jerries were shelling hard, going for the guns, because it was full of batteries round there'*. Private **Ernest Leonard Gays** was killed outright. Gays was from Leicester and cycling was his life. He had worked in a bicycle factory before the war, was a member of the local cycle club and on Saturdays he earned a bit of pocket money performing cycling stunts at the local cinema. He enlisted in the British army, where he ended up in the Army Cyclist Corps.[51] He was killed on 18 August. *'He was our only casualty'*, veteran Jim Smith remembered later: *'He was my best pal and I did feel bad about it – but felt worse about the next night. (...) Oh, I felt bad being detailed to bury my own pal. It was the hardest thing I ever had to do.'* He and two others dug a shallow grave. *'I remember feeling a bit upset, for the grave was only about four feet deep. I knew he probably wouldn't be there for very long, because of the shell-fire. (...) I felt bad'*[52] Jim Smith also sent a letter to Gays' mother. She replied a little while later, thanking him for it, but also asking him a lot of questions about what happened. *'Did you see my boy after he died, could you tell us how he was? I should like to know what time of the day or night it happened (or thereabouts). Was he up the doings (are you allowed to tell us?) or was he on Sentry?'*[53]. The 19-year-old's body was never recovered after the war and Private Gays's name is inscribed on the Tyne Cot Memorial.

22 August 1917: a forgotten action

The 61st Division had taken over the front line from the 36th Division on 17 August and set about preparing for the attack scheduled for 22 August. In the meantime an artillery duel ensued with each side trying to silence the other, causing regular casualties in the front lines. Lance Sergeant **Thomas Kilby Keeley** was killed on 19 August during one such bombardment. He was part of the 2nd/4th Battalion Gloucestershire Regiment. Keeley was from Chipping Campden in Gloucestershire and was married to Agnes Ellen Sharpe. He joined up as soon as war broke out in August 1914, as he had previously served with the territorials. His older brother George Charles also enlisted and was killed in early May 1917 during the Battle of Arras. The 29-year-old Thomas Keeley was buried after the war in New Irish Farm Cemetery.[54]

On 20 August seven tanks captured four pockets of German resist-

left: Lance Sergeant Thomas Kilbey Keeley (sitting) next to his wife and flanked by his brothers-in-law, brothers and cousins (Hughes)
right: Private Stephen Henshaw with wife and children and his private memorial (Hailstone)

ance on the St. Julien–Poelkapelle road which had held up the 48th Division on 16 August. The tanks cleared the area for infantry who were then able to occupy the captured positions. They went into action again two days later. In the case of the 48th and 11th Divisions, however, the men were only able to advance a few hundred metres with the tanks. Two German strong points were taken out: one east of the cross-roads at Keerselare (Vancouver Corner) and one east of Bülow Farm.[55] The men of the 48th Division pushed forward across the ground which their comrades of the 145th Brigade had tried to take on 16 August. In a shell hole they came across Private **Stephen Henshaw**, who was with the 1st/1st Ox and Bucks. Henshaw had been wounded by shrapnel on 16 August during the attempt to take Springfield and had crawled into a shell hole, where he waited for someone to come and get him. In the end he was not found until 22 August, but was then taken to the field hospital in Dozinghem. The 30-year-old Henshaw died of his wounds the following day. He left a wife and three young children behind in California, Birmingham. His youngest daughter, Dora, was only eight months old. A few years ago the present occupier of Springfield erected a private memorial on the spot where Henshaw was wounded.[56] Private Henshaw himself is buried in Dozinghem Military Cemetery. The brave attempt to

take Springfield was bloodily stamped on and not one of the group survived. The 1st/5th Battalion of the Warwickshire Regiment tried again on 22 August. Lance Corporal **Sydney Colloff** was among the dead. Colloff, who was twenty-five years old, came from Brookfields, Birmingham. He attended Camden Street Council School and went on to study at the Birmingham School of Art. Colloff was a talented jewelsmith and artist whose work was exhibited in the Birmingham Art Gallery. Lance Corporal Colloff's mortal remains were never recovered and he is remembered today on the Tyne Cot Memorial.[57]

The 61st Division attacked to the south of the 48th Division. They managed to push their front line forward some 550 metres and were able to take Somme Farm and Hindu Cottages. Corporal **Albert Clarke** was killed during the capture of these positions. Clarke was with the 2nd/1st Ox and Bucks and was mobilized in August 1914. He was a book binder with McCorquodale & Co in Wolverton, a major paper manufacturer with factories in, among other places, London, Glasgow and Wolverton. Corporal Clarke's name is inscribed on the Tyne Cot Memorial.

The 15th Division, north of the Ypres-Roulers railway, was also

Lance Corporal Sydney Colloff (de Ruvigny)

Corporal Albert Clarke
(McCorquodale Roll of Honour)

Private James Alcorn
(George Heriot's School)

Second Lieutenant Gideon Andrew
Forrest Renwick
(George Heriot's School)

Private James Finlayson Shaw
(Watsonians)

required to make attempts to improve the British jumping-off positions. The men went over the top at 4.45 a.m. under the protection of a creeping barrage. As soon as they went over, the German artillery rained shells onto them and they came under heavy machine gun fire. Both the 44th and the 45th Brigade had a hard time of it. *'On the right the fate of the leading companies of both the 13th Royal Scots and 11th Argyll & Sutherland Highlanders will never be known. So heavy was the machine-gun fire that no information could be sent back or supports sent up'.*[58] Among the dead was Private **James Alcorn** from the 13th Royal Scots. Alcorn was a 37-year-old commercial representative from Leith who was a widower with three children. His reasons for joining up are not known. He had only been at the front since the beginning of August 1917 and had almost no combat experience. His younger brother John Milles Alcorn, a Private with the 1st Battalion King's Own Scottish Borderers, died of wounds in early December 1917 in a French field hospital and was buried in Rocquigny-Equancourt Road British Cemetery, Manancourt, in France.[59] Private James Alcorn's body could not be recovered after

the war and his name is inscribed on the Tyne Cot Memorial. Second Lieutenant **Gideon Andrew Forrest Renwick** was listed as missing. When war broke out, Renwick was a pupil at George Heriot's School in Edinburgh and he immediately joined the school's Officer Training Corps. In 1916 he was allowed to serve in an Officer Cadet Unit, by which time he was almost nineteen. He was subsequently given a commission as a Second Lieutenant with the 13th Battalion Royal Scots and was sent to France. He went missing on 22 August 1917. An investigation was opened and Renwick's parents were able to obtain further information about the fate of their only son from a Scottish prisoner of war in Germany. *'He died bravely and cheerfully 'doing his bit'. Practically his last words were 'Come on, lads, we must be pushing on, follow me'. It will be at least a grain of comfort for you to know he had to suffer no pain, death being instantaneous. He died of bullet wound.'*[60] Second Lieutenant Renwick is also remembered on the Tyne Cot Memorial. Despite extremely heavy losses the men managed to advance. Potsdam, Vampire Farm and Borry Farm were taken, although further advance was not possible as losses were too heavy and the defenders were too strong. The survivors decided to pull back to a line between Railway Dump and Beck House.[61] One of the battalion's 114 missing was Private **James Finlayson Shaw** of the 11th Argyll & Sutherland Highlanders.[62] The *Memorial Record of Watsonians* reads: *'He was reported missing together with the bombing party which he was commanding.'* Shaw, an alumnus of the George Watson School in Edinburgh, worked for the Leith Dock Commission until November 1915, when he enlisted in the army, seeing action on the Somme in 1916 and at Arras in 1917.[63] Private Shaw is remembered today on the Tyne Cot Memorial.

The 8th Battalion Seaforth Highlanders also came up against very stiff resistance. German machine guns tore gaping holes in the Scottish ranks, but they pushed on and were able to advance to just in front of Iberian Farm, thanks to the help of the reserve company. In order to avoid the lethal German fire they made their way from shell hole to shell hole. The right company of the Seaforth Highlanders got lost, but still managed to get past Beck House, where almost the entire company was mown down by German machine guns.[64] Only a few men were able to advance a little further, one of whom was

Private **John Telfer Hiddleston**. Hiddleston was a 24-year-old smith from Sanquhar, Dumfriesshire, Scotland. In November 1919 his body was found at Bostin Farm, more than a kilometre east of Beck House. Private Hiddleston was subsequently buried in Tyne Cot Cemetery.[65] Private **Alexander Asher** was also buried after the war. He was originally buried with five others 150 metres north of Pommern Castle, at the foot of the slope leading to Hill 35. Four of these men were from the 8th Seaforth Highlanders and had also been killed on 22 August. Asher was from Bog'o'fern, Lhanbryde in Scotland and was a farmer, like his father. He joined up in early April 1917 and arrived at the front on 1 August 1917. Private Asher was killed three weeks later not far from Iberian Farm, which – despite repeated attempts – was never taken.[66] Hill 35 also proved a hard nut to crack as, from above, the German machine gunners had a clear view of the entire British attack. The 7th Cameron Highlanders could make no headway and even the extra platoons of the 9th Battalion Gordon Highlanders, who were supposed to consolidate and defend the hill after it had been taken, were not able to turn the tide. The men dug in at the foot of the hill and set up a line to Somme Farm via Pommern Castle with extra defensive points spread out at intervals. *'In carrying out this work the pioneers suffered rather heavily.'*[67] The trenches were dug in full view of the Germans. Sergeant **Alexander Ross** of the 1st Battalion Gordon Highlanders was among those killed while doing so. Ross was a veteran of the Boer war. He had also served in India and in Egypt and had been at the front since August 1914. He was wounded on 18 October 1914, probably during the Battle of La Bassée and was not able to return to the front until August 1915. Ross was wounded again in May of the following year and after convalescence he married Bella Thomson Wight in Huntly, in August 1916. He then returned to the front and was posted to the 9th Battalion, which was his unit when he was mortally wounded on 22 August. Stretcher-bearers took Sergeant Ross to an aid post at Aeroplane Cemetery where he died soon afterwards and was subsequently buried. *'He did fine work for the battalion, and his death is lamented by every one of us.'*[68]

Private John Telfer Hiddleston (standing) with his brother Samuel (Hiddleston)

Private Alexander Asher (de Ruvigny)

Tanks

The whole attack was to be supported by tanks. Eighteen tanks of the 3rd Tank Brigade, C and F Battalions, went into action with the 15th and 61st Division, but they did not have an easy time of it. *'The going was more than ordinarily atrocious, the whole of the Frezenberg-Zonnebeke road having been shot away'.*[69] Four tanks which were supposed to support the 45th Brigade did not even reach the start line, but got bogged down on the Ypres-Zonnebeke road. Of the other six tanks, four got stuck before leaving the British lines. However, the two remaining tanks did prove useful and supported the attack at Gallipoli Farm. Inevitably, there were a lot of casualties among the tank crews as direct artillery hits on the clumsy, heavy machines were fatal, which is probably how Captain **Duncan Innes Murray-Menzies** met his death. Murray-Menzies was from a military family. His grandfather, father, uncles and brother had all either served or were still serving in the British army. His brother, who had been commissioned as a Second Lieutenant in early August 1914, was with the 1st Battalion Black Watch, and had been killed in France

Sergeant Alexander Ross (de Ruvigny)

Front line tourists visit Tank C47 with a café hut on the left, 1919 (Deraeve)

Captain Duncan Innes Murray-Menzies (Perry)

Vancouver and Winnipeg also came under fire from the tanks. Many years after this attack Private J.L. Addy recalled: '*We were just coming to a place called Bulow Farm, which, of course, was a big pillbox, and the infantry were having a hard time there. Lieutenant Knight's tank was twenty yards or so in front of us and suddenly it just went boom. It was a direct hit from a heavy shell.*'[71] Lieutenant **Andrew Ralph Lawrie** was also killed that day near St. Julien while commanding one of the tanks of 'D Battalion', 1st Tank Brigade. Lawrie was the son of a bank clerk, from Dungoyne, Kirkintilloch, Scotland and studied at the University of Glasgow. He joined up in the spring of 1916, was commissioned as a Second Lieutenant and was posted to the 9th Battalion Scottish Rifles. He left for France on 22 August 1916 and at the end of December of that year was transferred to the 'Heavy Branch of the Machine Gun Corps', where he was promoted to Lieutenant shortly afterwards. He was slightly wounded in the face in May 1917, but was soon back on active service. The young Lieutenant was reported as missing exactly one year to the day after his departure to the front.[72] His name is inscribed on the Tyne Cot Memorial.

The British also went into action south of the Ypres-Roulers railway. Two battalions of the 14th Division were to attack along the Menin Road and take the high ground in front of Gheluvelt. Their objectives were limited, with Inverness Copse and Fitzclarence Farm as their furthest point of advance. The start signal for the attack was given at 7.00 a.m. While the 6th Battalion Somerset Light Infantry followed the creeping barrage and advanced strongly towards Inverness Copse, the 6th Battalion Duke of Cornwall's Light Infantry came under heavy fire from Fitzclarence Farm and the remains of a farm to its north. This meant that the Somersets had no protection on their left flank and were immediately attacked by the Germans on three sides. With the help of two tanks, however, they were able to form a defensive line which kept the German counter-attacks at bay. As the objectives had not been reached, the men were ordered to attack again the following morning. In the meantime, the whole line was consolidated and extended, but the operation was cancelled due to heavy rainfall during the night.

On 23 August it was much quieter on the front. The Germans

on 25 January 1915. He is remembered on the Le Touret Memorial. Duncan Murray-Menzies was born in March 1897 in what is now Sri Lanka, where his father was a serving officer and later commanded the Ceylon Mounted Infantry during the Boer war. Duncan attended Wellington College in Berkshire from 1911 to 1914, where he belonged to the Officer Training Corps and joined the army as an officer at the end of August 1914. He was posted to the 1st Battalion Black Watch, but in February 1917 he was transferred to the 'Heavy Branch of the Machine Gun Corps', which was to become the Tank Corps in July 1917. The 20-year-old Captain Murray-Menzies was killed on 22 August and was buried a hundred metres north of Iberian Farm, near Hill 35. However, his body could not be found after the war and his name is inscribed on the Tyne Cot Memorial.[70] That morning a number of tanks were deployed east of St. Julien. Most of them were already out of action before the attack had properly got going. Some got stuck in the mud and others sustained direct hits. A few tanks did, however, manage to advance with the infantry taking cover behind them, Bülow Farm and Springfield being two successes.

Lieutenant Andrew Ralph Lawrie (Glasgow University)

launched a small counter-attack along the Menin Road and on the 15th Division's front three battalions attacked Gallipoli and Iberian Farm, again without success. The 10th Battalion Durham Light Infantry of the 14th Division was also in the front line that day and by the evening was sustaining increasingly heavy German artillery fire.[73] Among the casualties was 24-year-old Corporal **Thomas Livermore**. He was the son of a carpenter from Bishop's Stortford, Hertfordshire. He had joined up in Hounslow in mid-August 1914 and was probably killed during an artillery bombardment. Corporal Livermore's body was found by a British exhumation company after the war some fifty metres south of the Menin Road, between Stirling Castle and Inverness Copse and was subsequently reburied in Tyne Cot Cemetery.[74] The following morning the rest of his battalion endured a heavy German attack with grenades and flame throwers. The 6th Duke of Cornwall's Light Infantry, who were south of Glencorse Wood, were forced to pull back to the start line on 22 August. At Inverness Copse the German attack was less successful and the ground which the Durham Light Infantry lost was immediately recovered. However, the British artillery did not know the exact position of their troops, as a result of which the men in the front line on the western edge of Inverness Copse were shelled by their own artillery. As there was no telephone connection from the front line they were not able to report this and were, therefore, forced to withdraw, whereupon the Germans immediately reoccupied Inverness Copse.[75]

Changes to the plan

By the end of August the front around Ypres had not moved very much. Despite repeated attempts the British had still not managed to capture the heights before Gheluvelt. German artillery observers continued to enjoy an excellent view of the British positions and could easily shell the entire area. Meanwhile, at British Headquarters, the high command was discussing the next stage of the campaign. The renewal of the offensive on 25 August was postponed. In the end, the general objective and the plan of campaign were retained, but its execution was entrusted to General Plumer instead of General Gough. Plumer abandoned the idea of a major offensive along the entire width of the front and instead proposed a series of attacks in depth with limited objectives. Plumer's new approach

Corporal Thomas Livermore (Warwick)

Two dead mules along the Menin Road, on the right of the photograph is the pre-war tramline, October 1917 (Deraeve)

based on 'step-by-step' advances and 'bite-and-hold' tactics meant that one battalion would advance to the first objective and immediately consolidate this, whereupon a second attacking wave would move through the front line and do the same with the second objective. A third wave would then pass through the first and second units and take the final objective. In order to break through on the ridge Plumer thought that four such offensive operations would be needed with six days in between to bring artillery forward. An important pre-condition to being able to break through successfully at Passchendaele-Broodseinde was the capture of the high ground at Gheluvelt from which the Germans dominated the entire British right flank. The ANZAC divisions, consisting of five Australian divisions and one New Zealand division, were moved to Flanders in order to spearhead this offensive. Unlike at the beginning of the campaign on 31 July 1917, there were now twice as many troops for scarcely half the breadth of front. There was also double the artillery firepower with respect to that of 31 July. Finally, in anticipation of a

German counter-attack, special reserves were also to be moved up to the front line. General Plumer asked for three weeks to complete the necessary preparations.

The troops who were now on the front line got no rest, however. In anticipation of the coming offensive small-scale attacks were ordered to tire the Germans out. The men of the 14th Division went in action again on 27 August at around 5.45 a.m. The plan was that they were to advance as far as Inverness Copse and Glencorse Wood with the help of four tanks. Unfortunately, the tanks got bogged down in the mud at Clapham Junction and the infantrymen who managed to reach the objectives were either killed or eventually had to fall back. No ground was gained, therefore. Just after midday the British divisions west of Zonnebeke also attacked. The men, who had come up to the front line in pouring rain, were already tired, having stood knee deep in water for more than ten hours waiting for the attack signal. Due to the poor state of the ground they were not able to keep up with the creeping barrage provided by the artillery. The men of the 15th and 61st Division got stuck between Gallipoli and Schuler Farm. Further advance seemed impossible and, here too, both divisions had to pull back to their start line. Further north, the 48th Division managed to capture Springfield and Vancouver with the help of a few tanks and the 11th Division was also able to extend its line somewhat. The 38th Division, on the other hand, came under a hail of machine gun fire from the outset and quickly had to return to their start line. The bad weather continued the following day and Haig decided not to carry out any more local attacks, except the one planned for 31 August. However, there was no improvement in the weather and this attack was also cancelled.[76] The 28 August was, therefore, a relatively quiet day on the front. Both sides reorganized themselves and set about recovering the missing from the battlefield and burying their dead. This was done under the protection of a white flag, but inevitably there were still a few casualties. The troops came under regular artillery shelling and snipers were active everywhere. Private **Ernest Alfred Bradford** was with the 1st/8th Battalion of the Worcestershire Regiment, near Springfield, which they had captured the previous day. Bradford, a 36-year-old postman from Easton, had survived the attack unscathed. He got married in April 1901 and had three young children. He had just finished showing a comrade some of his family photographs, shortly before he was shot by a German sniper. Bradford's wife Clara Jackson received the news from a postman who was a colleague of her husband and fainted when she heard that he was dead. It was to be many years before she got over the shock.[77] Private Bradford's name is inscribed on the Tyne Cot Memorial.

Towards a new offensive: September 1917

The start of the new offensive was set for 20 September. The preparatory artillery bombardments began on 31 August and continued until 13 September. From then on, the bombardments became heavier and more intense. On 1 September the C Battery of the 210th Brigade Royal Field Artillery was energetically engaged in shelling the German positions at Borry Farm. The battery was east of Preston House

Private Ernest Alfred Bradford (Bradford)

and south of the Bellewaerdebeek. Around 10.00 a.m. they came under heavy artillery fire themselves and both the battery commander, Major **Heinrich Helmutt Simon** and Lieutenant **Christopher Hartley** were mortally wounded by a German shell.[78] 31-year-old Hartley was married and lived in Aspley Guise, a village near Bedford. Lieutenant Hartley was buried in Ypres Reservoir Cemetery. Major Simon was taken to the field hospital at Lijssenthoek, where he died of his wounds on 8 September. The 36-year-old Simon was married to Edith and lived in Knutsford, Cheshire.

In the meantime, the infantry carried out small raids up and down the line in order to take prisoners and thus obtain intelligence about the enemy and their positions. In a few places along the line the British also tried to secure better jumping-off positions. To this end there were a number of fruitless attacks on Hill 35 at the beginning of September. On 6 September British artillery subjected the Germans in Borry Farm, Beck House and Iberian Farm to a heavy bombardment. The 42nd Division with the 1st/5th, 1st/6th, 1st/7th and 1st/8th Battalion Lancashire Fusiliers then tried to take these fortified farm houses one by one. The 1st/6th Battalion managed to take Beck House, but had to cede it to the Germans again shortly afterwards. The loss of Beck House meant that the attackers' left flank was now completely open to German fire from Hill 35. The German positions along the Ypres-Zonnebeke road also caused the British considerable losses. Among these was Private **Dixon Entwistle** of the 1st/5th Lancashire Fusiliers. He was the son of a miner from Hapton, Lancashire, and married Emma Sunley Rowland in 1913. They set up house together in Crawshawbooth in Lancashire. The 26-year-old Entwistle was a foreman at Holden's Alexandra Mill. The couple had two children: Edith, born in 1913 and Elizabeth, born in 1916.[79] Private Entwistle has no known grave and is therefore remembered today on the Tyne Cot Memorial.

left: Major Heinrich Helmutt Simon (Perry)
right: Lieutenant Christopher Hartley (Perry)

The British carried out a series of other small attacks at various points along the front, such as the attack on Hill 35 on 10 September. Most of these failed, however. The men now began to prepare themselves for the offensive of 20 September. The artillery increased its pressure on the German positions and practiced performing the

Private Bradford (second from the left in the middle row), who was with the 2nd/5th Norfolk Regiment when this photograph was taken (Bradford)

A wounded sergeant of the Argyll & Sutherland Highlanders receiving first aid treatment at Clapham Junction, 26 September 1917 (IWM)

British stretcher-bearers on the way to the battlefield, 21 September 1917 (IWM)

Private Dixon Entwistle (Ovans)

creeping barrages, which were intended to protect the infantry, on a daily basis. British units often made daring raids on German positions during these practice barrages as the prisoners of war obtained were always useful sources of intelligence. The final preparations were completed and the troops who were to spearhead the attack moved up to the front line on 19 September. The weather had also been good and the three weeks which Plumer had requested as preparation had certainly not been wasted.

20 August 1917:
Sergeant Jimmy Speirs
7th Cameron Highlanders

James 'Jimmy' Hamilton Speirs was a Scottish professional footballer. He was born on 22 March 1886 in Govan, Glasgow. His father, James Hamilton, had been a miner for many years, but gave up mining around the turn of the century and became a boilermaker. Jimmy was the fifth of the family's six children and had two sisters and three brothers. The 15-year-old Speirs left school just after the turn of the century and took a job as a clerk.

Football

The earliest references to Jimmy Speirs's footballing activities date from the spring of 1905. Maryhill FC spotted him not far from where he lived and Speirs's talent spoke for itself. Speirs frequently scored at decisive moments in the match, as when he scored the only goal in the final of the Glasgow Cup. At the end of the season he moved to Glasgow Rangers, which played in the Scottish 1st division. In his first season with them he scored seventeen goals.

On 24 October 1906 Speirs married Elizabeth Lennox Maden. He scored sixteen goals in that season and Glasgow Rangers ended up third place in the league tables. Top matches attracted as many as 80,000 spectators. Speirs's first child, James Hamilton Speirs, was born in late 1907. A few months later he played with the Scottish national team against Wales. The Scots won the game. In 1908 he left Glasgow Rangers for Clyde FC, another Scottish Division 1 team, not far from Glasgow. In that season his team also finished number three in the league. Even so, Speirs decided to leave the club and become a player with Bradford City, which was in the English First Division. His debut with the Bradford was on 1 September 1909 against Manchester United. He scored seven times that season and his team ended in the seventh place, but the 1910-1911 season proved to be his most illustrious year. Bradford not only obtained fifth place, its best league result ever, but also

made football history in the famous English FA cup competition. They managed to reach the final against cupholders Newcastle United. Neither of the teams succeeded in scoring during the match on 22 April 1911 and more than 65,000 spectators watched them replay the final a few days later. Speirs scored the only goal of the match and Bradford City won the cup. This goal, probably the most important of his entire career, won Speirs and his club a place in the annals of the English football history and as captain he was able to receive the cup himself. In November 2003 his FA medal was auctioned for the record sum of more than £ 26,201.

In early August 1912 James Speirs became a father for the second time with the birth of his daughter, Elizabeth Maden Speirs. At the end of the year he secured a lucrative transfer to Leeds City FC. Speirs was second in the league's list of top scorers twice in a row. The new football season had just begun when the war broke out. Leeds City ended fifteenth that year and did not do very well in the FA cup either. Speirs played his last match at the end of April 1915. League football was suspended for the duration of the war and Jimmy Speirs decided to join up. As a footballer he had played 285 official matches and scored 104 goals.

Volunteer

Speirs joined up in a recruiting office in Glasgow on 17 May 1915 and was told to report to the regimental depot of the famous Queens Own Cameron Highlanders in Inverness a week later, where he was posted to the 3rd Battalion. He was made a Lance Corporal at the end of July and served with the 7th Battalion in France on 29 March 1916, which was part of the 44th Brigade of the 15th Division. Speirs was promoted to Corporal at the end of July 1916. A month later he was wounded in the elbow and ended

Speirs at work, 1912 (Pickles)

Speirs's FA Cup medal, auctioned for a record sum in 2003 (Pickles)

Bradford City with the FA cup, 1911
(www.bantamspast.co.uk)

Sergeant James Hamilton Speirs, 1915 (Pickles)

up in hospital, but was able to return to his unit quite quickly. He won the Military Medal at Arras in late April 1917. Back home the newspaper reported: *'The numerous friends in Glasgow and the West of Scotland of Sergeant James H. Speirs, Cameron Highlanders, will be pleased to hear that in the big game across the Channel he is among the honours, just as he was wont to be when, as Jimmy Speirs, he played for Glasgow Rangers, Bradford City, and Leeds City.'* The article did not appear until June, by which time Speirs had been promoted to Sergeant.

Passchendaele

At the beginning of July 1917 Speirs returned to his unit after a brief period of leave in Scotland. On 20 August 1917 his battalion relieved the 8th Battalion Worcester Regiment at Pommern Castle. That day Speirs wrote a letter home in which he told his wife that they would be going *'over the parapet'* the following day. Speirs was wounded in the attack. At home the newspaper gave the news that: *'He was hit in the thigh during an advance, and managed to crawl into a shell-hole. There he was attended to for a short time, but the Cameron Highlanders did not return from their raid.'* The divisional history of the 15th Scottish Division does not mention this attack on 20 August, nor does the War Diary of the Cameron Highlanders and this date may well be wrong, therefore. The 15th Division did not attack at Pommern Castle until 22 August 1917. The objective was the capture of Hill 35, but the attack was only a partial success. The losses among the 7th Cameron Highlanders during the month of August were high, totalling 211 men, of whom 12 were dead and 59 missing. The 31-year-old Speirs was among them. His body was never found. *'A very large circle of friends will bear with the very keenest regret that Sergeant James H. Speirs, late captain of the Leeds City F.C. and formerly of Bradford City, is reported wounded and missing in France. (...) In the meantime, the greatest sympathy will be felt with Mrs. Speirs in her terrible anxiety. It seems only a week or two ago that Speirs called on us and had a long chat, and to many in Bradford the latest news will come as a great shock.'* It was not until October 1921 that Speirs' widow received the news that her husband's mortal remains had been found, although his body had

actually already been found in October 1919 between Pommern Castle and Iberian Farm, just south of Hill 35. The location also suggests that Speirs was killed on 22 August and not on 20 August. He was reburied at Dochy Farm New British Cemetery on the Zonnebeke-Langemarck road, one and a half kilometres from where he was killed.

Preserving his memory

His widow remarried in the 1920's and moved to the south of England. She died in the early 1930's and Speirs' daughter Elizabeth also died around the same time. His son James emigrated to Canada in 1929, where he married and had two children. He enlisted in the Canadian army in 1943, seeing action in France, Belgium and Germany. He died in 1993.

'Jimmy' Speirs' successful football career brought him immortal fame and ensured that he would never be forgotten. Speirs can be seen in countless photographs and special collecting cards and he was mentioned hundreds of times in newspaper articles. The Bradford City football club's museum also devotes a great deal of attention to his career. Finally, Andrew Pickles has created a superb website entirely devoted to James 'Jimmy' Hamilton Speirs.

Jimmy Speirs at Bradford City Football Club (Pickles)

4 The Battle of the Menin Road: 20–25 September 1917
9th (Scottish) Division

SITUATION: Although the campaign had been at a standstill for a while, the German positions and supply lines had been subjected to a continuous and heavy bombardment by the British artillery, transforming the terrain into a lunar landscape. The bombardment had not only razed the German positions to the ground but had also upset the area's centuries old drainage system causing its many streams to overflow their banks and become treacherous quagmires, although otherwise the ground was still relatively dry. In the last week before the offensive the shelling of German positions was further intensified: *'The scene was an indescribable universe of death – brown and pitted with shell-holes holding water, and how heavily laden infantry were to cross the inundations of the chocked Hanebeek and take the objectives at distances varying from 900 to 1,200 yards off was indeed a problem.'*[80]

OBJECTIVE: The prime focus of the attack was the area south of the Ypres-Roulers railway. The objective was to break through the *Albrecht-* and the *Wilhelmstellungen* in order to secure a good jumping-off position on the high ground in front of Gheluvelt and in Polygon Wood. The troops deployed to the north of the main attack were required to break through the *Wilhemstellung*. The Menin Road functioned as an axis along which the fighting developed.

COURSE OF THE BATTLE: The 23rd Division attacked just south of the Menin Road. Despite the presence of a few small pockets of resistance they advanced rapidly in the direction of Gheluvelt, but were unable to take their last objective, as a result of which Tower Hamlets remained in German hands. Two Australian divisions attacked North of the Menin Road and succeeded in reaching their objectives

20 September 1917: general situation (MMP) >

without undue problems. They made effective use of the thick mist to skirt around the German pillboxes and other defensive positions and to take these out. At the Menin Road the 23rd Division was able to take all its objectives. The 19th and the 41st Divisions also took all the ground that had been assigned to them, despite a few setbacks. North of the Ypres-Roulers railway almost all the units advanced according to plan. The 9th Division advanced quickly, despite the muddy ground conditions along the Hanebeek. The pillboxes which had previously held back earlier attacks could now be captured. The 55th Division encountered more serious problems. The men came under fire almost immediately and lost their protective artillery barrage. However, thanks to reinforcements, the division was able to advance further and eventually came to a halt 500 metres from its final objective. The 58th Division advanced without undue setbacks and took hundreds of German soldiers prisoner. The 51st Division initially encountered considerable resistance from the *Wilhelm-Stellung*, but after heavy fighting they were able to break through the German line and reached their final objective without undue problems. The northernmost division, the 20th, managed to penetrate the *Wilhelmstellung*, but further advance proved impossible.

All the German counter-attacks were successfully impeded by the British artillery and the defenders were only able to recapture small pieces of ground in a few locations. In the days which followed, the allied troops were able to improve their positions at various points along the new line. Only Tower Hamlets could not be taken.

RESULT: The first phase of the renewed offensive had been a complete success. General Plumer's new tactics proved to be highly efficient and dealt with the German system of counter-attacks with great precision. German losses were high: more than 3,000 of their soldiers had been taken prisoner and an even greater number had been wounded or killed. However, the numbers of losses on the allied side given by the official historian James Edmonds, are by no means inconsiderable. Between 20 and 25 September the allies lost at least 20,255 men – including a large number of dead. Nine Victoria Crosses, the highest British military distinction, were awarded.

According to the plan, the 9th Division was to attack east of the Frezenberg Ridge. Where the 8th and 16th Division had failed on 16 August, the Scots and South Africans now made another attempt to capture these objectives. Small scale attacks by the 15th Division on 22 August and by the 42nd Division on 4 September had only succeeded in moving the start position forward a little more than a hundred metres. The 28th Brigade prepared themselves for the attack on the right front, while the South African Brigade took charge

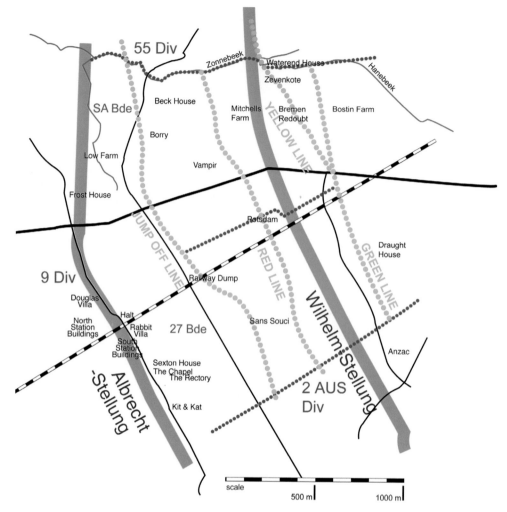

20 September 1917: 9th (Scottish) Division (MMP)

The 9th Division on 20 September 1917
   27th Brigade
      11th and 12th Royal Scots, 9th Cameronians (Scottish Rifles),
      6th King's Own Scottish Borderers (KOSB)
     South African Brigade
   1st, 2nd, 3rd and 4th South African Regiments

Strohgut, known to the British as Vampire Farm. A concrete pillbox was later built into the walls of the farm, 6 March 1916 (Deraeve)

Private Alexander Cowan (George Heriot's School)

of the left flank. The Red Line between Hanebeek Wood through Potsdam, Vampire Farm and Mitchell's Farm to the Zonnebeek constituted their first objective. In order to let the artillery do its job thoroughly, the men of both brigades were required to wait for an hour at this line. The 27th Brigade had to advance further to the Green Line, which ran just beyond the German *Wilhelmstellung*. The South Africans were also given the Yellow Line, an additional branch of the Green Line.

'Casualties on the march to the assembly area were regarded as inevitable, and there was nothing for it but to trust on luck.'[81] On 16 and 17 September the 9th Division relieved the 42nd at the Frezenberg Ridge. During the night of 19 to 20 September the men got ready for the attack and proceeded to the jumping-off area: *'Heavy rain descended for nearly three hours, but by rare good fortune the enemy's guns were unusually quiet and comparatively few casualties were suffered; this was taken as a good omen.'*[82] After the failed offensives of 31 July and 16 August the high command hoped that General Plumer's new tactics could tip the balance in the allies' favour.

The 27th Brigade: advance to the Green Line

The 6th Battalion King's Own Scottish Borderers were on the 9th Division's southernmost flank. Their first direct objective was Hanebeek Wood. Taking this copse, which was covered in pillboxes and fortified machine gun nests, promised to be no easy task. Under the protection of heavy artillery barrage they were required to advance to a position very close to their objective. Only one zone was not shelled so that the Scots were able to take up a position at the rear side of the wood. As soon as the artillery fire moved on to the German positions further forward, the Scottish Borderers would be able to attack the copse simultaneously from all sides.

When the attack signal was given at 5.40 a.m., the Scots stormed out of their positions in the direction of Hanebeek Wood. The artillery barrage did its work brilliantly and the men took up positions around the wood. Shortly afterwards, the artillery turned its attentions to other strong points and the Borderers were able to take the wood with relative ease. They were also helped by a few Australians of the 2nd Division, which attacked to the south of the 9th Division. The number of casualties was low, *'caused chiefly by rifle-fire and by our own shrapnel which was used on the right flank of the wood.'*[83] The men had now reached their first objective. After a halt of one hour the Scots pushed through to the Green Line. They also managed to take this without great problems, although they did suffer a number of casualties due to the German barrage and resistance from a stubbornly held machine gun nest. The men immediately began extending their positions.[84]

The 9th Battalion Cameronians (Scottish Rifles) went into action on the left of the King's Own Scottish Borderers. Their right company was able to reach the Red Line without encountering much in the way of opposition. The company on the left, however, took the full force of a machine gun installed in a pillbox on the railway line near Potsdam. The Scots were held up and several were killed. Private **Alexander Cowan** was one of the men of this battalion. Cowan, an alumnus of the George Heriot's School in Edinburgh, was heir to the two hundred year old family business 'Alexander Cowan & Sons', a major paper manufacturer and printing firm in Edinburgh. Cowan, who was unmarried, enlisted in the 9th Royal Scots in 1916 but later, in March 1917, left the regiment to join the 9th Scottish Rifles. The 27-year-old Private Cowan was killed on 20 September but his body was never found. He is remembered today on the Tyne Cot Memorial.[85]

Among the other casualties was Second Lieutenant **Alexander Currie Goudie** of the 9th Scottish Rifles, who was killed on 20 September. Before the war he had worked as a shipping clerk in Glasgow and had joined up on 1 September 1914 as a Private with the 1st Scottish Horse, a cavalry regiment with which he saw action in Gallipoli and Egypt. In December 1915 he was promoted to Lance Corporal and began officer training in Cambridge in November 1916. Goudie received a commission as a Second Lieutenant with the 9th Scottish Rifles at the end of February 1917. He left for the front in late April of that year and joined his unit at the beginning of May. The 23-year-old Second Lieutenant Goudie was killed near Zonnebeke on 20 September. His body was also never found and he is therefore remembered today on the Tyne Cot Memorial.

Their first objective, the Green Line, could only be reached with considerable delay, meaning that as soon as the troops got there it was time to press on again to the Red Line. For the 12th Battalion Royal Scots this was also their final objective. However, they were required to take out the pillboxes along the railway line, which proved to be a particularly difficult task. '*A row of five [pill-boxes], tucked in along the banks of the railway, was flanked on the north by the massive fortifications of Potsdam.*'[86] However, their many days of training in taking strong points of this kind proved its value and the pillboxes were taken out one by one. Naturally enough, the Germans did not cede their positions without a struggle, resulting in heavy fighting and giving rise to great acts of personal courage on more than one occasion. Captain Harry Reynolds managed to take one pillbox single-handedly and his one man action earned him the Victoria Cross.[87] The Royal Scots succeeded in taking the Red Line and dug themselves in, while the Scottish Rifles now tried to push on to the Green Line. The handful of pillboxes which still offered resistance were soon overrun and the Scots took a large number of prisoners of war.

Sergeant **Gerald William Walker**, a platoon sergeant with the 9th Cameronians, was killed during the advance to the Green Line. According to the platoon commander, who wrote to Walker's fam-

ily notifying them of his death, Walker was killed at the Bremen Redoubt, although this was actually in the South African sector. '*He died like a true soldier immediately after doing great work in capturing 80 German prisoners, for which he was recommended for the Military Medal.*'[88] The divisional history of the 9th Division only mentions forty prisoners and Walker was never awarded the Military Medal. Walker came from Barrhead, near Glasgow. After leaving school he worked as an apprentice with a cotton printer. He joined up in 14 August 1914 at the age of 21 and was sent to the front in May 1915. Sergeant Walker is remembered today on the Tyne Cot Memorial.

Another casualty was Lance Corporal **John Lavelle**. The 27-year-old Lavelle was from Burnley in Lancashire. His brother Joseph had been killed during the Battle of Loos on 26 September 1915, while serving[89] with the same battalion. Around the same time their father, James Lavelle, also died as a result of an accident at the Vickers' Wagon Works in Lancaster. Lavelle, who had previously served six years with the Royal Navy, joined up in 1917, leaving his wife and child behind in Burnley. Lavelle's mother heard the news of his death via '*a letter received from Pte. Blakey (...) who stated that his friend was shot through the head.*'[90] His body was never recovered and Lance Corporal Lavelle's name is inscribed on the Tyne Cot Memorial.

Lance Corporal John Lavelle (Otter)

The Scots of the 27th Brigade had succeeded in taking all their objectives. Success was in prospect. The task was now to fight off the German counter-attack.

The South Africans go into action

The South African Brigade were to be responsible for the northern part of the front line. The 3rd and 4th South African Regiments were required to push ahead to the Red Line, after which the 1st and 2nd Regiments would take over the attack and advance via the Yellow Line to the Green Line.

The 4th Regiment was able to reach the Red Line without difficulty. The German positions which had caused so much death and destruction among the advancing troops from the beginning of the campaign on 31 July were now overrun. The Germans in Borry Farm and Beck House did not even have time to grab their weapons. Although the South Africans reached the Red Line very rapidly, this

Second Lieutenant Alexander Currie Goudie (Perry)

Lance Sergeant Donald Gordon Douglas (de Ruvigny)

Sergeant Gerald William Walker (de Ruvigny)

Private Cyril William Arnot (de Ruvigny)

was not achieved without a number of casualties. Lance Sergeant **Donald Gordon Douglas**, who was killed at the Red Line, was one of them. Douglas was born in Northern Ireland in May 1886 and went to school in Ballymena and Londonderry. He joined the army in 1901, seeing action *inter alia* in South Africa, during the Second Boer War. When the First World War broke out in August 1914 Douglas was dispatched with his unit to fight the Germans in Southwest Africa, after which he was sent back to England for further training. He served in Egypt in 1915 and in 1916 he was one of the men who came through the action at Delville Wood, during the Battle of the Somme unscathed. On 20 September 1917, however, he was killed near Mitchell's Farm. In a long, moving letter, in which he also described his own experiences, his platoon commander gave Douglas's family in Portballantrae in Ireland the sad news: *'It is my painful duty to advise you that your son was fatally wounded at my side this morning (20 Sept.). He fell to a sniper's bullet when the position was captured and victory complete for the moment. Your son was my right arm in the taking of the objective that fell to the lot of my platoon. A moment or previously I had a marvellous escape myself, being struck by a bullet on the steel helmet. It was your son's great boldness and bravery that took him to the fatal spot to reconnoitre the resistance so as to deal with it. He was struck in the stomach and died almost immediately, but not before we had brought him into safety. Your son was buried in the neighbourhood of the 'strongpoint', and a cross put up bearing his name and that of his regiment. Killed in Action. I write to you with a full heart; your son was a brave and great-hearted man. I feel his loss very much indeed; he came into action as Platoon Sergt., being here to take charge in case of me falling. Sixteen men and myself were all that came out of that action, and all these wish me to express their sincere sympathy with you in your bereavement.'*[91] Lance Sergeant Douglas's battlefield grave was lost later on in the war and the 31-year-old professional soldier is now remembered today on the Menin Gate.

The 3rd South African Regiment advanced on the left of the 4th in the direction of the Red Line, but were to encounter much more resistance. German machine guns subjected the advancing South Africans to heavy fire from three pillboxes at Potsdam.

Private **Cyril William Arnot** was among those killed. Arnot was the second son of Frederick Stanley Arnot, a famous missionary and

Abandoned British positions on the Frezenberg Ridge, ca. 1919 (Deraeve)

explorer who had explored and opened up key areas of Africa for the colonial powers. After his travels in Central Africa, Arnot senior settled in Liverpool, where he helped coordinate the transport of supplies for missions to Africa. Cyril William was born in 1896. He originally went to school in Bristol, but it was not long before the entire family moved to South Africa, from where his father made various journeys into the African interior, while Cyril attended Jeppe High School in Johannesburg. After leaving school he became a clerk with the National Bank. His father, Frederick Arnot, died suddenly in May 1914, a few months before the outbreak of the war. Cyril joined up in August of the following year and left for England in October 1915 in order to undergo military training. He served in Egypt from January to May 1916 and – like Lance Sergeant Douglas – also survived Delville Wood. The 21-year-old Arnot was killed on the battlefields of Flanders on 20 September. He was buried on the spot where he was killed, but the reburial parties were not able to find his body after the war. Private Arnot is therefore remembered today on the Tyne Cot Memorial.[92]

It is probable that Corporal **Authbert Christopher Cedric Dutton** was also killed by the machine gun fire from Potsdam on 20

September. Dutton was the son of an Anglican vicar from Gargrave, a small village near Skipton in Yorkshire. He had only just turned nineteen when he lost his life near Zonnebeke.[93] Corporal Dutton's name is inscribed on the Menin Gate, as is that of Private **Harry Crockett,** who was also with the 3rd South African Regiment. Crockett, from Hawes, Yorkshire, was killed at the age of 18 near Zonnebeke.[94] Both had probably emigrated to South Africa with their parents as children, which would explain how they came to be with a South African unit.

With the help of the 12th Royal Scots the battalion was able to take the German defensive position at Potsdam, meaning that the 3rd Regiment had now also reached the Red Line.

At this point – and entirely according to plan – the 1st and the 2nd South African Regiments now took over the attack. It was their job to push on to the Yellow and the Green Lines. However, both regiments had suffered considerable losses from the German artillery and the murderous fire rained on them from Potsdam – and a few other enemy positions – during their advance to the Red Line. An account of this, which leaves little to the imagination, is preserved in the War Diary of the 1st South African Regiment. '*Almost immediately on my arrival at 1st objective I saw some men of both regiments move through the barrage and attack enemy strong point at D.26.a80.45 (Dressing Station). (...) I followed them and on calling on the enemy to surrender, 2 officers and between 30 and 40 men, (all Medical Corps), came out and were sent back as prisoners. The remainder refused to surrender. I ordered some men to blow in one of the loop holes, which they succeeded on doing, I believe with Mills Hand Grenades, then a 'P' bomb was thrown in. In a couple of minutes the whole place was in a sheet of flame with huge clouds of smoke issuing. I then formed two parties on N. and S. corner of L. end of the stronghold, and had the enemy shot down as he bolted. I estimate 40 enemy machine gunners were shot here. There are about 35 dead bodies in and about the entrance and 3 half burnt bodies inside the building. Besides this there is a string of dead trailing towards the enemy lines. No prisoners were taken.*'[95] This engagement took place just in front of the Yellow Line, which both regiments succeeded in taking without undue problems: '*The advance to 2nd Objective was uneventful and I was able to report at 7-50 am that the final objective had been*

Corporal Authbert Christopher Dutton (Craven's Part in the Great War)

Private Harry Crockett (Craven's Part in the Great War)

taken and consolidation was proceeding with touch on both flanks.'[96] The zone which the 2nd Regiment was required to take was considerably better defended, however. Above all the machine gun nests in Waterend House, Tulip Cottages and on Hill 37, all of which were within the 55th Division's area, caused many problems and hold-ups. The South Africans had to take the pillboxes on their own. Lance Corporal William Henry Hewitt captured two of them single-handedly, for which he was awarded the Victoria Cross.[97]

Yet despite such heroic actions, the 2nd Regiment still suffered a large number of casualties. Among them was Lance Sergeant **John Philips**, a South African citizen of Canadian origin. He was born in Montreal, where he was educated at Westmount Academy. He volunteered for service in the Canadian army in late October 1899 in order to fight in the war in South Africa and was posted to the 2nd Special Service Battalion Royal Canadian Regiment. The battalion, which was approximately a thousand men strong, arrived in South Africa at the end of November 1899, where the raw recruits were given two months intensive training. They were sent into action for

Lance Sergeant John Philips (de Ruvigny)

Ostermorgengut, known to the British as Low Farm. Here too a pillbox built with concrete blocks was constructed inside the ruins of the farm, ca. 1916 (Deraeve)

right: Sergeant Gordon Farquharson Wilson (Watsonians in the Great War)

the first time in February 1900 near Paardeberg, where the battalion immediately suffered heavy losses. Philips returned to Canada with his unit in late December 1900. The Boer War lasted until 1902 and in that same year Philips returned to South Africa to settle there permanently. He joined the Natal Border Police and saw action again in 1906 against the Zulu rebels. At the outbreak of the First World War he initially fought against the Germans in South West Africa and then volunteered for service overseas in 1915. Philips was sent to Europe in October of that year and was killed in Flanders on 20 September 1917, just one week before celebrating his 41st birthday.[98] Lance Sergeant John Philips is remembered today on the Menin Gate.

All the South African units had now reached their final objective, the Green Line, although both the new South African and Scottish positions still had to be consolidated and extended in anticipation of the expected German counter-attack. The allied artillery did a particularly good job, however: *'A terrific [German] barrage along our line about 5 P.M. seemed to be the prelude to an onslaught, and our men, surging forward out of the shelled zone, peered eagerly into the mist for a sight of the field-grey foemen, but all attempts of the enemy to mass were broken up by our artillery-fire. So accurate and stupendous was our barrage that it seemed like a solid, impenetrable barrier.'[99]*

The wounded

Despite the extremely poor state of the ground, the evacuation of the wounded went off quite well: *'numerous aid posts were established and the staff of stretcher-bearers was greatly increased by large parties from the infantry.'[100]* Sergeant **Gordon Farquharson Wilson** was one of the wounded who were taken off the battlefield on 20 September 1917. Wilson was born in Cape Town, but was of Scottish descent, which is why his family sent him to the George Watson School in Edinburgh. Wilson returned to the land of his birth in 1907, where he managed a large farm in the Transvaal. As soon as war broke out he joined the army in order to fight against the Germans in South-west Africa. In 1915 he left for Egypt and was sent to England for further training. Shortly thereafter he arrived in France with the 1st Regiment South African Infantry, where he was made a sergeant. The 25-year-old Wilson was wounded on 20 September. He was moved to a series of aid posts and eventually ended up in a Casualty Clearing Station in Poperinghe, where he died four days later. Sergeant Wilson was buried in Nine Elms British Cemetery.[101]

Private **Harold Hedley Art** was also with the 1st Regiment. Art was from Vereeniging in the Transvaal. He joined up with his brother Charles Herbert Art. They fought together in the trenches of the Western Front and were able to go to Nuneaton in England on leave a couple of times. Charles became a prisoner of war in 1916, probably during the Battle of the Somme, while Harold was mortally wounded at Zonnebeke on 20 September. He was taken to a Casualty Clearing Station, but died on 22 September. The 28-year-old Private Art was buried in Mendinghem Military Cemetery.[102]

Another casualty on 20 September was Private **George Thom**, who was of Scottish origin and had been educated at George Heriot's School in Edinburgh. Shortly before the turn of the century he swapped the inclement Highlands for the warmer climes of Ficksburg in the Cape Colony, where he worked as a magistrate for the British government. In 1900 he enlisted as a Trooper in the Imperial Yeomanry and saw active service with them during the Boer War. Thom then married and had two children. In 1917 he joined up again, this time as a private in the South African Scottish, which would ultimately become the 4th South African Regiment. He was seriously wounded on 20 September 1917. After passing through numer-

left: Private Harold Hedley Art (Davies)
right: Private George Thom (George Heriot's School)

ous aid posts he was finally taken to a field hospital, where a doctor treated his wounds. The 38-year-old Thom's agony did not end there, however. He was sent for further treatment at a Base Hospital in Boulogne, where he eventually died. Private Thom was buried in Boulogne Eastern Cemetery.[103]

While the wounded were being evacuated, the troops in the firing line were further consolidating their positions. Despite the temporary interruption of the offensive, both the German and the British artillery continued to shell the other and snipers looked for even the smallest of movements in the gaps along the enemy front lines, causing numerous casualties. On 21 September Brigadier General **Francis Aylmer Maxwell**, the commander of the 27th Brigade, made a tour of inspection of the newly extended positions. In the days before, he had gone up to the line on numerous occasions, in the heat of the battle, to lead and encourage his men. Maxwell was an experienced professional soldier. He had first received his commission in 1891 with the Royal Sussex Regiment, and two years later he was transferred to the Indian Staff Corps. Maxwell saw active service in various parts

The pillbox at Low Farm, photographed from the other side, after being captured by the British, and clearly built with pre-fabricated concrete blocks, September 1917 (AWM E759)

of India, where he was awarded the Distinguished Service Order in 1898 and also went on to serve with distinction during the war in South Africa. In March 1900 he and a group of other officers moved a number of guns to safety while under enemy fire, 'having shown the greatest gallantry and disregard of danger' and received the Victoria Cross for his bravery. After the Boer War he again served in India and in Australia. From June to October 1916 Maxwell commanded the 12th Battalion Middlesex Regiment. He was soon promoted to Brigadier General and was given command of the 27th Brigade. At the end of November 1916 he was awarded the Distinguished Service Order for the second time. In the early morning of 21 September 1917 Maxwell was keeping an eye on things while his men brought barbed wire up to the railway on the Green Line, when he was shot by a German sniper. Brigadier General Maxwell's body was taken to Ypres, where he was buried in Ypres Reservoir Cemetery on 23 September.[104] Maxwell's brother, Lieutenant-Colonel Eustace Lockhart Maxwell, who was six years younger, also lost his life during the war. Lieutenant-Colonel Maxwell was killed in France in 1916 and is remembered today on the Neuve Chapelle Memorial.[105]

Losses

The men of the 9th Division were relieved on the night of 21 to 22 September, an operation which took until morning to complete. An assessment could now be made of their achievements during the offensive. The number of casualties was relatively small given the size of the operation. The 6th Battalion King's Own Scottish Borders, for example, lost only eight officers wounded, with 26 men killed, 200 wounded and 27 missing, which was very good going by the standards of 1917. The 9th Division's total losses amounted to 2,111 officers and men, of which 395 were killed.[106] The South African Brigade suffered the heaviest casualties of the entire 9th Division. Out of the 91 officers and 2,488 men who went into the attack only half came through unscathed. 16 officers and 237 men were killed.[107]

Despite the chilling casualty figures, the offensive was a success. All the objectives had been taken and held and the German counter-attacks were shot to pieces before they could get off the ground. General Plumer could therefore look back on a particularly successful day. They still had a long way to go, but the allied train seemed to be on the right track.

Brigadier General Francis Aylmer Maxwell (Perry)

**20 September 1917:
Second Lieutenant Richard Taylor
2nd/8th London Regiment**

Taylor with his mother in Canada, after enlisting with the Patricia's (Parsons)

Princess Patricia's Canadian Light Infantry

Richard Hayward Taylor was born in January 1892 in Carbonear, a village – in what was then the British colony of Newfoundland – on the west coast of Canada. He was the only son in a family with seven daughters. Taylor attended the local school, later going on to the Methodist College in St. John, some 130 kilometres away. His father – who was also called Richard Hayward – was a sea captain. When he went to work for the Hudson's Bay Company in 1910, the family moved to Montreal in Quebec. Taylor began an engineering degree at McGill University in Montreal and in the meantime belonged to the 5th Royal Regiment.

In May 1914 Taylor, who was then in his second year at McGill, joined the 1st University Contingent of the Princess Patricia's Canadian Light Infantry. He left for England and joined his unit in the front line at Armentières at the end of August, transferring to the Divisional Signal Company of the 3rd Canadian Division in February 1916. He returned to England in late July 1916 as his name had been put forward for a commission and he was required to undergo officer training. A year later Taylor was made a Second Lieutenant with the 2nd/8th Battalion of the London Regiment, the Post Office Rifles. His mother wanted him to go to Canada on leave in August of that year: *'I beg to ask leave for my son 2/Lieut R. H. Taylor who left Canada two years ago (...). He is my only son and I certainly if it is possible want him back on leave as I am not well and I must see him.'* She did not receive an answer until 22 September. Sent from London, it simply said: *'it is regretted that under existing circumstances the leave applied for cannot be granted'.'* Second Lieutenant Richard Hayward Taylor had been killed two days earlier...

Post Office Rifles

The 58th Division, to which the Post Office Rifles belonged, was

to attack on 20 September from a position just east of St. Julien. The battalion had been able to train well and was ready for the attack: *'The assembly, which had been most carefully rehearsed, was accomplished with only one casualty; and the men, who were in excellent spirits and full of confidence, were 'out and over' the moment the barrage started(...).'* The attack went as planned and the positions which constituted their objective were taken. However, all the officers of A and C Companies were wounded or killed, Taylor being one of them. The army authorities listed him officially as wounded and missing, but stretcher bearer C. Saunders disagreed: *'I saw in the paper that he was reported Wounded & Missing early in October. He was actually killed on right of St. Julien 20th Sept. by shell fire. I found his body the same day (being stretcher-bearer) and took his property, including his watch and wallet (...). No time for burial. Ground held. We were relieved by the 10 Londons, who probably undertook the burials.'* The watch referred to was later destroyed. It had been heavily damaged and could no longer be returned to the family. The Divisional Burial Officer interred Taylor's body. His mother did not want to believe that her only son had been killed. As he was initially listed as wounded and missing, she maintained the hope that he had only been wounded and was suffering from amnesia. One of Taylor's sisters, Margaret, wanted to serve as a nurse with the Voluntary Aid Detachment and her mother initially refused to let her do so. However, when the news came that Taylor was missing, her mother did finally grant her permission. Margaret saw various *'awful places'* during her search but never found her brother. She stayed in Croydon, England until the end of 1918 .

Despite the fact that Taylor had been buried, his body could not be found after the war. Second Lieutenant Taylor's name is inmortalized on the Menin Gate.

Second Lieutenant Richard Taylor in England (Parsons)

South African Scots of the 9th Division in support trenches east of Frezenberg Ridge, 22 September 1917 (IWM Q11681)

5 The Battle of Polygon Wood: 26 September–3 October 1917
5th Australian Division

SITUATION: The offensive of 20 September had been a success. The men were able to take all their objectives and were now preparing for the next stage.

The artillery bombardment had played an important role in the success of the entire operation. On the afternoon of 20 September the first field batteries moved forward and soon began their heavy bombardment of the German positions, which was further intensified in the last 24 hours before the offensive began. A major German counter-attack in the early morning of 25 September threatened to throw a spanner in the works, but was stopped and driven back. Between 20 and 25 September the weather also remained dry, which made the preparations for the next step easier.

OBJECTIVE: The main focus of the attack now lay between the Ypres-Roulers railway and the Menin Road, where the Australians were required to push forward and capture the whole of Polygon Wood and the southern section of Zonnebeke. The Australian divisions were flanked on both sides by British units which were also required to advance a considerable distance.

26 September 1917: general situation (MMP) >

COURSE OF THE BATTLE: The 5th Australian Division attacked at Polygon Wood. They encountered little resistance and were able to take their final objective without undue problems. The German *Flandern I-Stellung* was breached just east of Polygon Wood. The men of the 4th Australian Division also reached their objectives without difficulty.

South of the 33rd Division, however, the 5th Australian Division had more problems. A day earlier the German counter-attack had pushed the 33rd Division back quite a distance and the lost ground

< Water carriers pass a burnt-out tank, 27 September 1917 (IWM Q2990)

could only be retaken with the help of the Australians. South of the Menin Road the 39th Division did not manage to break through to its final objective. The men came under fire from all sides and had no choice but to pull back. The 3rd Division attacked to the north of the 5th Australian Division. Its right-hand brigade was able to reach its objectives without too many difficulties, but the left-hand brigade was seriously handicapped by the muddy conditions of the Zonnebeek. The troops got bogged down and came under heavy fire. In the end they had to dig themselves in 550 metres from their final objective. The 59th Division was able to reach and consolidate its objectives without any problems whatsoever. Near Aviatik Farm the 58th Division tried to secure a good jumping-off position, but with little success and the men did not manage to reach their objective. Despite the mixed success of the British attacks the German counter-attacks were dealt with effectively and shot to pieces, especially due to the use of artillery.

RESULT: Most of the objectives were taken and for the second time in a row the offensive could be regarded as a relative success. The Germans again sustained a large number of casualties. They had hoped that a new attack would be longer in coming, as their reserves had been thinned out considerably. Moreover, the tactic of using *Eingreifdivisionen* now appeared obsolete as the allies had succeeded in adapting themselves very effectively to the defensive tactics which the Germans had been using up till that point. They now had to find another system of defence.

The 5th Australian Division on 26 September 1917
> 14th Brigade
>> 53rd , 54th, 55th and 56th Battalion
> 15th Brigade
>> 57th, 58th, 59th and 60th Battalion
> 8th Brigade (reserve)
>> 29th, 30th, 31st and 32nd Battalion

The 5th Australian Division attacked with its 14th and 15th Brigades. The jumping-off line ran diagonally through Polygon Wood. What still remained of the wood was to be taken in two stages. First of all the Australians of the 53rd and the 59th Battalion would push ahead to the edge of the wood, the Red Line, behind a protective curtain of artillery fire and once they got there the two battalions were to establish a defensive line. After a halt the 55th, 56th, 29th and 31st Battalions would take over and move on up to the Blue Line. This was just beyond the *Flandern I-Stellung*, which according to the plan, had also to be breached.

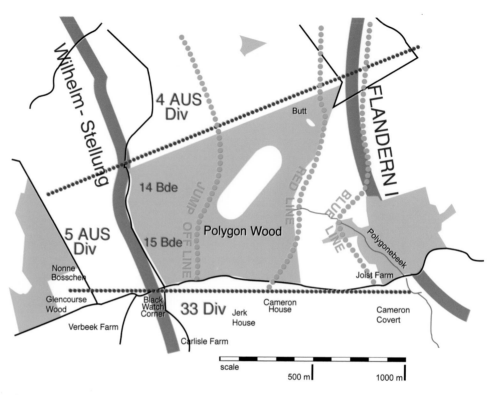

26 September 1917: 5th Australian Division (MMP)

The German attack on 25 September 1917

On the night of 22 to 23 September the men of the 14th Brigade took over the front line from the 1st Australian Division and the following night it was the turn of the 15th Brigade. The 14th Brigade also took over part of the line. *'All of the Division's preliminary arrangements were working admirably. Supplies of all kinds were reaching the front line in sufficient quantities, and the men were in high spirits; the artillery practise barrages were working splendidly; the engineers were outlining their forward communications. (...) In these circumstances, the situation was on the whole eminently satisfactory, and though casualties at the rate of about 100 per day were reported, these were unavoidable, and, perhaps, lighter than might have been expected.'*[108] In the early morning of 25 September the Australian and British positions came under a heavy German artillery bombardment. Shortly afterwards the Germans launched a major counter-attack on the boundary between the zones allocated to the 15th Brigade and the 33rd Division.

Private George Percy Taylor (Parnham)

Sapper William Alfred Fitch (AWM DA10092)

Classic photograph of the Anzac pillbox, where the Australian flag was planted on 20 September, 27 September 1917 (AWM E2321)

Plaque with the names of the Signal staff of the 29th Battalion, Fitch's name is the penultimate on the list, 6 June 1917 (AWM REL25338)

The men on the 33rd Division's right flank had a very hard time of it and had to give up part of the ground which had been won. Among the men of the 33rd Division was Private **George Percy Taylor**. Private Taylor was with the 9th battalion Highland Light Infantry, which tried to stop the German advance with a counter-attack. *'Many of the platoons who were ordered forward in support of the shaken lines disappeared for ever.'*[109] This was probably what happened to Taylor, a miner from Doncaster in South Yorkshire, who was only 19 when he was killed in the chaos of the attack. Taylor's father could not understand why his son had no identified grave and tried in vain to find out exactly what had happened to him. A framed version of this photograph of George Taylor, covered with a black veil, hung for many years in his sister Peggy's sitting room. Private Taylor is remembered today on the Tyne Cot Memorial.

After the German counter-attack had ceased, their artillery still continued to make its presence felt. The brunt of the bombardment was not only borne by the men in the front line. The supply lines and the support area also came under regular artillery fire.

Among the casualties was Sapper **William Alfred Fitch**, who was killed in the early evening. He was with the Signal Company of the 5th Australian Division, which had been working flat out all day laying communication lines to the forward trenches. Fitch was a 21-year-old carpenter from Middle Brighton, Victoria. He joined the Australian army in July 1915 and was posted to the 29th Battalion. He arrived in France at the end of June 1916 via the Middle East and on 1 April 1917 was transferred to the Signal Company of the 5th Australian Division. On 25 September he was one of the men who did not answer the roll call. He was listed as missing and the court of enquiry did not declare him officially dead until April 1918. They also interviewed thirteen men from Fitch's unit *'who were present or near the place where Sapper Fitch was last seen'*. Almost all of them told the same story: *'Towards dark he was sent to a Pill Box 10 or 20 yards away, used as an Advanced Signal Office, to obtain candles for lighting purposes.'* This was probably between Glencorse Wood and Polygon Wood. Soon afterwards a German shell killed various men just outside the pillbox. *'The bodies of these men were badly mutilated and buried on the spot.'* None of the men could confirm that Fitch was killed by this shell, although this seemed highly likely. The court of enquiry thus had no option but to declare him officially dead. His comrades put up a cross in his memory at Hooge Crater Cemetery.[110] Sapper Fitch is remembered today on the Menin Gate.

A large part of the 57th Battalion, which was heading through Glencorse Wood on their way to the front line as evening was falling, was caught by German artillery fire, causing at least 87 casualties. One of the three officers killed was Captain **John Thomas Hamilton Aram**, a 32-year-old accountant from St. Kilda, Victoria, who belonged to the 2nd Division's Signal Company. Aram was made an officer in early June 1916 and was sent to the Middle East. He subsequently sailed from Alexandria with his unit on *HMS Southland*, a Belgian ship which had been commandeered in 1915 and which had been obliged to change its name from the *Vaderland*. The ship was attacked by a German U-boat during the voyage and all on board were taken off except for ten volunteers who stayed on to bring the *Southland* safely to harbour. Lieutenant Aram also stayed on board, which earned him an honourable mention in despatches. On his return to Egypt he was transferred to the 57th Battalion and was promoted to the rank of captain in April 1916. His unit was sent to France shortly thereafter and arrived in Flanders a few months later. Captain Aram was killed on 25 September 1917 when he was hit by a German artillery shell, *'high in the side and [Aram] died almost at once'*.[111] The bodies of the two other officers who were killed, Captain Herbert Spencer Dickinson and Lieutenant Gerald Victor Woolcott Joynt, were taken out of the line a few days later and were buried near Dikkebus.[112] However, Aram's body could not be found and he is remembered today on the Menin Gate.

Private **Edward John Ryan** also lost his life in the same bombardment. Ryan was a 27-year-old farmer from Beulah, Victoria. He was initially sent to the Middle East, but eventually ended up in the trenches of the Western Front as part of the 57th Battalion. In early September 1916 he was wounded in the trenches by his own bayonet, which resulted in his being brought before a court martial, but was found not guilty of causing a self-inflicted wound. A severe bout

of bronchitis landed him in hospital at the end of December 1916 and he was sent to England to convalesce. He returned to his unit on 4 May 1917. In August of that year he spent two weeks' leave in England. Private Ryan was killed instantly by a German shell on 25 September 1917. A few days later a group of men went to look for his body, *'but were unable to find him. A shell must have buried him right out of sight so he was not buried in a cemetery but on the field.'*[113] His name is inscribed on the Menin Gate.

The German counter-attack was intended to recapture part of the ground they had lost and – in so doing – to cause serious disruption to the allied plans and preparations for a new attack. It had the desired effect as several Australian battalions took quite a beating and had to be replaced by fresh reserve battalions of the 8th Brigade, which were brought up in the middle of the night: *'The men's excellent physical condition brought them to the end of their journey in the early morning. The assembly on the jumping-off line had still to be completed, and the strictest silence had to be maintained lest the enemy's suspicions of the impending attack should be aroused.'*[114]

At exactly 5.50 a.m. the allied guns opened fire on the German positions: *'thousands of shells screamed through the air and burst in a long, straight line of flame and destruction about 200 yards ahead of the waiting infantry. Released simultaneously from the bonds that had held them silent and motionless, the 4,000 men of the six attacking battalions dashed forward at a run'*. A hundred metres from the artillery barrage the men stopped and waited until the barrage moved on to the next German line. Some couldn't control themselves and ran on into the line of fire to their deaths. *'But these were few: the rest restrained themselves and lit the cigarette that had long been held ready between the white lips. Hundreds of matches flickered feebly along the line in the misty grey dawn, and keen eyes watched the barrage as second after second of its three minute wait ticked away.'* As soon as the barrage had moved on, the men resumed their advance.

Captain John Thomas Hamilton Aram (AWM P00249.002)

Private Edward John Ryan (AWM DA13697)

Private Harry Wallace Brokenshire
(AWM H05891)

Private William Henry Pegrum
(AWM P02599.032)

Into battle with the 14th Brigade

The men of the 53rd Battalion followed right behind the barrage and the first pillboxes were attacked as soon as the bombardment moved on. Most of the defenders had been badly shaken up and were too dazed to offer much resistance. Many willingly surrendered. '*With hands raised and voices mumbling 'Kamerad, Kamerad', the long line of Germans with their field-grey uniforms and ashen-grey faces would file humbly out past the three or four grim Australians (...).*'[115] Those German defenders who did manage to open fire on the advancing Australians from within their pillboxes were quickly dealt with. The first objective had thus been reached quite easily and the number of casualties remained relatively low. It was now a question of waiting for the barrage which would soon be brought to bear on the next German line and for the arrival of the 55th and 56th Battalions.

In the meantime the 53rd Battalion set about consolidating the ground they had taken. It was at this point of the battle that Private **William Henry Pegrum** was killed. A comrade later explained: '*Pegrum was killed outright in the morning of 26th Sept. at Polygon Wood, being blown up by a shell which landed right alongside him.*' Pegrum had enlisted as a volunteer in the Australian army on 13 April 1915, leaving a wife and three children behind in Paddington, New South Wales. Private Pegrum went with the 17th Battalion to Gallipoli and then to the Middle East, eventually ending up in France, where he was posted to the 53rd Battalion. He was ill on numerous occasions during his service on the various fronts. Flu, a gastric infection and muscle pains landed him in hospital several times. In early September 1917 he was allowed to go to England on two weeks' leave. Not long after returning to his unit he was listed as missing after the attack on 26 September. Private Pegrum was not officially declared dead until the beginning of April 1918.[116] His body was never found and he is remembered today on the Menin Gate.

Just before 7.30 a.m. the barrage became heavier and moved on to the next German line. The men of the 55th and the 56th Battalions advanced and tried to push through to the final objective. They too encountered little resistance on the way, as most of the Germans scarcely fought back. Where they did, their positions were quickly encircled and taken out and they were able to reach the Blue Line

just after 8.00 a.m.. Here the Germans offered stiffer resistance, but with two attacking battalions this also proved no problem.

The men immediately began to extend and strengthen the positions they had captured. Yet the Australians were still not completely out of danger. The Germans now began shelling the area with artillery, while their infantry tried to get various counter-attacks off the ground. This proved unsuccessful, however.

It was probably at this stage of the battle that Private **Harry Wallace Brokenshire** of the 56th Battalion was killed. Brokenshire was a 20-year-old workman from Bishop's Bridge, New South Wales. He enlisted in the Australian army in September 1915 and joined the 56th Battalion in France in early December 1916. He was hospitalized a few days later suffering from painful feet. This happened again at the end of January 1917 and he was admitted to hospital in England with trench feet, where he stayed until March. Before returning to the front, he was given a week's leave in England during which he contracted gonorrhoea. In total, Brokenshire had been out of action for almost three months and was only able to return to his unit at the end of August. A month later Private Brokenshire was listed as missing after the attack of 26 September 1917 and the army authorities declared him officially dead in late December. Some time later his mother received a visit from a former comrade of her son, who claimed that Brokenshire had been killed by an artillery shell together with two other soldiers and a sergeant. Research into these three other men suggests that this cannot be what happened. All three were killed on 29 September and were with the 30th Battalion.[117] In September 1924 Brokenshire's mother received notification that the '*Imperial War Graves Commission has been successful in recovering the late soldier's remains which have since been interred with every measure of care and reverence in the Aeroplane Cemetery.*'[118]

Another casualty suffered by the 55th Battalion was Private **Albert George Pegram**, who was mortally wounded during the attack of 26 September, probably while the battalion was consolidating the Blue Line. Pegram was a railway worker from Bredbo, New South Wales. He enlisted in the Australian army in late September 1916 and joined his unit in France on 30 April 1917. Only a few days later he was hospitalized with diphtheria and could not return to the trenches

Private George Pegram (Pegram)

until 22 September. Four days later the inexperienced Pegram was shot in the stomach by a German sniper hidden in a pillbox, while he was helping to extend the battalion's positions.[119] Pegram was seriously wounded. He was taken out of the line via the Hooge, Birr Cross Roads and Menin House aid posts and received treatment the following day in a field hospital at Lijssenthoek, but died some days later from the consequences of his wound. Private Pegram was buried at Lijssenthoek cemetery.

The 14th Brigade had managed to take all its objectives and had suffered few casualties during the attack itself. The 15th Brigade, on the right flank, encountered more difficulties, however.

Into battle with the 15th Brigade

Private **Ernest Michael Penny** was killed even before the barrage had moved on to the next German line and the men could begin their attack. The 22-year-old Penny, from Coonabarabran, had joined the Australian army in May 1916 and left for England on completion of his training. He joined his unit, the 29th Battalion, in France at the end of March 1917. He became ill in July and had to be admitted to hospital, rejoining his unit in mid-August. A comrade in arms provided the following account of his death on 26 September: *'I was with Pte. Penny, when he was shot through the head by a sniper on Sept. 26th at Polygon Wood. We were half way across No Man's Land, waiting for the barrage to lift, when he fell. I was only two yards away, as he was a mate of mine.'*[120] Private Penny was subsequently buried near Polygon Wood, but his grave was later lost and his name was included with those of the other 55,000 missing on the Menin Gate.

After the barrage had moved on the men of the 59th Battalion started their advance. The 29th and the 31st Battalions also tried to break through and the three battalions advanced together to the Red Line, although they came under fire from a group of well-concealed German troops on their right flank. The previous day the 33rd Division had been obliged to cede a large area of ground here after a heavy counter-attack and had not yet managed to take it back. Various groups of Australians immediately attacked these strong points in order to silence their deadly machine gun fire. *'Usually the Germans*

Private Ernest Michael Penny (AWM P03492.001)

Private Patrick Bugden (AWM P02939.025)

Corporal Reginal Rowland (seated) is the second on the right (AWM P03633.003)

threw up their hands in the vain hope of mercy, but [Lieutenant] Gullet [29th Battalion] saw one German who kept his thumbs on the button until a bayonet drove into his chest.'[121]

A bit further on, in the 33rd Division's zone, a group of men of the 31st Battalion came under heavy fire from a number of pillboxes on their right flank *'causing severe casualties with machine gun fire from the direction of the Jerk House'*.[122] Several platoons stormed them and captured a number of machine guns. Private **Patrick Bugden**, the 22-year-old stepson of a hotelier from Tweed Heads in New South Wales, played an important role in this action. *'This man in face of devastating fire from Machine Guns gallantly led small parties to attack these strong points and successfully silencing the Machine Guns with bombs, captured the garrison at the point of the bayonet'.* Corporal **Reginald Rowland** also took part, but was not so fortunate. Rowland, a 25-year-old married man, was a fruit-grower from Bundaberg, Queensland, who had joined up in early January 1916. He arrived in England in October 1916 and was promoted to Corporal. He was sent to the front at the beginning of July 1917, where he was posted to the 31st Battalion. Rowland was killed by a German bullet during the storming of the pillboxes at Jerk House on 26 September 1917 and was subsequently buried.[123] As in the case of many others his body could later not be found. Corporal Rowland is, therefore, remembered today on the Menin Gate.

Somewhat later the Germans launched a minor counter-attack during which they took several officers and men prisoner. A few soldiers became separated from their unit. A group of three Germans managed to take Corporal Alf Thompson prisoner. The youngest of the three held a revolver against his temple. He later recalled: *'The eldest Fritz of the three started gibbering away in German and eventually made the young Fritz take his revolver away from my head (much to my relief!) A moment or so after (...) the Fritz who just saved me from being shot made a jump into the next shell-hole and got shot through the stomach. I looked up to see what was happening and saw a Private named Paddy Bugden charging up with a few men to my rescue. The other two Fritzes made to get away and Bugden quickly finished them off (...).'*[124] Bugden continually took the lead in almost all the actions he took

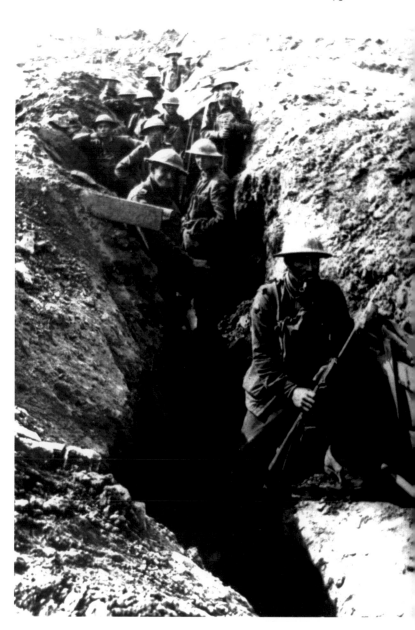

Australians of the neighbouring 45th Battalion at Garter Point, the second man on the left in the foreground is Private Arthur Bell who was killed on 13 October 1917 (AWM E842)

part in and volunteered for numerous dangerous missions. He rescued wounded men under heavy artillery and machine gun fire on 5 occasions, but on 28 September he was killed by German artillery fire. Bugden was posthumously awarded the Victoria Cross.

It is known that Corporal Bugden was buried *in situ*, although the exact position of his grave is not clear. His service record indicates two possible burial sites. The first is south of Chateau Wood, on the edge of the Menin Road. The other location is at the southern edge of Nun's Wood, at Glencorse Wood. In his book, *VCs of the First World War, Passchendaele 1917*, Stephen Snelling also gives a location at Glencorse Wood. Men of Bugden's unit made a cross and put a fence around his grave. After the war the numerous individual graves dug on the battlefield were transferred to larger cemeteries. Bugden's body was also exhumed and was eventually re-buried at Hooge Crater Cemetery.

The 15th Brigade also suffered heavily at the hands of the German artillery. One of their casualties was Lance Corporal **James Wilfred Harrap.** The 26-year-old farmer had enlisted in the Australian army together with his younger brother Ernest Merton in July 1915 and was promoted to Lance Corporal – and later to Corporal – while in the Middle East. Harrap turned in his stripes at his own request, however. In June 1916 he arrived in France with the 59th battalion and was seriously wounded in the thighs and back a month later. After convalescence in England and a brief period of leave, he returned to his unit. Early February 1917 found Harrap at the front again, but he was ill twice in a row and was not able to return to his unit till April 1917. He was promoted to Lance Corporal at the beginning of August but was killed on 26 September 1917: '*A H.E. shell exploded near [Harrap] killing him instantly*'. It is not known whether or not he was buried. Tragically, his brother James Wilfred was also killed on that day: '*His head was blown off from below the shoulders*'.[125] The same shell also killed Private **William Reeves Crossman**, a 34-year-old farmer from Milloo, Victoria. He had followed his younger brother in enlisting in the Australian army in July 1916 and sailed for England in late September of that year. He joined his unit, the 59th Battalion, in France at the beginning of February 1917. Private Crossman was killed on 26 September 1917. One of his comrades said: '*I*

saw his dead body lying in our front line trench at our objective at Polygon Wood on September 26th'. The following morning Sergeant Eason buried the bodies of Harrap and Crossman not far from each other in an adjacent trench, '*500 yards to the right of the mound in the road in Polygon Wood*'.[126] The graves of Crossman and the Harrap brothers were never recovered after the war and they are remembered today on the Menin Gate.

The men of the three battalions, who had now become completely mixed up, were able to forge on towards their objective without further significant hold-ups. '*For a time the scene was exciting, Germans running in all directions like so many bewildered rabbits, and resolute Australians rounding them up and shooting down those who refused to surrender.*'[127] They now also came under fire from a German position at Cameron House. Just as they had done with the other strong points, a group of Australians stormed it and managed to render the machine gun harmless. However, their right flank was still open and – for the time being – there was no sign of the 33rd Division. The commander of the 31st Battalion, therefore, decided to wait before advancing to their final objective.

Corporal **Ellis Eric Cork** took a bullet in the head, just before the barrage moved on '*and never spoke again*'. Cork was a 20-year-old civil servant from Arncliffe, New South Wales. He joined up on 31 December 1915 and sailed to the Middle East four months later. He was sent to England in June 1916 and joined the 31st Battalion in September. He was made a Lance Corporal in late March 1917 and promoted to Corporal shortly afterwards. At the beginning of September he was granted fourteen days' leave. Corporal Cork was killed at Polygon Wood six days after returning to the front. Cork was buried, but his body could not be found after the war. His name is inscribed on the Menin Gate.[128]

The 29th Battalion was also supposed to wait until the 33rd Division arrived, but in fact most of the platoons of the 29th followed the barrage.[129] The 33rd Division was able to be reinforced with an extra battalion and at 11.00 a.m. the Australians resumed their advance. Meanwhile, the final objective was already largely controlled by the men who had not waited and had pushed ahead anyway. The line was significantly further extended and consolidated and despite

*Corporal James Wilfred Harrap
(AWM DA11347)*

Private William Reeves Crossman (Sherree)

Corporal Eric Ellis Cork (AWM H06061)

various German counter-attacks the Australians refused to cede so much as a metre. However, the 29th Battalion took a considerable pasting and lost a very large number of men.

One of them was Private **Hugh McDonald**, a farmer (a 'Cocky'[130] as he put it in his letters), from Sealake, Victoria. McDonald was one of a family of twelve children, and was not yet 32 when he joined up in March 1916. His older brother Norman had preceded him and had served as a pioneer in Gallipoli, France and Belgium and the brothers had the chance to meet up in France on one occasion. Their sister Euphemia, who was a nurse with the Queens Alexandria's Imperial Military Nursing Service, was also in France. McDonald landed in England with the 31st Battalion in early August 1916, where he was to receive additional training before being sent to the front. The famous Stonehenge was not far from their camp: *'Some of my mates and myself had a look at it last Sunday. (...) When I used to look at the pictures of these stones in the old history I did not think that I would be forming fours and sloping arms along side of it a few years after.'* A little while later he left for France, where he was able to visit his sister at Le Tréport hospital. Shortly afterwards he joined the 59th Battalion at the front. His letters say very little indeed about the war: *'a lot of things which I cannot mention in a letter'*, although he did not conceal his admiration for the French countryside: *'France seems to be a very fertile country (...) just like a big vegetable garden with all sorts of green things growing.'* He was not quite so enamoured of the French themselves, however. He found their language difficult and was not at all keen on their mentality. *'They try to make all they can out of Bill -. They charge the highest possible prices for everything they sell; some locked their wells and refused to give us a drink of water at one place.'* At the end of March 1917 McDonald received a wound to his wrist and was sent to England to convalesce and it was not until late June that he could rejoin his unit.[131] Private McDonald was killed by an artillery shell on 26 September 1917. His body was found after the war and was reburied in Hooge Crater Cemetery.

By evening most of the positions had been taken and consolidated. The German artillery continued to shell the British without respite, causing numerous additional casualties. The shells not only fell on the forward line, but on the Australian supply lines as well. Among

Private Hugh McDonald (Rose)

the casualties was Company Quartermaster Sergeant **Arthur Heard**, who, like Captain Aram, was also from St. Kilda. The 31-year-old Heard had been a tram driver before the war and was married with one son. He joined up in July 1915 and came to France via Alexandria. A year later he was promoted to corporal and five weeks after that he was made Company Quartermaster Sergeant. *'At the time of his death he was taking up rations by a mule transport and he was in rear when a shell burst on top of him and he died with a broken spine a few minutes afterwards.'* This happened at Halfway House, southwest of Leinster House, on a wooden track which led to the front. Company Quartermaster Sergeant Heard was buried the following day. On 9 July 1919 his grave was moved about 400 metres to the Birr Cross Roads Cemetery.[132]

Casualties

The entire Blue Line, with the exception of a small area at the boundary with the 33rd Division, was now in Australian hands and this remaining piece of ground was captured by the 60th Battalion the following morning. *'Without that final advance the Battle of Polygon Wood, though still a fine success for the 5th Australian Division, would have lacked the perfecting touches that made it a complete and splendid victory.'*[133]

The entire 5th Australian Division was relieved on the night of 30 September 1917 and left the Salient. Despite the enormous success of the offensive they had suffered considerable casualties. The exact figures differ somewhat, depending on the source. According to Bean's Official History the infantry battalions of the 5th Australian Division lost 96 officers and 2,972 men.[134] *The Story of the Fifth Australian Division* specifies this further as 26 officers and 518 men killed.[135] On the subject of the 14th Brigade's casualty figures the author writes: *'So careful had been the preparations, so gallantly had all ranks fought, and so free had the left brigade front been from any untoward happenings that a success complete to the smallest detail had been achieved within a few hours. The losses had been light in the actual advance, but sustained shelling that was encountered for several days after the battle increased them considerably.'*[136] To a certain extent this is also true of the 15th Brigade. They lost more men during the fighting itself but the number of dead and wounded due to German artillery fire was just as great.

Company Quartermaster Sergeant Arthur Heard (AWM DA11539)

right: British soldiers at work on Buttes New British Military Cemetery, there is still no bronze plaque on the 5th Australian Division monument (Deraeve)

Photograph of the Butte and the German Ehrenfriedhof Nr 110, taken in Albania looking in the direction of Helles, 28 September 1917 (AWM E1912)

The remains of a German observation bunker in the vicinity of Polygon Wood (IWM Q2908)

William Robert Leathers as a young man (Elsom)

27 September 1917:
Corporal William Leathers
2nd Suffolk Regiment

William Robert Leathers was born in July 1883, the sixth child of Frederick Leathers and Harriet Campion. The family, which would eventually consist of eight children, lived in Bury St. Edmunds between Cambridge and Norwich. Leathers's father was an iron founder at Robert Boby, Ltd., St. Andrew's Ironworks in Bury. William Robert was also an iron founder in the same ironworks. He married the 22-year-old Alice Maud Norman in April 1905. Alice was then already pregnant with their first child, Gertrude Clarice, born in September of that same year. Phylis Evelyn, the second daughter, followed in January 1907. They went on have to six more children. Leathers belonged to the Territorial Force, volunteer soldiers who underwent regular training in the same way as in the professional army. In theory, they could not be sent overseas, but when war broke out in 1914 many territorials applied for overseas service. Exactly when Leathers joined up is not known. He was posted to the 4th Battalion of the Suffolk Regiment and later transferred to the 2nd Battalion. His seventh child, Gladys Violet, was born in December 1915.

Passchendaele
Leathers went home on leave for a few days at the beginning of September 1917. Afterwards, he returned to the front and rejoined his battalion, which was getting ready for an attack on the German positions. The men had trained extensively and were ready to smash the Germans on 26 September. For the 3rd Division, to which the battalion belonged, their objective was – among other things – the capture of Zonnebeke. The thick mist caused a bit of confusion at the beginning of the attack, but in the end everything went smoothly and the attack was a success. The Suffolks were on one line starting from the church at Zonnebeke, running via Zonnebeke Lake to point Tokyo, where the Australians were and they succeeded in consolidating the line. The Suffolks were still there the next day and needed fresh rations. On that day Cor-

Corporal William Robert Leathers before his departure to the front (Elsom)

Leathers' wife Alice and young son Harry, about 1918 (Elsom)

poral Leathers was in command of a small group of men who were responsible for bringing them up the line. During this action contact was lost with the 34-year-old Leathers. A local paper in the village where he was born announced the sad news: *'Much sympathy is felt for the aged parent in the loss of her son, while we hope that shortly she will receive assuring news of her son's safety.'* Leathers's brother, James Charles, who was three years younger than him and who was serving with the 1st/5th Battalion Suffolks in Egypt, died of his wounds in a hospital in Kanatara on 30 November 1917. Their father received a letter written by Captain Wilson informing him of how William had died: *'Leathers was in charge of a ration party going up the front line and he handed over the rations, and was last seen going back from the front line, since when nothing was heard of him. There was a certain amount of shelling going on at the time, but I hope before this you have some definite news of him turning up wounded (...).'* Corporal Leathers's body was never recovered and he was declared as officially killed a few months later. His name is inscribed on the Tyne Cot Memorial. His widow gave birth to their last son, Harry Alfred, in May 1918. His father never knew him.

6 The Battle of Broodseinde: 4 October 1917
New Zealand Division

SITUATION: At the front everything had gone according to plan. Twice in a row the allies had dealt the Germans a massive blow, they had succeeded in reaching their objective and the weather remained good. Haig planned the following offensive according to the requirements of the impending breakthrough at Passchendaele and extensive reserves, cavalry and tanks had to be kept at the ready for this purpose. On 25 and 26 September the Australians had reached Polygon Wood and Zonnebeke, while the British now held Kansas Cross. From 28 September to 2 October the ANZAC (Australian and New Zealand Army Corps) units took over part of the front line.

On 4 October the German high command employed a new tactic by packing the first line with large numbers of troops. The *Eingreif-divisionen* (counter-attack divisions) were brought forward with the intention of using them to recapture part of Zonnebeke. The 4th Guard Division was brought into position. After several failed attacks on previous days the German infantry was due to attack again at dawn on 4 October.[137] Yet on the night of 3 to 4 October the weather changed and it began to rain again.

OBJECTIVE: The objective of the third stage was to capture the ridge at Broodseinde, a task which was entrusted to the 1st and 2nd Australian Divisions. This meant pushing their way through the heavily defended *Flandern I-Stellung*. Various divisions were required to move forward on the left flank. The New Zealanders were expected to break through to their objectives via 's Graventafel. The objective assigned to the 3rd Australian Division was to penetrate the *Flandern I-Stellung* on the right flank of the New Zealanders and left of the 2nd Australian Division (left of the railway). The divisions of the 5th Army were to advance via Poelkapelle towards Spriet and

4 October 1917, general situation (MMP) >

< *Remains of a German 7.7 cm gun, semi-submerged in the mud before Passchendaele (Deraeve)*

Westrozebeke. On the right flank the men were required to advance via Reutel in the direction of Beselare.

COURSE OF THE BATTLE: The first minutes of the attack were fairly chaotic as the ANZACs came under heavy artillery fire just before the start. The Germans deployed their artillery as a preparation for an attack that they themselves were intending to carry out and as the ANZACs started to move forward to their objectives they saw the Germans advancing towards them. The result was a bloody series of bayonet fights. *'The area was soon littered with German dead, and the large number who bore bayonet wounds was evidence of the bitterness of the encounter'.*[138] Despite the presence of a large number of pockets of resistance the 1st Australian Division was able to advance rapidly to their final objective. The 2nd Australian Division forged ahead through the ruins of Zonnebeke and captured Broodseinde. The 3rd Australian Division advanced to the left of the railway line and captured the pillboxes at Tyne Cot. The New Zealand Division was also able to advance to the final objective without undue problems. North of the ANZACs a number of British divisions also went into action. The 48th Division was able to take almost all its objectives, while the 11th Division reached the church at Poelkapelle. The Germans (6th Bavarian Division) subjected them to heavy machine gun fire, but, thanks to the support of ten tanks, they were able to finish the job. The 29th Division also managed to take its objectives, unlike the 4th Division which encountered heavy resistance and could not reach its final objective. South of the ANZACs the 7th Division was able to push ahead to its objective without difficulties. The 21st Division came under fire, but thanks to the support provided by several tanks they were able to take out the German pillboxes. Later that day, however, it was nonetheless forced to withdraw. Despite heavy resistance the 5th Division managed to carry out the task they had been given successfully. Finally, the 37th Division was the only division which was not able to take its objectives.

RESULT: Under the circumstances, the new German tactic – packing their forward positions with men by bringing the counter-attack divisions as close to the first line as possible – proved to be an unfortunate decision. The timing of the German attack was also ill-fated: 4 October 1917 was to go down in history as Germany's blackest day. The allies were able to break through all over their line and reached almost all their objectives. Germans losses amounted to thousands of men killed, missing, captured or wounded, although allied losses were also high, however.

The New Zealand Division attacked from 's Graventafel-Abraham Heights across a front which was almost two kilometres wide and slightly more than one and a half kilometres deep. The plan was to be carried out by two brigades with four battalions each. The 1st Brigade attacked on the left, with the 1st Auckland, in the sector which bordered on the area allocated to the 48th Division and the 1st Wellington attacked on the right of the sector assigned to them, north of the Wieltje-'s Graventafel road. The brigade boundary lay approximately 200 metres north of this road and ran behind the fortified Riverside and Waterloo farms. The 4th Brigade attacked with the 3rd Otago on the left of their sector and the 3rd Auckland on the right near the boundary with the 3rd Australian Division. They were required to capture the Red Line.

After the first wave had dug itself in, the four remaining battalions were to push on to the Blue Line. The battalions chosen were the 2nd Wellington and the 2nd Auckland from the 1st Brigade and the 3rd Wellington and the 3rd Canterbury from the 4th Brigade.

The Germans had also made preparations for a major attack of their own in the early morning of the same day and had brought the *Eingreifdivisionen* forward. Normally these were held in the rear and their task was to carry out counter-attacks after enemy assaults on German positions.

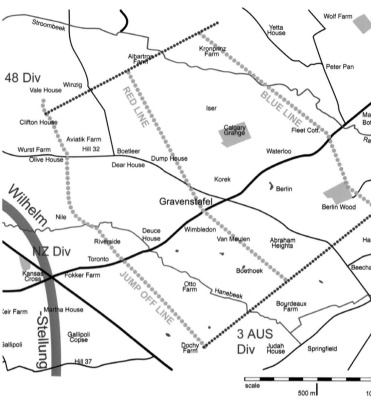

4 October 1917: New Zealand Division (MMP)

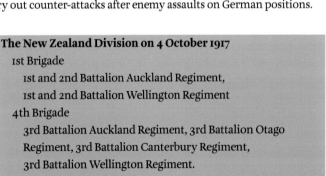

The New Zealand Division on 4 October 1917
1st Brigade
    1st and 2nd Battalion Auckland Regiment,
    1st and 2nd Battalion Wellington Regiment
4th Brigade
    3rd Battalion Auckland Regiment, 3rd Battalion Otago
    Regiment, 3rd Battalion Canterbury Regiment,
    3rd Battalion Wellington Regiment.

Second Lieutenant Allan Morpeth (de Ruvigny)

Private Norman Forde (Auckland Cenotaph)

Forward to the jumping-off lines

At the end of September the New Zealanders made their preparations for the coming offensive. The men troops arrived in Ypres after their training in France and the assault brigades left for the front in early October. British artillery shelled the German lines and the Germans were not slow to retaliate. Their response was relatively weak, however, with their guns being used only sporadically. 33-year-old Second Lieutenant **Allan Morpeth** was killed while the 2nd Otago Battalion was being relieved by the 1st Auckland. Morpeth was from Auckland, where he went to school and was later appointed Assistant Drainage Engineer by the local authorities. He worked on the Hauraki plains and later made a study of the Waikato, New Zealand's longest river. He joined up in January 1916 and was made a Second Lieutenant a year later. He arrived at the front at the beginning of May 1917. During the Battle of Messines in early June 1917 Morpeth had acted as supply officer and he fulfilled his first mission with the 1st Auckland to perfection: *'he failed us in no particular: wire, water, rations, and ammunition all came along in ample quantities, and Allan's work was the subject of complimentary remarks (...)'.*[139] Second Lieutenant Morpeth was buried in Oxford Road Cemetery in Ypres.

In the 1st Brigade, the 1st Auckland and the 1st Wellington took over part of the front line. *'The German artillery was comparatively inactive, responding but feebly to our practice barrage.'* [140] It was not long before they suffered their first casualties, one of whom was Private **Norman Arthur Forde**, a machinist from Saint Heliers Bay in Auckland. Like his older brother, Hugh Douglas, he attended Saint John's College from 1905. He joined up at the end of 1916 and was posted to the Otago Regiment. His brother also enlisted and ended up in the artillery. Forde arrived in England at the beginning of May 1917 and was transferred to the Wellington Regiment.[141] He was killed on 3 October. Private Forde's body was never found and he is remembered on the Tyne Cot Memorial. His brother died of his wounds a few weeks later.

The final preparations were made and on the night of 3 to 4 October the men moved up to their jumping-off positions under heavy enemy shelling. *'The men were heated, however, by the march and by the construction of their shallow trenches. Now, as they knelt down on the oozy soil in such protection as these shelters and shell holes afforded, a clammy drizzle began to fall, and a strong westerly wind chilled them to the bone.'* [142]

The attack

The start signal for the attack was planned for 6.00 a.m. and the German attack was timed to go over a few minutes later. At exactly 5.30 a.m. heavy artillery suddenly rained down on the Kiwis. The entire German artillery opened fire and shelled the lines with guns of various calibres. Most of the German shells fell just behind the lines, as a result of which the number of casualties among the New Zealanders was low. Half an hour later the allied guns opened up and laid a protective barrage along the whole line. The Germans, who were preparing to attack, *'were slaughtered by the tremendous weight of fire, and general confusion followed, from which they never recovered.'*[143] The New Zealanders clambered out of their positions and made their way towards the enemy line. An unpleasant sight awaited them when they reached the first German lines: *'The assaulting infantry had not gone more than 200 yards when they came on the first lines of the enemy which were to have carried out the attack anticipated some 10 minutes by our own. Another 200 yards in rear was the second, but both lines had been decimated by our artillery fire. On the 1st Auckland front alone were about 500 corpses, and generally along the whole line every shell hole held 1 to 4 dead Germans. Few wore steel helmets and only here and there was a bayonet fixed.'* The surviving Germans tried to hold them back, *'but when it came to bayonet work and close quarters, neither physically nor morally were they a match for their assailants.'* [144] Not all the German positions could be taken so easily, however. Many pillboxes had survived the barrage and the Germans inside did what they could to halt the New Zealanders' advance. Between the starting point and the first objective lay the Hanebeek valley. The heavy shell fire had transformed the stream into a broad quagmire and the men could only cross it in a few places and in single file. As they did so, the German artillery shelled them with deadly precision. Only the squelching mud into which the shells sank without exploding saved the New Zealanders from suffering very heavy losses.

To the Red Line with the 4th Brigade

The 4th Brigade was easily able to overrun the first German positions at Riverside, although the German defenders fired on the advancing New Zealanders from Otto Farm. The 3rd Auckland took the full brunt of this and a number of men were killed, including Second Lieutenant **Herbert Albert Edwin Milnes**, who was of English origin, having been born in Leeds, Yorkshire. He went to school in London and later graduated from London University, becoming a teacher after finishing his degree. In December 1905 he married Louisa Heath. That same month the couple left for Auckland, New Zealand, where Milnes became principal of the Auckland Training College. He was a man who left his stamp on New Zealand, excelling at numerous sports, such as golf, rugby, basketball and tennis. His wife died in October 1913. Milnes was made a Second Lieutenant with the Auckland Regiment in March 1916 and served on the western front from May 1917. He was killed on 4 October. *'Sincere and deep regret is felt throughout educational circles in this city at the loss which has been sustained by us in the death of your esteemed brother'*, wrote a former colleague to Milnes's brother. Second Lieutenant Milnes was buried at Otto Farm, although his body was subsequently exhumed in June 1920 and the 43-year-old Milnes was reburied in Tyne Cot.[145] There was heavy resistance on the other side of the Hanebeek, with groups of Germans everywhere trying to halt the advance. Some were completed demoralised and willingly surrendered, while others fought on bravely, although hopelessly.

The 3rd Auckland continued to advance through the muddy terrain. The New Zealanders were not able to take the remaining pillboxes without a fight either and Boethoek had to be taken by force. The 3rd Otago captured a machine gun and took fifty prisoners at Van Meulen, after which the ruins of 's Graventafel were wide open to the advancing New Zealanders. Here, too, they took several hundred prisoners of war.

Scarcely an hour after the start of the offensive the first men were already at the Red Line.[146] Sergeant **Henry Frank Warrington** was killed at this point. Warrington was a 23-year-old bachelor from Opotiki, Bay of Plenty and had seen a great deal of action before being killed on 4 October 1917. He fought at Gallipoli and on the Somme, where he was wounded and taken to England, being promoted to the rank of Sergeant on his return. His brother also fought, but survived the war.[147] Warrington is remembered today on the Tyne Cot Memorial. The 3rd Otago, which advanced side by side with the 3rd Auckland, was also able to reach the Red Line quite easily, but lost a number of men. Captain **Neville Henry Arden** was one of those killed during the attack. Arden, from New Plymouth, was an architect and had won a number of prizes for his designs and also excelled at cricket. He was quickly promoted and became a Captain. Arden was buried near 's Graventafel.[148] In February 1918 a British photographic team took a picture of his grave. Among the rubble of the bunkers, next to various up-ended rifles, a cross had been erected with his name on it. Captain Arden's mortal remains were transferred to Tyne Cot Cemetery after the war.

left: Second Lieutenant Herbert Albert Edwin Milnes (Auckland Cenotaph)
right: Sergeant Henry Frank Warrington (Auckland Cenotaph)

Battlefield grave of Captain Arden (IWM Q10700)

Captain Nevill Henry Arden (Auckland Cenotaph)

Private Ernest Frederick Evers-Swindell (Auckland Cenotaph)

Private Alfred Charles Sherlock (right) with his brothers Lawrence (middle) and Edwin (left) (Auckland Cenotaph)

To the Red Line with the 1st Brigade

At 5.00 a.m. the Aucklanders came under heavy German shelling, but most of the shells fell behind the waiting troops and losses were limited. Their advance to the Red Line was slow, however. This was particularly true in the case of the 1st Auckland as the men were not able to advance as rapidly as expected because of the poor state of the terrain. The Aucklanders pushed on to Aviatik Farm and Dear House where they suffered heavy losses. They were able to take these fortified positions, but the Germans did not surrender without a fight. Nor did they at Winzig: *'The garrison of this strongpoint were very brave men, and fought with desperate courage.'*[149] The 1st Auckland paid a high price for the capture of Winzig and several Aucklanders were killed. Among the dead was **Alfred Charles Sherlock**. He was from Collarbone Spur, Thames, and was a clerk with the New Zealand railways before joining up. His brother Edwin James had already left for the front in October 1914 and another brother, Lawrence Arthur, left for Europe in August 1916. Sherlock followed their example six months later. His two brothers survived the war, but for the 20-year-old Sherlock 's Graventafel was the end of the road.[150] His body was not found until after the war, when it was then transferred to Poelcapelle British Cemetery. Winzig could only be taken after it had been completely surrounded and the New Zealanders were able to fire on the position from all sides. Only now could they push on further towards their objective, but some of the British troops of the 48th Division had got lost and moved too far north with the Aucklanders following on behind them.[151]

The 1st Wellington which attacked to the right of the Aucklanders came under fire from Boetleer, but was able to capture the pillboxes. They suffered numerous losses on the slopes at Korek. The Wellingtons also strayed too far north in an attempt to keep in touch with the Aucklanders. Consequently, only half of the battalion was on the Red Line, creating a large gap in their front line, which also meant that the New Zealanders had still not occupied a large part of the ground they were supposed to take.

All the German pillboxes had to be captured one by one. Generally, these miniature fortresses could only be taken by an act of individual bravery. Private **Ernest Frederick Evers-Swindell** was killed in one such action at the beginning of the attack. When his unit was held up by a well-concealed machine gun, Private Tom Geange rushed towards it armed with a revolver. Evers-Swindell followed his example, but was shot. Geange was also wounded, *'but their gallantry diverted the enemy machine-gun and afforded the other men in the section the opportunity to push forward and capture the enemy gun, killing the crew'*. Evers-Swindell was a 23-year-old farmer from Moores Valley in Wainuiomata. He was born in Rodborough, England and emigrated to New Zealand at the age of 16 together with his two older brothers. He joined up in April 1915, was made a Lance Corporal and was sent to the front in Turkey, where he handed in his stripes and, after a spell in Egypt, ended up in France. He was killed on 4 October. His body was buried the following day, but could not be found after the war. Private Evers-Swindell's name is inscribed on the Tyne Cot Memorial.[152]

On the 's Graventafel ridge lay Korek, a strong defensive position with various pillboxes. When the 1st Wellington and 3rd Otago reached the Red Line, the Germans at Korek subjected them to heavy fire. A group of men from the Wellington and Otago Regiments risked their lives by moving through their own barrage in order to take out the concrete pillboxes, attacking them from behind, one by one, using hand grenades. One of these was relatively large and must therefore have been quite important, according to the Wellingtons' regiment book: *'Sergeant A. Paterson entered to find some thirty Germans dead or dying from the havoc our bombs had wrought. There seemed to be an inner recess in which was a German Major with some men. As soon as Sergeant Paterson entered, the German officer set fire to a mass of papers with some incendiary material. In a moment, the whole place was in flames, Sergeant Paterson came out; but the Germans were all incinerated. This dug-out burned for hours afterwards.'*[153]

A rapid advance was impossible, the German fire was too heavy and various men were killed. Private **William Wyndham Tosswill** was one of them. Tosswill was from Albany, Auckland, went to school in Wanganui and was a farmer before joining up.[154] Private Tosswill's body was never found and he is therefore remembered on the Tyne Cot Memorial.

Advanced Dressing Station at Abraham Heights, German prisoners of war helping to bring in the wounded, 9 October 1917 (MMP)

Private William Wyndham Tosswill (Auckland Cenotaph)

The New Zealanders had now taken the first objective and the four battalions which had led the first phase of the attack set about extending their positions. Meanwhile, the battalions of the second wave of the attack, who were required to push on to the Blue Line, forged ahead.

To the Blue Line with the 4th Brigade

The 3rd Canterbury was on the right of the Brigade's sector and on the left of the 3rd Australian Division. Immediately beyond the Red Line the men came under fire from several shell holes from which the Germans tried to halt their advance, although they were quickly able to overcome this resistance. The New Zealanders continued their advance without great difficulties, but near Berlin Wood they came up against two well-defended German pillboxes, which could only be taken after they had been completely surrounded and at a cost of 250 casualties, fifty of whom were killed. They reached their final objective just after 9.00 a.m. Private **George Smith**, a 39-year-old from West Eyreton, Canterbury, went missing during this part of the attack. His body was found south of Hamburg in March 1920, in the 3rd Australian Division's zone. Private Smith was reburied in Tyne Cot Cemetery.[155]

*Private George Smith
(Auckland Cenotaph)*

*Private Antoine
Spaccesi
(Auckland Cenotaph)*

*Private Thomas
Charles Webb
(Auckland Cenotaph)*

*Captain Hugh
Townshend
Boscawen
(Auckland Cenotaph)*

The 3rd Wellington attacked on the left, next to the 3rd Canterbury. They were required to advance through 's Graventafel to the Ravebeek valley, but suffered numerous casualties. Only one sergeant survived unscathed and all the other officers and NCOs were either wounded or killed. The fighting was heaviest at Waterloo Farm, where several men lost their lives, among them, Private **Antoine Spaccesi**, who was born in Bastia, Corsica. He emigrated to New Zealand without any family and became a fisherman in Levin, some ninety kilometres from Wellington. After his death a friend of his published a short obituary in the local paper: *'"Killed in action," say the cables; That is all the tale they tell Of the brave young lad who loved us, Of the lad we loved so well. How the life was sped we know not, What the last word, look, or thought; Only that he did his duty, Died as bravely as he fought. - Inserted by his loving friend, H. Cole, Levin.'*[156] The body of the young Corsican was never recovered and Private Antoine Spaccesi is remembered today on the Tyne Cot Memorial. The 3rd Wellington was held up for a while at Berlin by a strongly defended pillbox. Several other German pillboxes also tried to break the attack, but the Germans could not turn the tide against such overwhelming odds and were soon overcome. Thus, just after 9.00 a.m., the 3rd Wellington Regiment also found itself on the Blue Line. Taking it had cost them a great many casualties, however. Private **Thomas Charles Webb**, from Wellington, was among those killed. Back home, Webb was a well-known and much-loved figure in the fruit-growing community. He worked for the Orchards Division of the Ministry of Agriculture and was also secretary of the National Apple Show in Wellington in 1916. He joined up later that same year and sailed for Europe in March 1917 arriving in Devonport in May.[157] He was killed a few months later. Private Webb is remembered on the Tyne Cot Memorial.

The 4th Brigade was now on the Blue Line and immediately began consolidating its positions.

To the Blue Line with the 1st Brigade

In the 1st Brigade the 2nd Wellington and the 2nd Auckland had been assigned the task of carrying out the second phase of the attack. The 2nd Auckland and the 2nd Wellington were required to move on past the 1st Wellington and 1st Auckland on the Red Line and take the Blue Line. When the 2nd Auckland advanced towards the Red Line, the 1st Wellingtons were still fighting. *'One man lurches forward into a shell hole, another falls with a cry, clutching at the breast of his tunic, another stumbles to one side and gazes stupidly at a spreading red stain. The remainder take cover. Fifty yards ahead are a file of Huns(...). Rifle fire is opened at once, but it is amazing how many shots miss the mark, even at such absurdly short range. The morning mist, the battle-smoke, the excitement all have part in this.'*[158] It was not easy to advance rapidly to the Blue Line and there were many casualties. After the 2nd Wellington set off from near Winnipeg a German artillery shell landed among the men of Ruahine Company HQ. The company commander, Captain **Hugh Townshend Boscawen**, was killed instantly and two of his runners were also among the dead.[159] Boscawen was the only child from the first marriage of former army captain John Hugh Boscawen. Hugh Townshend was a veteran of the Boer War. He married Kathleen Crowe in 1909 and the couple had a daughter, Kathleen Patricia. They lived in Takapuna, Auckland. Captain Boscawen was buried close to where he was killed.[160] A number of other men from his company were also buried there: Private Albert August Olson, Private Wifred Denham Tunks, Private Ernest Ratcliffe and Private John Alexander Ferguson. The small battlefield cemetery was located between Winnipeg and Cluster Houses. At the end of August 1919 the exhumation units transferred them to Tyne Cot Cemetery, where they were also buried side by side.[161] The rest of 2nd Wellington were able to reach the Blue Line without many losses, however, the terrain they were required to advance through was covered with small pillboxes. A handful of Germans in a short stretch of trench at Kronprinz Farm made life very difficult for the Wellingtons, but they were able to surround the trench and the Germans defenders were either killed or taken prisoner. They reached the Blue Line just before 9.30 a.m. and set about consolidating their positions.[162]

The 2nd Auckland sustained heavy casualties when they were just beyond the Red Line. *'On approaching the pillboxes amid the chaotic jumble of brick heaps that had been Korek, our lines were checked by deadly Machine Gun fire at close range.'*[163] After few rounds of mortar fire were dropped on them, the Germans willingly surrendered. The Aucklanders continued their advance through the ruins of Korek to Calgary Grange, where, together with the Auckland and Wellington Regiment, they took a machine gun nest. 40-year-old Private **Percy Harold Maunsell** was killed nearby. Born in Waihakeke, he went to school in Wanganui and then became a sheep farmer in Wairarapa. Later on he moved to the north of Auckland where he worked at the station, probably as a porter. He joined up in 1917 and sailed for England in April. According to the *Memorial Book* of Wanganui Collegiate School, he had only been at the front for a week when he was killed. The entry reads: *'His grave is situated at a point north west of Gravenstafel'*, (...) *'close to the spot where he fell.'*[164] There was a cross over the grave. Private Maunsell's body was transferred to Tyne Cot Cemetery in late October 1919.[165]

Private Percy Harold Maunsell (Auckland Cenotaph)

Corporal Alexander Joseph Langford (Langford)

'One of the stiffest fights of the day was that of the 15th Company for a strongly-held trench at the foot of the hill, and right on the Blue Line.'[166] The advancing troops of the Auckland Regiment tried to push through to the Blue Line, but their ranks were becoming thinner and thinner. Corporal **Norman Ashton** was one of the casualties. The son of a New Zealand father and an English mother, he was born in Pendleton, Manchester, where he spent the first years of his life. The family subsequently moved to New Zealand, where Ashton initially attended the local school before going on to study at the Prince Albert College in Auckland. At the end of November 1915 he married Grace Florence Shrimpton from Mount Albert, Auckland. He joined up in early April 1916 and left for the Western Front that same month. Ashton never saw his son Desmond Norman, as he was born on 5 October 1916. The 36-year-old Corporal Ashton was killed less than a year later and was buried northeast of 's Graventafel, where his mortal remains were found at the beginning of June 1920 and were reburied in Tyne Cot Cemetery.[167] The Germans who defended their positions tooth and nail picked off the advancing Kiwis one by one. *'They were in the open – the Huns in a*

good trench'. The Aucklanders pushed on, however. *'It was an impossible task, and if the Germans had kept their nerve, every one of the attacking party would have been shot down (...). As it was their nerve failed at the critical moment, and they surrendered.'*[168] Corporal **Alexander Joseph Langford** was killed during this action. Langford came from South Hillend, Southland and had left Alexandria for France in May 1916. From then on he kept a diary in which he made a few notations every day. In France he wrote on 24 May 1916: *'Weather a little dull and close, went out the butts and put up record scores (I don't think) In the afternoon gas helmets were issued and damn rotten affairs they are to wear, if the gas is any worse it's a b.., after tea I went for the usual stroll had a look at one of the towers Napoleon built during his wars with England, sorry never had a chance to look inside it.'* The last diary entry dates from five days before his death: *'Sunday, went to confession last night to a Belgian priest, and went to communion this morning. Father O'Neil celebrated mass, heavy gun fire last night (...)'.*[169] The 23-year-old Corporal Langford was killed on 4 October and is remembered today on the Tyne Cot Memorial.

Corporal Norman Ashton (de Ruvigny)

German pillbox at Waterloo Farm, spring 1918 (Deraeve)

Private James Henry Heys (Otter)

Various objectives had been taken along the entire New Zealand front. However, the artillery continued to shell the German lines for a little while thereafter so that the New Zealanders could dig themselves in safely and extend their positions properly. *'The battle was won.'*[170] The Germans tried to establish a counter-attack at various points on the line, but the New Zealand artillery successfully broke it up.[171]

Wounded

A large number of soldiers were wounded during the advance. The medical units of the New Zealand Division had made effective preparations and had developed a complete evacuation chain. Two forward aid posts were to receive the wounded, from which they were carried to Spree Farm and Bridge House by stretcher bearers. From there they were taken to Wieltje, which was the last intermediate stop before the wounded arrived in Ypres. The evacuation of the wounded took place in the pouring rain, which meant that it was very difficult for the stretcher bearers to get all of the casualties off the battlefield quickly. Between 4 and 7 October more than a thousand wounded and sick men found their way via these aid posts to either a Casualty Clearing Station or a Base Hospital.[172] Not all of them made it and some died even before their wounds could be properly treated. One of these was Private **James Henry Heys.** Heys, a 33-year-old sales representative from Wellington, was with the 3rd Wellington Regiment. Heys was from Burnley, in England, where he had worked as a pastry cook. In April 1909 he exchanged his old life in England for a new life in New Zealand. He joined up in December 1915 and in June 1917 he was slightly wounded at Messines. He was soon able to return to his unit, but was wounded again on 4 October. Private S.W. Jones informed Heys's family and friends in England of what had happened: *'I am very sorry to tell you that our officer told us yesterday that Jim had died as a result of his wounds. It has come as a great shock to all us of, as we heard that he was not wounded very badly. It happened on the early morning of October 4th, as we were moving up to our objective. (...) Jim and I had kept together all the time, but got separated owing getting mixed up with another section whilst crossing a swamp. When we reached our objective and halted, I learned that he had been hit. It was fairly near to a forward dressing station, so we*

hoped that he would soon be fixed up all right. But the poor old chap must have died soon after and was buried either on the 4th or 5th October.' Heys is supposed to have been buried on the Frezenberg Ridge, probably near the aid post at Delva Farm. Private Heys is remembered today on Tyne Cot Memorial. Private Jones's letter continued: *'Jim was absolutely game all through, and we always shared the same billets, dugouts and shell-holes, being together all the time in the New Zealand and English camps. He was one of the best, and a better chum I never wish to have.'* [173]

Sergeant **David Gallaher** was born in late October 1873 and in 1878 his family emigrated from Belfast to Bay of Plenty in New Zealand. Gallaher moved to Auckland in 1890, where he played for the Auckland rugby team and his fame as a local sportsman spread. Gallaher always claimed to be three years younger than he really was and when he enlisted to fight in the Boer War in 1901 he gave his age as 24 instead of 27. His gravestone at Nine Elms British Cemetery gives his age as 41, whereas he was actually nearly 44. Gallaher became world famous as captain of the New Zealand national rugby team, the All Blacks. In 1905 he went on a world tour, winning all of the matches, bar one. He married in 1906 and had a daughter called Nora in 1908. When war broke out Gallaher was working as a foreman for the Auckland Farmers' Freezing Company. His younger brother, Douglas Wallace, was killed in France in June 1916,[174] whereupon Gallaher decided to enlist again himself. He was made a Sergeant with the 2nd Auckland Regiment on 1 June 1917 and was wounded in the face on 4 October. He was taken to an aid post on Abraham Heights and brought to a field hospital in Poperinghe soon afterwards, where he died the same day. Sergeant Gallaher is buried in Nine Elms Cemetery. Five Gallaher brothers served in the army: David and William in New Zealand units and Charles, Henry and Douglas in Australian units. Henry and Douglas were also killed.[175]

Second Lieutenant **Charles Edward Collins-Morgan** was also buried at Nine Elms. Like Gallaher, he was also wounded and taken to a field hospital. He, too, was a veteran of the Boer War. Collins-Morgan was an electrician and had joined up in October 1914. The end of December 1914 found him in Egypt with the rank of Sergeant.

He left for Gallipoli in April 1915, where he was wounded in August. He was sent to France in April of the following year and was made a Second Lieutenant with the Auckland Regiment a few months later. He was wounded again in September 1916 and was taken to a hospital in Brockenhurst, England, to convalesce. He won the Military Cross during the Battle of Messines in June 1917. In early September of that year he was granted ten days leave in England, where he married Lilian Emily Holden Smeeton in Richmond, near London, on 5 September. A month later the newly-married officer was mortally wounded. On 8 October the Chaplain Gavin wrote a letter to Collins-Morgan's young wife. *'I write just a line to tell you that your husband (...) passed through the Regimental Aid Post while I was there. His right thigh was fractured. I think it would be wrong to hide from you the fact that he is severely wounded but I may assure you that everything that could be possibly be done at the Aid Post was done. His leg was placed in a Thomas' splint, he was given a little brandy. A tourniquet was placed ready on the leg in case of need and the stretcher bearer warned to use it if necessary. He was attended to very soon after he was wounded. (...) In what hospital he is I do not know (...). He was conscious and able to speak and we must all hope for the best.'* He was taken to the field hospital at Nine Elms where he died from his wounds during the night. Charge nurse Ida O'Dwyer conveyed the sad news to his widow: *'He was brought into this hospital on the evening of the 5th [sic] suffering from a very severe compound fracture of the thigh – His leg had been very badly shattered and when brought in here was quite collapsed and suffering from shock and loss of blood. So immediately everything was done to revive him and as soon as possible he was operated on. But it was to no avail he sank rapidly and died at 2.30 a.m. the next day.'* [176] The 33-year-old Second Lieutenant Collins-Morgan had only been married for a month. His widow never remarried.

Sergeant David Gallaher (Gallaher)

Second Lieutenant Charles Edward Collins-Morgan (below left) during a shooting match in Hawkes Bay, 1907 (Morgan)

Sergeant **Ernest Nicholson Player**, a 29-year-old clerk with the Wellington Tram Corporation, was also wounded on 4 October. Player was married and came from Wellington. He had joined up at the beginning of June 1916, was sent overseas at the end of November of that year and joined his unit, the 3rd Wellington, in May 1917. He received several bullets in his left knee during the attack and was taken to a field hospital where a surgeon was obliged to amputate his left leg. The seriously wounded Player was transferred to Brockenhurst in England on 12 October so that he could undergo further treatment, but he died of his wounds four days later.[177] Sergeant Player was buried in Brockenhurst (St. Nicholas) Churchyard.

*Collins-Morgan with his new bride,
5 September 1917. He was killed a month later
during the Battle of Passchendaele (Morgan)*

*Sergeant Ernest Nicholson Player
(Auckland Cenotaph)*

Relief

There were regular exchanges of fire up and down the line during the rest of the day, but the number of losses was relatively small and the German counter-attacks at 3.00 and at 7.00 p.m. came to nothing. The New Zealand artillery immediately opened fire and the enemy action made no headway at all. The night passed without incident and the following day the New Zealanders were able to shoot the German counter-attack to pieces. By evening the 49th Division was able to be relieved. *'Though heavy, the price paid for these successes could not, in view of the magnitude of the results, be regarded as excessive.'* [178] The entire New Zealand Division lost 110 officers and 1,533 men, of whom approximately 320 were killed.[179] The 1st Auckland suffered the heaviest casualties, with 7 officers and 52 men killed.[180] German losses were much higher, however. The allied artillery had wreaked havoc in the packed German first and second lines. More than 5,000 prisoners were taken of whom 1,159 were taken by the Kiwis.

The entire attack was a great success. The allies had now been able to deal the Germans a sledgehammer blow on the third successive occasion. Between August 1914 and demobilisation in 1919 a total of 110, 386 New Zealand men and women served in the First World War, of whom 100,444 served overseas. 18,166 were killed and many more were wounded. 5,325 have no known grave. At the outbreak of war New Zealand had a population of only 1,089,825. This new nation made an enormous sacrifice which still has an influence on New Zealand society today.

Pillbox at Otto Farm, ca. 1920 (New Zealand Division)

4 October 1917:
Private Tom Rowbottom
22nd Manchester Regiment

Tom Prescott Rowbottom was born in December 1886, the second son of Jonathan Rowbottom and Jessie Robinson. His father, Jonathan, worked as a carder in the local cotton industry in Glossop, Derbyshire. Tom had a brother and two sisters. He grew up in this small village and was a printer specialized in the operation of Linotype machines, later working for the 'Glossop Chronicle', the local paper. He married Alice Garside on 13 September 1911 in the parish church of Glossop. Alice was the daughter of an architect from the same village. A few wedding photographs of the young couple survived. They set up home in Levenshulme, near Manchester, where Rowbottom was employed as a printer with C.W.S. Printing Works. Their only daughter, Gwendoline Mary, was born in 1914. Rowbottom joined the Lancashire Fusiliers Regiment in April 1917 and began his training in Scarborough, on the east coast of England. During his training he returned to the village of his birth on leave, 'and he looked the pink of physical fitness.' After eleven weeks of training he was transferred to the Manchester Regiment, where he ended up in the 22nd Battalion. He left for the continent 'to do his bit' and ended up in the trenches of France.

Polygon Wood

The 7th Division, to which his battalion belonged, had been at the front since early October 1914. They had seen action during the First Battle of Ypres, where they had been in position on Broodseinde ridge. This was not far from where the division was to take part in the battle on 4 October 1917. The division's front line was on the northern edge of Polygon Wood in Zonnebeke and their objective was a little over a kilometre away, just beyond the Broodseinde-Beselare road. Once another unit had captured the Red Line, the 22nd Battalion Manchesters were required to push on to the Blue Line, their final objective. Tom Rowbottom went forward with the other men towards In der Star Cabaret.

However, they came under heavy fire from Joister Farm, which held up their attack. The advance could not be continued until the battalion's reserves arrived to reinforce them. The attack was a success and they took the Blue Line, but losses were high: 1 officer and 44 men dead, 218 wounded and 28 others missing.

Between the end of October and the beginning of November Rowbottom's wife in Manchester received 'the distressing intelligence from the War Office.' Rowbottom had not survived the attack on the German positions. A friend of his from Manchester, who also took part in the attack, wrote that Rowbottom had been killed at his side. The local newspaper, for which Rowbottom had worked before the war, devoted a long article to their 'hero'. 'He was 31 years of age, he would have attained his 32nd birthday at the beginning of December, and he leaves a widow (...) and a bonny little girl of three years of age, to whom the fullest measure of sympathy will go out for their cruel and irreparable loss.' The body of Tom Prescott Rowbottom was never recovered and his name is inscribed on the Tyne Cot Memorial. Straight after Rowbottom was killed, his brother Frank – who was three years younger than Tom and had been a witness at his wedding – went overseas with the Army Service Corps. He survived the war.

Wedding of Tom Rowbottom and Alice Garside. The man on the right is Tom's younger brother, who was one of the witnesses, April 1913 (Copson)

Gwendoline Mary Rowbottom, born in 1914 (Copson)

‹ *Another, unfinished, pillbox at Waterloo Farm, 11 January 1918 (IWM Q8425)*

Private Tom Rowbottom (Copson)

7 The Battle of Poelcapelle: 9 October 1917
2nd Australian Division

Overall course of the battle

SITUATION: The offensive of 4 October had gone well and the most of the designated objectives had been reached. The next phase was the capture of Passchendaele, which was to take place in two stages. The first, on 10 October 1917, was to be a preparatory attack that would take the allies to just short of Passchendaele. In the second stage the village would be captured in its entirety by the Australians on 13 October. A few days afterwards the British would then take Westrozebeke and push on to Roulers and Torhout. Additional planning depended on the weather conditions. On 7 October several high-ranking British officers proposed halting the offensive in Flanders, but Sir Douglas Haig would not entertain any such suggestion: the demoralised Germans were to be driven off the ridge at Passchendaele. The light rain of 5 and 6 October now became showers. It rained harder the next day and on 8 October the heavy rain typical of autumn had set in. Bean wrote that *'in these circumstances Haig made the most questioned decision of his career.'*[181] The campaign had to be continued and could not be postponed. Haig brought both offensives forward by one day. Nevertheless, the condition of the battlefield did not look good. The artillery bombardments had covered the entire front line area in shell holes and the heavy rain had now covered it with a thick layer of mud. The artillery experienced great difficulties in taking up their required positions on time. Yet even then it was very difficult to carry out a proper bombardment. Munitions could only be brought up in drips and drabs. In normal circumstances getting the munitions from the railway trucks to the forward batteries took only an hour. It now took at least six hours and in some cases even sixteen. Moreover, with every round the guns sank deeper into the mud and the specially constructed artil-

lery platforms did not offer a genuine solution.[182] In these circumstances the infantry – deprived of the indispensable support of the field artillery – were as good as on their own against thick barbed wire entanglements and monstrous concrete pillboxes with their machine guns spewing death and destruction.

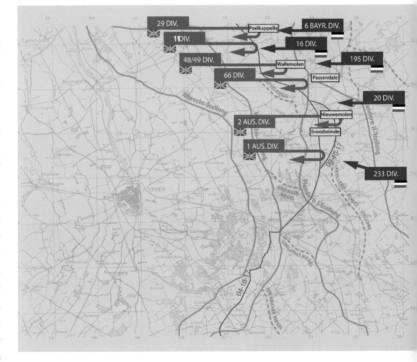

9 October 1917: general situation (MMP) >

< An MG-team of the 24th Battalion in the front line at Flinte Farm, the ridge in the background is the Keiberg, 5 October 1917 (AWM E947)

OBJECTIVE: During this first phase the British 49th and 66th Division were to attack in the direction of Passchendaele. The *Flandern I-Stellung* had to be breached and the men were to advance until just short of the *Flandern II-Stellung* in two stages. Other divisions would carry out flanking operations across the entire front and were given more limited tasks.

COURSE OF THE BATTLE: At the line near Ypres, on 9 October 1917 various divisions went into action along a front which was more than twelve kilometres wide. The 49th and 66th Divisions constituted the spearhead of the attack. The 49th Division attacked in the direction of Bellevue Spur, on both sides of the 's Graventafel-Mosselmarkt road, in a sector which began roughly at Kronprinz farm to a line which ran parallel to the Ravebeek, specifically that part of its course which flowed in a south-westerly direction. Its two brigades could hardly make any progress in the mud and only got as far as Peter Pan, near their first interim objective. The British attackers got stuck on the thick rows of barbed wire and then came under heavy fire from German machine guns from the *Flandern I-Stellung* at Bellevue. Reinforcements were brought up but could not turn

the tide. The 66th Division attacked with two brigades between the Ravebeek and the Ypres-Roulers railway. The offensive of the 198th Brigade was severely hampered by the mud and flanking fire caused numerous casualties. The 197th Brigade, which had its right flank along the Ypres-Roulers railway was initially able to advance effectively and even reached its objective, but then came under murderous fire from the German defenders. The men on the flanks made a partial pull back and the men at the centre of the attack were obliged to follow suit a while later. Eventually, the entire brigade installed itself on the first objective. Later on the whole division was required to pull back even further. The 2nd Australian Division attacked to the right of the 66th and they were required, above all, to protect the 66th Division's flanks. The 5th Brigade was able to reach the final objective, but came up against tough resistance. They too withdrew to the first objective where they made contact with the 66th Division. The 6th Brigade was initially able to advance effectively, but the exhausted Australians then came under fire from all sides. On the right of the 2nd Australian Division, the 1st Australian Division carried out a disastrous raid on the German trenches in Celtic Wood, which was intended to serve as a distraction. Scarcely 15% of the men came back in one piece.[183]

Further north, the 48th and the 11th Divisions were required to advance to Poelkapelle. They immediately came under heavy fire and had to cede the ground which they had won. On the flank, the 4th Division was also unable to reach its objectives. The 29th Division, however, which attacked from along the Ypres-Staden railway, did manage to reach its objectives, as did the Guards Division. The French Divisions, which attacked south of Houthulst Forest, also made progress.

South of the main attack, the 7th Division managed to gain some ground in the direction of the Zwaanhoek, while, at Gheluvelt, the 5th Division tried in vain to take Polderhoek Chateau.

RESULT: The whole offensive had achieved very little. A few divisions managed to gain some ground here and there, but the advance towards Passchendaele was delayed again. The number of casualties

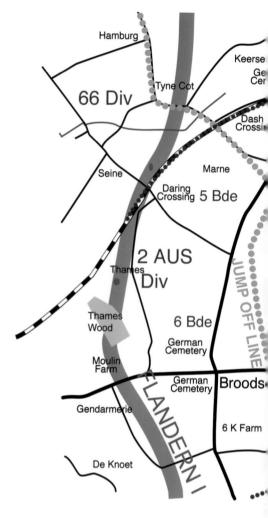

< Australian Field Artillery advanced observation post on top of Broodseinde Ridge, November 1917 (AWM E1155)

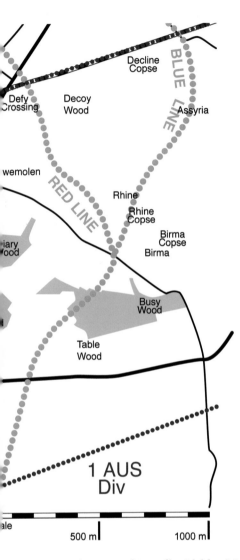

9 October 1917: 2nd Australian Division (MMP)

The 2nd Australian Division on 9 October 1917
5th Brigade
17th, 18th, 19th and 20th Australian Infantry Battalion
6th Brigade
21st, 22nd, 23rd and 24th Australian Infantry Battalion
7th Brigade (reserve)

was also high. The capture of Passchendaele now seemed very far off.

The 2nd Australian Division attacked with two brigades. The 5th Brigade made up the 66th Division's right flank. A single battalion was to advance parallel to the Ypres-Roulers railway to an interim objective – the Red Line – where the division would pause and another battalion would move on to the final objective, the Blue Line. This task was entrusted to the 20th Battalion with the 17th in reserve. The 6th Brigade attacked on their right. Its four attacking battalions had more limited objectives. The Red Line ran from the 66th Division's front across Defy Crossing through Busy Wood in the direction of Flint Copse. The Blue Line ran via Vienna Cottages in the direction of Assyria to Rhine House meeting up with the Red Line on the road between Nieuwemolen and Burma.

To the jumping-off lines

The 2nd Australian Division had already carried out an attack on 4 October 1917 and – like most of the units – the 6th and 7th Brigades had made excellent progress. The 5th Brigade was in reserve. As soon as the exhausted men were relieved in the newly captured positions, they were given all manner of fatigue duties: digging and strengthening new positions; laying duckboards; installing telephone cables; and numerous other tasks, all equally onerous. When they were allowed a few hours to get some sleep they had to do so in muddy, water-filled shell holes. They thus got very little real rest. Bean writes: *'Under such treatment the 6th Brigade, and the 7th also, simply faded away. Hundreds were evacuated through exhaustion, hundreds more with incipient trench feet.'*[184] On 7 October the exhausted Australians again occupied the front line as a preparation for resuming the of-

fensive. A hundred men from each battalion of every brigade were sent out of the line to rest and were replaced by fresh troops and new arrivals. As the 23rd Battalion had gone up to the front line earlier, they only received a handful of reinforcements. The battalion was not up to strength and this might cause problems. So the 21st Battalion, which had originally been designated as the reserve, had to take over part of the front line from the 23rd. The 22nd and the 24th Battalions were also not up to full strength when they went up to the first lines on 8 October. The 17th and the 20th Battalions of the 5th Brigade also arrived at the start line in a weakened condition.

Attacking with the 5th Brigade: Rhine House and Assyria Farm

The men got ready for the attack in the early hours of 9 October. The 20th Battalion made its way to the jumping-off line just south of Dash Crossing and the 17th Battalion moved back a few hundred metres. At exactly 5.20 a.m. the artillery laid a protective curtain across No Man's Land that would gradually move on over the German lines. The men of the 20th Battalion clambered out of the shell holes and tried to stay in one line parallel to – and just behind – the creeping barrage. However, due to the muddy conditions its batteries were operating in, the artillery had difficulty in dropping their fire onto exactly the right spot and as a result many shells fell short and landed among the men of the 20th Battalion. There were numerous casualties, but the battalion kept going.[185] The 17th Battalion, which was following almost directly behind the 20th, also sustained a few direct hits from their own guns, but likewise pressed on.[186] At the interim objective the 20th came under fire from Defy Crossing, where the Germans had a strong point. A small group of men managed to surround the position and overcome the defenders. Both the 20th and the 17th Battalions had now reached the interim objective, but had suffered numerous casualties. One of these was Private **Allan Marmaduke Crawley** a 20-year-old farmer from Wuluuman, New South Wales. He had enlisted in the Australian army in March 1916 and was already at the front in December of that year. He was hospitalized with a serious facial wound in late February 1917, but recovered quickly and – after two weeks – was granted a few days' leave. He returned to the trenches in early June 1916, rejoining his unit on 21 June 1916. Crawley was severely wounded during the attack on

9 October 1917 and was later listed as missing, after which nothing more was heard of him.[187] Like all missing Australians, Private Crawley is remembered today on the Menin Gate.

During the brief halt at the interim objective the German defensive positions were subjected to heavy shelling. The pillboxes, which were dotted across the terrain, took the full brunt of this. When the two Australian Battalions resumed their advance they encountered very little resistance from the German machine guns. A group of men from the 20th Battalion captured Rhine House close to the final objective. However, the 6th Brigade, which had to protect the right flank, ended up lagging behind. The men of the 23rd Battalion advanced too far to the north and came up behind the 17th Battalion. This meant that they missed Dairy Wood, which they were supposed to clear of Germans and it was precisely from Dairy Wood that well-concealed German troops were firing on the advancing Australians. The 23rd Battalion was still able to save the situation on reaching their final objective at Rhine House by protecting the 17th and the 20th Battalions' flank and by clearing the Germans out of Dairy Wood. When the allied barrage moved on again, the men were able to continue their advance. A group of about 30 men of the 17th Battalion pushed on towards the final objective at Assyria Farm. On the way they came under fire from the railway embarkment. Under the command of Lieutenant **John Maher Lyons** they were quickly able to take this pillbox out. They then moved on and headed towards Assyria Farm. *'So sudden and determined was the attack that the garrison barely resisted, several being killed and fourteen taken prisoner.'*[188] The group had managed to take Assyria Farm without undue problems. They were now on the Red Line, but later on they were forced to cede it again to the Germans. The Australians did not have enough men to consolidate the farmhouse and made a partial withdrawal. Lieutenant Lyons sustained a serious head wound later that day, when the Germans launched a heavy counter-attack . *'The enemy fire was heavy during this counterattack, so bad that Mr Lyons had to be carried into Rhine House, a large red bricked building, and left there,'* one of the men explained later to the Red Cross Society. An officer reported that Lieutenant Lyons *'was placed in a pill box and the stretcher-bearer had not time [sic] to evacuate him as they fell back.'*

When the position was subsequently recaptured, Lyons had disappeared. At the outbreak of war the 27-year-old tram driver had signed up to serve six months in the Australian army, but when his time was up, he immediately signed on for the duration. He fought at Gallipoli at the beginning of August 1915, where he was promoted to Sergeant and where he was decorated with the Military Medal: *'he showed great coolness and presence of mind when under fire, (...) he proved very efficient and intrepid.'* Lyons was also decorated by the French government for his actions on the Turkish peninsula. Together with several other soldiers he was awarded the *Medaille Militaire 'for general meritorious service with their battalions and gallantry in action.'* The 17th Battalion arrived in France at the end of March 1916 and he was to spend the rest of the war in the muddy trenches of the Western Front. In late June 1916 Lyons volunteered to take part in a night raid on the enemy trenches and a month later he was involved in an attack on Pozières in which he led his men through Munster Alley. He received the Meritorious Service Medal for both actions. In the second attack he was slightly wounded in the face and had to be admitted to hospital, returning to the front at the end of September. On 20 January 1917 he was made a Second Lieutenant. Six weeks later he was wounded again. A bomb exploded near him and Lyons was hospitalized with wounds to his entire body. It was not until late July 1917 that he could return to his unit, after which he was promoted to Lieutenant.[189] He was listed as wounded and missing after the attack of 9 October. For his actions on that day Lyons was awarded the Military Cross. It was originally thought that Lyons, an experienced officer, had been taken prisoner, but no trace could be found of him. Lieutenant Lyons's body was never recovered and he is remembered today on the Menin Gate. Sergeant **George Thomas Guinea** of the 6th company of the Australian Machine Gun Corps suffered a similar fate. The 23-year-old cabinetmaker from Glenthompson, Victoria, *'was hit through the lung near the heart and his mates dressed his wound and put him in a shell hole pending the arrival of the stretcher-bearers to take him to the rear.'* The German counter-attack made this impossible, however, as the Germans recaptured the spot where the wounded Sergeant had been left. Thereafter, nothing more was heard of him. Guinea had joined up in May 1915 and was posted to the 24th Battalion, with whom he departed for Egypt. From there

Private Allan Marmaduke Crawley (AWM P04086.001)

Sergeant George Thomas Guinea (AWM DA09537)

Private Edgar Athling Morris (Sullivan)

Lieutenant John Maher Lyons (AWM H05738)

left: Original grave cross of Lieutenant Campbell, who is remembered today on the Menin Gate (AWM H15317)
right: Lieutenant John Donald Campbell (AWM H15587)

he was sent to France, where he was transferred to the 6th Machine Gun Corps on 6 June 1916. In early August he won the Military Medal at Pozières. He twice managed to beat off a German counter-attack with machine gun fire single-handedly, *'killing many and forcing 30 to surrender.'* He was promoted to Lance Corporal shortly afterwards, became a Corporal at the beginning of May 1917 and was made a Sergeant a few weeks later. After the attack on 9 October 1917 he was listed as missing.[190] His body was not found until after the war. Sergeant Guinea was reburied at Passchendaele New British Cemetery. His brother John Leslie was killed at Messines in early June.[191]

No other unit of the 17th or the 20th Battalions managed to advance to the Blue Line. Their entire attack had got stuck at the interim objective. A great many officers had been lost which meant that the NCOs now had a vitally important job to do. The regimental historian was unstinting in praising them: *'When most of the officers were casualties, these men calmly took command, and by their coolness and soldierly initiative both encouraged and inspired their men.'*[192] He was

also full of praise for the medical units. *'The stretcher-bearers had a very trying task, and because of the terrible condition of the ground, four men were required to man each stretcher.'*[193] One of these stretcher-bearers – from the 20th Battalion however – was Private **Edgar Athling Morris**, who was the son of a policeman from Bankstown, New South Wales. Before the war he had found a job as a shunter with the railways thanks to the recommendations of former employers and prominent people from his neighbourhood: *'I always found him a thoroughly conscientious, honest and strictly trustworthy employee, always anxious to please and do his best. (...) I have never heard him use obscene language and I am sure he will succeed and will gain the confidence of anybody by whom he is employed'.* At the end of November 1915 the conscientious 23-year-old enlisted in the Australian army, joining his unit, the 20th Battalion, in the trenches in France on 2 October 1916. A few weeks later he was admitted to hospital suffering from trench feet and was not able to return to the battalion until July. Private Morris was killed at Broodseinde on 9 October. *'As far as can be ascertained this soldier was killed instantaneously, being hit by several pieces of shell mostly about the body. There is no record of the body ever having being buried.'*[194] Nor was it found after the war. Morris is remembered today on the Menin Gate.

Attacking with the 6th Brigade: Daisy and Dairy Wood

Unlike the 5th Brigade, the 6th Brigade was given a more limited objective and the 23rd, 21st, 24th and 22nd Battalions each took responsibility for taking part of this objective. According to Bean, the average strength of each battalion was only 7 officers and 150 men. The protective barrage offered insufficient cover and did not have much effect on the German positions. Despite heavy resistance, the 22nd Battalion was able to reach its final objective at the Broodseinde-Moorslede road, where it engaged in heavy fighting with a number of nearby German pillboxes.[195] Lieutenant **John Donald Campbell** was killed during the advance towards the final objective. He was with the 6th company of the Australian Machine Gun Corps, a unit which was dependent on the 6th Brigade. The 37-year-old farmer from Surrey Hills, Victoria, had joined up as a private in May 1915. He arrived in Gallipoli in late August 1915 and reported to the 22nd Battalion. He was quickly promoted and was already a Sergeant after only three months. At the beginning of March 1916 Campbell was made a Second Lieutenant. His battalion was still in Egypt, but the newly commissioned officer was sent to the 6th Machine Gun Company. From Egypt they were posted to France where he was promoted to Lieutenant in July in 1916. A few days after returning from leave in England Campbell was admitted to hospital in February 1917 and, after a period of convalescence in Le Havre, rejoined his unit. Lieutenant Campbell was granted another spell of leave in England at the end of August and was killed on the road from Broodseinde to Moorslede a month later.[196] The precise circumstances of his death have not yet been clarified. His body was buried and a cross was erected. Campbell's grave was destroyed by later bombardments, however, and no trace of it could be found after the war. He is remembered today on the Menin Gate.

Daisy Wood

On the left of the 22nd Battalion, the 24th tried to push through to Daisy Wood. The Division's War Diary reveals *'that progress was satisfactory despite the weak and irregular barrage until encountering enemy resistance at Daisy Wood.'*[197] They only advanced a derisory 200 metres from their jumping-off positions to Daisy Wood, but half way across the Germans got the Australian troops in their sights and opened fire. The Germans managed to take out all the officers of D company, who had tried, one by one, to take the German position with grenades. Captain Charles Morrice Williams, Lieutenant **Reginald James Pickett** and Lieutenant Norman Charles Nation were shot dead one after another.[198] Lieutenant Pickett, a 24-year-old bricklayer from Dandenong, Victoria, had joined up in March 1915. He was soon made a Sergeant and saw action with the 24th Battalion at Gallipoli in August of that year. Pickett ended up in a field hospital several times: in December 1915 with inflamed and infected fingers; in January 1916 with a shrapnel wound to the hand; and in March 1917 with scurvy. He had now been made a Second Lieutenant and in early April, after a brief bout of illness, was able to rejoin his unit. Hardly a month later a bullet went through Pickett's right arm, but he did not wish to leave his post and *'led repeated bombing attacks against the enemy for five hours doing most valuable work at a critical time.'* He was awarded the Military Cross for his ac-

Lieutenant Reginald James Pickett, then Sergeant (left), and Sergeant Jack Noble. (AWM D08870)

tions. Pickett was promoted to Lieutenant during his convalescence in England and returned to his unit at the beginning of July. He was cut down by German machine fire at Daisy Wood on 9 October 1917 and his men buried him a few hundred metres southwest of Daisy Wood.[199] Lieutenant Pickett's body could not be found after the war and his name is inscribed on the Menin Gate.

Of D company only two NCOs and a handful of men were left. The others were either wounded or dead. One of those killed was Private **Frederick William Bulling**, who was shot in the head by a German machine gun. He was not yet 20. Bulling, a young apprentice cabinetmaker from Prahran, Victoria, was killed instantly. He had joined up in December 1915 and six months later he was with the 24th Battalion at the front in France. In March 1917 he had to be evacuated to a hospital in England with a high temperature. He returned to his unit, which was by then at the front in Flanders, only

top: Private George Ernest Bolton (AWM H05674)
bottom: Private Frederick William Bulling (AWM H05688)

top: Lance Corporal James Horace Lane in the Middle East (AWM P00223.001)
below: Lane, probably in Egypt (AWM P00223.002)

Lieutenant Arthur Douglas Hogan (AWM H05765)

a few weeks before his death.[200] Private Bulling's body would have been buried where he fell, but no trace of it could be found after the war. The other companies also suffered enormous casualties, one of whom was Private **George Ernest Bolton**, a 25-year-old steam locomotive fireman from Collingswood, Victoria. He joined up in May 1915 and ended up in France in March 1916, via Egypt. At the end of the year he spent a few months in hospital suffering form muscle pains. He returned to his unit in late January 1917, but soon found himself back in hospital, this time with flu. Like Private Bulling, he did not rejoin the battalion until the end of September.[201] Nothing is known about either his death or his burial. Private Bolton's name is inscribed on the Menin Gate. Parts of A and C company dug themselves in on the edge of Daisy Wood and they too lost a lot of men. Among them was Lance Corporal **James Horace Lane**, who was a cabinet maker from Moonee Ponds, Victoria. He joined up in early 1916 and was sent overseas almost immediately. Although his service papers make no mention of it, he spent some time in the Middle East, probably in Egypt, and some photographs of him from this period have survived. In late September 1916 he joined his unit, the 24th Battalion, on the Western Front. Two weeks later he was hospitalized with bronchitis and it was just after Christmas 1916 when he returned to his unit. The 21-year-old Lane was promoted to Lance Corporal a month before he was killed at Broodseinde. He was wounded on 9 October. In February 1918 Lane's mother wrote to the Base Records that she had been informed '*that my Boy was seen put*

on a stracher [sic.].' Lance Corporal Lane was listed as wounded and missing. In June 1918 a soldier testified that Lane had been killed by a German artillery shell. He would then have been buried 500 metres from the lake at Zonnebeke, probably near a first aid post.[202] The grave could not be found after the war and Lane is remembered on the Menin Gate. Lane's brother, Arthur Jabez, had been killed at Bullecourt in May 1917.[203]

Later in the afternoon they managed to clear the Germans out of Daisy Wood, but there was no question of pressing on to Busy Wood, which was the 24th Battalion's final objective.[204] They had suffered appalling casualties and the men were in need of being relieved and taken out of the line to rest.

Between Daisy and Dairy Wood

The 21st Battalion was supposed to advance between Daisy and Dairy Wood and push through to just in front of Burma. The barrage hit the German positions on time, but '*all accounts proved it to have been light and ineffective, enemy snipers and Machine Gunners remaining in action over the whole area.*'[205] The attacking troops immediately came under heavy fire. As had happened to the 24th, the 21st Battalion now found that German defenders had managed to take out almost all the officers early on in the attack. One of those hit was Lieutenant **Arthur Douglas Hogan**, a jeweller and optician in civilian life, who was not quite 30. He '*fell gallantly leading the attack on the German positions over Broodseinde Ridge between Dairy and Daisy Woods.*' Hogan, who was a graduate of the Spencer Optical Institute and had a few years of previous military experience with a local militia unit, joined up in April 1915. He applied for a commission and was made a Second Lieutenant on 16 July 1915. Hogan left for Egypt with the reinforcements for the 5th Battalion in October 1915. He was admitted to a field hospital with a severe illness at the beginning of January 1916 and was later evacuated to Australia to convalesce. In early July he was on board the Ayrshire bound for England and he reported to the 21st Battalion in France at the end of October 1916. Hogan was promoted to Lieutenant a few weeks later. In March 1917 he was hospitalized for a week with bronchitis. He received a gunshot wound five days later and had to return to hospital. He was not able to rejoin his unit till the beginning of July.[206] Despite reports that he was buried in the German cemetery at the crossroads at Broodseinde, Lieutenant Hogan is remembered on the Menin Gate.

The death of so many officers caused chaos in the various companies of the 21st Battalion. The success of the attack and the job of leading the men now depended entirely on the NCOs. The battalion forged ahead and tried to reach the objectives as quickly as possible. A few units managed to make contact with the men of the 23rd Battalion at Rhine House. Other groups were able to reach the final objective under the command of NCOs, where they organized a defensive line, although *'with both flanks completely in the air and under heavy fire from Busy Wood where the enemy was extremely active.'*[207] The 24th Battalion was still lagging behind and not all the German pillboxes had been taken out. The 21st Battalion thus also suffered heavy casualties. One of those killed was Private **Herbert John Strong**, who was listed as missing after the attack. Strong was from Charlton, in England. His parents still lived there, having stayed behind when Strong emigrated to Australia, where he worked as a driver. He enlisted in the Australian army in July 1915 and was sent to Egypt after a brief period of training where he was posted to the 21st Battalion. In March 1916 he arrived in the trenches in France after disembarking in Marseille and was wounded in the thumb in November 1916. Strong was admitted to hospital and after a brief period of leave he was required to spend a few months with the 65th Battalion in England. It was not until late September 1917 that he could return to his unit in Flanders.[208] The 33-year-old Private Strong is also remembered on the Menin Gate. The same fate befell Lieutenant **Arthur George Walmsley**, who was also listed as missing after the attack and is now remembered on the Menin Gate. The 21-year-old clerk from Flemington, Victoria, had joined up in July 1915 and arrived in Egypt in October of that year, where he served with the 23rd Battalion. A month later he was hospitalized with a gastric infection and was not fit for active duty again until January 1916. While in France, Walmsley was made a Corporal and was promoted to the rank of Sergeant in October of that year. Shortly afterwards he was sent to England for officer training and was commissioned as a Second Lieutenant in March 1917, joining the 21st Battalion a month later. At the end of July 1917 he was made a Lieutenant. He was wounded

‹ Private Herbert John Strong (AWM DA 10221)

Lieutenant Arthur George Walmsley (AWM C01248)

during the attack on 9 October and made his way to a first aid post as quickly as he could. In early December one of the men explained: *'He had been hit in the shoulder as far as I could see. (...) I saw blood running down from his tunic at the back from his shoulder, but he did not seem too bad.'*[209] Even so, the young Lieutenant Walmsley probably died from his wounds shortly afterwards.

top: *Private Edwin St Clair Yeoman (in the middle) and his brother Leonard William (right) (AWM DA10212)*
bottom: *Sergeant George Goulburn Warren (AWM H18819)*

Dairy Wood

The 23rd Battalion went over with only 123 men, so the 21st Battalion took over part of its front line in order to make up for the shortage of men. The 23rd was supposed to advance through Dairy Wood towards Rhine House, the final objective. Each company – which on average consisted of only 30 men – was given its own objective. D and A companies were to push through to the interim objective and set up a defensive line there, while B company was to try to reach the final objective and it was C company's job to clear the terrain of all German pillboxes. The War Diary recorded: *'Little frontage opposition was experienced in the advance, but heavy M.G. and Rifle Fire was encountered from direction of Daisy and Busy Woods, causing approximately 50% casualties'*. Private **Edwin St Clair Yeoman** was one of those casualties. A soldier later told the Red Cross Society: *'I was not far from Yeoman as we went over No Mans Land and I saw him fall. He had been badly hit by a 5.9 shell which fell almost on him. I could not go up to him. I saw part of his body and he was killed instantly.'* Yeoman, who was not quite 22, was from Brighton, Victoria. He enlisted in the Australian army in September 1915 and joined his unit in Egypt in January 1916, from where he sailed to France. A few months later he was hospitalized with an infected facial wound. He rejoined his unit in June 1916, but was soon given a few weeks leave. Private Yeoman was listed as missing after the attack on 9 October and his mutilated body was never found again.[210] Like Sergeant **George Goulburn Warren**, Yeoman is remembered on the Menin Gate in Ypres. Warren was a 24-year-old farmer from Undera, Victoria, who joined up in late January 1915. At the end of August he was with the 23rd Battalion in Egypt and was later sent to France, where he was promoted to Corporal in 1916. He was admitted to hospital towards the end of the year suffering from trench feet and was not able to join his unit again until the beginning of May 1917. Warren was made a Sergeant in June. He was listed as missing after the attack on 9 October. *'Warren was seen suffering from shell shock, walking about 20 yards from the hopping off tape at Zonnebeke and no one ever heard anything of him after.'* After his death, Warren's family wanted to recover his engraved gold wristwatch, *'as I would value it immensely as a keep safe from my boy, who has given his life for King and Country'*. Warren had been given an expensive watch by friends on the occasion of his

British position recaptured by the Germans at Broodseinde, April 1918 (Deraeve)

departure for the front. The relevant authorities opened an investigation, but without success. As Sergeant Warren was missing, *'it is regretted that there is very little likelihood of the watch now coming to hand.'*[211]

Due to German flanking fire from Daisy and Busy Wood, the attacking companies had strayed too far north and thus missed part of Dairy Wood. When the first men reached their interim objective, they realized their mistake and formed an extra line to protect the flanks of the 17th and 20th Battalion. In the meantime, part of C company was able to clear the wood of Germans. They were to suffer a large number of casualties, one of whom was Lance Corporal **Russel Highfield Hawse**, a 25-year-old salesman and musician from Geelong, Victoria. He had joined up in late March 1915 and was posted to the 23rd Battalion at the end of August, which was then fighting at Lone Pine in Gallipoli. Via Egypt he ended up in the trenches

Lance Corporal Russel Highfield Hawse (AWM DA08937)

on the Western Front, where, in June 1916, he took part in a raid on a German position. In late July Hawse received a bullet in the foot and was evacuated to a hospital in England. He was able to rejoin his unit in early November and was made a Lance Corporal at the end of August 1917. He was killed on 9 October, *'sniped through the head during the attack at Broodseinde (...). The men who were with him at the time were all casualties. It is not known where he was buried.'*[212] Lance Corporal Hawse's body was recovered after the war by exhumation units of the British army and was reburied in Passchendaele New British Cemetery.

A little while later B company pushed on to the final objective. It was a short distance and the men were able to bridge it easily. They then built five fortified positions around Rhine House. At dusk the Germans carried out a large-scale counter-attack and the Australian units were forced to pull back from Rhine House. As soon as they had done so, the advancing Germans were subjected to a heavy artillery bombardment, which stopped the counter-attack in its tracks and avoided further loss of ground.

Relief

In the night of 9 to 10 October fresh, full-strength units were able to relieve the assault battalions. The 49th Battalion of the 4th Australian Division replaced the 21st, 22nd, 23rd and 24th Battalions, while the 45th Battalion replaced the men of the 17th and 20th Battalions. The men were sent to the rear for a period of rest. It was to be short, as they would be back in the front line at Passchendaele at the beginning of November. On that occasion, however, they no longer formed part of the attack. The battalions of the 5th and the 6th Brigade had been almost literally decimated and the number of casualties was high. The 5th Brigade lost 18 officers and 322 men while the 6th Brigade recorded the loss of 22 officers and 390 men.[213]

Yet Sir Douglas Haig still had no thoughts of giving up. On 12 October – as planned – he sent his troops into yet another attack, which he hoped would finally secure Passchendaele.

Two Australians of the 2nd Division watch the barrage from Westhoek, 9 October 1917 (AWM E1091)

German plank road to Broodseinde, seen from the Moorslede end, late 1917 (Deraeve)

9 October 1917:
Privates Charles and Reginald Herbert
2nd Lancashire Fusiliers & 23rd Battalion AIF

Stories of brothers, cousins, fathers and sons who fought in the war are legion. Often they joined up together or one served as an example to the other. Together they could endure the hardships at the front more easily, as they were not completely separated from their loved ones. Yet at the same time, they were exposed, just like everyone else, to the everyday dangers of trenches, bombardments and attacks. Many were killed or wounded and the Battle of Passchendaele was no exception. Here too, a great many family histories have been written. If they were in the same battalion, brothers would fight side by side on the muddy battlefields around Ypres. If they belonged to different units, they often did not know that their brother was going at the Germans with bayonet or rifle only a few kilometres away. Sometimes they were killed with only a few days difference between them and occasionally even on the same day, as in the case of the Herbert brothers, who had not only enlisted in different units, but also in the armies of two different countries.

Thomas Herbert and Martha Wilson were farmers in Stilton, a small village in Cambridgeshire. They had five sons. The oldest, Charles, was born on 24 March 1887 in Steeple Gidding. Reginald, their second son, was born in late December 1888. Their fifth son, Albert, came into the world in early September 1894.

Charles went to school in Hamerton and Denton and, like his parents, worked on the farm. In February 1913 he emigrated to Australia where continued the family farming tradition in Cootamundra, a former gold rush town. Reginald remained in England and went to school in Denton and Stilton. He later became a butcher. Albert, the youngest brother, went to school in Stilton and later went on to attend the Deacons School in nearby Peterborough. He was a schoolmaster.

A month after war was declared in August 1914, Albert joined the army in Northampton and was posted to the 2nd Battalion Northamptonshire Regiment, fighting on the Western Front from 1 April 1915. His career in the army was very short. Two weeks before the British offensive was due to start, the 20-year-old Albert was killed at Aubers Ridge in France on 26 April 1915. A comrade in arms and a close friend of his wrote to his parents: *'I have lost a true and dear friend, liked and respected by everyone in the regiment. He was a brave and fearless young soldier, and gave his life for his country, as only a British soldier can. I don't think he knew what fear was. I have been a great friend of his since we first met at Deacons School, over seven years ago. I came out with him on 1 April, and have been his constant friend ever since.'* Private Albert Herbert is buried in Rue-Petillon Military Cemetery, Fleurbaix.

Reginald had joined up in Liverpool a week before Albert was killed. He had previous military experience as a trooper with the 2nd King Edward's Horse, a cavalry regiment. From July 1915 he served with the 2nd Battalion Lancashire Fusiliers. Charles, who lived in Australia, enlisted in the Australian army on 9 October 1916. He also had previous military experience, having served with another cavalry regiment, the Northamptonshire Yeomanry, for three years before requesting to be discharged. He embarked for service overseas on 30 October 1916 and continued his training in England in early January. He was posted to France at the end of March 1917, where he joined his unit, the 23rd Battalion, at the beginning of April.

During the Battle of Passchendaele, both the 2nd Lancashire Fusiliers and the 23rd Australian Battalion went into action on 9 October 1917. Neither brother knew that the other was fighting so close by. Reginald's battalion was part of the 12th Brigade of the 4th Division and attacked northwest of Poelkapelle. At 5.20 a.m.

top: *Private Reginald Herbert (de Ruvigny)*
bottom: *Private Charles Herbert (de Ruvigny)*

the men left their jumping-off positions and advanced towards the German front line. They reached their first objective without undue problems, but then came under fire from Landing Farm, Compromise Farm and Millers Farm. They suffered appalling losses and were not able to reach their second and third objectives. Private Reginald Herbert was one of those killed. *'The best chum I ever had' (...) 'no man could have a better.'* Reginald was buried on the battlefield, but his body was not found after the war. He is remembered today on the Tyne Cot Memorial.

Charles was also sent to storm the German positions that day. His unit, the 23rd Battalion, set out through Dairy Wood, northwest of Broodseinde, towards their final objective, Rhine House, with too few men. Heavy machine gun fire on their flank caused numerous casualties among the advancing Australians and the Germans took out half of the already heavily depleted battalion. Private Charles Herbert was probably one of the casualties. The battalion succeeded in reaching Rhine House, but, in the evening, had to abandon the positions and pull back under pressure from a heavy German counter-attack. Like his younger brother Reginald, Charles was also buried on the battlefield and, after the war, a British exhumation party managed to find his mortal remains: *'Isolated grave in the Long Grass near a Sandy Topped Shell Hole'.* He was subsequently reburied in Aeroplane Cemetery. Charles's platoon commander wrote to his parents: *'I came into very close contact with him, and I valued him very highly indeed as a soldier and as a man. As a matter of fact, I had noted him for early promotion, and his loss to me will be hard to make good. He had always impressed me with his splendid personality and his gentlemanly conduct on all occasions (...). He was one of the best, more than that I cannot say.'*

The family Herbert lost three sons in the war. Two of them died on the same day scarcely seven kilometres from each other. They belonged to completely different units: Reginald to a British battalion and Charles to an Australian battalion.

8 The First Battle of Passchendaele: 12 October 1917
3rd Australian Division

Overall course of the battle

SITUATION: The 2nd Australian Division had suffered heavy losses on 9 October and the Australian troops, who served as the spearhead of the attack for more than three weeks, were almost at breaking point. The British 66th Division had also suffered heavy losses. The battlefield was strewn with the dead and countless wounded who had been left behind in the desolate landscape. The battlefield was in an appalling condition and in some places the mud was knee deep. This made it almost impossible to bring the artillery into position and to bombard the German lines effectively. In many places the pillboxes and the multiple rows of barbed wire were still intact. The allies had broken through the German's *Flandern I-Stellung*, but behind it lay the even stronger *Flandern II-Stellung*. The allied troops would have to take this line before Passchendaele could be captured. That the offensive on 9 October had been a complete failure did not stop the high command from attacking again on 12 October. The conditions had not changed, however and it was also still raining. After three months of artillery bombardments and rain, the idyllic heights around Zonnebeke and Passchendaele had been transformed into a genuine quagmire.

OBJECTIVE: The aim of the attack on 12 October was to capture Passchendaele. In order to do so the *Flandern I* and *II-Stellungen* would have to be breached. This task was entrusted to the 3rd Australian Division and the New Zealand Division. Other divisions along the front were either given flanking missions or were required to take more limited objectives.

COURSE OF THE BATTLE: The 3rd Australian Division and the New Zealanders were not to fulfil their mission, primarily due to the lack of artillery support. The failure of the artillery meant that the infantry came up against thick, impenetrable rows of barbed wire in which they were mercilessly mown down by German machine gun fire. The attack was stopped dead in its tracks with huge bloodshed. For New Zealand this was the blackest day in its history: until that time the country had never lost so many men in just one day. Almost 2,800 New Zealanders were killed, wounded, missing or taken prisoner. The 3rd Australian Division also had to contend with

12 October 1917: general situation (MMP) ›

‹ Roll call of C Company 40th Battalion, after coming out of the line, near Potyze, 14 October 1917 (AWM E4535)

heavy German resistance. The division's two assault brigades were initially able to advance quite far, but they were later pushed back to the jumping-off lines. The mud, the enormous scale of the German defence and the failure of the New Zealanders to advance caused genuine carnage in the Australian ranks. The 3rd Australian Division was flanked to the south by the 4th Australian Division, which attacked with only one brigade, but which still managed to take its, albeit limited, objectives. Yet the men of the 4th were to pay a high price for this small success and – due to the withdrawal of the 3rd Australian Division – they too were eventually pushed back to their jumping-off positions.

The 9th Scottish Division attacked north of the New Zealanders. They were also required to advance some two kilometres to the top of the ridge, just beyond Goudberg. The 18th Division was north of the Lekkerboterbeek. Here again the artillery support fell well short of expectations. Right from the very beginning of the attack both divisions came under murderous fire from the German positions, which enjoyed the advantage of height. The losses were huge and the attack literally got bogged down in the muddy terrain. The 4th Division's attack went better, with the left brigade managing an advance of 700 metres. The 17th Division also managed to take its limited objectives south of the Houthulst Forest, as did the Guards Division, west of the Ypres-Torhout railway line.

RESULT: Despite the success of the actions carried out by other British divisions in the north, the main attack of 12 October was again a complete fiasco. Passchendaele was still beyond the reach of the allied troops and would remain so for more than three weeks. Meanwhile the losses on both sides continued to mount.

The division's objective was simple: to capture Passchendaele in three phases. The first objective, the Red Line, was about 1,200 metres from the start line. The second objective, the Blue Line, was around 500 metres further on and was to serve as the jumping-off point for the assault on the third objective, the Green Line, which lay 400 metres behind Passchendaele. The village itself was to be captured by the 38th Battalion of the 10th Brigade and – according to the plan – ought to have been firmly in Australian hands by the afternoon. The men were to advance behind a creeping barrage.

The 3rd Australian Division on 12 October 1917

  9th Brigade

    33rd, 34th, 35th and 36th Battalion

  10th Brigade

    37th, 38th, 39th and 40th Battalion

  11th Brigade (reserve)

12 October 1917: 3rd Australian Division (MMP)

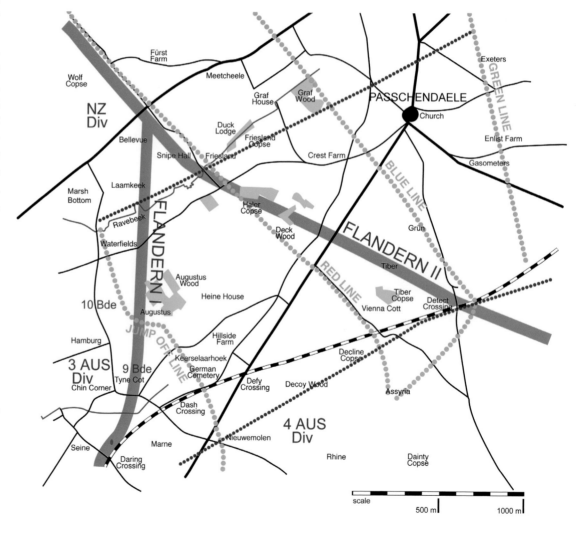

Private Robert Wilson (AWM P01920.005)

German photograph of the appalling condition of the terrain, looking in the direction of Zonnebeke, April 1918 (Deraeve)

Private Harold Thomas Sell (AWM H06663)

The 9th Brigade moves up to the front line

On the evening before the attack the 9th Brigade set out for the front line at 6.00 p.m., from its camp near Potijze, with the 34th Battalion at the head. The route had been reconnoitred beforehand by an officer. The brigade followed the Ypres-Roulers railway line to reach its assembly point. After midnight it began to drizzle, which soon changed into heavy rainfall. Combined with the strong wind this made the march very unpleasant for the Australian troops, although there were no casualties until they reached Zonnebeke station. From then on the going became a lot more difficult. At various points the duckboards had been shot to smithereens and the tapes had disappeared. The German artillery did not sit idly by and shelled the route with its heavy guns. Beyond the station the battalion halted just south of Alma. Captains Clarence Smith Jeffries and Telford Graham Gilder[214] of the 34th Battalion went on ahead to look for the assembly point, the battalion waiting patiently, while the two officers tried to beat a path through the morass. Among those waiting was Private **Robert 'Bob' Wilson** of C company, a 24-year-old miner from the district of Abermain, NSW. A German shell suddenly fell among the waiting troops. Four men were killed instantly – Wilson being among them[215] – and several others were wounded, one of whom died in a field hospital.[216] Lance-Corporal Green saw the whole thing. A year later he told the Australian Red Cross Society that Wilson had been killed outright: *'Bob Wilson was right close to me and was hit, his blood was all over the back of my tunic, he was killed instantaneously.'*[217] Green wrote a letter to Wilson's mother notifying her of the death of her son. No information has been found with respect to a possible burial.

The 33rd Battalion also suffered a similar incident. Private **Harold Thomas Sell** and two other men were killed as they made their way along the railway to the front line. A soldier explained: *'We were walking in single file along the main railway track. I was ahead of Sell. A high explosive shell fell and killed Sell and three others. Death was instantaneous.'* The bodies were probably not buried immediately: *'It was near the German Cemetery. Like many others, they were probably not buried at all, there was too much shell fire there.'*[218]

A little while later the two captains came back from their reconnaissance having found the tape. The 34th Battalion, and then the entire 9th Brigade, fell in and resumed their march. The 9th Brigade arrived at the assembly position around 3.00 a.m. It was still raining and the German artillery continued to shell the unprotected men. *'During the assembly and right up to Zero Hour, the battalion was subjected to heavy fire by 7.7s and 4.2 H.E. The greatest part of this fire appeared to come from S. and S.E. of Passchendaele. Casualties were heavy, principally on the right flank near the cemetery.'*[219] The other battalions of the 9th Brigade also had a hard time of it – even before the fighting began. *'Constantly shelled'*, notes the War Diary of the 35th Battalion, which, together with the 36th Battalion, was also heavily shelled by the German artillery and half of one of its companies was wiped out as a result.[220] One of the casualties was Second Lieutenant **Charles Teesdale Main**, a chemist from North Adelaide, NSW. The attack would have been his first experience of leading a platoon of soldiers in action, but the newly commissioned officer was dead even before the signal for the attack was given. *'Main was killed by a shell, when he was on the line of assembly, near the cemetery, in front of Passchendaele'*. His body would have been buried immediately by men of the battalion, but was never found.[221] Second Lieutenant Main is remembered today on the Menin Gate.

How the 10th Brigade fared

The 10th Brigade began its march to the front line around 9.00 p.m. The 37th Battalion was at the head of the column with the 40th and the 38th Battalions following behind. The 10th Brigade also set out from a camp near Potijze, but took another route. From the Ypres-Zonnebeke road they went via Bremen Redoubt to Van Isacker's Farm, Bordeaux Farm, Beecham Farm and finally to the front line.[222] Their losses were limited.

The 3rd Division's jumping-off line ran from the Ypres-Roulers railway line at Keerselaarhoek via the southernmost point of Augustus Wood towards Waterfields. The 9th Brigade was on the right and the 10th Brigade on the left, flanked by Australians of the 4th Division and the New Zealanders, respectively. To their left the New Zealanders were getting ready for the attack.

Second Lieutenant Charles Teesdale Main (AWM H05741)

To the first objective with the 9th Brigade

An hour before the bombardments, which began around 5.30 a.m., it stopped raining. The last men of the 33rd Battalion had finally reached their destination after a march of at least seven hours.[223] The men got ready for the attack. The War Diary of the 34th Battalion mentions the allied bombardment: *'It was very weak, and in many cases it was difficult to determine which was our barrage, and which was the fire from the enemy.'*[224] *'The greatest obstacle met in the advance, was the condition of the ground (...). The pace of the advance was slowed up, owing to the assistance it was necessary to give men who had sunk into shell-holes, and who could not extricate themselves without as-*

Private Joseph Varcoe (AWM P04514.001)

Captain Clarence Smith Jeffries
(AWM P01920.028)

sistance.'[225] According to Bean, the 9th Brigade attacked '*in the utmost confusion*'.[226] The Australians were hampered not only by the mud, but also by the German resistance. '*The tell-tale red and green rockets flew high above our heads, both to give our own artillery the chance to let rip, and as a sign of our heightened state of readiness: hold fast at the post that duty has brought you to, don't falter or give ground: the fate of thousands of comrades hangs on your fighting spirit and sharp observation!*'[227] The Germans were determined to hold their own positions, especially the *Flandern II*, at all costs.

The 35th Battalion was held up by machine gun fire at Defy Crossing, which was where the Ypres-Roulers railway line crossed the Broodseinde-Passchendaele road. The ruins were stormed and taken by men of the battalion under the command of Captains Carr and Dixon of the 35th Battalion. It was probably here that Private **Joseph Varcoe**, a 32-year-old grazier from Gunbar, NSW, was killed. According to his Service Record he was killed '*in front of the line to which the battalion afterwards retired.*' It is also likely that he was buried there, as Varcoe's brother received a letter from the chaplain saying that he would send him the notebook which his brother had on him when he died, '*which were in his possesion [sic] when killed in action.*'[228] If this is correct, Varcoe may have been buried the following day by a man of his unit. Private Varcoe's name is inscribed today on the Menin Gate.

The 34th Battalion had a fair degree of trouble from two pillboxes east of Augustus Wood and northeast of Heine House. These were captured by a group of men under the command of Captain Jeffries. He took 35 Germans prisoner and captured four machine guns. On their way to the first objective the 9th Brigade also came under heavy fire from Bellevue, Meetcheele, Tiber and Tiber Copse. The Germans also offered resistance for a while at Decline Copse. On reaching their first objective (the Red Line) the men of the 34th Battalion immediately began to dig in.

Major John Bruce Buchanan (left) in conversation with Major Howell-Price (right), who was also killed at Zonnebeke on 4 October 1917 (AWM A04038)

The 9th Brigade's second objective

The 35th Battalion immediately pushed on to the second objective. Due to the confusion at the beginning of the attack the various units of the battalions were all mixed up and men of the 34th advanced with the 35th Battalion. As the brigade had originally followed the Broodseinde-Passchendaele road instead of the Ypres-Roulers railway line, an opening had been created on the brigade's right flank. It was here, at Decline Copse, that Major **John Bruce Buchanan** of the 36th Battalion was hit in the stomach by machine gun fire from Tiber Copse.[229] He died from his wounds shortly afterwards. Buchanan's body was left behind and was probably buried at the beginning of 1918.[230] In November 1920 his mortal remains were found at Hamburg Farm by British exhumation units. Major Buchanan was subsequently reburied at Tyne Cot Cemetery.

Captain **Jeffries** assembled another team of twelve men in order to take out the German strong point from which Buchanan had been killed. Bean writes: '*It was shooting in short bursts, and he [Jeffries] was able to work up fairly close. Seizing a moment when it was firing to the north, he and his men rushed at it from the west. It was switched round, killing him, and sending his men to the ground.*' Shortly afterwards the other men in the group were easily able to take it. According to Bean, 25 Germans were taken prisoner and two machine guns were captured.[231] The War Diary of the 34th Battalion, on the other hand, gives the number of prisoners taken as forty.[232] Captain Clarence Smith Jeffries was posthumously awarded the Victoria Cross and was the last Australian to receive this high decoration during the Battle of Passchendaele. Jeffries' action ensured that the attack could be continued. Due to the large number of casualties the remaining officers of the 34th Battalion decided to take the second objective together with the 35th Battalion. They reached the Blue Line quite easily, although the German defenders in Tiber Copse caused some hold-ups. At the Blue Line, the men of the 9th Brigade came under heavy fire from Meetcheele and Bellevue Spur. It was now around 8.30 a.m. The 36th Battalion was supposed to take the third objective, but did not get that far. They too dug in around the second line. Yet both the left and the right flanks were wide open and the brigade now came under fire from all sides.

Due to a lack of reserve troops and the high number of casualties the surviving officers decided to fall back to the first objective. However, the Red Line had been completely abandoned because the men had helped reinforce the second objective. They pulled back too far and the 9th Brigade ended up back at its start line. It was during this withdrawal that Corporal **Rupert Milton Cross** of the 34th Battalion was killed. One soldier claimed that he was killed by a bullet which went through his right eye, whereas another soldier informed the Red Cross Society in a letter, that: *'As we were retiring I saw Cross laid dead on the ground. He was, at the time, half a mile in front of our trench on the right of a big cement dug out.'* Yet another soldier said that Cross *'was missing when we got back.'* Corporal Cross is remembered today on the Menin Gate. He was from Scone and joined up in Maitland on 1 February 1916, when he was not yet nineteen. His father was the editor of the *Scone Advocate*, a local newspaper which still exists today. In early September 1917 Cross was granted nine days leave in Paris. He was promoted to Corporal in the field on 9 October 1917. Cross was killed three days later.

The 10th Brigade on the offensive:
Augustus Wood and Waterfields

The 10th Brigade's attack went off in pretty much the same way. The 37th Battalion were in front, but came under heavy fire from Augus-

tus Wood and from various snipers near Waterfields. The men had to dash and jump from crater to crater in order to move forward. The 37th, 40th and 38th Battalions soon ended up on one line and with their companies all mixed up. There was thus no longer any structure to the attack. Augustus Wood was attacked from behind and taken by a group of men from different battalions. Waterfields was also captured. These actions claimed numerous casualties, one of whom was Sergeant **Lewis McGee** of the 40th Battalion. McGee had been awarded the Victoria Cross on 4 October for taking a German pillbox at Hamburg. Lieutenant Leslie Garrard wrote of him.[233] *'A machine-gun opened on us from the front, and some fell. Then another machine-gun took us in the flank. The sergeant-major's face was shining and his jaw was set. More men fell, and some took cover in shell-holes. No cover for him, the gallant man. Straight for the guns he rushed and might have taken them, but it was not to be. A bullet pierced his head and he fell dead.'.*[234] McGee was buried after the battle, just north of Waterfields. His grave, with its original wooden cross, was transferred to Tyne Cot Cemetery in January 1920.[235]

Another casualty during the attack on Augustus Wood was Lieutenant **James Roadknight** who was killed by artillery fire.[236] Roadknight was a 25-year-old teacher from Sale, Victoria, serving with the 37th Battalion and proved a true soldier from the very start.

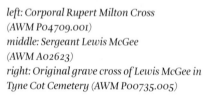

left: Corporal Rupert Milton Cross (AWM P04709.001)
middle: Sergeant Lewis McGee (AWM A02623)
right: Original grave cross of Lewis McGee in Tyne Cot Cemetery (AWM P00735.005)

Lieutenant James Roadknight (AWM H05603)

Captain Henry Southby (AWM H05566)

Private Charles Joseph Walsh (AWM H05590)

He enlisted as a Private almost as soon as hostilities commenced in Europe. He was quickly promoted and was made Company Quarter Master Sergeant at Gallipoli in 1915. He landed in Marseilles in 1916 and underwent officer training in Oxford. He joined the 37th Battalion as a newly commissioned Second Lieutenant in January 1917 and was made a Lieutenant in May of that year. He was wounded in the shoulder during the battle of Messines and was sent to England for convalescence. He was able to rejoin his unit again in late September, just in time for the attack on Passchendaele. He was buried in *'a shell hole about 70 yards from a pill box North of Augustus Wood.'*[237]

Captain **Henry Southby's** fate was also sealed at Augustus Wood. He was an experienced professional soldier and a veteran of the Boer War of 1902. According to Bean, he was mortally wounded by machine gun fire, which is confirmed by information from the Red Cross Society.[238] Captain Southby was slightly wounded and was taken away by two stretcher-bearers, but *'a shell landed right upon the stretcher, instantly killed Southby and the two stretcher bearers.'* Another soldier also confirmed this version of the facts. However, Corporal Crosthwaite maintained that he was with Captain Southby at the moment of his death: *'We got into a shell hole together, and a few seconds afterwards the Captain was hit by a bullet which passed through his wrist and cut the artery, and seemed to enter his side. He never spoke a word after he was hit, and was almost dead when we had to move on. I was wounded about 11 o'clock and on my way out I saw him again. He was quite dead and cold and black in the face.'* What Crosthwaith failed to inform the Red Cross Society, but did tell a friend of his in the battalion, was that he also removed Southby's watch and other personal possessions from his body. This is quite plausible, as the family wrote to Base Records in late December 1918 asking where his personal possessions where: *'the articles he was wearing at the time of his death, his watch, ring etc.'*[239] Southby's body was not found after the war and he is remembered today on the Menin Gate.

The capture of Augustus Wood had claimed many lives. The War Diary of the 40th Battalion adds the following observation to its account of the action: *'If the position of these strong points had been known beforehand, they could have been taken with much fewer casualties and less confusion to the attacking formations.'*[240]

The end of the battle: withdrawal battalion

Men from all the Brigades' various units had got mixed up with each other and arrived at their first objective chaotically and in dribs and drabs. The surviving officers decided to dig in. They received no reserve troops and the line was under heavy fire from Bellevue Spur, a strategic ridge which was in the zone that the New Zealanders should have captured. However, they had hardly managed to get out of their trenches and were subsequently unable to advance due to the thick rows of barbed wire entanglements and the heavy machine gun fire. The 10th Brigade's left flank was thus completely open and in the morning the Germans began a counter-attack from Bellevue Spur. The surviving officers gave orders to pull back to the jumping-off line, so that contact could be re-established with the New Zealanders. The withdrawal was completed around 3.00 p.m. It also started raining again. However, a small group of men managed to capture Crest Farm and was even able to advance to Passchendaele church, but turned back when no reinforcements appeared.[241]

Medical evacuation

While this was going on the medical units had been working flat out to evacuate the wounded from the battlefield. The doctors and stretcher-bearers also took their share of losses. One of the casualties among the medical units was Private **Charles 'Charlie' Joseph Walsh** of the 9th Field Ambulance, who was with the 9th Brigade. At around 5.00 p.m. a shell landed near a Regimental Aid Post.[242] '*An H.E. shell exploded near Walsh killing him instantly and Major Clarke[243] and another man.*'[244] This happened near a pillbox at Hamburg Farm. Private 'Charlie' Walsh's body was found at that location after the war and was reburied at Tyne Cot Cemetery in November 1920. Walsh was a speech and drama teacher before the war and had a passion for music. He worked in various music shops before joining up. His brother, Gunner Horace George Walsh, was wounded in November 1916 and died of his wounds in May 1921.[245]

Private **Daniel Joseph Hardy** served as a stretcher-bearer with the 37th Battalion. He was a sheep-farmer from Bulgoback, Victoria and had a brother in the same battalion.[246] Hardy had won the Military Medal as a stretcher-bearer during the Battle of Broodseinde on 4

Private Albert Edward Gundrill (right) and his brother Alfred (Blake-Gundrill)

Private Daniel Joseph Hardy (Blake)

Lance Corporal John Henry McDonald (AWM H06296)

October, where he had worked tirelessly and succeeded in evacuating numerous wounded men under heavy fire.[247] On 12 October he was again toiling to ferry wounded men away from the battlefield when he was hit by an artillery shell at around 8.30 a.m. He was killed instantly. Private Hardy's body was not buried until 19 January 1918, '*250 yds N of Hamburg*'. Another report refers to his having been buried at '*pill box Jab*'. The name of the pillbox is incorrectly spelt and should read 'Dab', being a reference to the adjacent 'Dab Trench'. Ultimately, however, both reports refer to the same spot. Hardy must have been buried by the roadside between Waterfields and Hamburg and his body was found in 1920.[248] There was still a wooden cross on the grave, which made identification easy.[249] Hardy was reburied in Tyne Cot Cemetery.

Private **Albert Edward Gundrill** was also buried at the Hamburg Farm aid post. In a letter to the Red Cross Society in June 1918, a soldier wrote: '*He was attached to our R.A.P. as a regimental Policeman for organising prisoners, into stretchers squads*'. Another soldier added to this information a year later: '*He was standing outside of the Dressing Station when an H.E. shell exploded near him, pieces entering his head and body, killing him instantly.*' Private Gundrill had been wounded in late January 1917, but was able to return to his unit in April.[250] His brother served in the same unit and survived the war.[251]

Other men were wounded and managed to reach an aid post, only to die later as a result of enemy fire or as a result of their wounds. Lance Corporal **John Henry McDonald** of the 36th Battalion was wound-

left: *Sergeant Hugh Madigan Ross*
(AWM DA13652)
middle: *Sergeant Joseph Henry Cock*
(AWM P04082.002)
right: *Private Leonard Parkes Holroyd*
(AWM P03641.001)

ed early on in the attack, but was able to make his own way to an aid post, where he was probably hit by a shell and died on the spot.[252] Lance Corporal McDonald is listed as missing. 12 October 1917 was his 24th birthday.

Sergeant **Hugh Madigan Ross** of the 38th Battalion died from his wounds in a field hospital in Poperinghe. On 12 October he was wounded at the beginning of the attack. He received first aid treatment at an Advanced Dressing Station just behind the lines and it was not until the early morning of 14 October that he was brought to the 2nd Canadian Casualty Clearing Station (Lijssenthoek), *'suffering from shell wounds in neck and compound fracture of the lower jaw and left thigh. He was operated upon immediately after admission, but died at 9 a.m.'*[253] He was buried in Lijssenthoek Military Cemetery. Ross was from Tambo Upper, Victoria, where he had worked as a bank clerk before the war.

Dead and missing

The attack cost many lives. All the battalions had suffered heavy losses and it was not known with certainty who had been killed and who was missing until the days immediately following the battle. Among those missing was **Joseph Henry Cock**, who was bookkeeper in civilian life. He served as a Sergeant with the 13th platoon of C company of the 36th Battalion and came from Wellington, NSW. The investigation conducted by the Red Cross Bureau revealed interesting information. The men questioned all said that Cock had been wounded in the foot or leg and had tried to reach an aid post. That was the last time anyone saw him. The interviewers' report gives a precise location: *'He saw Cock standing in a shellhole near the Churchyard at Passchendale [sic] where they hopped over. He had been badly wounded. As informant passed, he said 'Goodbye Sergeant' to Cock and saw no more of him.'*[254] The missing sergeant was

top: *The 3rd Division's 'track' through the totally devastated landscape,*
15 October 1917 (AWM E977)
bottom: *British troops burying the dead of the 3rd Australian Division,*
15 October 1917 (AWM E1042)

buried by the Canadian Corps near Tyne Cottage in April 1918, but his body could not be found after the war. His name is inscribed on the Menin Gate.

Private **Leonard Parkes Holroyd** was also listed as missing after the bloody attack and several other soldiers were interviewed by the Red Cross Bureau. All their statements say the same thing: Holroyd was in the trenches just before the attack, but no one had seen him after that. '*We then moved up to Ypres on the 11th October, and I saw him go into the line at Passchendaele between 5 and 6 o'clock on the 11th and that was the last I saw of him. I can't say what happened afterwards.*' A Sergeant stated: '(...) *just before we hopped over I lost sight of him, and subsequently heard he was killed.*' There is also a third statement, which was summarized by the Red Cross Bureau: '*Informant saw Holroyd in the line before the hopover and knew that he went over at the same time as he did.*'[255] Nothing more was heard of Private Holroyd thereafter. His name can also be found on the Menin Gate.

There are two versions of how Corporal **Albert Roy Barton Gibbs** of the 37th Battalion met his death: '*Gibbs was sitting in a shell hole with his arms folded and his head bent down, when the word was given to advance. Someone called out to him and as he remained quite still, some of us went to him and found that he was dead. We could not find any trace of a bullet or shell wound on him and we therefore concluded that he had died from concussion.*' Another soldier gave a different account: '(...) *He was severely wounded in the hip and I offered to dress it for him, but he told me to go on that he was alright. About ½ hour later I went over to him again but he was dead then.*' The precise spot on which he died also remains a matter of guesswork. Nevertheless, Gibbs would have been buried '*in the vicinity of Passchendaele – approximately ¾ mile south west therefrom.*' This is a point roughly between the Red Line and the Blue Line. However, his body was never found '*and in view of the particularly heavy shell fire to which this area was subjected in October 1917, it may be presumed at this juncture that all trace of the original grave site has been obliterated.*'[256] Corporal Gibbs is also remembered today on the Menin Gate.

Corporal Albert Roy Barton Gibbs
(AWM H04274)

Private Thomas William Kinneard
(AWM P01920.004)

Corporal Donald McIntyre McKillop
(AWM P03796.017)

13 October 1917

On the night of 12 to 13 October the front remained fairly quiet and the following day was also relatively calm. The 3rd Australian Division was licking its wounds and trying to reorganize itself as far as possible. It had paid a very high price for its efforts at Passchendaele in 1917. The 9th Brigade went over with 79 officers and 1,939 men, of whom 60 and 1,308 were lost respectively. The 10th Brigade had 64 officers and 1,800 men before the attack and only 23 officers and 767 men came out of the battle unscathed. The rest were killed, wounded, or missing or had become prisoners of war. The 3rd Australian Division had itself taken 351 German prisoners.[257]

They tried to bury the dead as best they could, while the wounded were evacuated and taken to the rear for treatment. Things were also quiet in the German lines as they too tried to take their wounded to safety. Yet more men died on 13 October. The German artillery was in action and subjected the trenches – little more than a series of water – and mud-filled craters linked together – to a continuous and heavy bombardment. Private **Thomas William Kinneard** '(...)*was killed instantly, by shell, got full issue and was hardly recognisable.*'[258] Kinneard was a wheeler from Abermain, NSW. Neither his body nor his grave could be found after the war.

More is known about Corporal **Donald McIntyre McKillop** of the 33rd Battalion. He was a 32-year-old teacher from Glen Innes and was killed during the attack on 12 October. In this case it is his burial, rather than his death, which is documented. On 13 October Sergeant G. A. Werner[259] and Lieutenant R. H. Blomfield[260] went looking for some of the men who were listed as missing. Blomfield later committed his recollections to paper: '*Captain Hinton*[261] *was amongst the missing and search parties had failed to find him. Bootmaker Sergeant Werner, promoted to acting Sergeant Major of 'A' Co., suggested to have another go. We missed each other among the hedges and debris, then I heard him call from a large shell hole: 'That's his boot, in the bottom'. Beside the shell hole, kneeling in the mud was the body of big Corporal McKillop. We had shovels, so we buried the Corporal with his Captain. By a strange coincidence, the first man I spoke to on getting back was McKillop's young brother, only a boy, who had just come up as a reinforcement. 'My brother?' he said, 'I knew he was out there somewhere'.*'[262]
Captain Hinton's mortal remains were exhumed near Dash Cross-ing in September 1920 and reburied in Tyne Cot Cemetery.[263] Corporal McKillop, despite having been buried next to Hinton, was never found.

Both men are remembered today on the Menin Gate in Ypres, together with the other Australians missing in action.

The ANZACs are relieved

The failed attack of 12 October 1917 was not the end of the Battle of Passchendaele, but the next day the British high command decided to postpone all new offensives around Ypres until weather conditions improved. The artillery also had to be moved forward in preparation for a new attack. The exhausted and decimated ANZACS were relieved by fresh Canadian Divisions under the command of Lieutenant General Sir A.W. Currie. From now on it was the Canadians who, together with a few British Divisions, would spearhead the attack. The next attack was finally set for Friday 26 October and would also be the start of the final phase of the campaign.

12 October 1917:

Private Albert Lovatt

8th South Staffordshire Regiment

Albert Ernest Lovatt was the son of James and Emily Lovatt and was born in Lawley Bank, Dawley, a mining village in Shropshire, in 1888. In August 1916 Lovatt walked into a recruiting office, enlisted in the British army and was given the service number 30557. Frederick George Rogers from West Bromwich also joined up around the same time and was given the service number 30533. Lovatt and Rogers met in their training camp and became inseparable friends from then on. Two weeks before both men left for the front, on 12 November 1916, Albert Lovatt married Elsie Bryce from Dawley. The newly-wed Lovatt was posted, together with Rogers, to the 8th Battalion of the South Staffordshire Regiment. The two men fought together through the British offensives at Arras in the spring of 1917.

Langemarck

The 17th Division, to which the 8th South Staffs belonged, was also to do its bit in the Battle of Passchendaele. On the night of 10 to 11 October they took over the front line on the Ypres-Staden railway line, between Houthulst Forest and Poelkapelle. The 8th South Staffordshires were required to attack just north of the railway line – which was their southern boundary. The Guards Division was on their left. The offensive began in the early morning of 12 October. Lovatt and Rogers advanced side by side towards the battalion's objective. They came under heavy fire and various men were killed, while others – Rogers among them – were wounded. Lovatt tried to get his wounded comrade to a first-aid post. That was the last time that either man was seen alive.

Lovatt and Rogers

As soon as Lovatt's wife received the sad news, she tried – using every possible channel – to get more information about what had happened to her husband. She corresponded with a soldier from the same battalion, but he was not able to tell her much

more. Private Rogers was reported officially killed in early December 1917, but there was no trace of Lovatt. In a letter to Elsie Lovatt at the beginning of December, J. Butler wrote: *'I could not say whether they was [sic] together but hope you will have some good news soon as he might be a prisoner of war'.* Shortly thereafter she received the official notification that her husband was missing. She also tried to obtain information via the British Red Cross and the Order of St. John. Official notification of Private Lovatt's death came in late December: *'It is my painful duty to inform you that a report has been received from the War Office notifying of the death of Lovatt A.E. (...) The report is to the effect that he was Killed in Action.'* In the meantime, J. Butler tried to find out what had happened, but many of the men had since been wounded and getting the right information was difficult. At the end of January 1918 he wrote: *'Well Mrs Lovatt I can't find the chaps yet but I think one or two of the old ones coming back as we are expecting a draft.'* More than a month later he reported: *'Well I made enquires [sic] of that Sergeant (...) and he said that Albert was not wounded when he saw him last as he went to take a wounded man to the dressing station and was not seen again.'*

It was not until the spring of 1920 that Elsie Lovatt received more news from the Infantry Record Office: *'I beg to inform you that an official report has now been received that the late soldier is buried at Cement House British Cemetery.'* Lovatt's body had been found near Langemarck. It is probable that the bodies of Privates Lovatt and Rogers were found together as the two inseparable friends are buried next to each other.

top left: Albert Lovatt (right) and Frederick Rogers (left) (Shaw)
right: Lovatt and Rogers: friends to the death (MMP)

Dead and wounded at the dug out railway bedding, between Tyne Cot and the Passchendaele-Broodseinde road, 12 October 1917 (E3864)

9 The Second Battle of Passchendaele(1): 26 October 1917
Royal Naval & 3rd Canadian Divisions

The Battle of Passchendaele had now been raging for almost three months and the allied troops had still not reached Passchendaele ridge. Little by little the hope of still being able to break through the German front line and to advance to the channel ports of Zeebruges and Ostend was fading. In the meantime the name Passchendaele had taken on a symbolic significance. For the high command the prospect of spending yet another long cold winter with Passchendaele within its reach was no longer an option. The village, with its dominating position, had to be captured – whatever the cost. This would not only be good for the morale of the troops at the front and the civilians back home, but would also give the army better and drier trenches. Furthermore, General Sir Douglas Haig needed another victory in Flanders. He had already started the preparations for a new offensive in France, at Cambrai and he had to keep German attention focused on Flanders for as long as possible. He replaced the exhausted Australians, who had already gone through their reserves, with the Canadian Corps. The divisions of which it was composed had first been sent into battle together at Vimy, where they had driven the Germans off the ridge as a single front. After Vimy Ridge these divisions were always to operate as a single Corps. They were brought to Passchendaele on 18 October 1917 in order to take their turn – after the British, Australian and New Zealand Divisions – at trying to take Passchendaele. On 22 October 1917 three British Divisions carried out a feint attack on the German positions at Poelkapelle and south of Houthulst Forest. The objective was to give the German defenders the impression that the offensive would continue to be focused on the entire front at Ypres and not just on Passchendaele.

The instructions given to the Canadian Corps on 19 October 1917 had been crystal clear and left no doubt as to why the offensive was to last until November. The fiasco of 12 October 1917 had sent an unequivocal message: the Germans would defend Passchendaele to the last man. The capture of Passchendaele was to be carried out in phases. *'The Canadian Corps will undertake operations for the capture of Passchendaele in conjunction with 1st Anzac Corps on the right and 5th Army on the left. The Operation will be carried out in three stages as follows: 1st stage – Capture of Red Objective; 2nd Stage – Capture of Blue Objective; 3rd Stage – Capture of Green Objective. There will be an interval of three and possible four days between the first and second stages, and an interval of four and possible five days between the second and third stages.'*[264] Passchendaele was thus to be taken in three stages. The first stage of what would eventually become the Second Battle of Passchendaele was executed on 26 October 1917; the second stage on 30 October 1917; and the third stage – somewhat later than originally planned – on 6 November 1917. Finally, there was to be a further, small-scale offensive on 10 November in order to improve some of the positions at different points of line.

Overall course of the Battle

SITUATION: By now the battlefield was in a terrible condition. The rain had transformed the entire area into a squelching, boggy mass. The route to Passchendaele was negotiable only with great difficulty. The Ravebeek valley was inaccessible due to the mud and the water, as the entire drainage system had been shot to pieces by the day in, day out bombardments. This meant that the Canadian Divisions were not able to attack shoulder to shoulder and – as a consequence – there was a gap in their front line. Moreover, the temporary im-

‹ This is also Passchendaele 1917 (CWM CO3757)

provement in the weather could not be exploited because the German artillery simply became more aggressive and its bombardments more intense. Night bombing from planes also sowed death and destruction from the air. On 25 October the sky was clear and it was apparent that the artillery had done a good job. The thick rows of barbed wire had been cleared adequately, but the pillboxes of the German *Flandern I- and II-Stellung* were mostly still intact. Only a direct hit could take these out, so the job was left to the infantry.

OBJECTIVE: The objective of the first stage of the renewed offensive was not to capture Passchendaele, but to secure a good start position for the second stage. Moreover, part of the *Flandern I- and II-Stellung* had to be taken in order to be able to get closer to Passchendaele. This task was entrusted to the 3rd and 4th Canadian Division. On the flanks other divisions would carry out smaller scale diversionary attacks so that Germans could not deploy all their reserves against the Canadians and their artillery would have to spread its fire over a much bigger front.

COURSE OF THE BATTLE: Ten divisions attacked in the early morning of 26 October. The 4th Canadian Division went over with only one battalion: the 46th. It succeeded in taking its objective, but – after three heavy counter-attacks in the afternoon – it was obliged to cede the ground it had gained to the Germans. They suffered losses of almost 70 %. It was not until the following day that the objective could be retaken – thanks to the 44th and 47th Battalions. The 3rd Canadian Division was initially more successful. The 43rd Battalion was able to make good progress, but the 58th Battalion immediately came up against heavy resistance. Despite some reports that the Red Line had been taken, the battalion was some 400 metres short of it. The men of 52nd Battalion were sent in as reinforcements and with their help the captured positions could be consolidated. The 4th Canadian Mounted Rifles were also able to reach this position and a section of the *Flandern I-Stellung* between Wolfe Copse and the Ravebeek was now entirely in Canadian hands. Other parts of the *Flandern I-Stellung* were still firmly in German hands, however. The front line which the 3rd Canadian Division was now manning was 500 metres from the objective, but the Canadians had succeeded in securing ground that was somewhat higher and drier.

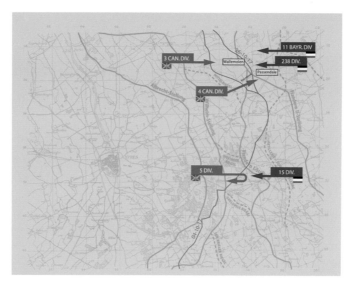

26 October 1917: general situation (MMP)

Further south the 5th and 7th British Divisions tried in vain to take Gheluvelt and Polderhoek Chateau. These attempts had to be abandoned early on due to the poor condition of the battlefield; the overwhelming strength of German resistance; and the excessively high number of casualties. The attackers in the north did not have much success either. The Royal Naval Division, to the left of the 3rd Canadian Division, attacked with the 188th Brigade, but its attack literally got stuck in the mud. The same happened to the 58th Division on its left and the men could only advance a very short distance. The 57th and 58th Divisions did not even get beyond their start lines. Two French divisions south of Houthulst Forest managed to gain quite a bit of ground, albeit at the cost of a large number of casualties.

RESULT: The first stage of the renewed offensive did not achieve very much. Only a handful of objectives had been taken in their entirety and in most places even the interim objective was not reached. In the days following the attack the men were able to take several pockets of German resistance up and down the line and thus strengthen and improve their jumping-off positions for the attack of 30 October. The allies had now taken large sections of the extremely important *Flandern I* and *Flandern II-Stellungen* which was a sine qua non for the further success of the campaign.
The objective for this stage of the offensive was to capture the Red Line, '*an essential preliminary to the capture of the whole Passchendaele*

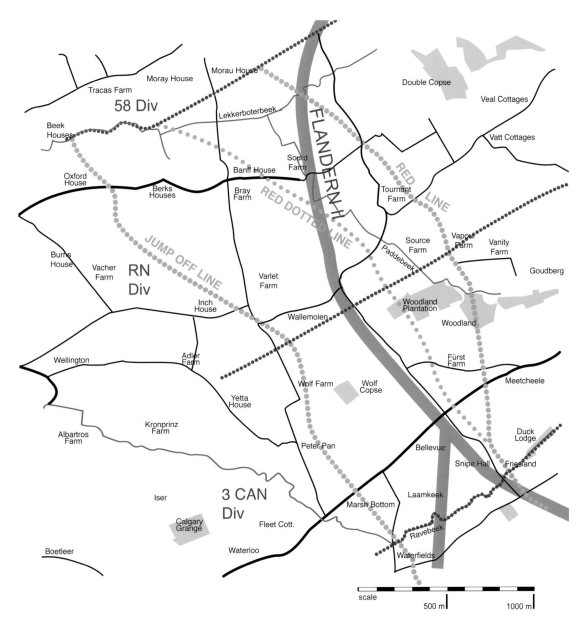

26 October 1917: Royal Naval and 3rd Canadian Divisions (MMP)

Ridge.[265] This meant that the Royal Naval Division would have to break through the *Flandern I-Stellung* north-east of Wallemolen and at the Paddebeek. The Red Line ran from Moray House across the Lekkerboterbeek via Tournant Farm to Source Farm. The interim objective – the Red Dotted Line – was to be taken by the 1st Battalion Royal Marines and Anson Battalion. The tasks of taking the Red Line and breaking through the *Flandern I-Stellung* were entrusted to the 2nd Battalion Royal Marines and Howe Battalion. Hood Battalion was in reserve and had to be able to step in at crucial moments, should the Germans launch a counter-attack. The 3rd Canadian Division was also required to breach and capture the *Flandern I-Stellung* and part of the *Flandern II-Stellung* along its entire front. Before they reached the interim objective – Red Dotted Line – they would have to take this highly fortified German line. The Red Line also crossed Woodlands Plantation, and ran via Furst Farm in the direction of Snipe Hall and then via Haalen and Deck Wood southwards to Decline Copse. This task was entrusted to two brigades. The 8th brigade attacked with the 4th Canadian Mounted Rifles, keeping the 1st Canadian Mounted Rifles in reserve. The 9th Brigade went into action with the 43rd Battalion on the left and the 58th on the right. The 52nd Battalion was in reserve.

Going up the line

In late September the men of 4th Canadian Mounted Rifles, who were in France, had already started their preparatory training for the offensive in Flanders. This was stopped on 4 October because of *'the success in Flanders'* and the battalion entrained on 20 October and set out for the front around Ypres.[266] They marched to Wieltje the following day, where they spent the night. On 22 October they moved to the vicinity of Pommern Castle, even nearer to the front. The next day they pushed on to the area around Albatross Farm and Kronprinz Farm, which is where the battalion suffered its first casualties due to *'rather severe enemy shelling'*.[267] On the night of 24 to 25 October the 4th Canadian Mounted Rifles relieved the 1st Canadian Mounted Rifles in the front line. This was no easy matter. The water-filled shell holes, boggy terrain and sticky mud made it difficult even for experienced guides to lead the new arrivals to the correct positions. The continuous heavy rain did not make it any easier. The relief was therefore not completed until around 5.00 a.m. The battalion suffered at least 18 casualties during the relief, one of whom was Captain **John Robinson Woods**, who was killed when a German artillery shell exploded near the dug-out he was in. He was killed instantly. Woods had been a student when war broke out. As soon as he graduated from the University of Toronto with a degree in 'Commerce and Finance', he enlisted in the Canadian army in September 1915. He was trained as an officer and was posted to the 35th Battalion. A month later he left for Europe with his unit where, after attending various training courses, he joined the 4th Canadian Mounted Rifles as a Second Lieutenant in June 1916. The battalion was then in Ypres. In 1917 he was promoted to Lieutenant and then to Captain.[268] The 25-year-old Captain Woods was buried on White House Cemetery. The 1st Canadian Mounted Rifles also sustained various casualties. When the battalion left the front line and tried to make its way to the rear along the narrow, muddy and slippery wooden tracks, battalion headquarters at Kronprinz Farm was hit by a German artillery shell which fell right in the middle of their ranks. Lieutenant **John Einarson** was one of the casualties. Einarson, from Saskatoon, had obtained a law degree from the University of Manitoba in 1914 and continued his legal studies until joining the 233rd Battalion in March 1916.[269] On arrival in France he was posted

to the 1st Canadian Mounted Rifles. Lieutenant Einarson's body was never recovered after the war and he is remembered today on the Menin Gate.

The other battalions of the 3rd Canadian Division and Royal Naval Division had similar experiences. They too had undergone extensive training and the Royal Naval Division *'was looking forward with confidence to the impending battle.'*[270] In the days before the start of the attack the men of the Royal Naval Division had already had to carry out heavy fatigue duties. Laying tracks and building dug-outs was exhausting work. On 17 October Able Seaman **John Ledger Reynoldson** was killed while carrying out these tasks. Reynoldson, a carpenter from Durham, had joined the Royal Navy in late November 1914 and had ended up in Howe Battalion. In June 1915 he was transferred to Nelson Battalion and was sent to Gallipoli. He arrived in France with the battalion in the spring of 1916, but in August of that year he was evacuated to a hospital in England with a severely infected heel. It was not until early December that he was able to rejoin his unit. On 17 October he was killed just southwest of St. Julien, probably on the Wieltje-St. Julien road. His body was found on 3 August 1920 and the mortal remains of the 26-year-old Able Seaman Reynoldson were officially buried in New Irish Farm Cemetery.[271]

Like the 4th Canadian Mounted Rifles, the battalions of the Royal Naval Division also took over their section of the front line during the night of 24 to 25 October 1917 and the medical units of the Royal Naval Division relieved their opposite numbers from the 9th Division. The headquarters of 148th Royal Naval Field Ambulance was at Vanheule Farm southwest of St. Julien, not far from the spot where Reynoldson had been killed a few days earlier. A few men lost their lives as they were taking over the evacuation routes and medical posts. One of them was Private **John George Welsh** of the 148th Royal Naval Field Ambulance, Royal Marines Medical Unit. Welsh had a wife called Sarah and three daughters: Mary, Agnes and Gwen.[272] Welsh, an insurance underwriter, was already 38 at the time he joined up at the end of March 1915. He was immediately posted to the medical units of the Royal Naval Division and left for

left: Captain John Robinson Woods (Pirie)
right: Lieutenant John Einarson (University of Manitoba)

Able Seaman John Ledger Reynoldson (Oxley)

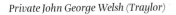

Private John George Welsh (Traylor)

Postcard from Welsh to his daughter Sarah, July 1915 (Traylor)

Private Frederick William Keen (Broom)

Memorial card for Frederick William Keen (Broom)

Gallipoli. Late May 1916 found Welsh on the Western Front where he was to serve until his death in October 1917.[273] Private Welsh's body was exhumed after the war and he was reburied in Dochy Farm New British Cemetery.

On 25 October the weather cleared up. It stopped raining and the men were able to do what they could to dry their wet uniforms and equipment. The final preparations for the attack were made and headquarters notified them of the start time for the attack on the following morning: 5.40 a.m.

Into battle with the Royal Naval Division

The weather changed again during the night and it began to rain heavily. When the signal to attack was given the men of the 1st Royal Marines and Anson Battalions clambered out of their muddy positions and tried to advance across No Man's Land behind the protection of a creeping barrage. They had to pick their way between the shell holes in order to do so. It was hard going, but '*substantial*

gains were recorded.'[274] The 1st Royal Marines made particularly good progress. By around 7.30 a.m. they were already at Banff House, just in front of their interim objective. This was certainly no stroll in the park for the attackers and well-concealed German positions rained machine gun fire onto the advancing British troops from several different points. Private **Frederick William Keen** of the 1st Royal Marines was among those killed. The 23-year-old Keen was from Chinnor, in Wallingford. A few weeks later his family received a letter from Second Lieutenant J R Jones informing them that: '*he died nobly having done his duty to his country.*'[275] Keen was an agricultural labourer who did casual work on the larger farms in his area. He joined up in Thame, Oxfordshire, in April 1917 and ended up in the Royal Marines at the end of August 1917.[276] Private Keen is remembered today on the Tyne Cot Memorial as is Private **Josiah Mitchell**. Mitchell, from Bristol, already had some experience at sea as he was a seamen on a merchant ship when he enlisted in the Royal Navy on 13 March 1917. At the beginning of August he was posted to the Royal Marines, who instead of going to sea, were sent to the trenches. The

25-year-old Private Mitchell, who was a married man, was listed as missing after the attack.[277] His body was never found.

Almost all the officers of the attacking battalions were taken out by the murderous German machine gun and artillery fire. One of them was Lieutenant **Francis Cedric Balcombe**, who was killed during the difficult advance to the interim objective. *'He took part in the operations on that day, and while leading his men forward was fatally wounded and died before it was possible to render him any assistance...'* Balcombe was only 24 when he died, but had already lived an adventurous life, being possessed of a *'roving spirit'*. He was educated

at Tonbridge School from September 1907 to December 1910 and, after having worked for his father for a while, emigrated to Vancouver, Canada, with his older brother. Vancouver did not really appeal to him and he set out on his own. He spent a while in San Francisco and then moved to Honolulu, although he did not stay there very long either. He went back to be with his brother in Vancouver and then decided to go north. When war broke out in August 1914 he hurried back from some inhospitable northern region in order to enlist in the Canadian army. He originally served as an ordinary soldier with the 29th Battalion and was with them in the trenches around Ypres in the winter of 1915-1916. He applied for a commission in the spring of 1916 and underwent officer training. In late October 1916 he was made a Second Lieutenant with the Royal Marines. He spent the winter of 1916-1917 in hospital with syphilis. Later that year he was admitted to hospital again with respiratory problems and shell shock and was only able to return to his unit at the end of August 1917. He was made a Lieutenant a few days before his death and exactly a year after he had been commissioned as a Second Lieutenant.[278] His body could not be found after the war. Lieutenant Balcombe is remembered today on the Tyne Cot Memorial.

Only small groups of men, on the left and right, managed to push through to their objectives and did not know whether the other groups had also reached their objectives. The men could only continue the attack on the flanks and if it were better organized. It was now the turn of the 2nd Royal Marines and Howe Battalions, who were required to advance to the interim objective, go past the two other battalions and try to push through to the Red Line. Here, too, only a few smaller groups of men managed to get to their objective. The protective artillery curtain had already moved on further than the men themselves and the number of casualties among the unprotected soldiers was very high. One of these casualties was Private **John Thomas Hopkins** from Coventry, who had joined up in his home town in early December 1915. He was a painter by trade and was therefore made a War Motor Ambulance Painter. Hopkins was not transferred to the 2nd Royal Marines until August 1917.[279] Private Hopkins was killed a few months later near Banff House. His body was never recovered and like that of many others his name is

‹ *Private Joshia Mitchell (Varlet Farm)*

Lieutenant Francis Cedric Balcombe (Tonbridge School)

Private John Thomas Hopkins (Sykes)

left: Sergeant Fred Parkin (de Ruvigny)
right: Lieutenant Francis Leonard Hunter Jackson (de Ruvigny)

inscribed on the Tyne Cot Memorial. Sergeant **Fred Parkin**, from North Molton in Devon, was also killed near Banff House. Parkin had joined up in November 1914 and had seen action with the Royal Marines in the Persian Gulf from February to August 1915. He became seriously ill in December 1915 and spent some time in hospital, but was back with 2nd Royal Marines, this time on the Western Front, from September 1916. Parkin gradually rose through the ranks and was a Sergeant at the time of his death. The 25-year-old Private Parkin would probably have been buried where he was killed.[280] His body was never recovered, however and he is remembered today on the Tyne Cot Memorial.

Howe Battalion's attack quickly ground to a halt. One of its companies got lost and ended up with the advancing troops of the 4th Canadian Mounted Rifles, *'leaving their own objective 'pill boxes' unengaged'*.[281] According to the plan of attack Howe Battalion was supposed to advance via Varlet Farm towards Tournant Farm. Lieutenant **Francis Leonard Theirter Jackson** – with his men – had probably ended up behind the Canadians, and tried to find the right direction by using his compass. *'Finding that his steel helmet was interfering with the working of his compass, he discarded it altogether, and so fell a victim to a sniper who shot him in the head.'* Jackson had joined up in February 1915 and was given a temporary commission as Sub-Lieutenant in late May. He was posted to Howe Battalion in August 1915, but was admitted to hospital a few weeks later suffering from flu. Jackson made a slow recovery and it was to be more than a year before he could return to active duty. In the intervening period he was a shooting instructor at a training centre while still unfit to return to the front. It was not until June 1916 that he rejoined the Howe Battalion. He was promoted to Lieutenant and was immediately given the command of a company. Jackson had just turned 26 at the time of his death. He was left where he was killed and his body was not exhumed until the early 1920s. It was found southwest of Woodlands Plantation, the spot where the 4th Canadian Mounted Rifles went into action and where a company from Howe Battalion got lost. Lieutenant Jackson's body could be identified from the compass he was holding when he was killed. He was reburied on Tyne Cot Cemetery.[282] Able Seaman **Harry Trollope** may also have

Able Seaman Harry Trollope (Varlet Farm)

been killed on 26 October 1917 on the same spot, at the same time that Jackson's company got lost. Trollope, who was also with Howe Battalion, was listed as missing. He had originally served as a cyclist with the London Regiment's Cyclist Battalion and had joined up in his birthplace, Todmorden, in February 1915. He had only been transferred to Howe Battalion at the end of August 1917.[283] Able Seaman Trollope's body was never recovered and his name is inscribed on the Tyne Cot Memorial.

By midday the Royal Naval Division's attack had got completely bogged down in the mud. Dotted up and down the line, there were a few groups of men who managed to keep going, but they were isolated and could do nothing. A few companies from Hood Battalion were moved up as reinforcements, but they could not turn the tide. On the German side Leutnant Ernst Jünger of the *Füsilier-Regiment 73* was reconnoitring the front line and reported that: *Here the enemy has broken through in depth, the pillboxes on the left flank of the II/73 is in enemy hands.*[284] His memoirs include an extensive description of what happened: *The enemy had broken through the front line and had captured the ridge from which they were to fire on the important Paddebeek, where the command post was. After I had marked the changes of positions on my map with some red lines in pen, I prepared, with my men, for the taxing march through the mud. (...) we came upon the traces of the dead everywhere, it was as if there was no living soul to be found in this wilderness.*[285] The British made no new attempts to continue their advance in the afternoon. *'To renew the attack it would have been necessary to bring up fresh troops, which could only be done by night, or to throw once more against the enemy disorganised and cruelly depleted units clinging to their slender gains.'*[286] A German counter-attack also made it clear that the positions captured would be difficult to hold. The attack had come to a complete standstill. The Germans also realized this: *The enemy fire has decreased and a new enemy attack is no longer to be expected.*[287]

When it eventually got dark, Commander Asquith ordered the relief of the battalions. Hood Battalion replaced Anson and Howe Battalions and Hawke Battalion was ordered to relieve the two Royal Marine battalions. The isolated units which had been able to advance a long way, now pulled back to their own positions. The ground gained was limited. Only a few hundred metres of soggy and devastated ground had been taken. Berks Houses, Bray Farm and Varlet Farm had been captured, but the interim objective could no longer be reached.

Into battle with the 3rd Canadian Division

The men of the 3rd Division also clambered out of their muddy positions and tried to make their way through No Man's Land towards their objective. At first, the attack appeared to have been more successful. 45 minutes after the start of the offensive *'our men could be clearly seen moving slowly over the skyline and around the two formidable looking Pill Boxes on the crest of the ridge'.*[288] These pillboxes were part of the *Flandern I-Stellung*. For the 58th Battalion the attack did not begin quite so well. The protective artillery barrage moved forward more slowly than planned, causing several casualties among the attackers. Lance Corporal **Charles Barcley Forrest** was one of the casualties sustained by the 58th Battalion on 26 October. He was from Bluevale, a small town in Huron County, Ontario. Huron County mostly consisted of farming communities and Forrest was also a farmer. Forrest enlisted in the Canadian army in May 1916, at

the age of nearly 33. A booklet about the war dead of Huron County tells that Forrest was *'killed in action somewhere in France'*.[289] Lance Corporal Forrest's body was never recovered and today his name is inscribed, together with those of thousands of others, on the Menin Gate. Private **Joseph Themry Barker** came from the same area. Born in Hampshire, England, he had emigrated to Canada with his parents. Like Forrest, Barker had also been a farmer before joining up in late November 1915. He originally served with the 161st Battalion, where he was a bandsman, although he served on the Western Front with the 58th Battalion.[290] Private Barker was listed as missing after the attack, but was only recorded in May 1918 as officially killed. He is also remembered on the Menin Gate. Despite this minor setback, the 58th Battalion was able to continue its advance and took several pillboxes and trenches. However, they now came under heavy fire from the *Flandern I-Stellung* at Snipe Hall and Bellevue and also took

Canadians at a German pillbox in Passchendaele, October-November 1917 (CWM CO3757)

Lance Corporal Charles Barcley Forrest (Huron County's Heroes)

Private Joseph Henry Barker
(Huron County's Heroes)

Private Clifford William Ruffell
(Croydon and the Great War)

fire from German troops in Crest Farm.[291] The entire battalion was forced to pull back to its start positions. Many men had already been killed, however. Among them was Private **Clifford William Ruffell** from West Croydon, near London. His parents still lived there, having stayed behind when he emigrated to Canada. Exactly when this was, is not clear. Ruffell enlisted in the Canadian army in Seaforth, Ontario, where he was a farmer, just before Christmas 1914. He embarked for England in early November 1916 and joined the 58th Battalion in France a month later. It was the beginning of winter and Ruffell was hospitalized with flu a few days after his arrival. Private Ruffell spent the entire winter in Le Havre working in the army depots. In March 1917 he was able to return to his unit and was to remain with them until he was killed at Passchendaele.[292]

The 43rd Battalion's attack was held up at Bellevue, where the first companies had suffered catastrophic losses. Private **Morden Earl Skinner**, from Selkirk, Manitoba, was one of those killed. He had obtained a law degree from the University of Manitoba in 1914 and was continuing his legal studies when he decided to join the Canadian army in November 1915. The day of the battle and the day of his death, 26 October 1917, was also his 25th birthday. His body could not be recovered after the war. Private Skinner is remembered on the Menin Gate in Ypres. Skinner is still remembered today, even in Canada. His family placed a gravestone in the local cemetery in Selkirk in his memory. The stone bears the inscription *'killed in action Passchendaele Ridge.'*[293] Like Skinner, Private **John William Stone** also had a degree from the University of Manitoba and was nearly 28 when he enlisted in the Canadian army at the end of November 1915. Private Stone reported to the 43rd Battalion in France on completion of his military training and was killed at Passchendaele on 26 October.

Due to the large number of casualties on Bellevue ridge, considerable sections of the 43rd Battalion pulled back to their start line. Only one group remained in their positions at Wolfe Copse. They had only been able to take it after heavy fighting and were not going to give it up just like that. However, no one knew they were still holding out until the group's commanding officer returned to bat-

left: Private Morden Earl Skinner (University of Manitoba)
right: Private John William Stone (University of Manitoba)

talion headquarters to make his report and ask for reinforcements. The 52nd Battalion, which had been held in reserve, was now sent forward to breathe new life into the attack which the 43rd and 58th Battalions had begun and to help strengthen the positions that had been captured. The 52nd Battalion advanced through the remnants of the 43rd Battalion and tried to attack the German flank, so that the 58th Battalion could also make a new attempt to storm the German positions. *'This operation was entirely successful. The fighting was heavy and continuous for several hours, resulting in the surrender of the enemy holding the 'pillboxes' on the spur, which had obstructed the advance of the 58th Canadian Battalion and what was left of the garrison of Lamkeek [sic] and Dad trench.'*[294] Together, the 52nd and the 58th Battalions were able to continue the advance. At around 3.30 p.m. the high command was able to take stock of what had been taken. On the left, contact was made with the 4th Canadian Mounted Rifles. The line now ran along the *Flandern I-Stellung*. With one or two exceptions, the interim objective had now been reached all along the line. However, this had taken an enormous toll in terms of casualties. Lieutenant **Edgar William Galbraith Patten**, who had obtained a degree in mathematics and physics in 1916, was among the dead. He had enlisted in the Canadian army in March of the year of his graduation and was made a Second Lieutenant a few months later. Patten went on to undergo certain additional training, including a Lewis Gun course and left for Europe in July 1917, where he reported to the 58th Battalion in Lens. *'On the day of his death at Bellevue Spur, Passchendaele, as he went forward with his platoon the officer on his left was killed and the advance was held up. After rallying his men he found that in order to make further progress it was necessary to bring forward a machine gun, the crew of which had all been killed or wounded. He carried it up and was getting it into position when he was instantly killed by a sniper.'*[295] Lieutenant Patten's body was buried where he fell, but could not be recovered later on. He is remembered today on the Menin Gate. The 52nd Battalion's losses were high. Among the casualties was Corporal **Reginald Walwin Fisher**. When his brother heard the news of Fisher's death, the local newspaper in Regina, Ontario ran the headline: *'Another happy young life is given for the cause.'* Fisher had joined up in February 1916 and was soon promoted to the rank of Sergeant. He arrived in Liverpool on 11 November 1916 and was sent to the 32nd Battalion. In January 1917 he joined the 58th Battalion with whom he served in France. A month later he resigned his stripes and returned to the rank of Private. He was admitted to hospital in March 1917 as a result of a gas attack and could not return to his unit until June, being promoted to Corporal in September. *'No details but the bare information of his death were received in the official notification yesterday.'*[296] Corporal Fisher is remembered today on the Menin Gate.

The 4th Canadian Mounted Rifles were initially able to make good progress through No Man's Land towards the German positions and went on to take the first pillboxes of the *Flandern I* line with relative ease. When they got there, however, a tough and bitter struggle ensued between the Canadian attackers and the German defenders, who were not inclined to give up the *Flandern I-Stellung* without a fight. However, the Canadians forged ahead and broke through the German positions all the same. A few units were able to advance a considerable distance beyond the interim objective and some even got as far as Woodlands Plantation, but here the losses began to mount up. The flanking battalions had not been able to keep up with them and the 4th Canadian Mounted Rifles now came under fire from all sides. They had no choice, therefore, but to pull back to the interim objective. One of the casualties was Sergeant **Hugh Buie** who, like many other Canadian soldiers, was from Scotland. He went

to school in Oban and Sandbank and emigrated to Montreal, Canada, together with his mother in September 1913. He was then just sixteen and found work with the Grand Trunk Railway Company. He enlisted in the Canadian army in Kingston in March 1916 and reported to the 4th Canadian Mounted Rifles in the trenches at Etrun, just outside Arras, some nine months later. He was made a Corporal in late January 1917 and promoted to Sergeant at the beginning of September. He was killed by an artillery shell during the offensive of 26 October 1917. Sergeant Buie was buried where he fell.[297] His name is inscribed on the Menin Gate.

At the interim objective the men of the 4th Canadian Mounted Rifles tried to consolidate the positions that had been won: *'A deep, continuous trench was successfully laid.'*[298] They were also able to make contact with the units on the right and left of their lines.

In the course of the afternoon the Canadians were able to hold off two large German counter-attacks with machine gun fire, but the Canadian attack itself made no further progress. Their objective, the Red Line, could now no longer be taken. *'The line occupied by our troops at the end of the day was a strong one and was chosen on account of the advantage it offered for immediate defence of the positions won and as a starting point for a further advance.'* The line now ran via Laamkeek to Bellevue to half way along the road to Wallemolen. The 4th Canadian Mounted Rifles had thus succeeded in taking and holding their interim objective.[299]

Lieutenant Edgar William Galbraith Patten (University of Toronto)

Corporal Reginald William Fisher (Pirie)

Sergeant Hugh Buie (de Ruvigny)

Private John Fraser Richmond (McRitichie)

Dead and wounded

While the attack was in progress the stretcher-bearers had been pulling out all the stops to get the wounded off the battlefield and take them to the rear for further treatment. However, the German artillery continually shelled the Canadians' lines of supply and access, causing – inevitably – a large number of casualties. Private **John Fraser Richmond** of the 43rd Battalion served as a stretcher-bearer on 26 October. Richmond was from Glasgow, Scotland, but had emigrated with his parents to Calgary, Alberta, in Canada, where he worked as a clerk and was married to Catherine Mary. Richmond joined up on 30 June 1916 and, three months later, he was already undergoing training in England. He reported to the 43rd Battalion in France on 3 November. In March 1917 he was able to begin a period of two month's training as a stretcher-bearer. A month before his death the 34-year-old Richmond was still in hospital with a high fever, being able to return to his unit after a few weeks. On 26 October 1917 Private Richmond was listed as missing after the offensive. As his body was never recovered, his name is inscribed on the Menin Gate.

The stretcher-bearers managed to evacuate all the wounded from the battlefield. By means of a chain of aid posts many men were eventually able to receive the treatment they needed in a hospital. Others were less fortunate, however, and died at an aid post or in the field hospital. This was the fate which befell **William Taylor**, a Private with the 43rd Battalion. Taylor was born in Bolton, England, where he grew up in a mining family with five sisters and four brothers and later worked as a miner in Lancashire, himself. At the age of 21 he married Ellen McDonnell with whom he had four children. His youngest daughter was born after his last leave before going to the front. She was still alive in 2006, but never saw her father. Taylor emigrated with his family to Winnipeg, Manitoba, just before the outbreak of war. He found work with the Canadian railways, but his dream was to start a farm. He joined up on 24 January 1916 and ended up in the 101st Overseas Battalion. He arrived in England in early July 1916, where his training continued. He was not to report to the 43rd Battalion until September of that year, however. In Poperinghe he frequented Talbot House – an informal 'soldiers' club' which was popular among the men – and was photographed there in full

William Taylor with his wife Ellen and sons Austin and William (Taylor)

Private William Taylor at Talbot House (Taylor)

Highlander's uniform. He received a serious head wound on 26 October 1917, but could not be evacuated by the 8th Field Ambulance until the following day. They finally took him to a field hospital near Poperinghe, where the 30-year-old Private Taylor died of his wounds the next day. He was buried in Nine Elms British Cemetery. Austin Taylor, one of Private William Taylor's sons, visited the grave for the first time in the summer of 1966 together with his wife. They were both deeply moved.[300]

All the units were responsible for burying their own dead, although various platoons of the 116th Battalion were detailed to help with this. The burial of the dead could not begin until night fall. '*Every care will be taken to identify the dead, to mark their graves, and to preserve their effects.*'[301] Three cemeteries were laid out. One in St. Jean, one at Wieltje and another at Squair Farm. However, in the muddy, lunar landscape it was difficult to remove the dead from the battlefield. Most were buried where they were killed and despite all the good intentions with regard to trying to identify all of them and mark their graves, many of the dead could not be recovered. This was the case with Private **James Russell Strachan**. Strachan was a telegrapher in civilian life and so ended up in the Signal Section of the 58th Battalion. He was born in Perth, Scotland, where he also went to school, but emigrated to Vancouver, Canada at the age of twenty-two. It is also known that he was married and that his wife's first name was Annie. Strachan joined up in Kingston at the beginning of 1916, but did not arrive in England until October of that year. He was given the rank of Acting Sergeant, but turned in his stripes in June 1917 in order to be able to go to France. He joined the 58th Battalion as a Signaller. The 35-year-old Private Strachan was killed at Bellevue on 26 October 1917 and was buried where he fell.[302] His body could not be found afterwards and Strachan is remembered today on the Menin Gate.

Relief and losses

The men were still in the front line the following day. There were no attacks , but the German artillery shelled the entire line and many men who had survived the attack of the day before were now killed. The long-expected relief was therefore more than welcome. That night the 116th Battalion, which had helped earlier with the burial of the dead, made its way up the line, where they relieved the 43rd, the 52nd and the 58th Battalions. The 2nd Canadian Mounted Rifles had already relieved the 4th Canadian Mounted Rifles in the evening. The first battalions of the Royal Naval Division were also taken out of the front line.

Once the attacking battalions, who had been in the firing line for more than 48 hours, were in a safer location, it was possible to make the first reports and hold the first roll-calls. For the Royal Naval Division no detailed figures are available.[303] Thirteen officers were dead. *'The losses in NCOs and men were equally severe, averaging more than five hundred a battalion in the 188th Brigade.'* [304] However, this seems enormously high in comparison with the figures of the Anson Battalion, which lost 10 officers and 260 men dead, missing or wounded.

The Canadian figures are more detailed. The 4th Canadian Mounted Rifles lost 17 officers and 274 men, of whom 8 officers and 80 men were dead or missing. The 43rd Battalion, which had come under such heavy fire on the Bellevue Spur, lost 13 officers and 336 men, of whom only 3 officers, but 102 men, were dead or missing. The figures for the 58th Battalion are somewhat lower. 17 officers and 289 men were lost, of whom 6 officers and 84 men were dead or missing. There are no figures known for the 52nd Battalion.

Private James Russell Strachan (de Ruvigny)

Passchendaele, 14 November 1917
(CWM CO2253)

Model of the Passchendaele-Broodseinde sector, made by the 33rd Battalion Machine Gun Company near Potijze, March 1918 (Hutchison)

4 and 26 October 1917:
Private John and Able Seaman Henry Joseph Dyde
1st Royal Warwickshire & Howe Battalion

William Dyde and his wife Anna Maria James lived in Chipping Campden in Gloucestershire. They had five children: George, John, Albert William, Henry Joseph, and Maria Lucy Elizabeth. John was born in late December 1894 and his younger brother, Henry Joseph, was born exactly three years later. All the children went to the local school and were still living at home when war broke out. John, better known as 'Jack', immediately joined the army. He was just 19 and ended up in the 1st Battalion of the Royal Warwickshire Regiment. He saw action for the first time in May 1915.

Henry Joseph, 'Harry' to his friends, worked as a barman in a local pub, 'The George and Dragon Public House' and also worked as a farm labourer. Two days before his 19th birthday he too decided to do his bit for King and Country and joined up. He finished his basic training in early June 1916 and was ready to join his unit. However, unlike his brother, he was not sent to a normal regiment, but to Howe Battalion of the Royal Naval Division. He also ended up on the western front.

4 October 1917 was a turning point in the Battle of Passchendaele. The allies believed that victory was finally in their grasp and it looked as if the German defenders could not possibly stop them. The 1st Battalion Royal Warwickshire was part of the 4th Division which attacked east of Langemarck towards Poelkapelle. Their orders were to take key points, such as 19 Metre Hill, Kangaroo Huts and Tragique Farm. The attack did not go as planned, however and the high command sent the Warwickshires, who were in reserve, forward to beat off a German counter-attack and to close the gap in the British front line. To do so, they had to take Hill 19. They succeeded and were able to advance a further 200 metres until just in front of the final objective. *'The advance was described by the brigadier-general as most opportune; it was well directed and executed, and had filled a gap which might have been serious*

in the event of a counter-attack.' The losses were not too bad. Two officers and ten men were dead and only two officers and 92 men were wounded or missing. Private John Dyde was one of those missing. He was not listed as officially killed until later.

Three weeks later his brother Henry Joseph went into action with the Royal Naval Division at Passchendaele, which was probably his first encounter with the horrors of the front. On 26 October the division attacked south of Poelkapelle. The Howe Battalion was required to advance through the ranks of the Anson Battalion at Varlet Farm and try to take the final objective. The attack was not a success and the men did not get very far. Many were killed, wounded or missing. Able Seaman Henry Joseph Dyde was killed by an artillery shell. His body was never recovered.

Neither brother has a known grave and both are remembered on the Tyne Cot Memorial. Their names are also inscribed on the war memorial in their home town of Chipping Campden.

top: Able Seaman Henry Dyde (Hughes)
right: Private John Dyde (Hughes)

Filling in a shell hole after the explosion. ›
The two wounded men in the ambulance at
least escaped with their lives (CWM CO2218)

10 The Second Battle of Passchendaele(2): 30 October 1917
3rd Canadian Division

Overall course of the battle

SITUATION: After the heavy rain on 26 October the weather had improved somewhat. A clear sky on 27 October meant that there was a good deal of aerial activity. Fighters of both sides carried out target spotting for the artillery; dropped bombs on the frontlines; or took aerial photographs, which occasionally resulted in dog-fights between allied and German machines. On 28 October it was still dry, but the mist hung like a shroud over the battlefield for the whole day. It didn't rain the following day either and the day of the offensive began with clear, cold, but dry weather. *'The two preceeding [sic] days had been fine and the shell torn ground had dried somewhat, enabling the men to pick their way over fairly solid ground around the lips of the shell craters. The craters themselves, with the exception of the very recent ones, being still full of water.'*[305] However, a strong wind got up and with it came more rain.[306] The constant bombardments were continually churning up the terrain and many places were still impassable due to the mud, even despite the brief let-up in the rain. Finally this time, the artillery managed to shell the German lines very effectively.

OBJECTIVE: The offensive on 30 October was aimed at capturing the objectives which the assault troops had not managed to take on 26 October. An additional – and important – objective was also to secure good jumping-off positions for the final attack on Passchendaele. The 3rd and 4th Canadian Divisions constituted the spearhead of the offensive and the line to be reached was designated the 'Blue Line'.

COURSE: The 4th Canadian Division attacked with only one brigade. Thanks to a brilliantly executed artillery barrage the 72nd battalion

< *Wounded Canadians take shelter in a German pillbox, October-November 1917 (CWM CO2211)*

succeeded in capturing Crest Farm. The 85th and the 78th battalions made good progress and the important area of high ground at Tiber Copse was also taken. The 3rd Canadian Division, on the other hand, had great difficulties in trying to push its frontline further forward. Its 7th Brigade managed to take Meetcheele, but with heavy losses. Further advance was difficult and the final objective – the Blue Line – could not be reached. The 8th Brigade attacked with the 5th Canadian Mounted Rifles, advanced 800 metres and was able to take Vapour Farm on the Goudberg. All the counter-attacks were repulsed. On the Canadians' left flank the British 63rd and 58th Divisions tried to seize more ground at the Lekkerboterbeek, but the men got bogged down in the mud and the entire attack was shot to pieces by German artillery. Their losses were enormously high.

RESULT: All the divisions suffered heavy losses and not all the objectives were reached. However, the Canadians did manage to secure a few key German strong points. The capture of Crest Farm, in particular, looked like the springboard for the final capture of Passchendaele that the grand plan required.

The 3rd Canadian Division on 30 October 1917

   3rd Canadian Division
      7th Brigade
         Princess Patricia's Canadian Light Infantry,
         42nd Battalion, 49th Battalion, Royal Canadian Regiment
      8th Brigade
         1st, 2nd, 4th and 5th Canadian Mounted Rifles
      9th Brigade (reserve)

The 3rd Canadian Division attacked with two brigades. The 8th Brigade attacked with only one battalion: the 5th Canadian Mounted Rifles, although two companies of the 2nd Canadian Mounted Rifles were on hand to provide support, if needed. After a brief halt of about half an hour at their interim objective – the Blue Dotted Line – the men were to advance to the Blue Line itself which they were to capture, consolidate and man. The Blue Dotted Line was also to be strengthened as far as possible. The Blue Line ran north of Vapour Farm across the Goudberg to just south of Graf Wood and from there it continued across the high ground at Crest Farm via Tiber to Vienna Cottages on the Ypres-Roulers railway line.

The assault battalions of the 7th brigade had the same objectives. The Princess Patricia's Canadian Light Infantry (known as 'the Patricia's' or the PPCLI) attacked on the left and the 49th Battalion on the right. Here, too, the Blue Line had to be consolidated and manned. *'This is very important this should be a distinct and definite line of defence, in view of the certainty of enemy counter attacks.'*

To the jumping-off lines

On the night of 28 to 29 October the 5th Canadian Mounted Rifles took over the frontline from the 2nd Canadian Mounted Rifles. Two patrols were sent out immediately into No Man's Land to reconnoitre the area around Woodland Plantation. On their return they reported that *'[the] ground is practically impassable, becoming worse as Woodland Plantation is reached.'*[307] Woodland Plantation *'is badly flooded in the centre, of which is a deep pond about 100 yards wide.'*[308] This information was of vital importance, given that this stretch of impassable terrain lay in the middle of the zone they had been allocated and their interim objective ran right through it. This valuable intelligence allowed them to make the final adjustments to the plan of attack.

On the same night the 7th Brigade also set out for the frontline, although under heavy German artillery fire. At around 1.30 a.m. they had taken over all the positions which the 9th Brigade, who they were relieving, had occupied. In the morning, a company of the Patricia's under the command of Captain Macpherson carried out a successful small scale attack on a German pillbox at Snipe Hall in or-

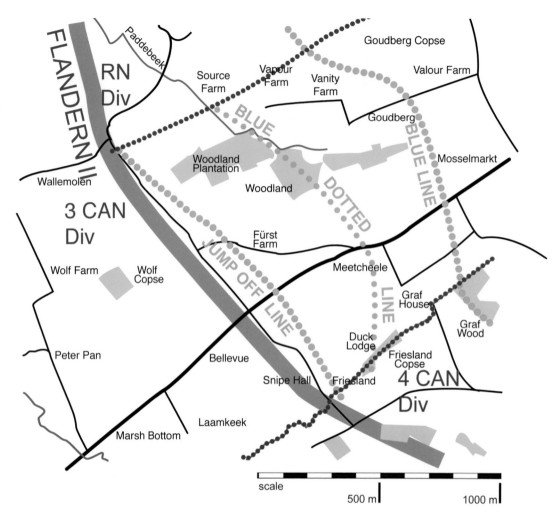

30 October 1917: 3rd Canadian Division (MMP)

der to straighten the frontline at that point. *'After manoeuvring over 500 yards of bad ground, he drove through strongly held positions and small isolated trenches, stormed the pill-box, surrounded and captured Snipe Hall and its garrison, and before daybreak was securely entrenched in line with the 49th Battalion along the cross-road.'*[309] Apart from the constant German artillery fire, it was relatively quiet for the rest of the day.

The following night the men got ready for the attack. It was a cold, but dry night. Under heavy German fire, they made their final preparations. The start positions which the men of the 3rd Cana-

Private John Cowie (Letters from the Front)

Private Jonathan Wade (de Ruvigny)

dian Division now occupied ran from the Ravebeek towards Snipe Hall and then ran in a northwesterly direction parallel to the road to Wallemolen. To their left the 190th Brigade of the 63rd Division was also waiting to go over the top, while the battalions of the 4th Canadian Division had taken up start positions to the right of the Ravebeek.

5th Canadian Mounted Rifles

The Canadian guns opened fire at 5.50a.m., *'followed one minute later by the enemy's barrage firing on our front and support lines. This was very heavy.'*[310] The 5th Canadian Mounted Rifles now went over the top. Despite the poor conditions of the ground they made quite good progress. The interim objective was reached fairly quickly and with reasonably low casualties. From this point on, however, things got steadily worse. Their own protective barrage was not providing the cover they had expected and in places fell short of its targets, *'some bursts occurring right over our trench.'*[311] Woodlands Plantation also caused problems and various companies lost sight of each other. The 30-minute-halt seemed unnecessary and even worked to the Germans' advantage giving them time to pull back and reorganize on higher ground, from where they again opened fire on the Canadians.[312] Around 8.00 a.m. C and D companies, who were on the battalion's left flank, managed to reach the Blue Line, which they now tried to consolidate. Source Farm, Vapour Farm and Vanity Farm were now in Canadian hands. The brigade's flanks were completely in the air, however. On their left the 190th Brigade had got stuck in the mud, with the Artists Rifles of the London Regiment, in particular, losing a lot of men. They were thus not able to keep up with the speed of the 5th Canadian Mounted Rifles's advance. There was also very little news of A and B companies, who were supposed to be responsible for the Brigade's right flank. A wounded Sergeant reported that *'A Coy has sustained severe casualties.'*[313] The brigade urgently needed reinforcements. Just before noon two companies of the 2nd Canadian Mounted Rifles were sent forward to support the men of C and D company: *'Can see them in small groups across towards Vapour Farm. Appear to be suffering heavy casualties but move on steadily and splendidly. Ground appears wet and sodden and very heavy going.'*[314] One of the casualties among the 2nd Canadian

Mounted Rifles was Private **John Cowie**. Cowie was born in Scotland in March 1896. He attended primary school in Pitsligo and also studied at Burnett's Civil Service College in Aberdeen. He emigrated to Canada at a fairly young age, although his parents stayed behind in Pitsligo. From June 1913 to his enlistment in the Canadian army in January 1916 he worked as a clerk with The Canadian Bank of Commerce. Private Cowie was sent overseas in July 1916, where he joined the 2nd Canadian Mounted Rifles in December.[315] Private **Jonathan Wade** had also tried to make a new life for himself in Canada and had said goodbye to the European continent in May 1909. In Nelson, British Columbia, he supported himself by working as a farmer and fireman. He enlisted in the Canadian army at the end of May 1916 and was also sent overseas the following winter.[316] Like Private John Cowie, Private Wade was also killed at Passchendaele when his unit came to the support of the exhausted men of the 5th Canadian Mounted Rifles.

The situation was now critical. Major Pearkes[317] reported the situation from the frontline: *'I have eight 2nd Canadian Mounted Rifles and twelve 5th Canadian Mounted Rifles. All very exhausted. Ammunition running short. Do not think we can hold out much longer without being relieved. Both flanks still in the air.'*[318] Pearkes did not have many men left and other officers on the new frontline were also facing the same problem.

After heavy fighting A company of the 5th Canadian Mounted Rifles also eventually managed to reach its objective. The first report of B company came in around 2.00 p.m. They were still south of Woodlands Plantation and were down to only fifteen men. It had now also begun to rain heavily. The 5th Canadian Mounted Rifles had taken all their objectives, but the entire battalion was completely exhausted. Their losses were estimated at 75%. They were therefore in dire need of being relieved and the order was finally given at around 8.30 p.m. The 2nd Canadian Mounted Rifles was ordered to replace the 5th Canadian Mounted Rifles along the whole line. Several companies of the 4th King's Shropshire Light Infantry (190th Brigade, 63rd Division) were also ordered to establish the link between the Canadians and the 190th Brigade. More men were killed during the night relief, of whom Private **Harry Choquette**, a furniture salesman from

Sherbrooke, Quebec, was one. He had joined up in December 1915.[319] Private Choquette is remembered today on the Menin Gate.

The relief was completed at around 5.00 a.m. and the exhausted men now got some rest just south of St. Julien. The following day, 1 November, the 5th Canadian Mounted Rifles marched to Watou. For them the offensive in Flanders was over, but for others the misery of the firing line continued. The 4th King's Shropshire Light Infantry was still taking numerous casualties, even on 31 October. One of them was Private **Thomas Godwin**, who was only 20 when he was killed at Passchendaele. His older brother Joseph had been killed during a German attack at Verlorenhoek between Zonnebeke and Ypres on 8 May 1915. Private Thomas Godwin's body was found near Kronprinz Farm in June 1920 and was reburied in Tyne Cot Cemetery.[320]

From the very beginning of the attack stretcher-bearers and medical officers had been working furiously to get the wounded off the battlefield to aid posts. This was extremely difficult, however: '*the forward area being at all times throughout the day subjected to intense enemy artillery and M.G. fire.*'[321] In the afternoon, the heavy rain '*added greatly to the sufferings of the wounded and the difficulties of the stretcher-bearers.*'[322] For men who had been wounded getting off the battlefield alive was no easy task. One such case was that of Private **Theodore William Seale** of the 5th Canadian Mounted Rifles. '*According to Platoon members, Pte Seale was hit by shrapnel, however still advanced. He was hit by another shell and fell on 30 October. However, he remained alive throughout the night and yelled encouragements to his platoon. He was later found dead on 31 October 1917.*' Seale, who was born in the United States in October 1894, but had grown up in Cookshire, Quebec. He enlisted in the Canadian army in February 1916, being posted to the 5th Canadian Mounted Rifles in December 1916. He had previously served two years with the 7th Hussars.[323] Private Seale's body was found after the war and buried at Passchendaele New British Cemetery.

The 24-year-old Major **Kenneth Locke Duggan** was wounded fairly early on in the attack. A runner brought the following message to battalion headquarters at Kronprinz Farm: '*7.04 a.m. Enemy is retiring over hill at extreme rear in large parties. Major Duggan, Lieut. Millar and Lieut. Dunning are reported wounded, the last seriously. Lieut. Hall is carrying on with A Coy.*' After the offensive Duggan's name was placed on the missing list: '*Reported wounded & missing.*' Major Duggan had probably been slightly wounded and had tried to make his way back to Canadian lines in order to get his wound seen to and was then, probably, either killed by enemy fire or drowned in the thick mud. It was not until June 1918 that Major Duggan was officially declared dead. '*Maj. Duggan Kenneth L. (...) has been missing since 30th October 1917. Reference has been made to the Unit, the Record Office and the Base, on the printed missing list, but no evidence of material value had been received which would indicate that he is not dead. In accordance with the decision of the Army Council, this soldier is to be regarded for official purposes as having died on or since the above date.*' Duggan was a talented officer from Montreal. Before joining in the Canadian army for the duration of the war he had already served three years with the 3rd Regiment Victoria Rifles of Canada and retained his rank of Lieutenant on enlistment in May 1915. Duggan was an engineer by training and it is therefore no surprise that he excelled in engineering and topography during the officers' training course, although he was also competent in all the other subjects, such as tactics, law and drill. He was sent overseas a few weeks after completing his instruction as an officer and joined the 5th Canadian Mounted Rifles in August 1916. Duggan was quickly promoted to Acting Major. He was wounded in the left leg by a piece of shrapnel during a raid at Arras in the winter of 1916 and was taken to hospital, where the fragments were removed. The wound failed to heal properly, however and Duggan was not able to return to his unit until the end of July 1917.[324] He was given command of A Company with the rank of Major. The location of his grave is not known and he is therefore remembered today on the Menin Gate.

49th Battalion

The 49th Battalion suffered its first casualties as soon as the men went over. '*We were under heavy machine-gun fire and rifle fire causing serious casualties at the outset. (...) My right front company lost practically all its effective strength before it crossed the road (...).*'[325] '*The enemy shelling steadily increased in intensity and, directed by a plane,*

Private Thomas Godwin (Dutton)

left: Private Harry Choquette (117e Battalion) right: Private Theodore William Seale (117e Battalion)

Major Kenneth Locke Duggan (Pirie)

*Private Robert George Angus
(George Heriot's School)*

came down on the line held by my men.'[326] The attack had scarcely begun, but there were already only four officers and 125 men left in the whole battalion. Private **Robert George Angus** was also killed during this attack. Angus was a 33-year-old Scot from Edinburgh, where he had been a pupil at George Heriot's School for four years just before the turn of the century. He emigrated to Canada in 1907, where he found work as a carpenter.[327] Angus enlisted in the Canadian army in April 1915 and was sent overseas. In late August 1916 he had to be evacuated to a hospital in Ypres with a dangerously high temperature and was not able to rejoin his unit till April 1917. Private Angus's body was not recovered after the war.[328] Like Angus, Private **Ian MacMillan** was also from Scotland. He had emigrated to Winnipeg in Canada together with his older brother, William McCall MacMillan, in 1912, where Ian worked as a clerk with the Union Bank. He enlisted in the Canadian army in February 1916. His brother William had already preceded him in May 1915 and was killed on the Somme in October 1916.[329] Private Ian MacMillan was killed at Passchendaele only four days after his twentieth birthday.[330] Private **Alexander Decoteau** was also killed on 30 October 1917. Decoteau was a famous and successful Canadian long distance runner and had represented Canada at the Olympic Games in Stockholm in 1912. The 29-year-old Canadian of Indian origin was killed by a sniper. Private Decoteau is buried in Passchendaele New British Cemetery.

The interim objective had still not been reached by afternoon and it was not until 6.00 p.m. that two companies of the Royal Canadian Regiment arrived to reinforce the remnants of the 49th Battalion. Furst Farm, which was near the Canadians' jumping-off positions, was still in German hands and could not be taken the following day either.[331] It also proved impossible to take the interim objective on 31 October. At dusk they were able to evacuate all the wounded, despite the German artillery fire. This stopped around 8.00 p.m. and the 49th Battalion were able to be relieved by the 42nd Battalion, which also belonged to the 7th Brigade and had been held in reserve at Abraham Heights, where they were continually shelled by German artillery. Among their many casualties was Private **John Harold Dennis,** a printer from Brampton, Ontario, who had enlisted in the Canadian army only few days after his 19th birthday. When

*left: Private Ian MacMillan (de Ruvigny)
middle: Private Alexander Decoteau (Heritage Community Foundation)
right: Private John Harold Dennis (Soldiers of Peel)*

he reported to the 42nd Battalion in France in 1916 he seemed to be jinxed, successively breaking his foot, getting ill and ending up in hospital with muscle pains. In 1917 he appeared to be fully fit again. Private Dennis was killed when a German shell fell on the spot where his battalion had bivouacked. Two officers were evacuated with shell shock, 'the other occupants being killed.' His body was exhumed from the side of the 's Graventafel-Mosselmarkt road at Waterloo, not far from Abraham Heights in March 1920. He is buried on Tyne Cot Cemetery.[332]

They were able to hold off various German counter-attacks thanks to the help of the artillery. The German Infanterie Regiment 172 describes one of these counter-attacks in its regimental history: *'The battalions attacked. They advanced up the hill in two waves. A heavy barrage with medium sized shells caused heavy losses. We left this behind us as quickly as possible. We soon ended up in a field full of shell holes. Sticky mud clung to our boots, making them as heavy as lead, we pressed on through shell holes filled with water, shattered treetrunks, a difficult route. The high ground north of Passchendaele was covered by murderous fire, the shells exploded very rapidly one after another. It was impossible to get through this curtain of fire (...). When the assault lines had taken this high ground, they came in sight of the enemy. The British artillery immediately targeted this new objective and the slope was covered by a heavy defensive barrage.'*[333]

German messenger on the Kraaiveldstraat in Passchendaele, 1917 (Deraeve)

Princess Patricia's Canadian Light Infantry

Like the two other assault battalions, the Patricia's also clambered out from their own series of joined-up shell holes which constituted their start line. They too, sustained casualties pretty well immediately. Private **Christian Fraser Dick** was hit in the back, collapsed and died shortly afterwards from his wounds. Dick was a bank clerk from Saskatoon, Saskatchewan. He had joined the army in May 1916 and was posted to the Patricia's at the end of December that year. Before the fatal 30th October he had only received a minor wound.[334] Private Dick is remembered today on the Menin Gate, where Private **Sydney Smith Sterns's** name is also to be found. Sterns, who was also from Saskatoon, Saskatchewan, was a 40-year-old banker who had only joined up in March 1917. He joined the Patricia's overseas in September 1917, but was immediately sent away for training. Private Sterns was finally able to join the battalion properly as a serving soldier on 26 October that year.[335] Private **Walter Livingstone Raynes** was killed on the 's Graventafel-Mosselmarkt road when he received a bullet in the stomach. Raynes, who was a protestant minister and a graduate of McGill University, had enlisted in December 1915 and had joined the Patricia's at Ypres in June 1916. He was granted ten days leave on 4 October 1917, which he spent in England.[336] Private Raynes was killed four weeks later.

The advance proved difficult. *'Beyond doubt the Passchendaele terrain was the worst ground fought over in the war. There was no cover whatever for the attacking troops wading through a sea of slime, and the pillboxes (...) were probably the most effective defence the enemy could have devised to meet such an advance.'* [337] The German artillery also did a particularly thorough job and the attacking Canadians came under heavy fire even before they had reached Duck Lodge. By the time the Patricia's finally reached the interim objective, only half the battalion was left and it had lost almost all its officers and NCOs. One of the NCOs killed was Sergeant **Arthur Roy Mutton**, a 23-year-old bank clerk from Mitchell, Ontario. He had enlisted in the Canadian army in late September 1915 and had joined his unit six months later. He was made a Corporal at the end of December and promoted to the rank of Sergeant in May 1917.[338] Like Major Talbot Mercer

left: Private Christian Fraser Dick (Letter from the Front)
right: Private Walter Livingstone Raynes (Pirie)

Private Sydney Smith Sterns (PPCLI)

Sergeant Arthur Roy Mutton (PPCLI)

Sergeant Hugh Farquhar Christie (PPCLI)

Captain William Hugoe Morris (Pirie)

Private Roy Broom (PPCLI)

Papineau, Sergeant Mutton was killed by an artillery shell at the start of the attack.[339] Private **Roy Broom**, from Kisby, Saskatchewan, was a 20-year-old bachelor who had been a clerk with the Canadian Pacific Railway before the war. He enlisted in the Canadian army in November 1915 and was hospitalized in September 1916 with a serious wound to his leg. His recovery was slow and he was continually plagued by illness, which meant that he was not able to rejoin his unit at the front until late April 1917. In June 1917 he was punished for *'writing a letter in which he endeavoured to disclose his whereabouts by means of a code'*.[340] Private Broom was killed on 30 October 1917 and is remembered today on the Menin Gate.

After reaching the interim objective the men who were left tried to push on to the Blue Line. As many officers had been killed and they had so far received no reinforcements, the NCOs took command. The regimental historian is full of praise for them: *'It was particularly on the gallantry and leadership of the NCOs that the issue depended.'*[341] Under their command the various units advanced slowly but surely towards the Blue Line, taking out German pillboxes. One of these NCOs was Sergeant Hugh Farquhar Christie. *'He made a daring reconnaissance of an enemy pill box which led to its capture.'*[342] When all the officers in his company had been killed or wounded, he took command and managed to guide his men to the Blue Line. *'With such leadership as this and gallant individual enterprise on every hand, the companies struggled on, desperately thinned and in no semblance of order, till before them stood only the pill-box on the crest beside the road, untouched by the artillery and raining death from every loophole. Heart had not failed, but strength was all but spent.'*[343] The pillbox was, in effect, blocking their advance to the Blue Line. Some 250 metres short of the line Captain **William Hugoe Morris** was killed by artillery fire. Morris had been a student at McGill University in Montreal and was made a Sergeant on enlistment in March 1915, one week before his 21st birthday. He went on to work himself up to the rank of Captain, winning the Military Cross on the Somme for *'conspicuous gallantry in action'*[344] in November 1916. His mortal remains were not recovered after the war and his name is inscribed on the Menin Gate.

In the meantime, Lieutenant **Hugh McDonald McKenzie** of the 7th Canadian Machine Gun Company had assumed command of a company of the Patricia's. Close to the pillbox he stopped to discuss the situation with Corporal Hampson: *'We talked the situation over for seemingly some time. I suggested something had to be done. A minute or so after, Mac got out of the shell-hole that we were resting in, got what men we had left going again (I won't mention how) (...).'* McKenzie organized the men into a series of small groups in order to attack the pillbox from all sides, *'he led on himself about 20 yards in front and was shot through the head by a sniper.'* His action was not in vain, however. A sniper of their own, Sergeant G. H. Mullin, was able to creep around the pillbox and eventually managed to capture it armed with grenades and a revolver. Both men were subsequently awarded the Victoria Cross, which in McKenzie's case was posthumous. McKenzie, of Scottish origin, was a married man and the father of two children. He emigrated to Montreal in 1912 and immediately enlisted in the Canadian army when war broke out. A few months later he was serving on the Western Front as a Private. In

May 1915 he won the Distinguished Conduct Medal at Bellewaerde, by which time he held the rank of Corporal, being promoted to Sergeant and receiving the French decoration the *Croix de Guerre* later that same year. He was given a commission as a Lieutenant with the Patricia's in January 1917, but was immediately seconded to the 7th Canadian Machine Gun Company. Lieutenant McKenzie's body was buried next to the German pillbox which had cost him his life. Corporal Hampson was one of those present: '*We put a cross up where we buried him. Came up after we were relieved and did this. Just showing how much we thought of him. You know, it was 6 miles of duckboards to do this. Seems crazy but we did it. Yes, Mac was blunt, said little, meant what he said, have a good laugh after. A man among men.*'[345] His grave could also not be found after the war.

The high ground at Meetcheele was taken and the attacking troops continued their advance. Just before they reached the road from Meetcheele to Graf, the companies came under heavy fire from Graf Farm and: '*from a strong-point on their left front*'.[346] The men dug in and tried to consolidate the line they had secured. '*We are established on the high ground in front of Matcheele [sic] with a line running approximately parallel with road running through Metcheele [sic] across our front. We are in touch with the 49th on our left. Our position is now definite.*' Two companies of the Royal Canadian Regiment were brought up to help the Patricia's, as the entire battalion now numbered less than 250 men.[347] Lieutenant **Harold Edward Agar** sustained a head wound while they were consolidating the position and needed to get out of the line to have his wound attended to. '*He was stopped by Captain MacPherson who bound up his wound and stayed there for half an hour before deciding to take his chances in going back.*' Lieutenant Agar left the shell hole and tried to make his way through the devastated landscape of No Man's Land to the rear. '*Fifty yards later he was sniped in the head and killed.*'[348] Agar was of British origin and had served with the 5th East Yorkshire Regiment before the war. When war broke out he immediately enlisted in the Canadian army and ended up as a Private with the Patricia's. He was seriously wounded at Bellewaerde in May 1915 and was wounded again in June 1916, but was able to return to the trenches after three weeks. Agar was made a Corporal and promoted to Sergeant shortly

German pillbox at Meetcheele, 1919 (CWM 0.4514)

thereafter, finally being made a Lieutenant in July 1917. He joined the Patricia's as an officer in October 1917.[349] Lieutenant Agar was killed a few weeks later.

At around 3.30 p.m., due to the large number of officers who had been killed and wounded, an extra company of the Royal Canadian Regiment was called up together with three extra officers, one of whom was Captain **Henry Ernest Sulivan**. They did not arrive at battalion headquarters at Waterloo Farm until 9.30 p.m. The situation at the frontline remained much the same, however. Except that the Patricia's strength had now been further reduced to 180 men. Attempts were now also made to get the large numbers of wounded off the battlefield, but only a handful of stretcher-bearers managed to get through the heavy German bombardment and reach the frontline.[350] At 1.30 a.m., on what was now the early morning of 31 October, battalion HQ at Waterloo received the following message

German hideouts before Passchendaele (Deraeve)

Lieutenant Harold Edward Agar (Newman)

Lieutenant Hugh McDonald McKenzie (PPCLI)

from Captain Sulivan: '*I find our line consisting of shell holes running about level with pill-box. Well held in small separate posts. (...) The enemy have apparently dug themselves in 200 yards in front of us. One of their patrols has just come up to our line but was beaten off. I figure I can hold this line against any counter-attack they put across. The sniping from our left is the worst feature. (...) We have about 15 stretcher cases in this Pill-Box as well as others outside. The enemy was using white flags today with their stretcher parties. I suggest that you send up stretcher parties by daylight to-morrow with white flags. We want water, S.O.S. Signals, S.A.A. and Bombs. Also a few rounds of blank.*' A few minutes later a second message came in reporting that Captain Sulivan had been seriously wounded. Sulivan '*was shot through the shoulder, chest and arm.*' The author of the message, Captain MacPherson, added: '*Very bad, I believe.*' Sulivan died a few hours later on a muddy duckboard track while being transported to an aid post near Wieltje. Captain Sulivan was buried immediately in Oxford Road Cemetery. Captain Henry Ernest Sulivan, who was born in Bristol, England, had emigrated to Canada in 1910. He enlisted in the Canadian army and was made a Lieutenant with the Patricia's in early August 1914. In February 1915 a German bullet broke the tibia and fibula on his right leg during fighting at St. Eloi. His leg took a long time to heal and Sulivan was *'very anxious to return to work'*. He was not able to rejoin the unit till June 1916, but when he finally did so, it was as a Captain.[351] Henry Ernest Sulivan was not the only member of his family to be killed in the war. His younger brother Eugene Gilbert was killed in May 1917 as a Captain with the British East Surrey Regiment.[352] Another younger brother, Philip Hamilton, had been a Second Lieutenant with the 2nd Battalion Royal Munster Fusiliers and was killed in August 1914.[353]

After Captain Sulivan had been sent to the rear, Major Niven took over the command of the frontline troops. It was not until early in the morning of 31 October 1917 that the stretcher-bearers could make a proper start on evacuating the wounded. Sergeant Hugh Farquhar Christie, who had brought his platoon up to the line the previous day, had been mortally wounded in the shoulder and right arm by a shrapnel shell. He was evacuated to the 44th Casualty Clearing Station, where he died. Christie was twenty-five years old. In March 1915 he had interrupted his studies to enlist in the Canadian army and went into battle with the Patricia's as a Private in July 1915. He was made a Corporal in September 1916, being promoted to Sergeant a year later.[354] He was awarded the Distinguished Conduct Medal for his bravery at Passchendaele, although posthumously. Sergeant Christie was buried in Nine Elms British Cemetery in Poperinghe. Private **James Davison** also died of his wounds at the 44th Casualty Clearing Station. He had been wounded in the head and left arm the day before. Davison, who was from Moneymore, Ireland, had emigrated to Canada with his parents around the turn of the century and became a commercial traveller. Before his enlistment in the Canadian army at the end of December 1915, he had previously served with 19th Alberta Dragoons for some six years and he did not join the Patricia's at the front until a year after his original enlistment. In September 1917 he was kept out of the frontline for one month due to illness. He was able to rejoin his unit at the beginning of October, by which time the Battle of Passchendaele was raging fiercely.[355]

Private Davison was buried next to Sergeant Hugh Farquhar.[356] It is likely that the stretcher-bearers brought the two men in together.

The men of the German *Infanterie Regiment 172* had a clear view of the Canadian stretcher-bearers: *'British stretcher-bearers searched the field, looking for wounded, under the protection of the Red Cross. They were working until after midday to evacuate the many casualties from the day before.'*[357] This could not be completed until 6.00 p.m. Captain Macpherson reported that: *'Only a line of shell holes held on frontage. No wire or trench'*.[358] Major Niven also sent a message back to headquarters: *'Quiet day so far, no casualties. Am arranging to have all dead buried before leaving.'*[359] Lieutenant John Egan Almon, Lieutenant Agar, Private **Walter Lawson Ruddy** and Lance-Corporal John Robert Newell were buried together, just behind the consolidated Canadian lines. After the war a British exhumation company discovered four bodies at this location. One could be positively identified as Lieutenant John Egan Almon, but the three others have only been partially identified: an unknown Lieutenant and two men from the Patricia's. Thanks to extensive research carried out by Steve Newman in the Patricia's regimental archives in 2000 a gravestone could be erected for Lieutenant Agar.[360] The two remaining men are still buried as unknown today. It has proved impossible to establish which one is Private Ruddy and which is Lance-Corporal Newell by archival research. Ruddy was a postman in Toronto, Ontario and joined up in May 1916 at the age of 26. He joined the Patricia's in December 1916. After undergoing a brief period of training in late September he returned to his unit on 12 October 1917.[361] He sustained a bullet wound to the elbow on 30 October while the Patricia's were consolidating their position. Like Lieutenant Agar, he tried to make his way to the rear, but was hit by an artillery shell on the way and was killed on the spot.[362] He is among the unknown Patricia's buried in Passchendaele New British Cemetery. Private **Lionel Victor Clare** was also buried near the new lines, not far from the Meetcheele pillbox which had sown such death and destruction in the Canadian ranks. Clare was from Cheltenham, England. He married Kathleen Margaret Gardner in November 1912 and was Secretary to the Municipal Railway in Saskatoon and enlisted in September 1916. His wife was living in England at the time. Private Clare

Private Lionel Victor Clare (PPCLI)

links: Private Walter Lawson Ruddy (PPCLI)
rechts: Captain Henry Ernest Sulivan
(de Ruvigny)

Private James Davison (PPCLI)

German print by Ernst Zimmer: 'Hinauswerfen der Engländer aus Passchendaele am 31 October 1917' (Deraeve)

joined the Patricia's at the front in February 1917 and was killed at the end of October 1917 during the attack on the pillbox at Meetcheele. His body was exhumed in August 1920 and transferred to Tyne Cot Cemetery.[363] The CWGC gives his age incorrectly as 27 instead of 30, however. Private **William McConnell's** body was also found and reburied at Passchendaele New British Cemetery. McConnell, a farmer from Fort Fairfield, New Brunswick, had joined up in February 1916, being posted to the Patricia's at the end of that year. Like many other men of the Patricia's he died at Passchendaele.

After the battle

What was left of the Patricia's were relieved on the night of 31 October to 1 November 1917 and did not reach Ypres until the following evening. Together with the remnants of the 49th Battalion they set out for Watou. The 7th brigade would return one more time to the hell of Passchendaele, later that month.

The English attack which was prepared with the use of strong artillery fire and undertaken with the deployment of enormous quantities of manpower resulted only in a small bulge in the front and not a major breakthrough. The 30th October represented a brilliant result by weakened troops against a superior force. This was acknowledged by an expres-

Private William McConnell (PPCLI)

sion of admiration on the part of the high command of the 4. Armee. The British had suffered heavy losses.[364] The losses were indeed extremely high. For the entire 3rd Canadian Division 75 officers and 1,706 went into the attack. Only 25% per cent came out unscathed. The 49th Battalion suffered the heaviest losses of all, with 80% killed, missing or wounded.

The second stage of the Canadian offensive to take Passchendaele had been only a partial success. Above all, the 3rd Canadian Division had not managed to take its objectives. The 4th Division had enjoyed more success, however and had been able to capture an important springboard into Passchendaele: Crest Farm. It was from there that the final phase of the offensive would be launched on 6 November.

Passchendaele, 18 April 1918 (Deraeve) >

30 October 1917:
Major Talbot Papineau
Princess Patricia's Canadian Light Infantry

Talbot Mercer Papineau was the son of a famous Canadian family. His great-grandfather fled to the United States after a failed rebellion against the British colonial occupier and his grandson married an American by the name of Caroline Rogers. Talbot Mercer Papineau, who was born in Monte Bello, Quebec, was the child of their marriage. Although Papineau had received the bulk of his education in English, he was completely bilingual. He attended Montreal High School and went on to study at the prestigious McGill University in Quebec. In 1905 Papineau was given one of the first of the much-coveted Rhodes Scholarships to be awarded in Canada, which enabled him to study law at Oxford University. He returned to Canada in 1908, where he served both at the bar and in politics. Papineau was a supporter of Canadian independence.

Princess Patricia's Canadian Light Infantry

As soon as war broke out in August 1914, Papineau enlisted in the Canadian army. He believed that the best way to free Canada from the grip of the British Empire was by fighting side by side with the British. Papineau was made a Lieutenant with the new Princess Patricia's Canadian Light Infantry and sailed for Europe in October. The end of January 1915 found him already at the front at St. Elooi. In late February of that year he won the Military Cross during one of the first Canadian trench raids, *'when in charge of Bomb throwers during an attack on the enemy's trenches. He shot two of the enemy himself, and then ran along the German Sap, throwing bombs therein.'* He was made a Captain in early March and, after the Battle of Frezenberg Ridge, near Bellewaerde, at the beginning of May 1915 he was the only surviving officer. At the end of February 1916 he left the regiment and was assigned to the Canadian General Staff in France, where – among his other duties – he was required to write press releases. In the meantime his political ideas concerning the Canadian question continued to evolve.

Papineau (left) with Major General Burstall (right) (Pirie)

He maintained an extensive correspondence with his mother and with an American woman sculptor, to whom he wrote in March 1916 *'The issue in Canada after the war is going to be between Imperialism and Nationalism. My whole inclination is towards an independent Canada with all the attributes of sovereignty, including its responsibilities.'* Papineau saw the Second Battle of Ypres in the spring of 1915 as the first step towards Canadian independence and he was regarded in many circles as a possible future Canadian Prime Minister. He was well aware of this. When, in May 1917, the Canadian divisions first went into action as a single corps and no longer as a component of British units, he decided to return to the front. He was motivated in part by a feeling of guilt

Major Talbot Mercer Papineau (Pirie)

after so many of his friends had been killed, but also by his political ambitions. Lieutenant Colonel Agar Adamson commented in a letter to his wife: *'Papineau (...) came to see me yesterday. (...) He wants to go to Oxford for five weeks to get fit rowing, playing tennis, racquets and running, then two weeks with his Mother in the country, then six weeks military training at some school in England. He said he intended to go into public life, after the war, in Canada and thought that he would have a better chance of getting the support of the public if he could show he had been with the Regiment through some big push like the last one. He wanted to become a Brigade Major as his Mother was very ambitious for him. I told him that if he came back he must do so as a Company Commander but he must make up his mind to stay, as I did not propose the Battn. a training school for the convenience of staff officers. He can think of nothing but himself and annoyed me very much though I did not comb him down as much as the self-seeking bounder deserved.'* Papineau rejoined his unit in June. He was promoted to the rank of Major and given the command of a company. Adamson was well satisfied with the performance of his new officer: *'Papineau is really very good.'*

Passchendaele

In late October the Canadians were getting ready for an attack on Passchendaele. On 29 October Papineau wrote a final letter to his mother: *'There seems so little to say when if only I knew what was to happen. I might want to say so much. These would be poor letters to have as last ones, but you must know with what a world of love they are written. You have given me courage and strength to go very happily and cheerfully into the good fight. Love to all, and a big hug for you, dear, brave Mother.'* In the early morning of 30 October, a few minutes before the attack began, Papineau was visited in the forward trenches by Major Hugh W. Niven. *'Moments before his company was to begin their attack (...) Papineau turned to the second-in-command Major H. W. Niven, DSO, MC, and remarked, You know, Hughie, this is suicide.'* His observation proved tragically correct as the 'big push' which Papineau had hoped to take part in was indeed to result in his death. He was cut in half by a German artillery shell almost as soon as he went over.

He could not be buried initially and it was not until the Patricia's returned to man the same stretch of line again, some weeks later, that his body was found. Adamson told his wife in a letter: *'A pair of feet with revered putties was seen sticking out of a shell hole full of water. (...) Major Papineau always wore his putties that way, they pulled the body out and by examining the contents of the pockets, found it to be Papineau. He had been hit by a part of shell in the stomach blowing everything else above away, poor fellow. He could not have known what hit him.'* They buried him and placed a cross on the grave. Major Papineau may have been reburied in Poelcapelle British Cemetery after the war, but this is not known with certainty. Papineau is remembered today on the Menin Gate.

Bei Paschendaele (K.T.

11 The Second Battle of Passchendaele (3): 6 November 1917
2nd Canadian Division

Overall course of the Battle

SITUATION: The repeated Canadian and British attacks on 26, 30 and 31 October had definitively opened the way to Passchendaele. The high ground at Crest Farm was now firmly in Canadian hands and the men were still fresh. It had rained without stopping since October and early November brought no respite. The terrain that in October had been transformed by the continuous rain and the unrelenting artillery bombardments into a fiendish quagmire was now in an even worse condition. Large sections of the Ravebeek valley were now totally impassable morasses covered in shell holes filled with water and sludge. The ubiquitous mud was even a major problem on the high ground of Passchendaele and – just as on 30 October – there was no linkage between the assault troops. The front line no longer ran in a single line, but Passchendaele was in sight.

OBJECTIVE: On 6 November 1917 the Canadian Corps was required to capture a broad arc around Passchendaele. This task was entrusted to the 1st and 2nd Canadian Divisions, who were flanked on the right by the I Anzac and on the left by the II Corps. Smaller attacks were to be carried out further south, where the British 5th Division south of the Polygon Wood mounted an attack on the German positions. The Germans were all too well aware of the importance of the heights: *'It has now become very clear that the British objective is to capture Passchendaele and the heights to the east of it, at whatever cost, in order to be able to attack the positions at Houthulst Forest from the flank. They have deployed countless divisions and an immeasurable quantity of artillery and material.'*[365]

6 November 1917: general situation (MMP) >

< Pillbox belonging to a German Kampf-truppenkommandeur in Passchendaele (Deraeve)

COURSE: In contrast to many other offensives a number of successes were achieved during the Third Battle of Ypres on 6 November. The 6th Brigade of the 2nd Canadian Division took Passchendaele with relative ease. The job was done in slightly less than three hours. The 1st Canadian Division took its objectives in the space of only two hours. Despite stiff German resistance the entire attack went like clockwork.

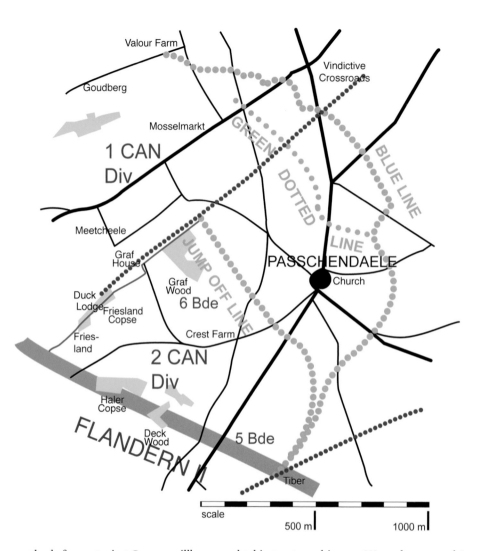

6 November 1917: 2nd Canadian Division (MMP)

The 2nd Canadian Division on 6 November 1917

2nd Canadian Division
  6th Brigade
    27th (City of Winnipeg) Battalion,
    28th (North West) Battalion
    and 31st (Alberta Regiment) Battalion, 29th Battalion.
  5th Brigade (flanking)
  4th Brigade (reserve)

RESULT: The ruins of the tiny village of Passchendaele were now finally in allied hands and the British imperial forces had captured it in less than a hundred days. Despite the successful offensive on 6 November the cost in terms of human life was still high. Many were killed or wounded.

The 2nd Canadian Division's objectives

The 2nd Canadian Division had been ordered to capture Passchendaele in one go. The plan did make provision for a temporary halt, but the Canadians were only to avail themselves of this if it proved absolutely necessary. The main thrust of the attack was entrusted to the 6th Brigade, while the 5th Brigade was only required to carry out a flanking operation. The three assault battalions were to advance side by side to the Green Line behind a protective curtain of allied artillery fire. The Green Line lay just beyond Passchendaele and the terrain to be captured was less than a kilometre deep. This was very different from the objectives of 31 July. The entire attack was to be preceded by a heavy artillery bombardment which would systematically clear the German barbed wire. The artillery was further required to complete *'the destruction of the remaining houses in Passchendaele'*.[366] If the entire attack were to prove a success, a number of advanced positions would have to be established which were required to hold back any German counter-attack.

To the jumping-off lines

The attack had been prepared perfectly. The entire 6th Brigade had spent hours studying the plans and numerous practice attacks had been carried out. They had particularly concentrated on the various methods for capturing German pillboxes and taking out machine gun nests. All units and all ranks now knew exactly what they had to do.

The brigade had arrived in Flanders on 3 November. On the night of 4 to 5 November 1917, while the other battalions were still able to spend a few quite days near Ypres, the 29th Battalion took over the entire front before Passchendaele from the 4th Brigade. The battalion had orders to prepare for the attack, which above all meant getting the assembly positions and jumping-off positions ready. By the

Canadian pioneers carry duckboards with wounded and prisoners of war. October-November 1917 (CWM CO2205)

is remarked that the night was especially dark, that the enemy kept up a very heavy harrassing [sic] fire all night, and that the men had never been in the area before, this assembly of the Brigade, within 150 yards of the enemy line without discovery, may well be considered in such a short space of time, without any appreciable casualties. The ground conditions under which it was accomplished were also most difficult.'[371] The German troops in their own front line had no idea that only a few hundred metres from where they were, almost 2,500 heavily armed Canadians were calmly preparing themselves for the attack. Most of the men tried to get some sleep or wrote one/a last letter. In the meantime, the 29th Battalion, which had made all the preparations, withdrew to act as reserve.

Jumping-off line

The area which the 29th Battalion had prepared as the start line was actually in No Man's Land, between their own and the German forward lines. This meant that the waiting troops would escape the deadly German artillery fire that was rained on the front line every day and would be able to stay closer behind their own barrage when the attack started. At around 3.00 a.m. the three battalions made their way to the jumping-off zone. The Germans were still unaware of what was in store for them.

evening of 5 November these preparations were complete and the assault battalions were able to move up to their assembly points. The 28th Battalion spent one more night near Potijze, but the 31st Battalion set off for the Abraham Heights and the 27th Battalion marched to Hill 37.[367]

On 5 November the 31st Battalion was the first to head up to the front line and had reached its designated position by about midnight.[368] The 27th Battalion, which was at Hill 37 came under heavy enemy artillery fire as it made its way up the line *'causing a number of casualties'*.[369] Just how many casualties there were and who these were is not known, however. By just after midnight the 27th Battalion had also reached the front line. The 28th Battalion was the last to set out for the forward lines. Following a small diversion around Hill 37 the 28th also arrived at the forward line, without incident.[370] *'When it*

The jumping-off line ran from the Broodseinde-Passchendaele road (just outside the centre of Passchendaele village) beyond Crest Farm to the northernmost point of Graf Wood. The Canadian 1st Division was to attack on the left and the 5th Brigade was to carry out its flanking manoeuvre on the right of the Broodseinde-Passchendaele road.

Through the ruins of Passchendaele with the 6th Brigade

The allied guns opened fire at exactly 6.00 a.m. on the morning of 6 November: *'It seemed as if every gun on the Western Front had opened up. Our troops immediately climbed out of their trenches and shell holes (...) and advanced behind the line of smoke rolling forward.'*[372] The German artillery immediately answered the Canadian fire, but their shells did not harm the Canadians who, by then, had already reached the German forward lines. The first wave of the 27th

Battalion was only fifty metres from the German positions.[373] The defenders were taken completely by surprise and were initially only able to offer limited resistance. Few prisoners were taken and after the battle the Canadians found numerous German dead: *'most of them bore the mark of the bayonet.'*[374]

The Canadians did not encounter the first genuine pockets of resistance until they entered the devastated village. Concealed in concrete cellars and hidden behind hedges, the Germans fired on the advancing Canadians, but were quickly disposed of. They came up against more resistance just outside the centre of Passchendaele village, where several strongly-manned pillboxes and machine gun nests sowed death and destruction among the attackers. Despite the fact that the assault troops had undergone exhaustive training in the capture of pillboxes, taking these strong points often required acts of individual heroism. In the 6th Brigade's report on the action an officer noted: *'Many very gallant acts are recorded of the hand to hand fighting at these points.'* One of these gallant acts was that of Private **James Peter Robertson** of the 27th Battalion. Just outside the centre of Passchendaele his platoon came under heavy fire from an entrenched German position. While the other men tried to take it out from the front, Robertson crept up from behind. He jumped in among the Germans and killed several of them with his bayonet. The others panicked and ran away, whereupon Roberston took over the machine gun and fired on them as they fled. By this time the rest of his unit had now appeared and they continued their advance towards the Green Line. Robertson took the captured machine gun with him and went on firing on the fleeing Germans.[375] Private **William Ralph Gray**, a farmer from Golden Plains, Saskatchewan, son of emigrants from the United States, belonged to the same unit as Robertson. He had joined up in March 1916 at the age of twenty, reporting to his unit just north of Arras at the end of November 1916.[376] Private Gray was killed in the ruins of Passchendaele on 6 November. His body was not recovered after the war and he is remembered today on the Menin Gate, with the other men of his battalion.

left: Private James Peter Robertson (Snelling)
middle: Lieutenant Thomas Yates (Pirie)
right: Private Albert Hamill (Pirie)

The Germans also offered heavy resistance at other points on the battlefield from machine gun nests, pillboxes and from organized groups of defenders hidden in shell craters. The resistance was particularly strong in front of the Green Line, just outside Passchendaele. The Germans had now recovered from the initial shock and were doing all they could to stop the Canadians and push them back. Their efforts were in vain, however, as several Canadians crept around the positions and attacked them from behind. Other strong points were disposed of with rifle grenades and shells.

Private William Ralph Gray (Pirie)

Even so there were still many casualties, particularly among the officers of the 28th Battalion. Three of their four company commanders were wounded early on during the attack. *'The next senior officer of each Company immediately took command and as officer after officer fell the chain of responsibility was passed on, 'C' Company finally reaching their objective with Sergeant Prescott in charge.'*[377] Lieutenant **Thomas Yates** of the 28th Battalion was also killed, although his death is not mentioned in any report. Yates, born in England on 11 November 1890 and a bookkeeper before the war, had served from the very beginning of hostilities, having enlisted in Valcartier in September 1914.[378] He quickly rose through the ranks and eventually ended up as an officer with the 28th Battalion. Lieutenant Thomas Yates is also remembered today on the Menin Gate.

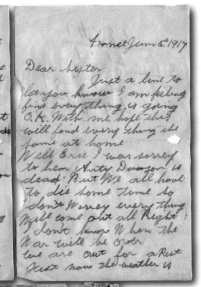

Private Roland Thomas Heath (St Denis)

top: *Letter from Heath to his sister, 6 June 1917 (St Denis)*
left: *Silk embroidered postcard from Private Heath to his brother,
3 May 1917 (St Denis)*

German planes also tried to halt the Canadian attack, strafing the advancing troops from the air. While unable to turn the tide, their actions were not without effect. At around 7.30 a.m. the commander of B company of the 28th Battalion sent a note to battalion H.Q.: *'Objectives all reached. Consolidation. (...) Casualties very heavy. (...) Enemy aeroplanes doing terrible work.'*[379] One of the men killed of B company was Private **Albert Hamill**, who had worked for the local post-office in Whitewood, Saskatoon, where his father was post-master. He enlisted in the Canadian army In August 1915 and was already in the muddy trenches of the Western Front only a year later. Until October 1917 he belonged to one of the Salvage Companies, which were units responsible for clearing up the battlefield after an offensive and collecting any useful material. He had only been transferred to the 28th Battalion on 13 October 1917 and had just turned twenty-four when he was killed at Passchendaele on 6 November.[380] Like many other Canadians Private Hamill has no identified grave and is remembered today on the Menin Gate. Private **Roland Thomas Heath** of the same unit was also killed. Heath, a farmer from Moose Jaw, Saskatoon, had enlisted in the Canadian army two years earlier on 6 November 1915, at the age of thirty-two. Despite having sustained a serious bullet wound to the chest in September 1916, the war still seemed to be a great adventure to him, which is reflected in his letters home: *'Well Greta, Jack is pretty sore because Ontario went dry but it is a good thing. We have a wet canteen it opens from 12 to 1 & 6 to 9, so it is not so bad here for beer. You can tell auntie Dawson I will tell he [sic] all about the War when I get back. I have been all over England & up to Edinburgh Scotland for my leave and had a good time their [sic]. There is about ten Girls to every man here so you see one has to be careful not to get kidnapped.'* These letters also clearly reveal his optimism: *'Well I have had a dandy good trip hope will home soon. (...) Well kid, cheer up, I wil soon be back in Canada.'* His last letter was dated late September 1917. The next news that his family was to receive about him came in a night telegram: *'Greatly regret [to] in form you 105153 pte Roland Heath (...) officely [sic] reported killed in action November 6/1917'.*[381] Private Heath is remembered today on the Menin Gate.

Around 8.00 a.m. – only two hours after the start of the attack – the three assault battalions had reached their objective, the Green Line.

'*The spirit and fighting qualities shown by the men was magnificent and the supervision and leadership exercised by the officers was of the highest standard. All ranks made the assault with the greatest dash.*' The entire attack appeared to have been a success. The Germans had been taken completely by surprise and had sustained heavy losses. After the attack the Canadians found the bodies of almost seventy Germans strewn around the church.[382] Canadian losses, on the other hand, were relatively small by comparison to the previous offensives at Ypres. The 28th Battalion, for example, had lost barely 35% of its men.[383] The day had only just begun, however.

Consolidation

So far everything had gone according to plan and the units set about extending their defensive positions just beyond the Green Line. This advanced position had to serve as a first line of defence against the German counter-attack, which would not be long in coming.

Snipers

Consolidating the ground that had been won turned out to be more difficult than expected. German snipers plugged away at the Canadians '*and caused severe losses in our forward companies.*' Furthermore, a few remaining German pockets of resistance ensconced in concrete pillboxes still had to be taken out in the 31st Battalion's area. C company's commanding officer, Major **Gordon Douglas Powis**, discussed the plan for taking two of these pillboxes with some other officers from B company. The men of B company were to open fire on the pillbox, while a group of men from C company would skirt around it and attack it from behind. '*The most regrettable circumstances delayed the success of this enterprise. It was in getting under way the arrangements for this final advance that Maj. Powis, regardless of danger, exposed himself in order that the final objective be secured with absolute certainty, and his gallant conduct could not have been more praiseworthy.*'[384] Major Powis was hit by a German sniper while he was trying to convey the instructions to the men. He was killed instantly. The 30-year-old Powis was from Edmonton, Ontario and had graduated from McGill University in Montreal with a degree in electronic engineering. He was married and his wife's first name is known to have been Mona. Powis had belonged to a local militia

unit, where he held the rank of captain and retained this rank when he enlisted in the Canadian Expeditionary Force at the beginning of July 1915. Powis was not sent overseas with his unit till April 1916 and was promoted to Major in May 1917.[385] His body was never recovered after the war and Major Powis is also remembered today on the Menin Gate.

The pillboxes which Powis wanted to take were subsequently captured with relative ease. One of them was big enough to serve as a first aid post.[386] There were also a few other pillboxes that had still not been taken scattered within the battalion's zone, but the Germans inside realized that there was no point in continuing to resist as this would only result in their deaths and, therefore, willingly surrender. In one well-concealed concrete German dugout the Canadians accepted the surrender of six German officers, among whom were the battalion commanders of the *10. Grenadier-Regiment König Friedrich Wilhem II* and of the *7. Bayerische Infanterie-Regiment* respectively. The latter unit was supposed to launch a counter-attack in the event that the enemy succeeded in breaking through at Passchendaele. In isolated points across the battlefield the Germans did indeed try to put together a poorly organized counter-attack, but were hindered by the Canadian artillery.[387] The *Königlich Preussische 4. Niederschlesische Infanterie-Regiment Nr. 51* took part in one such counter-attack at Passchendaele on 6 November. '*The enemy must have seen the attack coming early on from their good observation posts, and pulled out all the stops to impede this. In particular, they wanted to hold on to their favourable positions for an advance the next day. It was a question of feeling one's way, crawling, staggering and falling in mud and water amid a hail of shells and blood. The rain bucketed down without respite. We then came under heavy fire from British naval guns, our number 12 company taking a direct hit. (...) There, on the main road north of Passchendaele the attack came up against the British infantry. However, before things had been decided, we received the order to advance. The line which had been reached with such great losses had to be maintained.*'[388]

Major Powis was by no means the only casualty of the German's murderously accurate fire. Canadian snipers tried to do the same to them, but this proved no easy task. Some of them were wounded just

Major Gordon Douglas Powis (Pirie)

Private Stanley Richard Shore (Christie)

Prisoners of war receiving tea and bread, Passchendaele 6 November 1917 (CWM CO2216)

outside the Canadian line of defence. Private James Peter Robertson, who had previously driven a group of Germans out of a strongly defended position, immediately went out into No Man's Land in an attempt to save two wounded snipers and managed to get one of them back to the safety of the Canadian lines. *'In spite of a veritable storm of bullets, Robertson went out again. He fell before reaching the second man – he was probably hit – but picking himself up, he continued on his way, and secured his second comrade. Slipping on the sticky mud, nearly exhausted, he stuck to his man, and had put him down close to our line, when an unlucky shell exploded near by, killing him instantly.'* Robertson was from Medicine Hat, Alberta and had been an engine driver with the Canadian Pacific Railway before joining up in early 1915. He was awarded a posthumous Victoria Cross for his actions at Passchendaele on that day. The medal was formally presented to his mother, amid great public interest, in April 1918. Private Robertson's was buried 420 metres north-east of the ruins of Passchendaele

church, a location which was just in front of the Green Line on the left flank of the 27th Battalion's area. His body was found after the war and reburied in Tyne Cot Cemetery.[389]

Another man killed from the same unit was Private **Stanley Richard Shore**, a 19-year-old bank clerk from Saskatoon, Saskatchewan. Before joining up in March 1916 he had belonged to the 105th Saskatoon Fusiliers, a local militia regiment. In England he was originally posted to a transport unit, the 5th Divisional Train, but joined the 27th Battalion in May 1917. He spent two weeks in hospital due to illness in August 1917, but on 12 September he signed himself as present with his unit.[390] Private Shore is remembered today on the Menin Gate.

The job of consolidating the new line of defence was completed quite easily. According to the 31st Battalion's War Diary the Germans were unable to carry out a counter-attack in their zone and were also having difficulties doing so in the other zones. *'In front was a practically impassable swamp. It was only on the Battalions on the flanks that the enemy could counter-attack and that only on very exposed ground and through confined approaches.'*[391]

Evacuating the wounded

While the positions were being consolidated, the stretcher-bearers began their work. It was their job to get all the wounded off the battlefield and take them to a dressing station or field hospital. *'This was rendered doubly difficult on account of the low marshy ground and shell torn ground over which the parties had to work.'*[392] The whole area also came under

German artillery fire, which caused many additional wounded and dead among the Canadians. Private **James Alexander Blackwood**, from Moose Jaw, Saskatchewan, was with the 5th Canadian Field Ambulance. Blackwood had been born in Ireland and had only been living in Moose Jaw for a year when war broke out. He was a pharmacist at the time of his enlistment in the Canadian army. The 5th Canadian Field Ambulance was responsible for picking up and transporting all the wounded of the entire Canadian 2nd Division. Prior to the attack an extensive network of Regimental Aid Posts (RAP's) and first aid posts had been established, including Tyne Cottage, Levi Cottage, Thames Farm, Frost House, Bavaria House, White Chateau, Bremen House, Mitchell Farm and Otto Farm. On 6 November Blackwood was transporting a wounded man from Tyne Cottage to Levi Cottage. The track had been laid that same day with special mats which were supposed to make the journey easier. Private Blackwood sustained a serious head wound just before reaching Levi Cottage. He was taken out of the line as quickly as possible, but died of his wounds in Vlamertinghe later that same day.[393] The 29-year-old Blackwood was buried in Vlamertinghe New Military Cemetery. His commanding officer wrote of him, after his death: *'[He was] always doing cheerfully whatever he was called upon to do, no matter what the nature of the duty was, always with the idea of helping to bring this terrible war to a successful conclusion.'*[394] His brother Corporal Joseph Blackwood also died of his wounds in March 1918. He was only twenty-two.[395]

The German prisoners of war did not have any easy time of it when they were taken out of the line and more than forty were killed by their own German artillery fire. The conditions under which the evacuation took place were extremely difficult. Even so, the War Diaries of the 27th and the 28th Battalion[396] report that all the wounded were removed from the battlefield.[397] One of the aid posts was a pillbox at Tyne Cottage. Private **Frank Rogers** of the 27th Battalion had been seriously wounded and was picked up on the battlefield by a team of stretcher-bearers who took him to Tyne Cottage to be treated by a doctor. Rogers, who was born in Chicago, in the United States, came from Regina, Saskatchewan where he was a repairman. He was only eighteen when he enlisted in the Canadian army in January 1917 and had his first taste of trench warfare in June of that year. Two months later he was picked up by the 4th Canadian Field Ambulance after receiving a gunshot wound to the

Canadian stretcher-bearers evacuate a wounded man through the mud of Passchendaele, October-November 1917 (CWM CO2215)

left: Private James Alexander Blackwood (de Ruvigny)
right: Private Frank Rogers (Pirie)

left: David Donaldson (George Heriot's School)
right: Private Wilfrid Wild (Pirie)

Lance Corporal Francis John Quesnell (Pirie)

shoulder, but was able to rejoin his unit after a week. Private Rogers died of his wounds at Tyne Cottage on 6 November 1917 after having served only ten months. He was buried immediately afterwards and was one of the first men to be buried in Tyne Cot Cemetery.[398]

Burying the dead
The Canadians' attempts to evacuate all the wounded men from the battlefield were fairly successful and when the battalion was relieved the following day all the wounded had been taken off the battlefield. Special attention was also paid to the dead, but burying them or transporting them to a cemetery was a lot more difficult. The 27th Battalion's War Diary records that: '*Owing to the length of the trail and the terribly 'going' it was impossible to carry out the dead other than officers. However, the dead in advance of the original front-line were all buried where they fell before the Battalion was relieved in the line.*'[399] The 28th Battalion also managed to bury all its dead before going out of the line.[400]

One of those buried was Lance Sergeant **David Donaldson**, who was born in Edinburgh, Scotland, in September 1891 where he attended George Heriot's School from 1904 to 1907. He later emigrated to Canada with his younger brother William Duncan, finding work with the Canadian Pacific Railway. Donaldson enlisted in the Canadian army in September 1915. On joining the army he gave his brother as his next of kin. His brother, who was a commercial representative, also enlisted in the Canadian army in January 1916 and both were sent to Europe. David ended up as a Sergeant with the 82nd Battalion in May 1916 and his brother William became a Gunner with the 6th Canadian Field Artillery. David married a woman called Henrietta, from Edinburgh, in July 1916, after which the name of his new wife replaced that of his brother as his next of kin on his Attestation Paper. David was very eager to see action at the front and turned in his Sergeant's stripes in September 1916 so that he could join the 31st Battalion, which was to due to embark for France. He sustained a wound to his left hand at Vimy Ridge on the night of 14 April 1917 and was not able to rejoin the battalion until a month later. He was made a Corporal in July 1917 and – one month later – received the news that his brother had been killed in France.[401]

Private George Frederic Furley
(Tonbridge School)

David Donaldson was made a Lance Sergeant with D company on 6 November 1917, but was killed later on that same day. His body was exhumed at Tiber in the early 1920s, which is south-west of Passchendaele and quite far outside the zone in which the 31st Battalion attacked. It is not clear how he came to be buried so far beyond his own area. Lance Sergeant Donaldson's body was transferred to Tyne Cot Cemetery where he received his final resting place.[402]

Another man buried on 6 or 7 November 1917 was Lance Corporal **Francis John Quesnell**, a 29-year-old railway worker from Regina, Saskatchewan. He was a keen bowling enthusiast, but was best known for his prowess at baseball: '*Frank was known as the "Flying Frenchman" and when he connected with the pellet, that at least did fly.*' Like many other young Canadians he had joined up in the spring of 1916. The doctor who conducted his physical examination recorded his condition as *Excellent*. However, once at the front, he proved not so healthy. He was regularly absent from duty due to illness, shell shock or – on one occasion – a twisted ankle. Lance Corporal Quesnell was probably killed early on in the attack. On 29 November 1917 a local newspaper wrote of him: '*He had all requisites of a fine soldier and had done wonderful work for his country prior to the time that a Hun bullet laid him low.*' Three days later his photograph appeared in the same paper with the legend: '*Friends of Quesnell were shocked to read that in Monday's Leader that he had been killed* *in action on November 6th.'* Quesnell's body, which was found after the war east of Graf Wood, close to the 28th Battalion's jumping-off line, could be identified on the basis of his identity disc. His mortal remains were subsequently transferred to Tyne Cot Cemetery.[403]

The same newspaper which imparted the sad news of Quesnell's death to friends and family at home had also earlier announced the death of Private **Wilfrid Wild**. *'Word reached J. Wild, of North Regina, Thursday evening, that his son, Pte. Wilfrid Wild, was killed in action on November 6 in France.'* Wild, who was born in England in the summer of 1898, worked on a farm near Winnipeg. He was not yet eighteen years old when he enlisted with the 179th Battalion in March 1916. He left Canada in October 1916 and sailed for Europe with his unit, reporting to the 28th Battalion in May 1917. Private Wild was killed during the capture of Passchendaele, after having served only five months at the front.[404] It is likely that Wild's body was also buried, but it was never subsequently recovered. As one of the missing, Private Wild is remembered today on the Menin Gate.

Days following the attack, 7 and 8 November 1917

The night passed without incident, but the German artillery shelled the newly acquired Canadian positions for the whole of the next day. The Canadians, meanwhile, concentrated on trying to extend and reinforce their positions.

The following night the 5th Brigade was able to relieve the 6th Brigade. The entire brigade marched to Brandhoek in the direction of Poperinghe. At 5.30 a.m. a German plane dropped various bombs onto them. Two officers were killed outright and three others were wounded. Five other ranks were also wounded, one of whom was Private **George Frederick Furley**.[405] He was a man who cut a striking figure. Not only was he – at 1 metres 93 – quite tall for the period, but he also bore a large scar over his right eyebrow. Finally, his right leg was shorter than the left. He was already forty when he enlisted in the Canadian army in February 1916. His nephew, Bernard Edward Furley, was a Major with the East Kent Regiment and had been killed at Loos in October 1915.[406] Furley's younger brother had also been killed.[407] Furley had attended Tonbridge School from January 1892 to Christmas 1894 and emigrated to Canada in 1903 where he

mostly earned his living as a farmer. He arrived in England at the end of August 1916, but could not join his new unit till February 1917. He had survived the offensive on 6 November, but sustained serious wounds to his left arm when the German plane dropped its bombs: *'GSW left arm, compound fract[ures].'*[408] Private Furley was taken to a Casualty Clearing Station in Poperinghe as quickly as possible, but died later of his wounds. He is buried today in Lijssenthoek Military Cemetery.

It was not until they arrived in Brandhoek that the brigade could work out the number of casualties it had suffered. Compared with the other offensives in Ypres in 1917, losses, though high, were still relatively light. Around 30% of the 6th Brigade was dead, missing or wounded or had been made prisoners of war.[409] The War Diary of the field hospital at Lijssenthoek in Poperinghe also refers to casualties figures as being low: *'apparently the casualties from todays [sic] fight have been fairly light as our normal routine has hardly been disturbed.*[410] *Some 15 German officers and 230 German NCOs and men were taken prisoner.'*[411]

Assessing the outcome

The offensive of 6 November was a resounding success across the whole line. The attack did not secure much ground, but all the objectives set had been reached and consolidated. The commander of the 2nd Canadian Division was proud of his men: *'Vimy Ridge, Hill 70 and Passchendaele are victories of which every individual in the Division may be justly proud and the Division has made a name for itself as a first class fighting Division.'*[412] The commander of the 6th Brigade was equally unstinting in his praise, describing their actions on that day as: *'a most worthy record'.*[413]

More importantly, the village of Passchendaele had finally been taken and the Germans had now been almost entirely driven off the ridge. On 10 November the Canadians were to make one last attack to finish the job.

Primitive German shelter in Passchendaele, spring 1918 (Deraeve) ›

172

6 November 1917:
Lance Corporal Norman Chadwick
3rd Battalion CEF

Ireland

Norman Francis Chadwick, the fourth child of William Henry Chadwick and Mary Jane Gloyns, was born on 11 October 1896. The couple had seven children in all. The family was from Ireland, where a series of failed potato harvests, between 1845 and 1848, caused famine and dire poverty, better known as The Great Hunger. Hundreds of thousands died and approximately two million others emigrated to England, Australia, America or Canada – the Chadwicks among them. The family decided to move to Canada in the hope of finding a better life and a new future. Norman's father, William Chadwick, became a printer in Toronto.

France

Norman Francis Chadwick followed in his father's footsteps and became, in his turn, a printer with the Orange Sentinel, a local Toronto newspaper. He enlisted in the Canadian army in August 1915. On completion of basic training Chadwick left Halifax aboard the SS Olympic bound for England, where he disembarked in Liverpool with the 83rd Overseas Battalion in early May 1916. He ended up in the 1st Battalion and continued his training in England. According to a newspaper cutting preserved by the family, Chadwick was offered the chance of becoming a Drill Instructor, but wanted to serve at the front and therefore refused the promotion. He finally ended up with the 3rd Battalion in the trenches in France in December 1916. He was made a Corporal in early April 1917, but was wounded during the fighting at Vimy a few days later. A bullet grazed his chin, landing him in a hospital in Boulogne, but was back to his unit two weeks later. In September 1917 he was awarded the Military Medal, *'for conspicuous gallantry and devotion to duty'* after the fighting at Hill 70. He celebrated his 21st birthday in the trenches on 11 October *'and I hope to spend the next at home',* he wrote in a letter home, *'we have old Fritz beaten'.* The battalion left for Ypres two weeks later.

Lance Corporal Norman Francis Chadwick (right) (Boos)

CHADWICK—Won his victory of November 6th, 1917, on Passchendaele drive, now officially reported killed, Corp. Norman Francis Chadwick, late of the 83rd, dearly beloved son of Mr. and Mrs. William Chadwick, 9 Grove avenue, in his 20th year, and nephew of Private George Gloyns, now overseas, late of Toronto waterworks.
But the hardest part is yet to come,
When his comrades they return,
And he'll be sleeping far away
And we are left to mourn.
—Grandma Gloyns.

Newspaper cutting with his grandmother's eulogy (Boos)

CORP. CHADWICK WOUNDED.

Mr. and Mrs. Wm. Chadwick, of 9 Grove avenue, received a cablegram to the effect that their son, Norman C. Chadwick, had received a face wound and was admitted to hospital at Boulogne, France, on April 13. Corp. Chadwick went overseas with the 83rd Battalion, and while in England was appointed drill instructor, but, thinking that was not doing 'his "bit," gave up his stripes and went to France.

Chadwick wounded (Boos)

Belgium

In the early hours of 6 November 1917 the 3rd Battalion, which was part of the 1st Brigade of the 1st Canadian Division, was getting ready for an attack on Passchendaele. Their assault positions were near Fürst Farm and their objective was to capture Goudberg. They succeeded in doing so, but many were killed or wounded. Lance Corporal Chadwick was one of those killed. Lieutenant R. Montgomery notified the family of his death: *'He was always very consistent and whole-hearted in whatever work he was required to do, whether it was in the line or training behind the lines. I considered him a very valuable and efficient soldier. He was accidentally killed by a German 59 howitzer shell. As we could not bring the body out he was buried where he was killed.'* The body of the 21-year-old Chadwick could not be recovered and his name is inscribed on the Menin Gate. Chadwick also had a cousin at the front. The family was devastated by the fate of their young men. Several members of the family placed brief obituaries in the local paper. His parents, brothers and sister submitted the following poem:

'A mother's heart is aching for the son she loved so well.
Oh, no, the voice that now is still keeps ringing in my ears
If I could have only raised his dying head or heard his last farewell,
The grief would not have been so hard for those who loved him so well.
In the still hours of the night, when sleep forsakes our eyes,
Our thoughts are far away in France where our darling hero, Norman lies.'

A Canadian soldier at the entrance to a dugout, Passchendaele 14 November 1917 (CWM CO2256) >

12 The End of the Battle of Passchendaele: 10 November 1917
1st Canadian Division

Overall course of the battle

SITUATION: Passchendaele had finally been captured on 6 November. The Canadian plan – to take Passchendaele in three stages – had been a success. Of the village itself, however, only rubble remained. It had been completely destroyed. The Canadians were now on top of the ridge, but one more attack would be able to improve their positions considerably.

OBJECTIVE: On 10 November three divisions were to try to improve the allied positions on Passchendaele ridge. This meant advancing further north, in the direction of Westrozebeke.

COURSE OF THE BATTLE: Three divisions took part. The 1st Canadian Division spearheaded the attack and was completely successful in achieving the objectives it had been given. It was flanked on the left by the British 1st Division, which succeeded in capturing part of the Goudberg. The 2nd Canadian Division was deployed on the right of the 1st Canadian Division, but was not required to participate in the attack.

10 November 1917: general situation (MMP) >

RESULT: Despite heavy losses, the entire attack was a success. Together with the British, the Canadians succeeded in reaching their objectives. Passchendaele and a part of the road to Westrozebeke were now in allied hands.

< What was left of the church itself... (MMP)

The 1st Canadian Division had been ordered to take various strategic points: Vindictive Crossroads and the ridge just north of it. This was entrusted to the 7th and 8th Battalions of the 2nd Brigade, helped by the 20th Battalion of the 4th Brigade. The line to be taken ran along the highest points of the ridge. Once taken, the new line would have

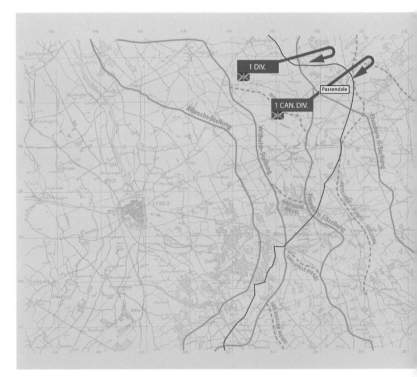

The 1st Canadian Division on 10 November 1917
>   2nd Brigade
>   5th, 6th 7th, 8th and 10th Battalion
>   4th Brigade
>   18th, 19th, 20th, 21st Battalion
>   1st Brigade (reserve)
>   3rd Brigade (reserve)

to be properly extended and strengthened. The 5th Battalion provided immediate support at Meetcheele and the 10th Battalion was in reserve at Duck Lodge. The terrain to be taken was only 400 metres deep at some points and at others points slightly more than a kilometre.

To the front line

On 9 November 1917 all the battalions set off to their jumping-off positions. The 7th, 8th and 20th Battalions took up positions in the front line, while the 5th and 10th Battalions took up positions behind the front line. During the afternoon, however, both the front and the support lines came under heavy shelling. The Germans knew that the Canadians were planning a new attack and so did their best to impede their preparations. The artillery fire was continuous and lasted the entire night. In the early morning the Germans increased the pressure and an infernal tornado of shells was released upon the waiting troops. Thirty men were killed and more than 100 others were wounded. Despite this setback the Canadians were determined to carry out this last mission, *'it was felt, that all possible had been done and there was a feeling of confidence throughout that the operation would be successful.'*[414]

In the attack

In the early morning of 10 November it was misty, with the low clouds threatening rain. At exactly 6.05 a.m. the men crawled out of their positions and followed behind the artillery barrage. None of the battalions had significant problems at the start of the offensive. The 7th Battalion had to deal with a German position at Vindictive Crossroads and also came under machine gun and rifle fire just before the final objective, causing numerous casualties. They were quickly able to deal with this resistance, however and the battalion advanced to beyond their objective. With the help of the 20th Battalion they were able to take an enemy trench. The Canadians came under heavy fire from a pillbox on the road to Oostnieuwkerke. The pillbox was rendered harmless, but the Canadian troops had to pull back to their original objective. Likewise, the 20th Battalion also encountered little resistance at first, yet there were still a great number of casualties. One of these was Private **John James Byers** of

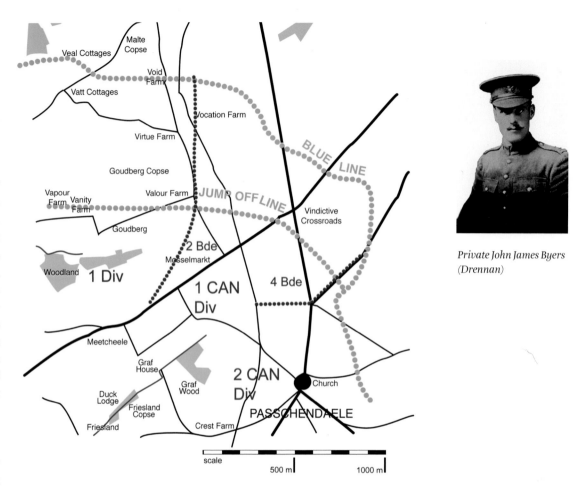

Private John James Byers (Drennan)

10 November 1917: 1st Canadian Division (MMP)

the 20th Battalion. Byers was born in September 1891 in Killinkere in County Cavan, Ireland and had three sisters and six brothers and got on especially well with his older sister, Sarah. It is not known exactly when he emigrated to Ontario, Canada, but probably he did so together with his older brother, Robert. Byers found work as a labourer. He enlisted in the Canadian army in December 1915 and was sent overseas. He regularly wrote to his sister Sarah in Ireland. *'You are still alive'*, wrote Sarah to him, to which Byers replied: *'I am still alive and so is my shirt!'* On 10 November Private Byers was killed north of Passchendaele. When the family in Ireland received the news it came as bitter blow and his sister Sarah was completely distraught.[415] Byers's body was buried at Passchendaele New British Cemetery after the war. The 8th Battalion encountered no further

left: Private Herbert Stanley Ferguson (University of Manitoba)
right: Lieutenant John Cochrane Smith (University of Manitoba)

Sergeant James Nicol (George Heriot's School)

top right: Panoramic view of the battlefield seen from the positions of the 2nd Canadian Division (CWM CO2265)

problems. At around 7.00 a.m. the battalion commander spotted a large number of men withdrawing *'in considerable disorder from the objectives.'*[416] An extra company was forward in order to improve the situation. Soon afterwards it became clear what had happened. The South Wales Borderers of the British 1st Division, who were supposed to advance towards the objective on the left of the Canadians, had got lost and pushed the Canadians's left company to the right. The South Wales Borderers then returned to their jumping off positions, which created a large gap in the front line. The 8th Battalion had lost too many men to be able to fill this gap and so were reinforced by the 5th Battalion, which sent a company forward. The situation had now improved considerably, but the men were exhausted. One of the 8th Battalion men killed was Private **Herbert Stanley Ferguson**, from Dauphin, Manitoba. He had graduated from University of Manitoba at the beginning of 1916, but joined up in late February of that same year. On completion of basic training he was sent overseas and was posted to the 8th Battalion. The 23-year-old Private Ferguson was listed as missing after the attack on 10 November.[417] His body was never found. Ferguson is remembered today on the Menin Gate.

The 5th Battalion, which provided the immediate support, took a terrible pasting from the German artillery. Several German planes had spotted the troops in the early morning and their positions immediately came under heavy shellfire. Sergeant **James Nicol** was one of the casualties. Nicol was born in April 1892 in Edinburgh, Scotland and attended George Heriot's School between 1905 and 1907. He emigrated to Canada in 1911, where he worked as an inspector. Four years later, in October 1915, he enlisted in the Canadian army in Edmonton. He embarked for Europe with the 63rd Battalion in April 1916 and was posted to 5th Battalion in France in June 1916. Nicol was made a Lance Sergeant just before the end of the year. The 25-year-old Scottish Canadian was wounded in the right leg during the Battle of Vimy Ridge and was taken via Boulogne to a hospital in Taplow, England. His wound healed quickly and he was released from hospital on 1 June 1917 and was able to return to the front, where he was promoted to Sergeant at the end of September 1917. He was listed as missing after the attack of 10 November 1917.[418] His body was never found and Sergeant Nicol's name is inscribed today on the Menin Gate. Lieutenant **John Cochrane Smith** was also killed. Smith was from Inverness, Scotland. It is not clear when he emigrated to Canada, but he obtained a Bachelor of Science degree in Agriculture from the University of Manitoba in 1911. Before enlisting in the Canadian army, Smith worked as a cattle inspector. He joined up in late July 1915 and received a commission as a Lieutenant. He was originally posted to the 63rd Battalion, but was later transferred to the 5th Battalion in France. Lieutenant Smith also has no known grave and is therefore remembered today on the Menin Gate.

The Canadians had dealt with a strong German counter-attack along the entire front. In some places they were able to beat this off with the help of the artillery. Elsewhere the men had to stand on the parapets of the freshly dug trenches in order to keep their weapons out of the mud, but they too managed to repulse the attack and to drive the enemy back with rifle fire.[419]

Passchendaele village seen from on top of the ruins of the church (Deraeve)

The men of the 5th Battalion were not the only ones to get a rain of shells over their heads. The 10th Battalion, in positions slightly further forward, also got the same treatment. Lance Corporal **George Kirkpatrick Johnston** of 10th Battalion was severely wounded. Johnston, of Scottish origin, was the son of a town councillor. He sang in the choir and was a keen bowling enthusiast. He emigrated to Canada in 1911, where he worked as a bookkeeper and secretary in a small firm. He enlisted in the army in October 1915 and sailed for England in April 1916. He originally held the rank of Company Sergeant Major, although had to turn in his stripes on being transferred to the 10th Battalion, but was quickly promoted again to Lance Corporal. Johnston was wounded on 10 November and was taken to a first aid post. Lance Corporal Johnston died on the way to the aid post at Wieltje and was buried in the adjacent Oxford Road Cemetery, the point from which the allied offensive started on 31 July 1917.

The bombardments went on all day and the entire front line came under heavy shelling. By evening the troops in the forward trenches had been so depleted and were so exhausted that they were in urgent need of being relieved. The problems were acute: *'three men dying in Dressing Station of exhaustion and two others on the way out were drowned in the Ravensbeek [sic], not having the strength to cross the little stream.'*[420] The 10th Battalion relieved them and they made their way, exhausted, out of the line.

From 10 to 11 November

Burying the dead proved difficult as the Germans continued to shell the entire area. The few who could be buried did not get a cross due to lack of materials. It was important to get the wounded off the battlefield as soon as possible. The men who were relieved had to do their best to evacuate their wounded comrades from the field. This job lasted the whole night and the whole of the following day. On 11 November the German artillery was relatively inactive, with only a few heavy explosions putting the men at risk in the morning and afternoon. One of these cost the life of Captain **Cyril Knox Barrow Mogg**, who was killed by an artillery shell in one of the reserve trenches, together with Lieutenant Harry Carter.[421] Mogg was from Bishop's Canning, Devizes, England. He had emigrated to Canada with his brother, Aubrey Barrow Mogg, who was two years younger than him. Cyril worked for the Canadian Bank of Commerce and Aubrey had a chicken farm. Cyril Mogg enlisted in the Canadian army in October 1915 and his brother did the same a few months later. His brother was sent to the front almost immediately and was killed at St. Eloi near Ypres in August 1916. Cyril left for Europe at the end of March 1916 and ended up as Lieutenant with the 7th Battalion. He was hospitalized in April 1917 with a severe case of flu and was not able to rejoin his unit until August, by which time he had been promoted to Captain. The 30-year-old Captain Mogg was killed on 11 November. Like his younger brother he is remembered today not only on the Menin Gate, but also in their home town of Bishop's Cannings, where a special memorial was erected. The parish church features a copper cross on which the names of both men are engraved. Their father, the Rev. Canon Mogg, was the parish priest.

Lieutenant **Lawrence 'Larry' Lavell Davidson** and his company were responsible for the wounded of the 5th Battalion. It was their

left: Lance Corporal George Kirkpatrick Johnston (Wight)
right: Lieutenant Lawrence Lavell Davidson (Pirie)

Captain Cyril Knox Barrow Mogg (Letters from the Front)

Sergeant Charles Blair Smillie
(Letters from the Front)

Private Robert Frank Fane
(Letters from the Front)

job not only to ensure the evacuation of the wounded, but also to make sure that supplies reached the troops. Davidson was born in Canada and went to school in Regina, later going on to study at the University of Toronto. While a student he had taken various military training courses and was immediately made an officer on his enlistment in the Canadian army in 1916. He embarked for England in September 1916, ending up in the 32nd Battalion and was posted to the 5th Battalion in France in early November 1916. After the heavy fighting at Vimy Ridge, Davidson was given ten days leave in Paris and was able to spend a further ten days in England in late October. He rejoined his unit on 4 November and was wounded a week later by a gas shell. Davidson was evacuated by the 6th Canadian Field Ambulance to a field hospital in Poperinghe. The next day he was admitted '*seriously ill*' to the 14th General Hospital in Wimereux near Boulogne. His condition did not improve and became critical ('*dangerously ill*') on 20 November. Lieutenant Davidson died on 25 November 1917 as a result of his wounds and of gas inhalation.[422] He was buried near the hospital in Wimereux Communal Cemetery.

Other soldiers who had been wounded were also able to be evacuated for treatment. Private **Charles Blair Smillie** of the 8th Battalion sustained a head wound on 11 November. He was taken to a field hospital, where he died of his wounds on 14 November. Smillie, like many other soldiers in the Canadian army, was of Scottish origin and his parents lived in Glasgow when Smillie left Scotland to try his luck in Canada. He worked for the Canadian Bank of Commerce from May 1911 until his enlistment in the Canadian army in December 1914 at the age of twenty-two. He was made a Lance Corporal with the 32nd Battalion in March 1915 and was promoted to Corporal soon sfterwards, but resigned his stripes in November. Smillie was transferred to the 8th Battalion and made a Sergeant two weeks later. He was mortally wounded on 11 November and is buried in Nine Elms British Cemetery.[423]

The 10th Battalion spent the whole day in the front line. It was relatively quiet, with only occasional artillery bombardments, but, even so, a fair number of men were killed. One of them was Private **Robert Frank Fane** from Earslfield in London. He emigrated to Canada and found a job in a bank in February 1915. Scarcely a year later he was bored of this and decided to enlist in the Canadian army, arriving in England with the 151st Battalion in October 1916. He was promoted to Lance Corporal, but turned in his stripes in August 1917. Prior to his promotion he had spent a spell in hospital suffering from an oedema caused during bayonet training.[424] Private Fane was killed at Passchendaele on 11 November 1917. Like many other Canadians he has no known grave and his name is inscribed, like theirs, on the Menin Gate.

Relief

In the evening the exhausted men of the 1st Canadian Division were relieved and an assessment of the casualties sustained in the heavy fighting of the previous days could finally be made. The 2nd Brigade had spearheaded the attack and had therefore suffered correspondingly high losses. The brigade went over with with 99 officers and 2,610 men, of whom only 58 officers and 1,383 men came out unscathed. There were more than 170 killed, 859 wounded and 232 missing. The brigade's strength had thus been reduced by more than 45%.[425]

However, all the objectives had been reached and the Canadians had achieved a major victory, just as they had at Vimy Ridge. Despite their heavy losses, 1917 had been a successful year for the Canadian Corps. Winter would soon be upon them, the period of the major offensives was now finally over and the front was again stagnated. This was the end of the Battle of Passchendaele.

Passschendaele 1917:
Died of Wounds

When the Battle of Passchendaele officially ended on 10 November, its full consequences could not yet be appreciated and they were to be felt long afterwards. Not only had the British and German armies lost large numbers of men and huge quantities of material, but the civilians at home had also been hit hard. Tens of thousands of soldiers never returned and there seemed to be no end to the daily stream of returning wounded. The lightly wounded were treated in British hospitals and then sent back to the front. Others took longer to recover and were still in hospital even after the armistice was signed in November 1918. Many were to battle for survival for a very long time and there are known cases of men wounded at Passchendaele who died of their wounds in the spring of 1918 or even later.

Private **Thomas Wilson**, who was studying humanities at the University of Edinburgh, joined the British army in October 1916 and was posted to the 9th Highland Light Infantry. He arrived at the front in June 1917 and served with the 15th Royal Scots. He was wounded on 22 October in an attack on German positions north of Poelkapelle and was listed as missing. However, German stretcher-bearers brought Wilson to one of their own first aid posts, where he received medical attention. He was later transferred by train to a hospital in Ghent, but died of his wounds as a prisoner of war on 4 January 1918.[426] The 20-year-old Wilson from West Calder near Edinburgh is buried in the *Westerbegraafplaats*, in Ghent.

Lieutenant **Arthur William Edmett** was from Maidstone. He attended Tonbridge School from 1904 to 1907 and later became an engineer. In May 1915 he decided to join the Officers Training Corps and received a commission as a Second Lieutenant. He was posted to the Queen's Own Royal West Kent Regiment at the end of December 1915 and was sent to the trenches in France as

left: Private Thomas Wilson
(University of Edinburgh)
right: Wilson's Grave in Ghent (MMP)

a novice officer in May 1916. He was admitted to Guy's Hospital in England for convalescence in September that year, having suffered a severe wound to the thigh. His brother, who was a Private with the 1st Auckland Regiment, was a patient in the same hospital and was later killed on 7 June 1917 at Messines. Arthur Edmett's convalescence proved to be very long and he was not able to return to the front until August 1917. He was promoted to the rank of Lieutenant and joined his former battalion, which, on 21 September, attacked south of the Menin Road in the direction of Tower Hamlets. The attack was a success, but Edmett *'was shot through the abdomen whilst attacking in command of his company'*. He was in urgent need of medical attention, but was only given a dressing to cover the wound *'and he lay for twelve hours without shelter or protection in the midst of a terrific barrage with shells bursting all round him'*. When it was eventually possible to move him, he still had to endure the long painful journey to a field hospital. He was subsequently sent to a larger hospital in France, where *'a very critical operation was performed''*. Six weeks later he was transferred to a clinic in London and later admitted for the second time to Guy's Hospital, where he underwent yet another operation, but his heart arrested on 16 March 1918.[427] The 28-year-old Lieutenant Edmett was buried in Maidstone Cemetery in Kent with full military honours.

Private **Stanley Whittal Harding** did not make it to England, but died of his wounds in Boulogne. Harding was from Wandsworth

Lieutenant Arthur Edmett (Tonbridge School)

Private Stanley Harding (de Ruvigny)

left: Rifleman William Charity (de Ruvigny)
right: Private William Evans (de Ruvigny)

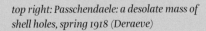

top right: Passchendaele: a desolate mass of shell holes, spring 1918 (Deraeve)

and had attended Battersea Grammar School. He married Grace Lilian Dunstan in July 1913. Harding joined the 28th Battalion London Regiment, better known as the Artists Rifles in October 1915. During the attack on Passchendaele on 30 October 1917 the battalion was shot to pieces by German artillery and Harding was one of the wounded. He was taken to a Canadian hospital in Boulogne,[428] where he died on 30 March 1918 aged 29. Private Harding is buried in Boulogne Eastern Cemetery. Rifleman **William Henry Charity,** who was with the 9th Battalion Rifle Brigade, died the following day (31 March 1918) in a hospital in England. Charity, a grocer from Gloucester, was born in Hereford and joined up in June 1916. He was severely wounded on 24 August during a German artillery barrage at Inverness Copse, south of the Menin Road. Charity was successfully evacuated from the front line and subsequently ended up in Graylingwell Hospital in Chichester, where he died, as mentioned above, on the last day of March 1918. The 40-year-old Rifleman Charity is buried in Hereford Cemetery. He left a wife and two young daughters of 10 and 11 respectively.[429]

Private **Williams Harkeness Evans** was wounded at Zillebeke on 17 August 1917 in at least 14 places in the head, arms and legs. However, this was not the first time that the young bank clerk from Walhamstow had been wounded. He had previously sustained wounds to the head and knee at Neuve-Eglise at the end of October 1916. After his recovery he refused the offer of a commission and returned to the front, where with his unit, the 14th Battalion London Regiment, he saw a great deal of heavy fighting. He was wounded again at Zillebeke and was sent to Gloucester Red Cross Hospital in England, where his brother Leslie Wilson Evans was also a patient, having been severely wounded in Italy. Private Harkeness Evans was granted his final discharge from the army on 20 December 1918 as his wounds were too severe to permit continued service. Evans, who was then twenty years old, died in hospital three weeks later on 11 January 1919.[430] He is buried in Barnwood (St. Lawrence) Churchyard.

13 The war in the air 1917

The war in the air

When the First World War broke out the role played by aircraft was very limited indeed. Flying was still in its infancy in 1914 and reconnaissance and observation were then the most important tasks. By the end of the war, however, aircraft were an integral part of warfare and would remain so until the present day. Not only could planes obtain useful information about the situation on the ground; they could also guide the artillery; provide support to ground troops; and carry out bombing raids. 1917 was a major turning point in the role of aircraft in the war. From then on the army high command consistently involved the aerial arm in the preparation and execution of every offensive.

Crashed German Gotha G.IV bomber in Berg op Zoom near Torhout. Two of its crew of three (all from Fliegerabteilung 40) did not survive the crash, 17 August 1917 (Deraeve) >

The planes the army had at its disposal in 1914 had been totally surpassed by 1918. The need to have faster and better planes with ever more powerful engines than those of the enemy led to a rapid evolution of new technologies and successively improved models. Yet it was not only the aircraft industry which underwent an exponential expansion. The air forces of the various countries also expanded on a similar scale. Britain originally had two separate air arms: the Royal Flying Corps (RFC) for the army and the Royal Naval Air Service (RNAS) for the navy. These two air services were combined in April 1918 to form an independent branch of the armed forces: the Royal Air Force (RAF). Weaponry likewise underwent a rapid evolution: from hand guns to several different models of machine gun specifically designed for aerial combat. Like any other branch of the armed forces, the Royal Flying Corps also had a clearly defined hierarchical organization. Every Brigade of the Royal Flying Corps had a Corps Wing and an Army Wing, each with a number of Squadrons. The

Corps Wing concentrated on guiding the artillery, reconnaissance and observation, while the Army Wing concentrated on offensive operations against the enemy air force.[431]

Pilots also became increasingly important during the war. Originally, they still waived to each other in the air, but soon began to take weapons with them in the cockpit. When the first machine guns were installed, the era of genuine aerial combat had begun. Originally pilots made high-altitude, solo patrol flights, but they soon began to fly in formation. New tactics were taught in training and battle-hardened and experienced pilots regularly came to demonstrate new techniques. The pilots were on the whole very young: most of them were barely twenty. In 1917 the average life expectancy

< Probable remains of the Spad 7 single-seater fighter flown by Second Lieutenant Harry Ronald Hicks of no. 19 Squadron, which crashed on 12 October at Broodseinde. The photograph was taken on 17 October 1917 (AWM E4648)

of a recently trained flyer amounted to only a few weeks. Despite the popular image that airmen lived a life of luxury and were scarcely exposed to the dangers of the front, they came under fire every day and numerous pilots and planes were lost.

The Battle of Passchendaele

During the Battle of Passchendaele the air forces of both sides played an important role. They had a twofold mission. In the first place they were required to keep enemy planes out of the air so that the allies enjoyed absolute dominion over the skies. Secondly, all the lines of the German defensive positions had to be photographed and mapped. The reconnaissance patrols undertaken for this purpose and the escort missions required to protect them began several weeks before the ground offensive itself.[432]

Reconnaissance, observation and aerial photography

One of the RFC's most important tasks throughout the entire war was that of observing the enemy. Pilots flew thousands of reconnaissance flights and their observers took countless aerial photographs. They photographed not only the enemy trenches, but also took extensive photographic series of their own positions. Nor did they restrict their attentions to the front lines: supply lines, troop encampments, railways and other important points were also photographed. Once on the ground these photographs were developed and their contents meticulously transcribed onto detailed maps. In this way the allies knew exactly where the German lines were in relation to their own positions. During these missions pilots and their observers were easy prey for German fighters. Their planes were slow, making them vulnerable to fighter aircraft built for speed and manoeuvrability. After considerable losses escort patrols were eventually sent to protect them.

Lieutenant **Cecil Dunbar Hutchinson** of No. 57 Squadron was barely 26 when he died of his wounds. Hutchinson had been a student at University College Nottingham and had belonged to the Officers' Training Corps (OTC) since August 1914. At the end of November 1914 he applied for a temporary commission as an officer with the infantry. The university's letter of recommendation described him

as: *'an excellent candidate – quite fit to take charge of a platoon'*.[433] In early December he received a commission as a Second Lieutenant with the 7th battalion of the South Staffordshire Regiment with whom he sailed to Mudros, Greece in July 1915. He participated in the landing and early hostilities at Sulva Bay in Gallipoli, Turkey, on 7 August. After heavy fighting on the Turkish peninsula, the battalion was evacuated and transferred to Egypt. From July 1916 he was on the Western Front, where he was promoted to Lieutenant in August and made a Temporary Captain in September 1916. When he returned to England he underwent extensive training as an observer. This also included training and practice in operating machine guns during the flight.[434] At the end of May or early June 1917 he was posted as an observer to No. 57 Squadron, which was then based in Boisdinghem near Saint-Omer. On 10 August he took off around 6.00 p.m. with Second Lieutenant Arthur Norman Barlow (aircraft no. DH.4) on a reconnaissance flight and with orders to take aerial photographs of the German lines. The inexperienced young officers in their slow two-seater were shot down by *Leutnant* Max von Müller above Ingelmunster.[435] It was his second kill of that day and the 21st in his flying career.[436] A few days later Hutchinson's family received a telegram from the War Office: *'Regret to inform you Lt C.D. Hutchinson (...) was reported missing August 10th.'* It was not until 3 October 1917 that they received more news: *'now reported wounded Prisoner of War.'* Hutchinson's father, Arthur, replied immediately, wanting to contact his son, who had fallen into German hands: *'[we] shall be very grateful if [you] will give us the address of the Hospital or Camp in Germany where we may communicate with him. Can you do this?'* However, the authorities did not have any further information. At the end of the month the news came from Germany that Lieutenant Hutchinson had died of his wounds on 12 August 1917, although it was to be the beginning of January 1918 before official confirmation was received. The German Red Cross sent a message via neutral Denmark saying that Hutchinson *'died on 12.8.17 as a consequence of his severe stomach wound in the field hospital at Meulebeke.'* The unfortunate Hutchinson was subsequently buried in Meulebeke. His pilot, Arthur Barlow, had more luck, however. He survived both the dogfight and the crash and was taken prisoner. In late February 1920 the family received Hutchinson's possessions from Germany: a cigarette

Lieutenant Cecil Dunbar Hutchinson (Perry)

Second Lieutenant Frederick Ewen Baldwin Falkiner (College of St Columba)

Lieutenant Leslie Glendower Humphries (Lloyds Bank)

case, a whistle on a cord and other personal effects which had been carefully preserved by the German authorities and which they were now able to return to the family after the war.[437] In the mid-1920s Hutchinson's body was exhumed and reburied in Harlebeke, New British Cemetery.

Reconnaissance planes were slower and more difficult to defend than other aircraft and many of those sent on reconnaissance missions never returned. Like Hutchinson, Second Lieutenant **Frederick Ewen Baldwin Falkiner** and Lieutenant Cecil Barry also belonged to No. 57 Squadron. Both men were from Ireland: Falkiner was from Dublin and Barry was from Kanturk, near Cork. At the outbreak of war Falkiner already had some military experience. He was a member of the College of St. Columba Officers' Training Corps and of Dublin University Officers' Training Corps. Falkiner enlisted in Dublin as a private with the 7th Royal Dublin Fusiliers in September 1914 and was made a corporal that same month, later seeing action in the Middle East. He landed with the 10th Division in Sulva Bay, in Gallipoli, as a machine gunner on 7 August 1915, where his unit besieged the Turkish positions on Chocolate Hill. After a week, however, he was hospitalized with a severe case of diarrhoea and remained in hospital until September, when he was posted to the Base Depot in Mudros.[438] In early October he rejoined his unit which had then arrived in Salonika.[439] Falkiner was then sent to the Balkans, where he was made a Lance-Sergeant in the first week of the new year. In June 1916 he embarked for Egypt, from where he was sent to England for officer training and was made a Temporary Second Lieutenant with the 15th Royal Irish Rifles at the beginning of 1917. In the spring of that year, however, Falkiner was trained as an observer with the Royal Flying Corps and subsequently posted to No. 57 Squadron. His brother, George Stride Falkiner, who was a Second Lieutenant with the 2nd Battalion Royal Dublin Fusiliers was killed on 16 August 1917, not far from Vampire Farm in Zonnebeke. In the early morning of 21 August 1917 Barry, who was piloting the machine, and Falkiner, as observer, were on a reconnaissance mission above the border town of Ascq when their plane was intercepted by *Oberleutnant* Ernst Udet of *Jagdstaffel* (Jasta) 37. The Irishmen's plane was shot down and shattered into pieces on impact. Neither Falkiner, aged 22

nor Barry, aged 20, survived the crash. This was Udet's 9th kill of a future total of 62.[440] In early October Falkiner's mother was notified by the War Office that *'a message has been dropped from a German aeroplane into our lines'*, stating that Falkiner was dead. Yet it was not until March 1920 that more details were known concerning the fate of the two men. The British Military Mission in Berlin gained access to German documentary sources. *'According to the German records this officer died on 22-8-1917 and was buried in the cemetery Praet-Bosch, grave no. 339 together with Lieutenant C. Barry.'*[441] The German cemetery where both men were buried after being shot down is better known today by the name of *Deutscher Soldatenfriedhof Vladslo*. In the early 1920s the British dead were exhumed and transferred to British cemeteries. Second Lieutenant Falkiner and Lieutenant Barry thus found their last resting place in Tyne Cot Cemetery.

Planes that were shot down did not always fall behind the German lines, however. On 16 September a biplane carrying Lieutenant **Leslie Glendower Humphries** and his observer Second Lieutenant F. L. Steben was shot down above Glencorse Wood in Zonnebeke.[442] Their aircraft, a reconnaissance plane, was probably shot down by *Hauptmann* Rudolf Berthold, who downed two reconnaissance planes above Zonnebeke that same day,[443] being respectively his 18th and 19th kills in a career total of 44.[444] The plane and its two occupants fell right behind the Australian lines northwest of Glencorse Wood. Steben was wounded, but Humphries was killed outright. The young Lieutenant Humphries was not yet eighteen when he enlisted in the British army in June 1916 . He was then too young for active service and was placed in the reserve. Humphries had attended King Edward's High School in Birmingham for four years and could handle a motorcycle, for which he did not, however, have a driving licence. When war broke out he was working for Lloyds Bank. In October he was finally able to join the 28th Battalion Artists Rifles Officers' Training Corps with the rank of Private and was accepted for officer training in early March 1917. He was commissioned as a Second Lieutenant at the end of April 1917 and underwent training as a pilot, later being posted to No. 4 Squadron, which was based in Abele, near Poperinghe. He had probably not been at the front very long when his plane was shot down. Humphries's parents received a telegram informing them of his death on 9 October, but it was not until March 1918 that they learned where their son had been buried. After the crash Humphries had been buried *'near Pill Box, Westhoek Ridge, Zonnebeke'*. In late August 1919 the family received further news about their son's last resting place: *'(...) it has been found necessary to exhume the bodies buried in this area and to re-inter them, and the body of the above mentioned officer has been removed and buried in Hooge Crater Cemetery East of Ypres. The new grave has been duly marked with a cross bearing all particulars and registered in this office.'*[445] The grave does not give Humphries' correct rank, however. He appears to this day as Lieutenant instead of Second Lieutenant.

Aerial duels and patrols

Protecting reconnaissance missions automatically resulted in aerial combat. The Royal Flying Corps carried out daily offensive patrols aimed at shooting down German planes so as to secure dominance and superiority in the air. Ace pilot Rhys Davids[446] explained: *'Our job is to see that the Boche does not get a chance to do any work in the air at all – I mean useful work like bombing and observation. What advantage do we gain? We just gain the supremacy of the air, bless you, that's all: we'll 'ave a notice board put up to the effect. AERIAL PARK. PRIVATE. HUN TRESPASSERS WILL BE PROSECUTED. And we keep our machines safe.'*[447] These daily patrols almost always ended with dangerous and acrobatic aerial duels. Initially the planes would fly in neat formation, but as soon as the enemy was spotted the pilots split up in order to adopt the best possible position from which to engage the enemy. This usually ended up in lethal individual dogfights, although these were often indecisive. Attacks sometimes had to be abandoned when the one or both planes ran out of ammunition or when their guns jammed. These duels could also become personal. The planes flew so close to each other that it was easy to see the face of the enemy and eye contact was often made. The impressive acrobatic stunts were actually not for show, but only a technique for surviving in the air. Pilots with poor flying skills or of with insufficient knowledge of their machines were not likely to survive a dogfight. In the air the weakest were the first to be eliminated. Successful pilots were seen as genuine heroes. Aircraft and dogfights could be seen from the ground and earned great respect and pilots were soon known as the

knights of the 20th century. Nevertheless, it was still a war in which the smallest mistake could cost the life of even the best and most experienced pilots. The Germans sometimes dropped lists of dead pilots and their observers onto the allied lines. The British authorities never regarded these lists as official, although they were generally accurate. These death rolls often included the names of some of the best pilots. Even those who seemed immortal pilots were still vulnerable to the machine guns of an equally strong enemy.

In 1917 Major Blomfield collected the best flyers together in No. 56 Squadron, which was to consist only of ace pilots. Most of them had a great deal of experience, which made them less likely to commit beginner's mistakes.[448] Among the men of No. 56 Squadron were Major James McCudden, Captain Albert Ball, Captain Reginald Hoidge, Lieutenant Arthur Percival Foley Rhys Davids, Second Lieutenant Robert Hugh Sloley and many others. At the end of the war No. 56 Squadron had at least 427 kills to its name.[449] Despite this great success, however, the unit also lost many pilots, of whom forty were killed. One of these was Captain **Wilfrid Alan Fleming**, an

Two crew members of a British plane, after being shot down, probably in Beveren-Roulers, October 1917 (Deraeve)

Captain Wilfrid Alan Fleming (Perry)

Second Lieutenant Robert Hugh Sloley
(www.theaerodrome.com)

experienced officer, who had registered to sit the entrance examination for the Royal Military College at Sandhurst in August 1908. He was then eighteen years old. His father, Allan Stafford, had been a civil servant in Pakokku in the British colony of Burma and lived in Woolton, Liverpool, during the war. Fleming was a boarder at Harrow School in Middlesex from 1904 and at the beginning of February 1909 passed the examination as a Gentleman Cadet and began his training as an officer. A year later he was given a commission as a Second Lieutenant with the Devonshire Regiment and was already a Lieutenant when war broke out. He sustained a minor wound to his right leg at the end of September 1914 and was admitted to a hospital in Nantes. The War Office notified his family: *'condition quite satisfactory.'* Fleming joined the 14th Infantry Brigade as a Captain in late 1915. Exactly when he underwent training as a pilot is not clear, but this was probably in 1916. On 10 August 1917 Fleming set out on patrol towards Roulers, Izegem and Kortrijk. Just after midday he became involved in a dogfight above Dadizele, probably with Leutnant Stock. The German bullets found their target and Fleming's plane went down. He did not survive the crash. On the British side no one knew what had happened, however. Fleming was listed as missing and the family were sent a telegram to that effect. Soon afterwards a German plane dropped a message over the British lines *'in which it is stated that he is dead.'* The *Norddeutsche Allgemeine Zeitung* also published Fleming's name in September 1917 in their *'list of English Air losses'*: *'Sopwith: One-seaters. – No. A8923: Capt. Fleming.'* The accuracy of the newspaper announcement clearly shows that pilots enjoyed a considerable status in 1917. Shooting down an enemy plane was seen as a great victory. The German newspaper even gives the serial number and model of the plane concerned. When the family were notified of this they immediately wrote to the War Office requesting that Fleming's name *'shall not be published as having died in German hands.'* The reason for their objection to this is not known. It was not until January 1918, however, that an official letter arrived from Germany with the precise circumstances of Fleming's death. Information about missing pilots was routinely obtained via the British Red Cross and at the end of January 1918 a communiqué from the German Red Cross sent via Copenhagen conveyed the news that Fleming *went down with his plane on 10.8.17 at Dadizeele. He was bur-*

ied in Ledeghem cemetery. In early August 1917 the War Office also received a report from a Belgian soldier who claimed to be able to identify his grave and said that *'Captain Fleming's relations could also obtain the wristlet watch, he wore when killed, from a man who bought it of a German soldier a few moments after the aviator's death, with the idea of finding one day the friends of the deceased.'* How this Belgian soldier from Dieppe came upon this information behind the lines is not known. Nor is the War Office's reply to this letter. After the war Fleming's grave was indeed found in the German military cemetery of Ledegem.[450] As in the case of Hutchinson, Fleming's body was eventually reburied in Harlebeke New British Cemetery.

Second Lieutenant **Robert Hugh Sloley**, another talented pilot from the same Squadron as Fleming, was also killed. Sloley, a South African, was the son of Sir Herbert Sloley and came from an upper class background. He originally served in the Royal Artillery, but, after training as a pilot, he was posted to No. 56 Squadron in 1917 and notched up eight kills in only two months in Flanders. On 20 August he managed to escape an attack from a German Albatros fighter above Moorslede and – using acrobatic flying – was ultimately able to shoot down his attacker. This was his second kill. Two days later he shot down another German machine during a morning patrol above Houthulst. His successful patrols came to an abrupt end, however, when he was attacked by four German planes above Westrozebeke during a mission on 1 October 1917. Flight Commander James McCudden saw what happened. Sloley was *'circling inside four Albatros scouts, and as I glanced I saw a Hun, who was turning inside the SE at twenty five yards range, shoot the SE's left wings off and the British machine went down in a spin with one pair of wings left. It was poor Sloley, who was, as usual, where the Huns were the thickest.'*[451] Sloley's body was never recovered and he is remembered today on the Arras Flying Services Memorial, Faubourg d'Amiens Cemetery, Arras.

The German pilot who shot Sloley down was *Leutnant* Xavier Dannhuber, who proved quite successful in Flanders and obtained at least ten kills during the Battle of Passchendaele. Eight days after shooting down Sloley he brought down yet another British machine. This time his prey was Captain **William Victor Trevor Rooper**.[452]

Rooper had been made a Lance Corporal on his enlistment on 5 August 1914. He was only seventeen, but had some previous military experience with the Officers' Training Corps of Charterhouse School in Surrey and was given a commission with the 24th Denbighshire Yeomanry just before Christmas 1914. After training he joined no. 1 Squadron, which was based in Bailleul on the French-Belgian border near Loker in the summer of 1917. He shot down his first German *Albatros* above Beselare in late July 1917 and was made a Captain in mid-September. However, Rooper himself was shot down above Polygon Wood on 9 October. He managed to land the plane behind the allied lines, but died of his wounds later that same day.[453] He was buried in Bailleul.

Other famous German flyers also brought down many allied planes. *Oberleutnant* Otto Schmidt, Hauptmann Rudolf Berthold, *Leutnant* Kurt Wüsthoff, *Leutnant* Julius Buckler and *Leutnant* Werner Voss are only a few of the best known. Voss had at least 48 kills to his name. On 16 August 1917 he shot the Sopwith Camel piloted by Captain **Noel William Ward Webb** out of the sky over the battlefields of Flanders. Webb was an experienced pilot, who had originally been posted to No. 25 Squadron after completing his training at the end of June 1916. From July 1917 the 20-year-old Ward, who was from London, was a member of No. 70 Squadron. Just three days before his death he had brought down three enemy planes over Diksmuide and damaged four others, for which he was posthumously awarded a second Military Cross. *'By his spirit and gallantry he has set a fine example which has inspired the pilots of his flight to successfully attack enemy formations many times more numerous than their own.'*[454] His body was never found and he is thus remembered today on the Arras Flying Services Memorial.

Accidents

That young, newly trained, pilots only survived a few weeks at the front is no tall story. The stories of pilots who were killed almost as soon as they arrived due to their inexperience are legion. The enemy was quick to spot them in a dogfight and they often got into difficulties because of their limited flying abilities. Some flew too close to the ground and crashed or collided with other planes in full flight.

This was the fate of Second Lieutenant **John Machaffie** and Second Lieutenant **Robert Dudley Wilson McKergow**. Machaffie was from Manitoba, Canada, where his father was with the Home Bank of Canada in Toronto. Machaffie received a good education, attending Trinity College School from January 1913 to January 1914 and when war broke out in August 1914 he was a pupil at the Kelvin Technical High School. He probably enlisted in the Canadian army in the autumn of 1915, when he was eighteen. In late December 1916 he was recommended for transfer to the Royal Flying Corps and Machaffie was sent to a training camp for *'elementary instruction in aviation'* at the end of April 1917. In May he was given a temporary commission as a Second Lieutenant with the Royal Flying Corps.[455]

McKergow, whose father was a Lieutenant Colonel with the British army, was also from a good family. Before his transfer to the Royal Flying Corps, McKergow had been with the 5th Dragoon Guards. He was made a Second Lieutenant and flew five months as an observer in No. 70 Squadron in 1916. He was not yet twenty. After undergoing training as a pilot, he – like Machaffie – was also posted to No. 29 Squadron, which was then based in Poperinghe. Both flyers had been at the front for exactly a month. On 21 September they went out on patrol with other planes, but on the way back to base they collided with each other in mid-air, both machines going into a fatal spin. Neither man survived the crash. The families were notified that their sons had been killed in action.[456] Their limited flying experience was probably one of the causes of the accident. Machaffie and McKergow are buried next to each other in Ypres Reservoir Cemetery.

Second Lieutenant **George Cowie** had also not been at the front very long when he crashed behind German lines on 22 October. Cowie, whose father was a Captain with the Royal Army Medical Corps, was from Mortlach, Banffshire. He joined the Officer Training Corps at Rugby School in Easter 1913 and held the rank of Lance Corporal when he left school in December 1916 and was recommended for the Royal Flying Corps. He had just turned 18 *'and is well reported on.'* He began his training as a pilot in the spring of 1917 and was made Second Lieutenant. It is not known when he first arrived at the front, but this was probably during the summer of 1917. He was posted to No. 54 Squadron, which was then engaged in heavy aerial fighting

Captain William Victor Trevor Rooper (Perry)

left: Captain Noel William Ward Webb (www. theaerodrome.com)
right: Second Lieutenant John Machaffie (Perry)

with the German air force. On 22 October Cowie disappeared behind the German lines with his Sopwith Pup and was listed as missing. It was to be a number of months before more was known about the fate of the missing officer, however. During the war information about missing pilots was often sought via diplomatic channels. In this case liaison between the Red Cross and the *Bureau International de la Paix* in Bern, Switzerland, succeeded in shedding more light on what had happened to Cowie. The information was sent directly to Cowie's father, who then informed the War Office: '*on 22nd 10-17 two sopwith pup flying machines were destroyed. In one of them Lt Percy Goodbehere born on 10-3-92 at Manchester now in Karlsruhe a Baden was found. The aviator in the other was found dead family name is unknown the only name that could be stated was 'George'. We therefore suppose that the date being the same it concerns the missing Lt George Cowie R.F.C.*'[457] The pilot of the other Sopwith Pup was made a prisoner of war (both planes had come down behind German lines). Cowie was dead, however, and was buried in the German military cemetery *Praet-Bosch*. As in the case of Falkiner and Barry, Cowie's body was also exhumed in the early 1920s and was transferred to Tyne Cot Cemetery in Passchendaele.

The remains of Machaffie and McKergow's planes after their fatal collision (O'Connor)

Guiding ground troops and artillery spotting

The Royal Flying Corps also had other tasks apart from reconnaissance, aerial photography and patrolling, which included guiding troops on the ground and artillery spotting. Guiding troops on the ground was no easy task. Pilots had to fly at a low level over the battlefield while fighting was going on below and find where troops had advanced. On the featureless lunar landscape of No Man's Land it was often very difficult for the infantry to establish exactly where they were. The Royal Flying Corps provided support to the troops on the ground during every phase of the Battle of Passchendaele. Special symbols were painted onto the fuselage so that the planes could be recognized. The instructions for the ground troops were simple: '*The most advanced Infantry will signal their positions on the aeroplane calling Klaxon Horn or showing white lights by lighting WHITE flares and signalling with Watson fans. Flares must be lit in the bottom of the trenches or in the bottom of shell holes.*'[458] The infantry was generally not very keen on being ordered to fire white flares as these would,

after all, reveal their position to the enemy as well to their own planes.[459]

Artillery spotting was a completely different task. The Royal Flying Corps used techniques which had first been used during the Battle of the Somme. Artillery barrages were of fundamental importance to the success of every ground attack and when it came to taking out strong points precision of fire was absolutely vital. The job of the Royal Flying Corps was to provide accurate guidance to the artillery from the air. By precise aerial observations RFC observers overflying the battlefield could pass on very precise data allowing the gunners to make re-adjustments to the gun settings after an initial few rounds had been fired. Specialized personnel on the ground forwarded these coded wireless messages to the artillery batteries which could then immediately act on the information provided.[460]

Predictably, these spotter aircraft came under heavy attacks from German planes, who had every interest in seeing them driven from

Second Lieutenant Robert Dudley Wilson McKergow (O'Connor)

Second Lieutenant George Cowie (Perry)

British Havilland DH.4 of no. 57 Squadron, which made an emergency landing in Roulers after a dogfight with a fighter from Jasta 18, killing the observer-gunner Second Lieutenant Inglis (Deraeve)

left: Captain A.L. MacDonald (Perry)
middle: Second Lieutenant Francis John Ashburton Wodehouse (Perry)
right: Second Lieutenant William Harold Trant Williams (Perry)

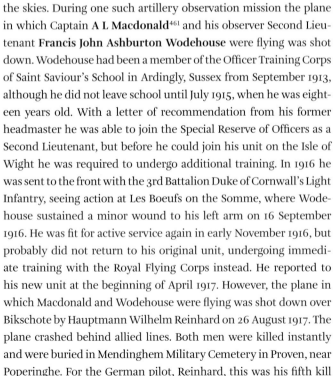

the skies. During one such artillery observation mission the plane in which Captain **A L Macdonald**[461] and his observer Second Lieutenant **Francis John Ashburton Wodehouse** were flying was shot down. Wodehouse had been a member of the Officer Training Corps of Saint Saviour's School in Ardingly, Sussex from September 1913, although he did not leave school until July 1915, when he was eighteen years old. With a letter of recommendation from his former headmaster he was able to join the Special Reserve of Officers as a Second Lieutenant, but before he could join his unit on the Isle of Wight he was required to undergo additional training. In 1916 he was sent to the front with the 3rd Battalion Duke of Cornwall's Light Infantry, seeing action at Les Boeufs on the Somme, where Wodehouse sustained a minor wound to his left arm on 16 September 1916. He was fit for active service again in early November 1916, but probably did not return to his original unit, undergoing immediate training with the Royal Flying Corps instead. He reported to his new unit at the beginning of April 1917. However, the plane in which Macdonald and Wodehouse were flying was shot down over Bikschote by Hauptmann Wilhelm Reinhard on 26 August 1917. The plane crashed behind allied lines. Both men were killed instantly and were buried in Mendinghem Military Cemetery in Proven, near Poperinghe. For the German pilot, Reinhard, this was his fifth kill

of a future total of twenty. In early July 1918 Reinhard himself was killed in a plane crash in Germany.[462]

Ground support and bombing

The other major tasks of the Royal Flying Corps were providing support to ground troops during attacks and the bombing of tactically significant targets. Supporting troops on the ground was relatively straightforward: flying low over the enemy lines and doing as much damage as possible with machine guns or small bombs. Bombing important tactical targets was a job that was entrusted exclusively to bombers. However, their objective was not – as it was later to be in the Second World War in the days of Bomber Command – to destroy the entire German war machine, but rather to destroy or seriously damage major German installations just behind the front line. This was also a dangerous job, as the enemy planes responsible for protecting German air space were in a constant state of readiness.

Second Lieutenant **William Harold Trant Williams** was fired on by a group of German planes during a support mission above Polygon Wood on 16 August 1917. The enemy bullets finally hit his machine above Houthulst Forest and he crashed behind enemy lines. Williams, who had been wounded in the crash, was picked up by Ger-

Lieutenant Hew Wardrop Brooke Rickards (de Ruvigny)

Second Lieutenant Ronald Heathcote Corbishley (Hill)

man soldiers who took him to a field hospital, but he died of his wounds six days later. Williams was buried in a German military cemetery, but his body was exhumed by the British authorities after the war and taken to Harlebeke Military Cemetery. Williams was an intelligent young officer, who had just passed his first year at Liverpool University. However, rather than continue studying, he decided to join the British army. Having previously been a member of the Officers' Training Corps he was immediately able to undergo officer training and then went on to train as a pilot with the Royal Flying Corps. In the summer of 1917 he joined his new unit at the front at the age of only nineteen. The shooting down of Williams's plane was claimed by none other than *Rittmeister* Manfred Freiherr von Richthofen, better known as 'the Red Baron', who had no less than 80 acknowledged victories over British machines! He was the terror of the skies from September 1916 to April 1918.[463] Later in that same month, however, von Richthofen was himself shot down over France.

On 28 July 1917 Lieutenant **Hew Wardrop Brooke Rickards** and Second Lieutenant **Ronald Heathcote Corbishley** were on their way back to their base in Boisdinghem, together with several other bombers of No. 57 Squadron, aboard their Airco DH.4 bomber (Airco is an abbreviation of *Aircraft Manufacturing Company*). They had just carried out a successful raid on the German airfield at Ingelmunster when they suddenly came under fire from a group of German fighters. Three British Airco DH.4s were eventually shot down. Leutnant Tuexen and Leutnant Czermak both claimed a victory that day against a British bomber, but which of them it was who shot down Rickards and Corbishley is not known. Both officers were listed as missing. Rickards' wartime career is an interesting one. He attended Uppingham school until December 1913, after which he went to France with the idea of learning the language and then using his French to secure a job with the Egyptian Civil Service. When war broke out a few months after his arrival in France he immediately joined the French Foreign Legion, with whom he served until February 1915. Rickards then received a commission as a Second Lieutenant in the Royal Field Artillery and served with them at the front in France until May 1916. At his own request Rickards was then

posted to the Royal Flying Corps as an observer. On 26 November 1916 he was wounded in the left thigh by a German bullet during a flight over the German lines at Puisieux, south of Arras. He was fit for active service again at the end of January 1917, but, instead of returning to the front, underwent training as a pilot. He rejoined the Royal Flying Corps as a Lieutenant in May 1917. Corbishley's career was equally distinguished. He had joined the 12th battalion Royal Fusiliers as a Private in September 1914, was quickly made a Lance-Corporal and received a commission as a Second Lieutenant with the 8th Battalion Devonshire Regiment in late July 1916. He probably joined the Royal Flying Corps some time in 1917. The circumstances of surrounding the deaths of two men were not to be clarified until after the war, although a great deal of the documentation then compiled has been preserved to the present day. A report of a '*Special Mission Searching for Missing Soldiers*' is perhaps the most interesting. Investigations were undertaken in the area around Roulers, '*resulting in the discovery of the graves of three unknown aviators at Wielsbeke (...) It was ascertained that these three men had been brought down with their machines on 28.7.17.*' One plane had crashed in the village itself. The pilot was killed, but the observer, Lieutenant A.C. Malloch, was made a prisoner of war and sent to Ghent. According to the report the pilot had a tobacco pouch and a cheque book on him from which his name could be established as: 'De Corbishley'. The other plane had crashed just outside the village. '*It's [sic] two occupants were both killed. Monsieur Brabandere*[464] *had been able to preserve some portions of underclothes, i.e. 1. A shirt with the initials 'H.N.S.' and a collar marked 'Skeffington.'*[465] *2. A sock marked with the initial 'R', a 15 in. collar and an unmarked shirt made by Harrods.*' The two planes mentioned in the report, were two of the three bombers intercepted by German fighters on their way back to base after their successful mission. Exactly where Rickards and Corbishley crashed is difficult to establish as the report mixes up the names of the pilots and their observers. Corbishley was an observer with Rickards and not with Skefftington. The two dead pilots and the observer were buried behind the church at Wielsbeke. However, once their identities had been determined in January 1920, a further difficulty arose. Rickards' parents appreciated the problem: '*I must point out however that it is impossible for the grave to be registered until it has been defi-*

nitely ascertained in which of the three graves that have been discovered my son's body lies. As I understand thro' friends of our's [sic] who have visited the spot (...), that the graves are simply marked as those of "three unknown Airmen".' After consultation with what was then the Imperial War Graves Commission (IWGC), it appeared that the bodies of the three Britons would have to be exhumed in order to identify them.[466] When this was done is not clear, however. The three British pilots are still buried in the churchyard of Wielsbeke.

The day before the bombing mission over Ingelmunster the same Squadron had carried out another raid on the German airfield at Heule. On their way back to base a German plane fired on the British machines above Houthulst, bringing one of them down. The two occupants of the British plane did not survive the crash. The observer, Second Lieutenant Noel Roderick Rayner was killed instantly.[467] His companion, Lieutenant **Arthur James Lewis O'Beirne**, was severely wounded and was taken to a hospital, where he died of his wounds the following day. O'Beirne, the oldest son of a British army recruiting officer from Warwick, had enjoyed an excellent education: Summerfields School, Radley College and Exeter College in Oxford. May 1914 found him on his plantation in Nairobi in British East Africa and when war broke out he immediately enlisted in the East African Mounted Rifles as a Trooper, but was back in England nine months later where he was given a commission as a Second Lieutenant with the Queen's Own Oxfordshire Hussars. O'Beirne was transferred to the Royal Flying Corps in November 1916, joining No. 57 Squadron as an aviator in mid-July 1917. O'Beirne's brother, who was as an observer with the Royal Flying Corps[468], was also killed when his plane was shot down over Vimy Ridge during an observation flight on 3 April 1917.[469] O'Beirne and Rayner were buried in Coxyde Military Cemetery.

Lieutenant Arthur James Lewis O'Beirne (de Ruvigny)

Wreckage of the British Martinsyde 'Elephant' fighter G/102 of the no. 27 Squadron, brought down after a direct hit over Sleihage, Lieutenant Goodwin did not survive the crash (Deraeve) >

The war in the air:
Lieutenant Arthur Rhys Davids
56th Squadron Royal Flying Corps

Eton College

Arthur Percival Foley Rhys Davids was born on 27 September 1897 as the second child of Thomas Rhys Davids and Caroline Augusta Foley. His father Thomas was a prominent professor of Indian civilization and his wife had a university degree in Indian languages and religions. Arthur proved a particularly intelligent child and his parents sent him to Doctor Summerfields Preparatory School in Oxford in 1907. From that year onwards he began an extensive correspondence with his mother and two sisters which was to continue until just before his death. He started at Eton College in May 1911 where he obtained extremely high marks in Latin and Greek. In July 1913, despite the impediment of a stutter, Rhys Davids got the highest examination results in the entire school. He joined Eton's Officers Training Corps at the beginning of 1914. He was then sixteen years old.

Royal Flying Corps

In July 1914 Rhys Davids volunteered to serve in the Royal Flying Corps. In a description of his first flight he wrote to his sister: *'It's absolutely ripping!'*. Although he enjoyed flying he missed school life. Moreover, life in the army was not for him and he particularly missed the lack of companionship of people of his own social class: *'My darling Ma, you also can't imagine how much I loathe the army (...). I just drift on quite mechanically. Nobody except the little few I have collected around me understands me in the least: above all nearly everybody is so common and so sordid – especially after Eaton (...).'* Rhys Davids got his wings in January 1917 and was selected in early March of that year for the newly formed 56th Squadron, which was intended to be an elite unit and only ace pilots were eligible. He expressed his joy in a letter: *'Gee! ain't I bucked? Just think Mums: I shall be with my friends Muspratt and Potts; we have for flight commanders the two best fighting pilots in the RFC and, on top of it all, as you know, the best scout machine that has yet been brought out. Oy!'*

France

At the beginning of April 1917 the 56th Squadron moved to France. Rhys Davids's landing after the first test flight on French soil was nothing if not dramatic. His plane broke in two and had to be extensively repaired. Despite being in the best squadron of the entire Royal Flying Corps, he was not wildly enthusiastic about the other pilots. *'I really am getting along jolly well, but (...) there are only one or two people in the squadron I have the faintest hope of making a real pal of, and it is next to impossible that I can do even that. They are all just the 'ordinary good fellows' with nothing remarkable about them; none of them have any real intellectual ambitions. BUT I AM IN FRANCE AND DOING THE REAL THING AT LAST!!!'* Rhys Davids's first dog-fight gives pause for thought as a number of pilots from the 56th were killed that day. Rhys Davids also came under fire from *Leutnant* Kurt Wolff, who was on patrol with *Leutnant* Werner Voss. Rhys Davids's plane was severely damaged and he was forced to make an emergency landing. Three pilots were still missing that evening, including the famous Captain Albert Ball, with 44 kills to his name. A few weeks

‹ Second Lieutenant Arthur Rhys Davids
(Revell)

Rhys Davids (middle) with Keith Muspratt (left) and Maxwell Coote (right) (Revell)

and cricket into a cocked hat'. He liked to take risks and was berated for his reckless behaviour by his Flight Commander on more than one occasion. He confessed to his mother: *'But, O my old Ma, one can't lay down rules while on mere earth for people in fighting patrol in the air. You are a different man – at least you aren't a man at all, that is I am not – you are a devil incarnate filled with the dazzling thrill of playing the best game God ever created, mad after Huns and just forget everything else but showing the old Hun that there's only one man fit to be in the air and not two. And the only way you are sobered down is when you see fifteen red beggars coming for three of you, on which occasion you beetle off for dear life. And I can say I have been a cunning foul, and I have given the old Hun little chance of shooting straight.'* His behaviour in dog-fights was eccentric: *'when he went into action he shouted out Greek warriors' cries from the siege of Troy which raised him right up above himself.'* Rhys Davids's unshakable confidence in his own skill as a pilot and his daring brought him a string of victories. In four months he netted at least twenty-five kills, most of them over Flanders. On various occasions he shot down more than one plane a day and was soon given a bar to the Military Cross. Once again he expressed his surprise in letters to his mother and sister. Despite his success, Rhys Davids cut an improbable figure in the RFC, where he was, basically, a fish out of water. When the weather was too bad for flying or on a day off, he preferred to pass the time reading or writing. *'The dear old CO very sportingly said I could take a day in bed, which I did, and finished off the little pamphlet on the Poetic View of the World, which is a good reading. (...) Then I read some 400 lines of Euripides and wrote 3 or 4 letters, altogether very delightful, though my little garret was a bit dingy.'* He always took *'a small volume of Blake's poetry'* with him when he flew in case he was taken prisoner.

later Rhys Davids shot down his first German plane over Lens. He bagged another three the next day and another two on the two days thereafter, making six in less than a week, for which he was awarded the Military Cross. Later he wrote to his mother: *'I suppose I might as well tell you at once that for some absurdly inadequate reason they have deemed fit to give me the Military Cross.'*

Passchendaele

At the end of May the 56th Squadron was sent to Estrée Blanche, the new assault base for aerial combat above the front in Flanders. Rhys Davids loved flying and dog-fights, *'it beats football*

On 23 September 1917 Rhys Davids made his most spectacular kill. The celebrated *Leutnant* Werner Voss had five British planes on his tail, but with his Fokker triplane managed to hold out for more than ten minutes. Rhys Davids reported later: *'I got in several bursts at the Triplane without any apparent effect, and twice* placed a new drum on my Lewis gun. Eventually I got east and slightly above the Triplane and made for it, getting in a whole Lewis drum and a corresponding number of Vickers into him. He made no attempt to turn until I was so close to him I was certain we would collide. He passed my right-hand wing by inches and went down. I zoomed. I saw him next with his engine apparently off, gliding west. I dived again and got one shot out of my Vickers; however; I reloaded and kept in the dive. I got in another good burst and the Triplane did a slight right-hand turn, still going down. I had now overshot him (this was at 1,000 ft), zoomed, but never saw him again.' James McCudden saw Voss's triplane go down: 'I saw him go into a fairly steep dive and so I continued to watch, and then I saw the Triplane hit the ground and disappear into thousands fragments for it seemed to me that it literally went into a powder.' Voss's plane crashed at Plum Farm north of Frezenberg Ridge on the boundary between Zonnebeke and Langemarck. The 20-year-old Voss was killed and is now buried in the *Kameradengrab* in the German military cemetery at Langemarck. It was Rhys Davids's nineteenth kill. The Engineering officer of the 56th Squadron later recalled: *'You know, he always stammered after a fight, but when he landed after the Voss fight he stammered so badly that we couldn't understand him at all, he was so excited.'*

Missing

Rhys Davids was awarded the Distinguished Service Order in early October 1917: *'For some curious reason they have given me a DSO.'* That 'curious reason' was: *'For conspicuous gallantry and devotion to duty (...). He is a magnificent fighter, never failing to locate enemy aircraft and invariably attacking regardless of the numbers against him.'* On 11 October he notched up his last kill above Beselare. Rhys Davids was soon due to go home for a few weeks of leave, but on 27 October he failed to return from a patrol and was last seen in a dog-fight with a number of German planes southwest of Roulers. His apparent death or capture was the most severe loss that the 56th squadron had suffered until then. His mother was heartbroken at the disappearance of her only son. She could not accept that he was dead and retained the hope

that he had only been taken prisoner, writing to all the relevant authorities and using her connections to obtain more news of what had happened. It was not until late December that the War Office notified her that a German plane had dropped a message behind the British lines stating that Lieutenant Rhys Davids was dead. German newspapers also announced the news. His mother Caroline only abandoned her hope of his still being alive when the War Office declared Rhys Davids officially dead. More news emerged in 1920, when – via diplomatic channels – the family secured the return of Rhys Davids's personal effects. There was no information, however, as to his grave or where he died and this information was never to be forthcoming. Much later it emerged that he had been shot down by *Leutnant* Karl Gallwitz northwest of Dadizele. Rhys Davids's body was never recovered and he is remembered today on the Arras Flying Services Memorial.

On leave in August 1917 (Revell) >

Rhys Davids at the controls of an SE5a, summer 1917 (Revell) >

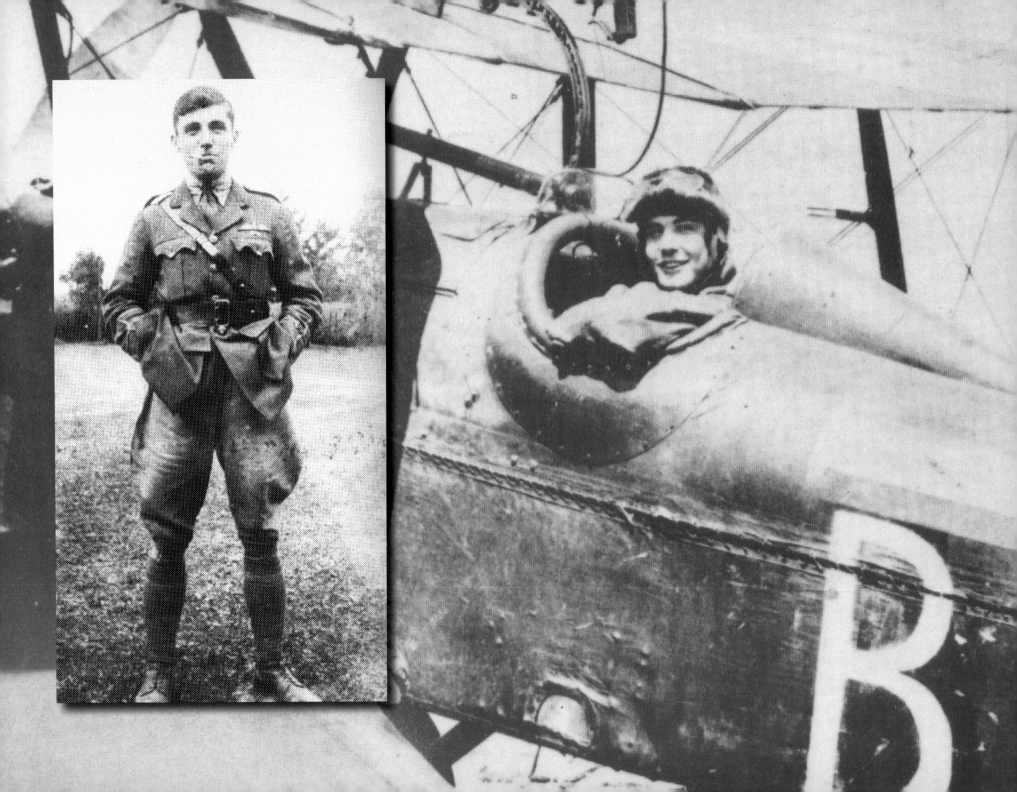

Epilogue

On 10 November 1917 Haig's Flanders offensive bled to death on the top of Passchendaele Ridge. Shortly thereafter the Canadians were withdrawn and again replaced by British troops. The allies were now on top of the Mid West Flanders Ridge, but the small part of it that was now in their possession was less than three kilometres wide. In the final weeks of the battle the fighting had gradually squeezed itself into a bottleneck with Passchendaele church as its most important objective. As a result, the British had acquired an almost untenable salient in which they were shelled and fired on from three sides. Fighting was to continue on the northern flank of this salient for the entire winter 1917-18 in the most degrading conditions. Heavy fighting also continued around Polderhoek, south of Polygon Wood. The situation at both points was so precarious that all the ground won in 1917 had to be given up in April-May 1918 under pressure from the German spring offensive. From a tactical point of view the Battle of Passchendaele was, therefore, a complete failure. Zeebruges and Ostend had not been reached and even the first phase of the offensive, breaking through on the ridge, was not achieved. The only result after 100 days of fighting was that the British had acquired a completely devastated terrain no more than eight kilometres deep, which they would then have to give up again a few months later.

The second failure of the offensive was in terms of human life. According to official army statistics there were 245,000 casualties between 31 July and 12 November 1917 of which almost 106,000 were sustained in the final month. These figures are not broken down into killed, wounded and missing (of whom some were also prisoners of war), although such figures do exist for certain divisions and certain episodes of the battle. In its cemeteries in Belgium, the Commonwealth War Graves Commission currently has 33,716 identified servicemen who died in the same period. On the various memorials to the missing the names appear of a further 43,316 other dead who have no known grave. The actual number of dead is undoubtedly somewhat higher, as those who died in the following weeks, months – and even years – as a result of wounds sustained during the battle were often buried behind the lines and in 'Base Hospitals' in France and in Great Britain. 64% of the wounded were able to return to the front after medical treatment and a further 18% were given non-combatant duties in the rear. For completeness's sake we should also note that in Belgium, the Commission also preserves the memory of 15,722 war dead for the period from 7 June up to and including 30 July 1917 in Belgium. There has been a great deal of speculation regarding German losses during the battle, but recent historical research has revealed that these were around 215,000.

The various chapters of this first part of the book have also demonstrated how the Battle of Passchendaele eventually led to the total destruction of the physical fabric of the battlefield. Aerial photographs clearly show that the landscape had been preserved pretty much intact prior to the summer of 1917. Yet the artillery hurricane of the last two weeks of July left almost nothing standing. Entire villages, houses, trees and streets were erased from the face of the earth. All that remained were millions of shell holes: one next to the other and superimposed one on top of the other. From as early as August the offensive began to be hindered by brief periods of heavy rainfall which rendered the churned-up earth sodden and boggy. It was not until 4 October that the rain became torrential. The shell holes were so flooded that, when observed from the air, more water than land

< Remains of a German gun before Passchendaele, late 1917 (Deraeve)

could be seen. In a very short period of time the area changed into a squelching quagmire in which men, animals and machines sank and drowned. Rupprecht von Bayern was surely not exaggerating when he described the mud as his best ally. While the allied troops tried to make their way through this morass, they were systematically fired upon with machine guns from German pillboxes. It is also interesting to note that the successful German defence tactics of 1917 were later to be the basis for developing other defensive systems such as the *Atlantikwall* during World War Two.

Even before the end of the offensive questions were being asked from various quarters in Britain about the way it was being directed. To begin with there had been no element of surprise whatsoever. The Germans had been able to prepare themselves to the best of their abilities and were ready for the great *Abwehrschlacht* from the middle of July onwards. In order to have had a genuine chance of succeeding, the breakthrough on the Ypres salient should have followed immediately after the explosions of the mines at Messines-Wytschaete. A second criticism was Haig's initial disregard of the experienced Plumer in favour of the younger Gough. The fact that Haig was later forced to fall back on Plumer's Second Army in any case, meant that even more valuable time was lost. As indicated above, what the preparatory artillery bombardments really shot to pieces was any possibility of a successful breakthrough rather than the German defences. It is, at all events, difficult to understand how Haig could assume that the German resistance had been broken by the artillery. His previous experiences in 1916 and 1917 should, in fact, had convinced him to the contrary. Equally questionable is his insistence on continuing the campaign after the catastrophic attacks of 9 and 12 October. He used the pretext of securing better assault positions for the winter, but Haig, of course, also needed a symbolic victory which was the capture of that seemingly unreachable village on the top of the ridge, the name of which had since acquired mythical proportions: 'Passion-dale' or 'valley of suffering'.

The Battle of Passchendaele was therefore a disastrous campaign in almost all aspects. Yet for the allies it did have two positive consequences. In the first place the offensive obliged the Germans to move

15.06.1917
Passchendaele

all their reserves to Flanders, which would otherwise had been deployed in the south against the exhausted French. It was also Pétain, the new French Commander-in-Chief, who repeatedly urged Haig to continue the offensive. Passchendaele thus gave the French time to reorganize themselves after Verdun and the ill-fated Nivelle offensive. The second positive consequence was of a strategic nature, although it was certainly not intended in this way by Haig. As a battle of attrition, Passchendaele 1917 had broken the German military apparatus. In the German literature the *Flandernschlacht* 1917 is thus also often associated with the concept of *Materialschlacht* (battle of material attrition). German industry was never able to replenish the huge quantities of materials and munitions which were lost during the campaign. Passchendaele also became an unprecedented drain on materials and resources on the British side too, but Britain still had colonies and in 1917 the Americans also entered the war. During

10.10.1917
Passchendaele

10.11.1917
Passchendaele

their successful Spring offensive of 1918, the Germans were to find themselves short of exactly those resources which they had lost in 1917. Using new tactics they were able to break through the frontline to a depth of up to twenty kilometres at some points in Northern France, but they almost completely lacked the munitions and logistics to exploit this. Thus, although the German defenders actually won the Battle of Passchendaele it is our firm conviction that their logistics were broken at Passchendaele and that Germany lost the war in Flanders.

PART II TYNE COT CEMETERY

In the first part we saw how the death toll of 1917 grew exponentially the closer the battle came to the village of Passchendaele. From the stories of many of the victims it was clear that in the space of 100 days an entire generation had been all but mutilated. But what happened with those tens of thousands of dead? How did their bodies come to be buried in their present graves and what about the many missing? In this second part we endeavour to provide an answer to these questions through new investigations into the most significant last resting place for those who died in the Battle of Passchendaele: Tyne Cot Cemetery. With 12,000 graves and 35,000 names of missing soldiers this is the Commonwealth's largest cemetery in the world. With some 230,000 visitors a year, it is also the most visited. In the following seven chapters we will discuss in turn the history of the site, the burial of the dead and the work of the Commonwealth War Graves Commission, the architecture of the cemetery, the different types of stones and their meanings, a new statistical analysis, the Memorial to the Missing and, finally, past and present remembrance of those who lost their lives.

< *Two British soldiers washing themselves in a shell hole surrounded by grave crosses at St. Julien. One of the graves is that of Sapper Frank B.B. Vickery, 475th Field Company Royal Engineers, who was killed on 16 August 1917 and whose name is now inscribed on the Memorial to the Missing at Tyne Cot, photograph dated 13 March 1918 (IWM Q11562).*

1 History of the site

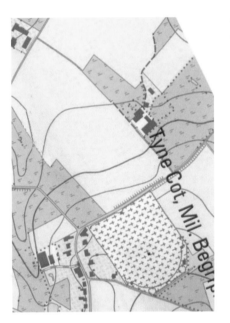

Extract from a topographical map dated 2001. Scale 1:10,000 (NGI).

‹ *Aerial photograph of Tyne Cot and Vijfwegenstraat, ca. 1965 (IFF).*

The 'Rozeveld'

Tyne Cot Cemetery lies at the heart of an old feudal estate which was once known as 'Rozeveld' ('Rose Field') and is situated on the border of Zonnebeke and Passchendaele. It was dependent on the Manor of Passchendaele and, according to Karel De Flou, was already mentioned in the Rent Book of 1576. The Ypres-Roulers railway line, laid in 1868, runs over a small part of 'Rozeveld' and now forms the border with the hamlet of Kerselaar to the east. To the southwest the demarcation line was probably somewhere around the old inn 'De Vijfwegen' ('The Five Ways') better known locally as De Muis ('The Mouse'), which is situated at the crossing of the Schipstraat and the Vijfwegenstraat. Geographically Rozeveld is on the western slope leading to the crest of the Mid West Flanders Ridge, which virtually follows the Passchendaele-Broodseinde-Becelaere road. Tyne Cot offers a good view towards Ypres and the West Flanders hills and hence the area is of major strategic importance.[1]

To provide a good understanding of what the area around the current cemetery looked like before and during World War One, a complete survey has been made of all houses in the corner formed by the Vijfwegen and Tyne Cot streets (formerly Spilstraat). This was no simple task given that the Passchendaele council archives were totally destroyed by fire in 1914. In the end it seemed that prior to the war there had been buildings in about 10 locations. We will take a look at those from the northwest to the northeast, anti-clockwise, and therefore first along the Spilstraat and then along the Vijfwegenstraat, according to addresses provided in the 1914 electoral roll. We can see that the closest buildings along Tyne Cotstraat all date from after World War One and mostly even from after the 1950s.[2]

Spilstraat 4 – At the earlier exit from the Debruyne farm to the Tyne Cotstraat there was a small one-building farm that was demolished in 1883 and replaced by a larger one. In 1914 this was the home of the unmarried brothers Karel and Alfons Cappelle. The farm was not rebuilt after the war.

Spilstraat 5 – In front of the exit from the Deleu farm lived Engel Lescouhier, originally from Langemark, who worked as a hoop cutter (hoop iron was used among other things for vats and kegs). This house was not rebuilt either. When ditches were being dug along Tyne Cotstraat some five years ago, the remains of walls made of red bricks were found.

Spilstraat 6 – The current Deleu farm is the only property situated on the west side of Spilstraat. The Calmeyn family lived there for more than 100 years until 1905. In 1914 the family of Henri Vanhee and his wife Leonie Nollet, arrived. When they fled the war they first went to family at Crombeeke and then on to Steenvoorde where Henri and his two horses worked for a French farmer. The farmer had an aunt in Oudezeele whose son was drafted into the army. So they moved to that farm and remained there until 1923. Following the war, Henri Deleu, grandfather and namesake of the current owner, came to work in the newly rebuilt farm. The pre-war manor was one of the most important in Passchendaele and had already appeared on maps made by the Count of Ferraris in 1774. Until 1867 the farm was owned by Maria de Trammecourt, a descendant of the last squire of Zonnebeke who had sold the manorial properties to the abbey in 1698. The farm then covered an area of 31.56 hectares. From the Popp map we can see that the farm buildings were in a sort of U-shape and that there were also three remains of an earlier wall. Next to the current entrance way, which runs to Beecham Farm further to the east, there were also exits to the northwest and south. According to a British intelligence report from the summer of 1917, the farm, known to the British as Hamburg Farm, was completely burned out. It was here that the Australian Serjeant Lewis McGee won his Victoria Cross on 4 October of the same year for his capture of a bunker, which is still preserved today and located behind the farmhouse. According to the report mentioned above there had been an oast house for chicory there which was rebuilt after the war and today is one of the few such facilities still working in Flanders. The current manor house dates from 1922 and is sited closer to the entrance way.

Spilstraat 7 – To the northwest of the present cemetery we can see that in 1774 there was a farm existing of two buildings, a garden, an orchard, three sections of land, two meadows and some woods, as well as parcels of land lying further away. The last occupant prior to the war was Karel Verfaillie, not related to Richard, who, in addition to farming, also traded in coal. His third wife was named Lucie Vandenbroucke and together they had seven children. In 1914 the farm underwent major renovation which resulted in three rather than two buildings. It was not rebuilt after the war because a large part of the land was taken for the establishment of Tyne Cot Cemetery.

Spilstraat 8 – Around the turn of the century, Hendrik Markey built a house with a bakery as an annex on the south-western bend in the Spilstraat. He was married to Marie-Thérèse Decuypere and had two sons and three daughters, one of whom died during the war. During the reconstruction of the area there came a larger building with a bakery, barn and a stall for his horse, which he used for his bakery rounds. The house was later separated from the other buildings. In the former living area there was also a shop for a time and during this period Alice Deneut kept an inn at the side of the cemetery named 't Rozeveld. Rosa Demeyere rebuilt this as Bed & Breakfast De Klaproos, which has a good view over Tyne Cot Cemetery. Today these are numbers 24 and 26 of the Tyne Cotstraat.

Henri Vanhee and Leonie Nollet, the last occupants of Hamburg Farm before the war, ca. 1930 (Vanhee).

Spilstraat 9-10-11 – The land to the south of the current cemetery, enclosed by Vijfwegen and Tyne Cot streets, was still completely wood land in 1774. In 1914 there were three working peoples' cottages situated to the south of the current cemetery. These were the property of Bernard and Maria Malfait from Zonnebeke. Jules Santy lived at number 10, his son Cyriel Santy-Desmedt lived at number 9 and his daughter Octavie, married to Hendrik Patteeuw, lived at number 11. After the war the land was bought by a society for cheap housing, which built two terraced houses closer to the Spilstraat.

Spilstraat - Vijfwegenstraat – On the north-eastern side of the corner formed by Spilstraat and Vijfwegenstraat in 1914 stood two terraced houses which were owned by the town clerk, Arsène Vandenweghe-Dochy. It is unclear who lived there, or what the numbers of the houses in Spilstraat were. After the war the land was converted to farmland between this point and the railway line, now the property of Frans Cools. In 2004 a six-metre wide piece of land beside the Vijfwegenstraat was taken for the entrance to the new Visitors' Centre. During these works at the beginning of August 2006 a pre-war floor of red brick was found close to the electricity cabin, which was on the corner of the two streets and indicated the positions of the missing two-house terrace.

Bruno Dierick and Pharaïlde Deleye, who lived in the now disappeared farm on the site of the new visitors' centre from 1911 (Verfaillie)

top: The Heveraet family just before their return from France. Standing from left to right: Marie-Louise, Marcel, Kamiel and Henri. Seated from left to right: father Emiel, Germaine and mother Leonie, ca. 1919 (Deneut)

top right: Jules Debruyne's family – Alida Taillieu with their five oldest children in Normandy, ca. 1917 (Debruyne)

Vijfwegenstraat 11 – In 1857 Louis Herreman bought a piece of land in the northwest corner of Spilstraat and Vijfwegenstraat. He built a house which was later used by his daughter Leonie Herreman and her husband Emiel Heveraet, who made his living sawing wood. In 1912 there was a totally new building with a smaller second building which was probably his workplace. In 1914 the Heveraet-Herreman family fled to Poperinge and later via Steenvoorde to Pitgam. When they returned to Passchendaele they built a wooden shed not far from a bunker, of which a photo still exists. The house itself was rebuilt in 1923 at the corner of the Vijfwegenstraat. Following the death of daughter Germaine Heveraet, it was sold to Nico Geldof-Maes. In 1960-62, the grandson Andre Deneut built a house near the rear wall of Tyne Cot Cemetery on the site of the earlier house. At the beginning of the 1990s he found a pre-war brick water well and the remains of a basement complete with a stack of coal.

Vijfwegenstraat 10 – Facing the back of the current cemetery in 1914 was a house used by August Tyvaert of Ichtegem and his wife Elodie Deblauwe. All sections to the east of the Vijfwegenstraat were then the property of the Passchendaele town clerk, Arsène Vandenweghe. The house was not rebuilt after the war.

Vijfwegenstraat 9 – A British intelligence report dating from the summer of 1917 describes the site as "Farm Dierinck - Newly built and strong. Fairly high position. Small cellar under dwelling house." In December 2005 during foundation works for the entrance wall to the new Visitors' Centre, the remains were found of a shallow cellar measuring 4.30 x 6.30 metres. This was made up of red bricks and finished with cement, indicating construction shortly before the First World War. The farmhouse was occupied by Pieter Verbeke's large family until October 1905. In 1911 Bruno Dierick and Pharaïlde Deleye lived here with their seven children. Their son Cyriel was killed in action on 23 August 1914 near Verbrande Brug in Vilvoorde. Their daughter Marie died in Houtkerque during the evacuation of war refugees. After the war three buildings appeared on the site, two of which were built against the original farmhouse. In 1931, another daughter named Madeleine married Richard Verfaillie, with whom she had seven children, and together they extended the farming business. In the 1930s the farmhouse, together with the Debruyne farm, became the property of the notary Andre Camerlynck from Passchendaele. Following his death, his daughter Agnes and her husband Patrick Depuydt demolished the buildings in 1983 in order to build a new residence. This however, was never built and in 2005 the family donated part of the land for the construction of the new Visitors' Centre beside Tyne Cot Cemetery. The Visitors' Centre was built on what was the western side of the demolished Verfaillie-Dierick farmhouse.

Vijfwegenstraat 8 - Before the war, two farms, each of some 3.5 hectares, stood close to each other to the north of what is now Tyne Cot Cemetery. The one furthest to the west was occupied by Jules Debruyne and his wife Alida Taillieu. When the war began they had four children. They first fled to Poperinge and later to Falaise in Normandy, where two more children were born. Around 1923 the farmhouse was rebuilt and the Debruyne family was able to return to Passchendaele. From 1959 the farming business was established further by their son Gerard and is today run by their grandson Bart Debruyne. Before the war a zig-zagging path through the fields connected the farmhouse with both Vijfwegenstraat and Tyne Cotstraat. A second exit to Vijfwegenstraat ran via the Verfaillie-Dierick farmhouse and remained until a new entrance was built alongside the cemetery. The only current entrance takes a right-hand course across the shortest distance between the farmhouse and Tyne Cotstraat, with the present house number 28. Before the war the buildings were in an L-shape, but now they are parallel to a barn added at the rear of which the foremost part stands on the site of the pre-war house. The Debruyne farm is the only one remaining between Vijfwegenstraat and Tyne Cotstraat and thus rightfully bears the name 'Rozeveld'.

Vijfwegenstraat 7 – To the east of the Debruyne farmhouse stood a second house with stables. This was not rebuilt after the war. Jules Descamps and Louise Latruwe lived there from 1891 and had six children.

In 1774 a major part of the Rozeveld was still in its original state of woods and heath lands. Around 1850 much of this disappeared. In 1914 there were only a few areas of wood land to the northeast of the Debruyne and Dierick farms. During the First World War, these were known as Augustus Wood. A stream rises there and runs northwest into the Ravebeek. After the war a small area of woodland re-established itself behind the Debruyne farm and became known locally as 'Faaljes bosseltje'. It was later felled by the Debruyne family but never really levelled off.[3]

Passchendaele Ridge

Because this study is focused on the cemetery itself we will not provide a full overview of all events that occurred here during the war. These will be dealt with in a separate publication concerning the nearby Ypres-Roulers railway as the physical link between the town of Zonnebeke and Tyne Cot Cemetery. Here we provide only the most important facts relevant to the development of the current cemetery.

On 20 October 1914, during the First Battle of Ypres, the site was just behind the foremost German trenches and it remained so throughout the winter of 1914-15. During construction of the most northerly section of the new parking area, the remains of an early Ger-

man trench were uncovered on 4 and 5 April 2006. Over a distance of 18 metres, two planks with a maximum width of 0.4 metres were found at a depth of 0.8 metres. The absence of further construction works suggests that this was a very basic earthen trench with sandbags above ground level, which, by its west-east orientation, served as a communication trench. Nevertheless, the large numbers of spent German 7.92 mm cartridges and French bullet tips point to this being a particularly dangerous position. Beecham Farm, 500 metres away, was firmly in French hands. The remains of two leather, spiked helmets were found in the trench. One of these proved to be Bavarian. Other objects found were two beer bottles in green glass, one of which was from Maracaibo (Venezuela), a German boot which could not be preserved and the remains of a cowhide backpack. From a historical point of view perhaps the most important find was an aluminium drinking cup bearing the mark of the No. 2 Battery of a Fuss-Artillerie-Regiment (Wilhelm Berg) that cannot be further detailed. Despite the fact that the wood was very poorly preserved it is, however, notable that a section of Passchendaele trench originating from the first winter of the war was found despite the battle of 1917 and the intensive groundworks of the 1920s. A well-preserved Signal Lamp Mark I made by Christopher Durnell, 19790, Birmingham 1916, was found just to the south of the trench in a 1917 shell hole.[4]

left: Andre Deneut finds the pre-war stone well of the Heveraet's house, then Vijfwegenstraat 11, ca. 1990 (Deneut)
right: Photograph of part of the pre-war Dierick farm uncovered in December 2005 during the building of an access wall to the visitors' centre (MMP)

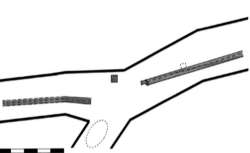

Excavation of a German communication trench, winter 1914-15 (MMP)

top right: The remains of a German spiked helmet and a drinking cup from a Foot Artillery Regiment (MMP)
bottom right: 1916 Signal Lamp Mark I, found in a shell-hole under the new car park (MMP)

The Second Battle of Ypres resulted in Tyne Cot being almost six kilometres behind the new frontline in May 1915. The Germans began to build the Flandern I Stellung in the late summer of 1916. The main characteristic of this line was that the heavily manned trenches were almost completely replaced by strongly constructed concrete bunkers in which several men were congregated around a machine-gun post. With a covering of reinforced concrete between a metre and 1.5 metres thick they were protected against the heaviest fire. These bunkers were placed an average of 100 to 250 metres apart and were therefore positioned to provide a perfect field of fire. To the west of the foremost bunkers at Tyne Cot lay Dab Trench with, on the other side of the Tyne Cotstraat, a large amount of barbed wire and several forward posts. Given its strategic position close to the crest of the ridge, Flandern I was split here with a second line of bunkers.[5]

On 4 October 1917, the 40th Battalion of the 3rd Australian Division broke through the Flandern I position at the present Tyne Cot Cemetery. New offensives here by the 66th and again the 3rd Australian Division, on 9 and 12 October respectively, resulted in an unprecedented bloodbath and no meaningful results. Only after the relief by the 4th Canadian Division did the front again move in the direction of Passchendaele on 26 October. The closer the Allies came to the village, the heavier the resistance from the German bunkers became because the height difference provided better command of the lower ground. The lower lying areas over which the Allies had to attack had been transformed into a morass of mud. At the end of the battle the 2nd Canadian Division was relieved by the 33rd Division. In the winter of 1917-18 they put in a great deal of effort to make the bunkers the Allies had taken usable again and to provide access across the land via duckboard tracks, plank roads and light railways.[6]

Between 13 December 1917 and 5 January 1918, the 50th Northumberland Division temporarily took the place of the 33rd Division. A map dating from this period and made by the 7th Field Company RE shows some six bunkers and shelters as a Regimental Aid Post (RAP). War diaries also provide the coordinates of various aid posts on or around the present cemetery, from which we can only assume

left: he 33rd Battalion Machine Gun Corps at the central pillbox at Tyne Cot, then converted into 'Machine Gun H.Q. Left Group', seated (with moustache) Captain Cross MC, February-March 1918 (IWM Q56253)
right: 33rd Battalion Machine Gun Corps, providing anti-aircraft fire with a Vickers MG mounted on a wooden pole, February-March 1918 (IWM Q56239)

that the RAP was spread about in various buildings. By far the most frequently mentioned coordinate is D.17.a.0.3, the bunker on which the Cross of Sacrifice now stands. In addition, according to the 7th Field Company, Hamburg Camp was above this, in fact on the other side of the similarly named farmhouse, with '26 shelters completed'. On 21 March 1918, the 33rd Division was relieved by the 49th and from April 30 by the 6th. In the meantime the German Spring Offensive had begun in earnest to the south of Ypres and, in order to avoid being cut off, Haig decided on a general withdrawal on 16 April. This offensive also died down and from August 1918 the opportunities were completely reversed. Tyne Cot Cemetery was again several kilometres behind the German frontline and remained so until the beginning of the final Allied offensive of 28 September 1918. The 12th Bavarian Division was again defending the old 1917 line, which was then designated the first line of the Flandern II Stellung. The German position was very weak and the Allied forces so overpowering that the site was taken on the first day of the offensive by Belgian units of the 2nd Grenadiers and the 16th Infantry Regiment.[7]

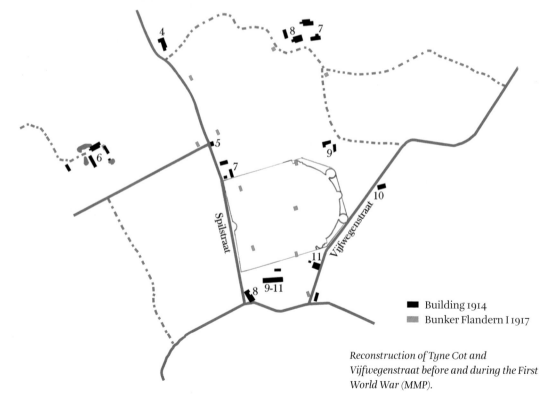

Building 1914
Bunker Flandern I 1917

Reconstruction of Tyne Cot and Vijfwegenstraat before and during the First World War (MMP).

View of the northern pillbox at Tyne Cot and (in the distance) the still surviving pillbox at Hamburg Farm, where Lewis McGee won the Victoria Cross on 4 October 1917, ca. 1920 (Reed).

Bunkers

'Stellungskarten' and Trench Maps were mainly intended to chart enemy positions. Only occasionally do we come across 'Secret Editions' which shows a side's own positions and even then there are varying degrees of precision. As a result, tracing bunkers becomes very difficult as regards to making out if something is a concrete construction or an ordinary shelter. For battlefield reconstruction it is therefore necessary to place British and German staff maps side by side and compare these with the topography of the land itself and with what, for example, farmers can provide about absolute positions. In this way we can place some 10 bunkers, with a clear disposition of two rows, on the map between Vijwegenstraat and Tyne Cotstraat. On the opposite side from the earlier Spilstraat stood a further two constructions in front of and behind Hamburg Farm. The exact positioning of all bunkers makes it possible to obtain a clear view of the great strength of the Flandern I Stellung and the difficulties the Australians experienced in taking it. The siting of the bunkers is also important because the lay-out of the cemetery was to a great degree influenced by this.

After the breaching of the line in October 1917 the concrete bunkers that were still usable were given names and numbers, presumably at the end of the year. Although there is no map showing them, we do know that the bunkers around Tyne Cot were No. 8 (which was worked on at the end of March by the 11th Field Company), No. 10 named 'Infernal' (where the remains of the Australian Frederick N. Inglis were found after the war), No. 13 'Insane', No. 14 'Indigo', No. 15 'Irksome' and No. 16 'India' (sited near Dash Crossing at 28.D.16. d.60.44). In the 1920s a large number of Flandern I bunkers were dismantled. Blasting of the concrete at Tyne Cot would have caused too much damage to the cemetery and these were therefore symbolically integrated into the lay-out. Between 1930 and 1932 hundreds more bunkers in Zonnebeke and Passchendaele were demolished at the cost of the Belgian state. Elsewhere, the last remnants of Flandern I disappeared around 1950 when the metal they contained again became worth a great deal of money at the time of the Korean War. Today only some 15 bunkers of this once infamous position remain preserved and visible, three of them within the walls of Tyne Cot Cemetery.[8]

The two foremost bunkers within the cemetery are perhaps the most well-known of the entire Western Front. On 2 January 1918, the most northerly, 'Indigo' or 'Barnacle' at position 28.D.16.b.7.4, was described in the War Diaries of the 50th Division as 'Support Battalion Headquarters' with four Lewis guns. In the second half of the month, the 212th Field Company carried out infrastructure works at the southern bunker named 'Irksome' in connection with a cookhouse. It is likely that this did not occur in the bunker itself but alongside it in a specially constructed shelter. In the frightening May days of 1940 the Tyne Cot bunkers were used by the residents of the Rozeveld as shelters. At the beginning of the 1980s they were closed off by concrete plates without a plan of them ever being drawn. Externally the concrete structure is built between a wooden framework with woven steel and fine to middle grade gravel as aggregate for the concrete. The outer measurements of 11 x 3.65 metres are close to the four bunkers we investigated along the old railway line, which formed part of the same Flandern I Stellung. There, constructions comprised three rooms and an outbuilding, the latter not in concrete, for use of a machine-gun. Here the fourth room seemed to be fully integrated with, in each case, a conical narrow opening up to 0.15 metres high and 0.2 metres through the 1.2-metre thick western wall. At the rear of the southern bunker and between the four door openings we also found three square air vents with a cross-section of 0.15 metres. Today the concrete structures are 1.5 metres above the surface. During the war they were probably covered with earth to divert attention from enemy air observers.[9]

The third and central bunker at Tyne Cot Cemetery is completely covered by the Cross of Sacrifice and, according to a British article from 1923, would have been about 2.7 metres in height. A plan of the bunker, preserved with the original designs of the Cross, shows that the original western and southern sides were almost seven metres long. Two entrances opened into a narrow corridor with two rooms behind, protected at the front by a wall of reinforced concrete more than 1.5 metres thick. The bunker was part of the locally doubled Flandern I Stellung and, after its capture on 4 October 1917, was used by various units as a Regimental Aid Post. At the beginning of November 1917 this was described as "a pill-box, behind the walls of which was a 3ft. x 9ft.

10in. excavation with a canvas roof, designed as the regimental aid post in the attack on Passchendaele". On 5 January 1918, it was mentioned as an aid post 28.D.17.a.0.3 for the last time. Data concerning the battlefield cemetery behind suggests, however, that it remained so until the end of March. There is nothing left to see of the two other bunkers in the cemetery. They rose only slightly above the field and totally disappeared during the laying of the gradient for the Memorial to the Missing. The roof of the most southern one was rediscovered in October 2002 at a depth of about 0.7 metres when a grave was dug at plot 45, row G, for the interment of an unknown Briton. For many years the workmen had asked themselves why, at this particular place, three gravestones were missing… At the end of October 1917 the structure at 28.D.16.b.95.26 provided a roof to the company staff of the Canadian 46th Battalion. In the 1990s the most northerly bunker also saw the light of day during the laying of a water main. In the Visitors' Centre one can see clearly from a plan dated March 1921 that the structure measured about the same as the two foremost bunkers and today is beneath the non-public area between the outer wall and the northern pavilion which, for a large part, is built on.[10]

Northern pillbox with (left) '14 INDIGO' painted on, 1926 (Daniel)

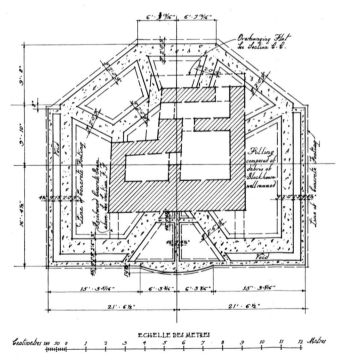

top: The imposing central pillbox with the reconstructed Dierick farm on the left, 1922 (CWGC)
top right: North-east corner of the central pillbox with entrance and 'Tyne Cot, 8th Coy' painted on, 1919 (Attree)
bottom right: Plan of the central pillbox with design for the erection of the Cross of Sacrifice, 1923 (CWGC)

Between Tyne Cotstraat and the rear of the cemetery there was a sixth bunker in the Heveraet family's garden, of which the south-eastern corner opened on to Vijfwegenstraat. Gerard Deneut (husband of Germaine Heveraet) demolished the structure at the time of the Korean War with the help of his son Andre. The southern front wall and two parts of the side walls remained in place until 1997 when Germaine Heveraet moved to a nursing home and the house was sold. During road works on Vijfwegenstraat in December 2005 workmen again came across the south-eastern corner of the bunker. Sadly enough we were not called to carry out further investigations. It was heard that some four German helmets were found. Thanks to Andre Deneut and Rachelle Heveraet a good reconstructive drawing of the bunker was possible. It quickly appeared that this was a mirror image of the bunker beneath the Cross of Sacrifice. The struc-

Plot 45 with the uncompleted row G. The reason for this gap remained a mystery for many years until an unknown British soldier was buried here on 17 October 2002 and the remains of the fifth Tyne Cot pillbox were found, at a depth of approx. 70 cm (MMP)

ture was built with fine gravel and there were railway sleepers in the roof. In May 1940 the Heveraet family sheltered in it and later in the Second World War a German officer who had served here in 1917 visited.[11]

Gerard Debruyne (born 1921) still remembers four concrete shelters that were demolished near his farmhouse around 1930. No. 13 'Insane' was some 125 metres to the north of the left-hand bunker in the cemetery and 35 metres to the east of Tyne Cotstraat. The construction was of the same type as the two foremost structures at Tyne Cot Cemetery and connected by means of a concrete trench. This could have been the previously mentioned Dab Trench, but no traces of a trench were found during foundation works for the new path beside the northern wall of the cemetery. The soil structure was certainly disturbed to a depth of almost a metre as a result of intense shelling during the war and levelling of the fields after the war. Some 150 metres further north, at what was the pre-war entrance to the Debruyne farm and close to the lost Cappelle house, there was a fourth comparable bunker about 50 metres from Tyne Cotstraat. At Rozeveld, a few second line bunkers were constructed running paralell to the main Flandern I-Stellung, which connected the previously mentioned site on the Vijfwegenstraat from north to south with the three rear bunkers in the cemetery and ran to a fifth about 220 metres from the northerly pavilion. This bunker was located in the previously mentioned 'Faaljes bosseltje' as the furthest extension of Augustus Wood, now a strip of meadow which is still uncleared. Between this concrete structure and the first-line bunker at the former Cappelle farm, stood, some 60 metres to the north-west of the present farm buildings, another large structure which was squarer in shape and a smaller version of the one beneath the Cross of Sacrifice.[12]

Finally, there were another two concrete bunkers on the western side of Tyne Cotstraat and sited in front of the Flandern I Stellung. The first stood just to the north of the drive to the Deleu farm, which was better known as Hamburg Farm during the war. The staff of the Canadian 44th Battalion sheltered in this bunker, 28.D.16.b.55.70, at the end of October 1917. The second is still situated behind the

A sixth pillbox, just outside the cemetery, at the corner of Vijfwegenstraat, which was partly demolished around 1950 and which completely disappeared in 1997, ca. 1992 (Deneut)

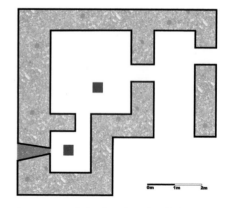

Reconstructed plan based on descriptions by Rachelle Heveraet and Andre Deneut, the pillbox appears to be a mirror image of the one under the Cross of Sacrifice (MMP)

present house and between the foundations of the pre-war buildings. This was known for its capture by the Australian Serjeant Lewis McGee on 4 October 1917. It is a small concrete structure of the one-room type with an entrance and a window opening. The owner, however, does not allow anyone to visit or even survey it.[13]

For the sake of completeness, the Imperial War Museum has three photos which show men at one of the Tyne Cot bunkers, put into service as headquarters of the left group of the 33rd Battalion Machine Gun Corps. In the unit's war diary we can indeed read about machine guns at Tyne Cot, but it is unclear which of the structures described above relates to this account.[14]

Name

The question which arises during every visit to Tyne Cot Cemetery is one concerning the meaning of the name. As in many cases, the cemetery got its name from a toponym that was applied during the war. The generally accepted explanation is that 'cot' is derived from 'cottage' and refers to a farm cottage which once stood on the site. Other cemeteries with similar usage of the word are Bard Cottage and No Man's Cot in Boesinghe and Lancashire Cottage in Ploegsteert. On early maps it was always spelled 'Cott.' with a double 't' and a full point, something which later changed to the simpler 'Cot' as it is now written. The further afield Vienna Cottages were also abbreviated to Vienna Cot. We have noted that the name almost always appeared on the southeast of the Heveraet house and its associated sawmill of wooden construction. The Tyne is the name of a river in Northumberland, not far from the Scottish border. In the close neighbourhood are various other farmhouses that have been given the name of a river, such as Marne, Seine and Thames. These are all sited in the area around the Nieuwebeek, which was perhaps the source of inspiration.[15]

Tyne Cot appeared on staff maps from the middle of 1916 and therefore cannot have denoted bunkers that bore a resemblance to cottages as is often stated and written. The influential 'Ypres Times' of October 1923 provides the first mention that the name Tyne Cot was given by the Northumberland Fusiliers. The British historian Rose Coombs specifies the 50th Division from Northumberland but

Surviving pillbox of one room type, at Hamburg Farm, captured by Lewis McGee on 4 October 1917 (MMP)

gives no timeframe in which this could have occurred. The division only came to the Rozeveld in December 1917 but fought for the first time in the area in May 1915. The latter is also the period in which many houses, heights and crossroads acquired their names. If the naming actually does go back to 1915 and the 50th Division it must be attributed to the 4th, 5th, 6th or 7th Northumberland Fusiliers. But how does this work with Marne, Seine and Thames Farm? It is clear to us that – if there is any link with units of the 50th Division – they, in the best case, named the cemetery site in 1917 after one of the nearby ruins of the much earlier Tyne Cot. After the war it would have been obvious that the ordinary name of a river was just a bit too ordinary for the largest British cemetery in the world. As part of its remembrance character Tyne Cot Cemetery required a much more powerful etymology, an association with something that was known to many visitors and which also arose spontaneously from the 1920s. An important element in this is that at the same time, in the original registers of the cemetery, there is not a single link to the soldiers from Northumberland and the resonant 'cottages beside the Tyne'.[16]

Another explanation, which used to be heard among the local Passendale people, is that of 't Hinnekot, Flemish for chicken coop. The British could have converted this to a form familiar to them in the same way they converted Ploegsteert to Plugstreet. But it seems much more likely to us that it was the people of Passchendaele who could not pronounce the British name 'Tyne Cot' and - as they still do - read it as 't Hinnekot. A comparable example is Switch Road at Poperinge which the local population pronounce as 'Zwitserse route' ('Swiss route'). Another local story says that there was a sign for 'Lammertyn' farm on which only the last letters were legible, leading the British to make the association with their own Tyne. But there is absolutely no person of that name mentioned in either the 1914 electoral roll or in an excellent study about Passchendaele farms. We can therefore only decide that the name Tyne Cot is, in fact, quite banal: the ordinary name of a river that was used to identify and clarify the position of some buildings, as happened in other places in the immediate neighbourhood. All further interpretations say more about the symbolism of the cemetery itself than they do about the history of the site.

Collective grave 2/A/2 for 27 dead under seven stones (MMP)

Battlefield Cemetery

The original battlefield cemetery was sited to the east of the central bunker - that is, between the Cross of Sacrifice and the Stone of Remembrance. It was here that those who had died at the Regimental Aid Post before they could be evacuated by the field ambulances were buried. These are now plots 1 and 2 where, according to the old register, 343 men were interred. When carrying out his inventory, Frans Descamps counted 344 graves, of which 258 are identified, 40 partly identified and 46 not identified. The first graves date from 9 October 1917. The last addition was that of 19-year-old Private Henry H. Dilks of the 1st Queen's, who died on 26 March 1918 (2/A/4). One in three of those identified belonged to the 33rd Division, 61 identified were with the 2nd Canadian Division, followed by 30 from the 50th and 29 from the 4th Canadian Division. All except seven came from divisions which used the central bunker and several nearby shelters as a Regimental Aid Post. The seven include the Privates Albert E. Gaulton of the 16th Division (1/H/15) and the 18-year-old G. Nairn of the 9th Division (2/A/3). The five others are all airmen whose bodies were brought here from Praetbos in Vladslo after the war (1/AA/18-22). The row in which they are buried is designated as AA implying that this was an addition to the original row A. The first five rows (AA-D) of plot 1 are also notably more regularly arranged than the remainder. The numbering of rows and stones is not easy to follow, but Frans Descamps managed to put it into a structured focus.[17]

A photo of four Canadians who were buried in plot 1 of the battlefield cemetery was also found. These are the Privates Hugh MacInnes (1/B/31) and Frank Rogers (1/D/14) and Lieutenants Percy L. Barber (1/C/28) and Francis T. Pendergast (1/D/24). On 30 October 1917, Private Hugh MacInnes was declared 'killed in action, after being wounded twice and voluntarily remaining on duty'. He was born in Scotland in 1893 and began work with the Canadian Bank of Commerce. MacInnes died in service with the 78th Battalion. Lieutenant Francis T. Pendergast worked in the merchant navy in civilian life. He died on 4 November 1917, while serving with the 21st Battalion whose staff occupied the bunker at Hamburg Farm.[18]

Private Hugh MacInnes, buried in the original cemetery (Canadian Bank of Commerce)

The Canadian Lieutenant Francis T. Pendergast, who died at Tyne Cot on 4 November 1917 and is also buried here (Princess of Wales' Own)

*Two stones for four Germans, one of whom is
Otto Bieber of Infanterie-Regiment 79,
killed here on 4 October 1917 (MMP)*

There are also two gravestones in the battlefield cemetery for four Germans, only one of whom is identified: Musketier Otto Bieber of Infanterie-Regiment 79. He was born on 25 October 1896, in Gr. Werder/Osterode and died on 4 October 1917, while serving with the 11th Company close to the present cemetery. Two of the four Germans were originally buried beside the northern pavilion where they were probably found at the time of the dedication of the cemetery in 1927. Today they are a symbol of reconciliation in death, something that until the 1950s also occurred in various German cemeteries: 'Im leben ein Feind, im Tode vereint'. Just behind the Cross of Sacrifice is a collective grave for 27 dead (2/A/3), buried under five gravestones marking three identified bodies, one for eight unknown Britons and one for four unknown Australians. According to a note in the burial return sheets they were originally buried together under a wooden cross. In row E of plot 2 are two Canadians with the surname Hatt whom it is often said were brothers. They died on 6 and 7 November 1917, and belonged to the 25th Battalion from Nova Scotia. Research into their service files showed that in fact Frederick Hatt (II.E.11), born in 1878, was not the brother of the 21-year younger Creighton W. Hatt (II.E.10), although there is a real chance that they were related. Sometimes relatives could be buried together following a special request from the family.[19]

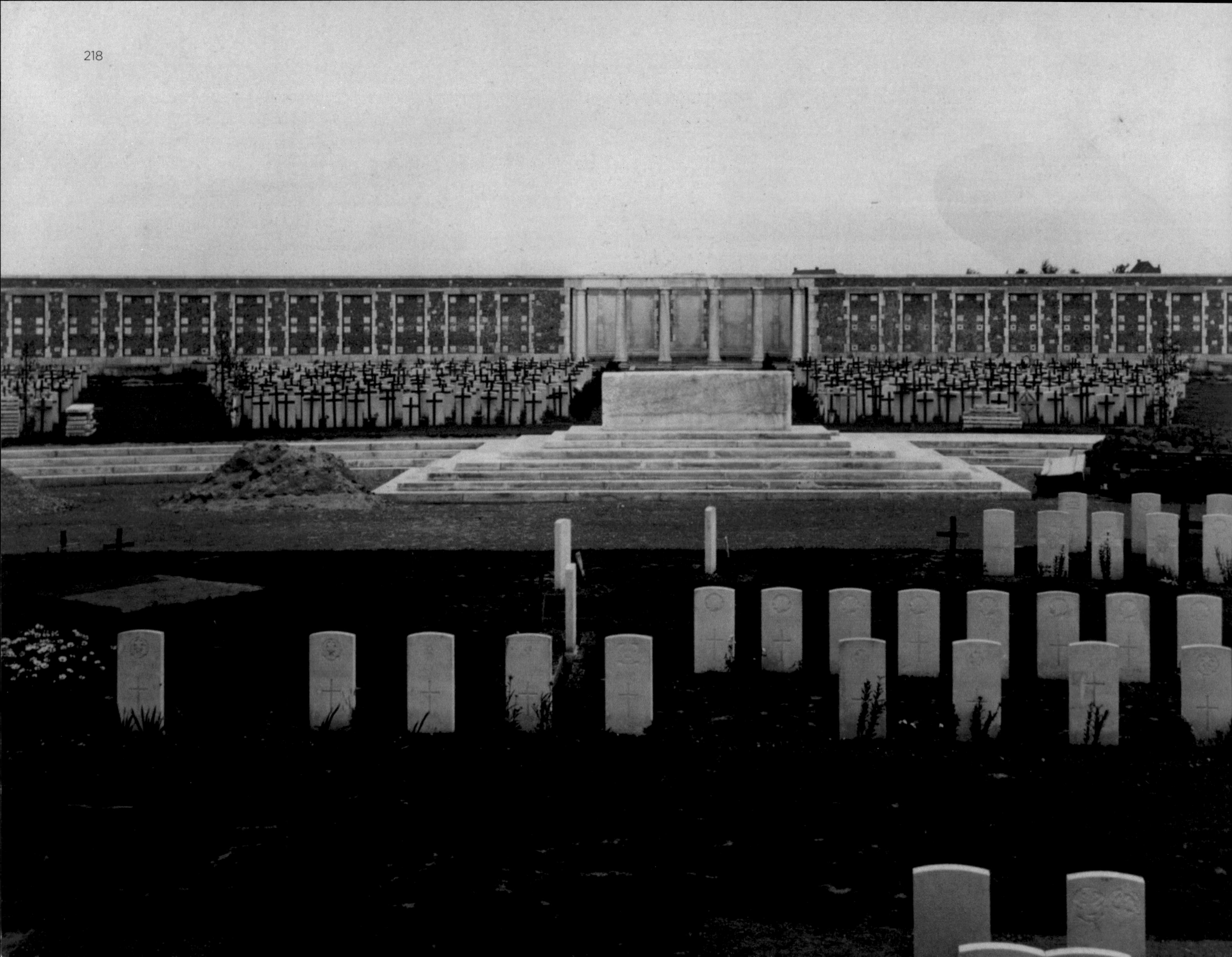

12 October 1917:
Private Matthew Austin
35th Battalion AIF

Matthew Austin on his bicycle (MMP)

‹ *The oldest graves during the final stages of laying out the cemetery with the Memorial to the Missing still under construction and the Stone of Remembrance already finished. New headstones have been put next to the wooden crosses, ready to be put in place, 1926 (Daniel)*

Miner

Matthew Herbert Austin was born in March 1893 in Clifton, a small mining town between Sydney and Wollongong in New South Wales. His parents had emigrated to Australia from Wolverhampton, England, in 1875 and his father, Emanuel, found work as a miner in Clifton. Matthew had two brothers and two sisters. Not long after Matthew was born the family moved to Helensburgh, a village where a major coal-seam had been discovered a few years before. It is known that Austin attended Helensburgh Public School and that his father died of pneumonia in 1899. His mother, who was left a widow with four children, later remarried. With her second husband, Thomas Coulson, she went on to have more children. Austin left school in 1907 at the age of 15 and became a sailor on a merchant ship. Four years later he gave this up and decided to try his luck in Kurri Kurri, a small town some 200 kilometres north of Helensburgh, which had been founded in 1902 to accommodate the influx of miners. Since then a large number of new coal-seams had been discovered in the area and by 1911 it had a population of almost 6,000. Austin found work as a miner in the Stanford Merthyr colliery, a large mining complex where 'Pie' Austin was to stay until he joined up. It was also in this period that Austin took up cycling, at which he proved to be quite good, excelling particularly at track events. He went on to win numerous local and regional races.

Volunteer

A few months before the outbreak of the war Austin married Elizabeth Ellenor Roberts and on 14 December 1915 they had a son, Donald Hugh Austin. Two weeks later, Austin enlisted as a volunteer in the Australian army. He had probably already decided to do so much earlier, but chose to wait because his wife was pregnant and he wanted to wait until the baby was born. On 29 December 1915 he presented himself at the barracks in Newcastle, a town 45 kilometres east of Kurri Kurri. He was by no means the only miner to join up at this time and at least 1,845 other men from the region did the same, of whom almost 300 came from Kurri Kurri. The 'March of the Wallabies', a famous recruiting march from Walgett to Newcastle, which took place between 1 December 1915 and 8 January 1916, encouraged a large number of young men to enlist.

At the beginning of March 1916, Austin was posted to C company of the newly formed 35th Battalion, which was part of the 3rd Australian Division. He received training at Broadmeadows and he was soon promoted to the rank of Lance Corporal and afterwards to Corporal. Just before leaving for Europe he was given a few days leave and used the opportunity to go home, where the last known photographs of him were taken. On 1 May he boarded *H.M.A.T.* Benalla in Sydney. He appears to have lost his corporal's stripes at some point shortly after this, but the reason for this is not known. He kept a diary and after a few days at sea he wrote a long letter home. His experience as a merchant seaman stood him in good stead, as many of the men were seasick despite the good weather, *'but I don't think that complaint will trouble me'.* The journey was extremely boring, but this was part of military life: *'all the troops on board will be glad when they get off this boat, everybody is fed up of her (...) but its all in the game, & will have to make the best of it, experience teaches, but a man has to pay for it mighty dear on this ship, whether we will get any better when we get ashore remains to be proved.'* There was a good atmosphere on the ship, however, and the men were in good spirits: *'They had the flags flying yesterday & gave three cheers for the King & Empire.'* The ship made a stopover in Cape town, South Africa on 10 June 1916. Austin noted in his diary: *'10th arrived Capetown South Africa. Went on a route march through the City.'* The next day the whole battalion was given a few hours leave: *'11th 35th Bat-*

Austin with his wife Lizzie and young son Donald, 1916 (Austin)

talion on leave in Capetown from 12 p.m. to 4 p.m. Invited inside by Capt. Murphy (Hilldrop) returned officer from German West Africa.' Austin was back late and was put on fourteen days fatigue duty as a consequence. On 16 June the men resumed their journey and at the end of that month the ship docked in Dakar, which was then the capital of French West Africa. The next day they sailed for England with an escort of several warships. '9th. Sighted English Coast 9.00 a.m. Arrived Plymouth 3.00 p.m. disembarked 6.00 p.m. left 7.00 p.m. arrived Exeter 9.30 p.m. & received refreshments from mayoress & committee of the town.' The battalion then set off for the training camp at Lark Hill, where they were to receive further instruction. In August Austin was posted to the battalion's Signal Section. The rest of his stay in England largely consisted of training, visits to London, short excursions in the local area and inspections by senior officers. The 35th Battalion left for France on 21 November 1916. Austin came through the cold winter of 1916-17 unscathed and even survived the first offensive which the 35th Battalion was involved in, the Battle of Messines on 7 June 1917, without a scratch, although in mid-July he spent two weeks in hospital due to illness.

Passchendaele

On 12 October 1917 the 35th Battalion went into action again in Flanders. This time the objective was to take Passchendaele. Between what is now Tyne Cot Cemetery and Crest Farm the battalion, as part of the 9th Brigade, suffered appalling losses. The attack did not result in any ground being gained and Austin was listed as missing. His grandfather in Manchester wrote to the Red Cross Society at the beginning of March 1918 asking for more information about his grandson. The Red Cross began an investigation which very quickly yielded results. A soldier explained: 'We made an attack at Zonnebeke on Oct. 12 which was not a success and we had to come back. We were relieved on the morning of the 14th October and I saw him at an old Pill Box which had been made into an Aid Post. As far as I could see he had been killed by a M.G. Bullet in the head. Someone passed the remark to me "There is poor old Pies".' The Red Cross Society replied to Austin's grandfather at the beginning of May 1918: 'We deeply regret to in-

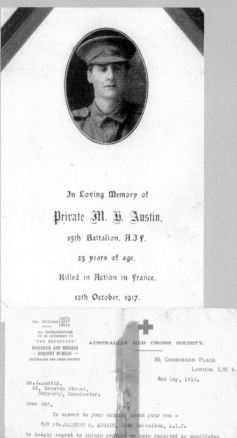

top: *Mourning card for Private Austin with the battalion colours (MMP)*
bottom: *Letter from the Red Cross concerning Austin's death (MMP)*

form you that we have received an unofficial report which we fear leaves little hope that he is alive.' The official notification followed only a month later, and gave Austin as *'now reported Killed in Action on 12-10-17'.* Austin's wife, Lizzie, who was temporarily living with her parents, was also informed. Austin's tragic death did not go unmarked by family and friends and the numerous condolence cards received by his wife are a vivid testimony to this. Almost all were decorated with the British and Australian flags.

Families could publish death notices in local newspapers in remembrance of relatives who had been killed. Given that around fifty other men had been killed on 12 October 1917 there were a considerable number of these published and Austin's family placed several, of which this - placed by his son - is an example: *'In loving memory of my dear daddy, Private Matthew Herbert Austin, who was killed at Passchendaele October 12th, 1917. You are not forgotten, daddy dear. For true love never dies. The dearest spot on earth to me is where my dear daddy lies. Inserted by his little son, Hughie.'* Other members of the family also placed their own notices. Austin's body was later recovered, *'from a point about 2 miles S.W. of Passchendaele',* northeast of the walls of Tyne Cot Cemetery and therefore not far from the 'jumping-off line' from which the battalion went into action in October 1917. Austin was reburied in the newly laid-out Passchendaele New British Cemetery.

Austin's widow remarried in the early 1920s with a man named Stoker, while his son, Donald Hugh, was brought up by his grandmother in Kurri Kurri. He followed in his father's footsteps and was a successful cyclist in the 1930s. Interestingly, the newspapers still made references to his father: *'Young Harry Austin, who on Saturday won the Weston Amateur Cycling Club's five mile road race, comes of a cycling family. His father, the late Mr. Herb Austin, will be well remembered by older residents of the town as one of the best riders in this district in pre-war days. "Pie" Austin, as he was popularly known among his fellows, lost his life during the Great War. (...) More will be heard from this lad in the future in cycling circles.'* At the age of twenty the talented Donald Hugh was hit

by a car during the Charlie Taylor Road Race and spent several weeks in hospital recovering from his injuries. It was not until 1975 that he was able to visit his father's grave in Passchendaele and this has now become a family tradition. His own son (Austin's grandson) has already visited the grave three times and his two sons (Austin's great grandsons) have also visited both the grave and the battlefields of Passchendaele.

Donald Austin at his grandfather's grave, September 2005 (Austin)

2 Commonwealth War Graves Commission

Graves Registration Units (1915-1918)

For centuries, Flanders has been the battleground of Europe, a situation that applies particularly to the Mid West Flanders ridge which forms the final natural barrier to the channel ports of northern France. Nothing remains today to remind us of the tens of bloody battles that were fought here before the First World War and the thousands of soldiers who lost their lives. After a battle, the dead were usually burned or buried in mass burial sites. In fact, many wars were fought by mercenaries who were more feared and despised than respected. In southern Europe, the burial tradition favoured ossuaries, which held the bones of the fallen and include, for instance, the chapel dedicated to the memory of the dead at Solferino. The World War I ossuary at Verdun, France, is the largest of its kind and holds the remains of 130,000 soldiers. Mass graves were used mostly by the French, both during and after the war. As late as 1915, a French regulation required the bodies of soldiers to be buried in communal graves (literally, ditches) with a maximum of one hundred men per grave and a separate place reserved for officers. On the British side, many officers were buried individually during the Boer War while low ranking soldiers were buried collectively, albeit in the face of rising criticism. Even in 1914 many British soldiers were consigned to collective graves, in many cases buried by the German forces in captured territory. Victorian mores led increasingly to individual burials even among the working classes. On the front, friends of the fallen spontaneously began to arrange individual burial sites. From 1915 on, this became compulsory if circumstances allowed.[20]

In September 1914, the 45-year-old Fabian Ware was sent to France to take command of Mobile Unit A of the British Red Cross. On discovering the many graves, he noticed that their positions were not registered and that no one was responsible for them. Fabian Ware started to compile lists with his own unit. These were very useful to the Red Cross in answering the many enquiries made by relatives of the deceased. Ware's work was much appreciated and, in March 1915, his unit gained recognition by the British Army as the Graves Registration Commission. At the end of September, the unit was effectively transferred from the Red Cross to the armed services, a move which immediately allowed for extra personnel, mainly men deemed unfit for service. In February 1916, the Commission was reformed to the Directorate of Graves Registration and Enquiries (DGR&E). The officers of the Graves Registration Units received full army status and the soldiers were paid. Fabian Ware was promoted to Lieutenant Colonel and had more than 700 men under his command by the end of the year. By April 1917, 150,000 graves had been registered in Flanders and northern France and 12,000 photographs of graves had been forwarded to next of kin.[21]

At the front, care for the dead was left mainly to the soldiers in their own sector. Special burial parties were formed and sent out at night to bury as many bodies as possible. After the battle of 26 October 1917, the 4th Canadian Division sent out a burial party consisting of 150 men - 50 from every brigade, each group led by one officer. During the battle, the men evacuated the wounded and as dusk fell they began burying the dead. This was usually limited to consigning the bodies to bomb craters and gathering a few personal effects for later identification purposes. Wherever possible a soldier's grave was marked by an inverted rifle on top of which hung the victim's helmet, or by binding together some pieces of metal and wood found near the spot. In several cases a bottle containing the deceased's

‹ Two Canadian graves under water, ca. 1917 (CWM CO2349).

personal information was buried alongside the body. The position of the temporary grave was recorded on a map and later processed by an officer or army chaplain and handed over to the Directorate with the soldier's possessions. Men from the Graves Registration Units were not allowed in the battle zone. When the frontline shifted, they could start making permanent field graves.[22]

The study of tens of files from the Passchendaele Archives revealed a clear pattern of how next of kin were informed of a relative's passing. In a great many instances the first announcement came by telegram. It was followed shortly afterwards by a letter written by an officer from the soldier's unit. The letter generally mentioned how the soldier died a quick death and how much he was missed by his comrades. A few weeks later came the official announcement by way of a completed standard form. Later still, the Directorate communicated the whereabouts of the deceased's final resting place, and this in turn was followed by a similar form from the War Office. When there was no known grave, as was graphically the case in 1917, correspondence lasting many months could ensue with the Directorate and the Regiment. Indeed, next of kin were determined to find out what had happened and where their loved father, son or brother lay buried. The Australian Red Cross Society created the Wounded and Missing Enquiry Bureau for the very purpose of finding out the exact circumstances of the death of as many Australians killed or missing in action as possible. They achieved this mainly by searching for living witnesses of a deceased soldier's final moments. This unique source material has recently been made available online by the Australian War Memorial. The Wounded and Missing Department of the British Red Cross also interviewed four to five million troops, which resulted in 385,000 reports. It is not known to us whether these files still exist today. When a body was discovered, personal objects such as identification tags, a wallet, a watch, letters and the like were usually handed over to the family of the deceased. After the war, the closest next of kin of each of the fallen soldiers were each sent a bronze memorial plaque, commonly called a 'Death Penny', which bore the deceased's name and the inscription: 'HE DIED FOR FREEDOM AND HONOUR'. It was accompanied by a special scroll and a pre-printed note of gratitude signed by King George V.[23]

Fabian Ware soon began to think of what was to be done after the war. Early in 1916 the National Committee for the Care of the Soldiers' Graves was created with the Prince of Wales as president. This advisory body was to examine the question of burial grounds. Following France, Belgium agreed in September 1917 to take ownership of the burial sites through dispossession. They were then to be relinquished in the name of the Belgian people. Fabian Ware strongly felt that the fallen from the entire Empire should be treated equally. This explains why the National Committee was transformed by Royal Charter on 21 May 1917 to the Imperial War Graves Commission (IWGC) with the Prince of Wales as its president and the Minister of Defence as chairman. The IWGC's main tasks included marking all the graves as well as building and maintaining burial sites. Initially the IWGC was greatly dependent on the services of the Red Cross. The IWGC was also tasked with publishing the registers and, after the armistice, gradually took over the Enquiries Department from the Directorate. This department went on to employ more than a hundred staff who had to find their way through 3,000 card cabinets, stacked four high over a total length of 150 metres. The Directorate, for which the War Office was responsible, stuck to identifying and (re)burying the remains. Both the Commission and the Directorate were commanded by Fabian Ware, now a Major General, which greatly facilitated co-operation. Even today, the identification of discovered remains is still the responsibility of the ministries of defence of the Commonwealth countries while the CWGC is responsible for reburials.[24]

Exhumation Units (1919-1921)

After the Battle of Passchendaele, the situation in the battle zone was so horrendous that thousands of bodies had been ripped to pieces even before they were buried. The incessant artillery fire had destroyed temporary graves to the point where they were completely obliterated. After the war urgent efforts were needed to search for, identify, register and rebury tens of thousands of soldiers who had been temporarily or partly buried, or had not been buried at all. Because of demobilisation, the Directorate was able to send only a few hundred men. When it was estimated that 15,000 were needed, a new contingent was recruited from the demobilised forces. A report

Fabian Ware (1869-1949), founder and driving force behind the Imperial War Graves Commission (CWGC)

Dead Scottish troops, some belonging to the
Gordon Highlanders, August 1917
(IWM Q7814)

top right: Australians making grave crosses in Ypres, 31 October 1917
(AWM E1405)
right: Flowers on the grave of Corporal H.E. Knowles, 235th Brigade Royal
Field Artillery, who died on 31 May 1917 and is now buried in Bedford House
Cemetery, photograph dated 1 October 1917 (IWM Q6037)

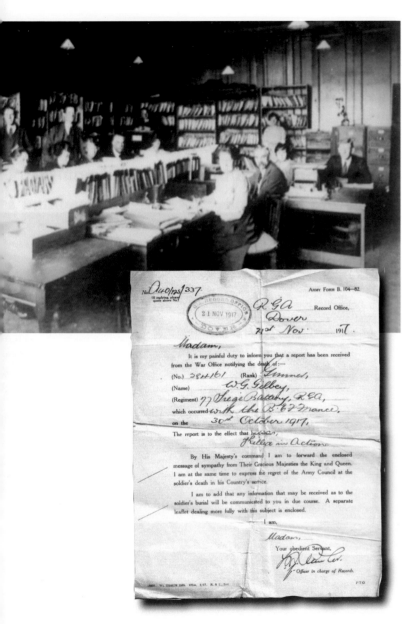

top: Gunner W.G. Gilbey from Hornchurch (Essex), 77. Siege Battery Royal Garrison Artillery (Schayes)
bottom: Photograph of the grave of Gunner W.G. Gilbey, The Huts Cemetery Dikkebus (Schayes)

Handwritten notification of Gilbey's death issued by his unit, 1 November 1917 (Schayes)

A British soldier looks for the papers of a fallen comrade in what was left of Chateau Wood, 29 October 1917 (AWM E4599)

Unburied body during the battle of Passchendaele, September 1917 (IWM Q11688).

from early 1920 indicates that 8,559 men eventually worked at un-earthing remains. How these men fitted into the army structure is not at all clear, the more so because no War Diaries appear to have survival. The burial return sheets for some of the collective burial grounds in the Zonnebeke-Passchendaele area seem to indicate that these men were organized in labour companies. Due to the nature of their task, they were called 'Exhumation Companies' but this term cannot be traced to any official army chart. Photographs show that the men usually wore the uniform of their previous war unit. They fell under the British supreme command for Flanders and northern France, and under the Directorate of Graves Registration and En-quiries. Their base camp was located at Remy Siding near Poperinge. In June 1920 their commanding officer was Colonel Sutton.[25]

The search for victims was carried out according to set procedures. Services in London first divided the battlefield into sections of about 500 m² onto which was added all possible information from the burial sheets. A special survey officer marked out these sections in the field with flags. The units were subdivided into squads of 32 men who worked in groups of four. Their standard gear consisted of two pairs of rubber gloves, two spades, a pair of pliers, stakes to mark the graves, tarpaulin and rope to wrap bodies in, stretchers and the dangerous disinfectant cresol. All possible graves on the deline-ated terrain were first marked out with stakes. This task required a great deal of experience because there were virtually no crosses left. Prominent indications of a possible burial were rat holes dug around the remains, pieces of military gear, sudden concentrations of wild grass (broad and dark sprigs) and blue-grey-black discolouring pat-terns in the soil. A commonly used instrument to prod the earth was a sharpened machine-gun cleaning rod.[26]

Only after the survey could the men proceed with exhumations. The pockets of uniforms were searched and the necks and wrists of the decomposing bodies examined for identification tags. Pieces of gear or garments such as leather belts, spoons and ground sheets could also contain numbers. From time to time legible papers were found and on a rare occasion a pocket watch enabled identification of its owner: Second Lieutenant Frederick William Putney (16/H/9), an Australian who died 12 October 1917: 'Silver wrist watch, presented by Alderman Carrington Council 1916'. According to instructions, exhumations were always to be carried out in the presence of a burial officer who collected personal possessions in separate ration bags and saw to it that the bodies were wrapped in canvas soaked with cresol. When the men came upon the body of an officer, dental records were made for matching with such information, which was more readily available in the case of officers. The exhumation was concluded by an 'A Form' in duplicate - one copy was meant to accompany the remains and the other was included with the personal possessions. These were sent to London for final examination. The slightest doubt meant a comparison with the original service files. After the identity of the deceased had been established, the regiment and family were contacted for the entry of information into the register of the new cemetery. Files were drawn up for tens of thousands of fallen men but were all destroyed in the 1930s. Today, all there is left are the published registers of the burial sites and the burial return sheets, written weekly on the basis of the A Forms which accompanied the remains. These documents specify for all post-war cemeteries where each grave originated from, on what basis the identification had been validated and whether personal objects had been sent to base.[27]

During their investigations, the exhumation units found not only British dead but also German victims. Article 225 of the Versailles Treaty stipulated that only commissions of the allied forces had the right to develop burial sites. In the British sector, the British were responsible for reburying German war dead, most of whom were given a grave behind the existing Ehrenfriedhof No. 103, at the southwestern corner of Broodseinde crossroads. At the beginning of 1925 there were 5,163 burials in that cemetery including, according to a

certain source, only 400 identified soldiers. When the cemetery was being cleared in the 1950s, 1,353 identified bodies were transferred to Menin and 3,833 to the Kameradengrab in Langemark. Even so, British efforts at identification were close to minimal. Maintenance of the Broodseinde German Military Cemetery by the IWGC left much to be desired. 'The English are absolutely not interested in the maintenance of German cemeteries in their zone,' said Lieutenant Remy just before taking over command of the cemetery under sector III of the Belgian War Graves at the beginning of 1925. Captain Stiles of the IWGC promised to do the necessary, but it is not clear who eventually did get the wooden crosses in order. The final implementation began shortly before 1930 when the cemetery was eventually transferred to the privately held Volksbund Deutsche Kriegsgräberfürsorge, which had previously taken on patronage. During this process the cemetery built by the British was fully integrated with the German cemetery Broodseinde No. 103, a cemetery which numbered 646 graves, with another 200 or so graves from three smaller burial sites that were also concentrated here. The new Ehrenfriedhof finally covered 27,135 m² and contained the remains of more than 6,000 German servicemen.[28]

left: Systematic search for human remains, Passchendaele, 1920 (CWGC)
top: Note the boggy conditions of the ground, 1920 (CWGC)

A corporal of the Labour Corps carries out the necessary formalities, 1920 (CWGC)

left: Skeleton in exposed grave, 1920 (CWGC)
top: The empty grave is filled in again, with the mortal remains on a stretcher (CWGC)

By May 1920 the Exhumation Units on the Western Front had already recovered more than 130,000 bodies and toward the end of that year the workforce was systematically reduced. One of the rare surviving reports, dated 24 June 1921, shows that there was only one Exhumation Company consisting of three platoons still operating. The first platoon worked in Flanders and numbered six officers, 135 men and 60 additional Belgian locals, and was still able to re-inter 215 British and 135 German soldiers a week. In one of the last notes by the GRUs we can read that in July and August 1921 'isolated graves have been reported by civilians and gardeners to so great an extent that two small flying squads have been kept busy on this work en-

tirely, and have not been really sufficient to deal with all the work reported'. On 31 August 1921 Great Britain officially put an end to the First World War which meant that the British troops were effectively withdrawn. A few days before his units ceased all activities on 10 September, Colonel Dick Cunyngham, Commander of the British troops in France & Flanders, delivered the following document: 'I certify that the whole of the battlefield areas in France and Belgium have been cleared of such isolated British and German graves (with the exception of German isolated graves North of Ypres-Menin Road) as were marked in any way above ground which was accessible, or could have been found by reasonably careful search. Graves so found have been concentrated, and all available particulars of identity and full information of the places of original burial and re-burial have been furnished to the Imperial War Graves Commission.' The efforts of the Exhumation Units had enabled more than 200,000 dead to obtain a final resting place.[29]

The search continues (1921-2007)

From September 1921 on, the Imperial War Graves Commission took over responsibility for the war dead. Without the help of the military it was impossible, however, to carry out systematic searches. Added to this were the facts that new remains would always be found and that the search operations could not last forever. A rare surviving report of 29 April 1922 written by Lieutenant Colonel Gell, Assistant Director of Records IWGC, shows how the former British battlefields were divided into eight sectors, with each assigned an exhumation team. The team for Area No. 1, the Ypres Salient, consisted of one Area Registration Officer (at that time a certain Major Williams), seven field assistants, one part-time office assistant and 14 workmen (of whom 10 were British and four were Belgian). They followed the last months of levelling works carried out by the Belgian state with nine teams of 30 men and 20 teams of 10 men. The document clearly indicates what ground had not been levelled: extensive pieces of land between 's Graventafel and Black Watch Corner, isolated strips of land which were in such bad condition that the budget for the works was insufficient, all the woods, all the water-logged ground, and finally, allotments or plots where there were difficulties concerning ownership. Around half of the remains recovered by then, were exhumed during the official levelling works. The other half were reported findings by farmers and contractors working on reconstruction projects.[30]

The local population was regularly instructed to report all findings to the IWGC or to the local authorities. At the end of 1919 each finding was compensated by the sum of two francs, a figure which was later raised to five and eventually 10 francs. Compensation covered only the remains of deceased servicemen from the British Empire, a fact which obviously limited the official number of recovered remains of German soldiers. As soon as reconstruction was well on its

way a new phenomenon occurred in the second half of the 1920s: the so-called 'diepgronden' (deep ground works). Hundreds of workers attracted by the high price of metal spread out across the recently levelled fields to dig for treasure. Most farmers gave permission for this for the reason that the ground was being cleared to a depth of three spades. Needless to say, many remains were found in this way. When these were not compensated they were simply looted of their valuable effects and thrown back into the ground. On 4 January 2005 we found one of those dumped German soldiers from whom the skull was missing close to Polygon Wood. Between September 1921 and the end of 1925, 9,401 remains of British servicemen, of whom 3,502 have been identified, were officially recovered on the Western Front. From time to time major discoveries were made as was the case in April 1928 on land belonging to Baron de Vinck near Sanctuary Wood, Zillebeke. The discovery involved two missing burial sites containing 80 and 82 bodies presumably from 1915 and 1916 respectively. The bodies were buried at a depth of 1.8 to 2.7 metres and were perfectly preserved. Tags had been removed from the necks but the cords were still present. In several cases a regiment could be identified and in one case the identity. The bodies were re-interred at Sanctuary Wood Cemetery. By April 1935 the number of British soldiers recovered since the operation was taken over by the Imperial War Graves Commission had risen to 26,530.[31]

Even today remains from the First World War are occasionally found. Of the estimated 200,000 missing casualties of all nationalities in Flanders, only half have found a final resting place in a cemetery or 'Friedhof'. Unfortunately not all findings are reported and many exhumations are performed unprofessionally. Contractors particularly tend to look the other way when staff come across bones because they fear that work could be halted. Collectors of militaria roaming the battlefields with metal detectors are another problem. All too often little consideration is applied when looking for pieces to add to their collections. Yet there are well-documented findings such as that of the three British servicemen discovered in 1999 in the hamlet of Molenarelst in Zonnebeke. One was identified as John R. Thomson, killed in action on 4 October 1917 while serving with the 2nd Gordon Highlanders. On 21 October 2004, he was re-interred at

Burial Return Sheet Tyne Cot Cemetery, 18 June 1920 (CWGC).

Remains separated for identification, clearly those of an Australian, 1920 (CWGC).

Burial of three unknown Canadians at Passchendaele New British Cemetery, 9 June 2003 (MMP).

Polygon Wood with full military honours and in the presence of two family members. On 17 October 2002 the remains of an unknown British soldier, found by a farmer in Schipstraat, were re-interred at Tyne Cot Cemetery. On 9 June 2003 three unknown Canadians were laid to rest at Passchendaele New British Cemetery. During archaeological excavations at the former Ypres-Roulers railway, on 27 May 2005, 400 metres from Tyne Cot Cemetery, we found the well-conserved remains of a Lancashire Fusilier who had been killed on 9 October, 1917, and buried in a shell crater between the rails of the track. At the beginning of September 2006 in Zonnebeke we were able to recover the remains of five Australians of the 50th Battalion who had died between 25 and 28 September 1917. The bodies were wrapped in blankets and tied with copper wire, a fact that enabled us to deduce historically that they had been at burial site J.7.b.7.9, which had since disappeared. The Lancashire Fusilier was reburied at Tyne Cot Cemetery on 4 July 2007, while the five Australians will be re-interred at Buttes New British Cemetery on 4 October, 90 years after they were killed in Flanders.[32]

Very soon after the war ended, the IWGC was frequently requested to re-open certain graves, because for example, people thought they could put a name to a partly identified grave or because one person had two graves. On 14 December 1921 the Commission answered a similar question put by the Australian war graves service in the following way: 'With regard to the general question of examining the contents of the unaccepted graves in every case, experience shows that in many cemeteries where the bodies are buried (or have been re-buried) in 'trench graves', the crosses are not positioned exactly over the bodies of the soldiers whose particulars they bear. The result is that if we dig under a cross to 'B', it is more likely we shall hit upon the remains of his neighbours 'A' or 'C'. This has been proved in numerous cases. For evidential purposes, I may refer to the cases of Lijssenthoek Military Cemetery and Duhallow A.D.S. Cemetery where the Americans have removed bodies of British soldiers from under crosses bearing the particulars of American soldiers. In each case it has been found that the cross to the British soldier concerned was immediately adjacent that of the American. Except in very special cases exhumation is inadvisable and would possibly, if not probably, cause confusion. We have continually before us the result of the investigations in Hooge Crater.' The Hooge Crater case must have been important because it is also referred to in other documents. Since then post factum identification can only result from historical research.[33]

After the war, identification of recovered victims was almost exclusively based on additional material findings and through a comparison with the official death lists and service files. Only in a few cases did identification arise from historical research. The most famous example at Tyne Cot Cemetery is the grave of an unknown brigadier general who up to the Second World War had been identified as James F. Riddell (34/H/14). Essential in this kind of investigation are the burial return sheets which indicate for every grave where they were found and what was found with them. This is how, in 1991, CWGC Records Officer Norm Christie was able, post factum, to assign names to four existing graves at Passchendaele New British Cemetery and the following year to another at Tyne Cot Cemetery. The latter case involved an 'Unknown Canadian Officer' buried at site 36/E/24. He served with the 47th Battalion and had been found west of Vienna Cottages. Only one officer of the unit had gone missing in that area: Lieutenant John W. Hinckesman, who died officially on 27 October 1917. Most post factum identifications involve officers as attributing a name by elimination is obviously easier because there are considerably fewer candidates. Nevertheless, the CWGC treads carefully in its approach, particularly since the questionable attribution of the grave of Rudyard Kipling's son in 1992.[34]

We are convinced that by re-studying the burial return sheets a number of graves can still be attributed. A first case we are introducing is that of Captain William M. Kington of the 1st Royal Welsh Fusiliers, who died on 20 October 1914, east of Broodseinde. The burial return sheet indicates that his remains were found at site D.23.d.10.20 together with insignia of the Royal Welsh Fusiliers and ribbons of the Distinguished Service Order, as well as the Queen's and King's South African Medals. This combination is so rare that he must be the officer involved. Another case, handed over to us by Clive Harris of Battle Honours Ltd, is about Second Lieutenant William R.S. Smith of the 28th Squadron Royal Flying Corps. On 22 October 1917 he was flying a one-seater Camel aircraft over Becelaere when he was shot down by anti-aircraft gunfire. From the burial return sheets and documents owned by the family, which had been completed by Captain G. de Trafford of the War Graves Enquiry Bureau in Ypres, it appears that he had been buried at site 60/F/16. The gravestone, however, reads: 'A Soldier of the Great War, Unknown Second Lieutenant, Royal Air Force, 1918, Known unto God." Smith himself is now commemorated as missing at the Arras Flying Services Memorial in France.[35]

Repatriation

Whether or not to repatriate the fallen servicemen became one of the most emotionally charged debates of post-war Britain. Having a grave to mourn at is indeed an important part of the grieving process. Just as the survivors were demobilized, it was argued, the dead should be able to come home as well. Fabian Ware himself insisted that the remains should not be repatriated because the process was financially and logistically impossible. As early as January 1918 the

John R. Thomson, 2nd Battalion Gordon Highlanders, missing at Molenarelst on 4 October 1917 (Thomson)
left: Reburial of John Thomson at Polygon Wood Cemetery, 21 October 2004 (MMP)

newly created IWGC declared that there was no question of repatriation after the war. Furthermore, leaving the matter to individual choice would have favoured the well-off and shattered the strongly held principle of equality in death. The heated debate escalated repeatedly even in Parliament and in the end was settled by the government. In Canada, opposition to the ban on repatriation was possibly even greater, in part because it was virtually impossible for most people there to visit a grave. For many, illegal repatriation seemed the only way out. Several French and Belgians saw a financially rewarding opportunity and stole various bodies from cemeteries such as Voormezele Enclosure No. 3. In 1920 the body of Private Grenville Hopkins, who died on 15 November 1917, north of Passchendaele, was found together with that of Private L.J. Macewen. Both had served

Discovery of the body of a Lancashire Fusilier in the railway cutting, 27 May 2005 (MMP)

Artefacts found with the Lancashire Fusilier (MMP)

with the Princess Patricia's Canadian Light Infantry and were buried at Tyne Cot Cemetery in Row A of Plot 56. In January 1921 the Hopkins family had asked in vain to repatriate the remains to Canada. On the night of 17-18 May, 1921, Private Hopkins' body was illegally disinterred and transferred to a mortuary in Antwerp from where it was to be shipped to Canada. The body was traced, impounded and reburied at Schoonselhof Cemetery in Antwerp.[36]

Remains which had been given a final resting place could in principle never be disinterred again, not for additional research or investigation and not for repatriation. The only rare exceptions applied to deceased family members who, at the request of next of kin, could

be buried together. This occurred with the Gavin brothers from Longreach, Queensland, Australia. Lance Corporal James T.B. Gavin and his brother Private G. Gordon B. Gavin, both served with B Company of the 26th Battalion and died on the same day, 4 October 1917. Their unit was stationed a little outside Zonnebeke to the right of the Ypres-Roulers railway. James, 23, was killed around 5.40 am by German fire on the frontline. His brother, two years older, was fatally shot in the head at around 9 am close to the Passchendaele-Broodseinde road. His remains were not found until 1921 and were buried at Tyne Cot Cemetery 59/C/12. At his family's request he was re-interred three years later at Ypres Reservoir Cemetery (7/B/12), not far from his brother James's last resting place (7/B/3).[37]

Excavation of the remains of five Australians at Westhoek, early September 2006 (MMP).

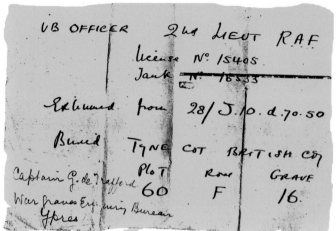

Document from the War Graves Enquiry Bureau in Ypres giving Smith's final resting place (Harris)

top: Second Lieutenant William R.S. Smith, probably buried at 60/F/16 (Harris)
bottom: Newspaper cutting of a memorial service held in his honour (Harris)

In France the call to repatriate the dead was equally forceful but the practice was also initially forbidden. Even during the war hundreds of clandestine exhumations took place, mainly with the help of shadowy figures. This shows how great the need was to have the physical presence of a grave to grieve over. As a result of public pressure from September 1920 the body of a deceased could be repatriated at the state's expense. In the following years, 30 to 40 per cent of all identified fallen were transferred to civilian cemeteries. The remaining bodies were concentrated in huge concentration cemeteries or ossuaries, the maintenance of which was at the cost of the state. In Belgium too the government hesitated a long time before taking a final stand on the matter. At the beginning of March 1921 repatriation was finally allowed and about half of the fallen Belgians were reburied in civilian cemeteries. The other dead were regrouped in official war cemeteries by the 'Service des Sépultures Militaires'. Many towns have a special burial ground for their war dead, but in smaller villages they were interred among civilian graves. In this way, quite a number of war graves have been lost during the clearing of civilian cemeteries in recent years. Belgian graves have not been centrally registered as was the case with the British. Since control of the cemeteries was transferred from the Belgian Ministry of the Interior to the Ministry of Defence at the beginning of 2004, a great deal of effort has gone into improving the remembrance process for Belgian casualties of the war. Germany, having lost the war, was also not in a position to demand that their dead be repatriated. They had been buried across some 600 cemeteries, a number which was already reduced to 177 by 1923. In the following years several more small burial sites were regrouped. Finally, in the mid-1950s it came to a draconian reduction to the four concentration cemeteries we know today: Langemark, Vladslo, Menin and Hooglede.[38]

The decision of the British not to repatriate the dead is essential to a full understanding of remembrance in our region. Hundreds of thousands of families remained separated from the graves of their loved ones. This is why no other nation has sacrificed so much to remember its dead. Massive repatriation would have caused remembrance to fade a lot faster or even to disappear altogether.

Tyne Cot as the world's largest CWGC cemetery

The decision to develop the small Tyne Cot graveyard into the largest of all IWGC cemeteries was undoubtedly inspired by its strategic location just below the crest of the Passchendaele Ridge on the 1917 battlefield. By studying the burial return sheets we could make out three distinct phases in the development of the cemetery. The first bodies were brought in in the week of 18 June 1919 by the 728th Labour Company. The remains came almost exclusively from Sheet 28.D, which is more or less the square area formed by the east of Keerselare, Passchendaele village, Molenarelst and Frezenberg. Until 23 September 1920, the unit commanded by Captain H.C. Woolley had developed plots 3 to 32. At the beginning of March 1920 the 126th Labour Company also started reburying remains at Tyne Cot Cemetery. Some of these came from that same D sector but many more came from 28.J, an imaginary square between Frezenberg, Molenarelst, Kruiseke and Klein Zillebeke, including the villages of Becelaere and Gheluvelt. The 126th Exhumation Company developed plots 33 to 57 and was last mentioned in December 1920. The third phase lasted until the beginning of April 1921 and involved plots 58 to 67. This development was executed by the No. 1 Platoon of the only remaining exhumation company, a unit which was active over a much larger area. In February-March 1921 the remains from several German cemeteries were also brought in. More on this subject can be found elsewhere in this book.[39]

The burying mostly occurred through so-called trench burials which were long trenches of 1.2 to 1.5 metres deep, in which the dead were laid to rest separated by a gap of about 60 cm. Remains which had been found in close proximity were kept together as much as possible in regard of future identification. Pending their reburial they were laid out in barracks, around which hung an all-pervading smell according to several witnesses. Given their large numbers, the bodies were wrapped only in canvas by the exhumation units. A note from 1935 indicates that, after the IWGC took over, burials occurred almost always in lined coffins of white wood. When coffins were delivered to the burial site they were covered with the Union Jack. After the remains were laid in the trench, an Army chaplain would say a prayer and the crosses would be placed in position. A Registration

Officer ensured that the right bodies were buried beneath the right crosses. The crosses were of a type that had been in use during the war by the Graves Registration Units. The identification details were stamped onto an aluminium strip which was then cut to nameplate size. Original crosses from transferred graves were re-used as much as possible. This was followed by a certain standardization by the IWGC. Starting in 1924 the crosses were systematically changed to Portland gravestones. Family members could take possession of the original wooden crosses and, if their deceased relative was missing, could ask for the cross of an unknown soldier. According to a 1997 list, there are still original crosses to be found at 236 locations in Great Britain, mainly at Churches and semi-public buildings.[40]

Given that the new cemetery was located on an historically important battlefield, remains were also discovered during reburials. These discoveries occurred almost exclusively during the first phase of the development by the 126th Labour Company. Almost all cases involved the dispersed field graves of Canadian and Australian soldiers who had been buried outside the actual battlefield cemetery at the end of October and beginning of November 1917. Very near to the cemetery the well-known Australian cyclist Matthew H. Austin was exhumed. He was killed during the catastrophic attack of 12 October 1917 while serving with the 35th Battalion and was reburied at Passchendaele New British Cemetery. The post-war logic that decided which dead should go to which cemetery is difficult to follow. During the research involving the five recently discovered Australians mentioned previously, we discovered a small burial site at 28.J.7.b.7.9. The other dead who were interred at this location had been dispersed to three cemeteries: Tyne Cot, Buttes New British and Poelcapelle New British Cemetery. In the Tyne Cot Visitors' Centre there is a silver frame with a picture of Lieutenant Randal A. Casson, 2nd Royal Welsh Fusiliers. His remains were found at Polygon Wood on 14 June 1923 by forest ranger Leon Kindt. Thy were not re-interred at one of the two closest cemeteries but at Poelcapelle New British Cemetery.[41]

The fact that identification and registration during reburial did not always proceed smoothly is illustrated by the fact that several

Gordon Gavin (right) was transferred from Tyne Cot to Ypres Reservoir in 1924 where he is buried next to his brother James (left). Both were killed on 4 October 1917 (AWM P03174.002).

Exhumation of a German war dead, Westrozebeke, 1916 (Deraeve)

dead appeared to have two graves. Second Lieutenant John Larkin of the Australian 41st Battalion died on 5 October 1917. His remains were found at 28.D.20.d.8.7 and reburied at 57/F/11. Identification was made on the basis of his disc, rank badges and watch, on which was engraved 'Jack Larkin from Mother and Father'. At 16/E/9 there was also a cross bearing his name which had been relocated from 28.D.21.d.60.40. On 14 December 1921 the IWGC decided to keep the first grave and to re-assign the second to an 'Unknown Australian Soldier'. A similar problem arose with the last resting place of the Australian Charles R. Campbell of the 37th Battalion. In this case too a body was found under a cross bearing his name, reburied at 34/J/14. However, based on an identification disc, a second cross with his name on was placed at 20/E/1, next to his friend Alan Rudge David. Both had belonged to the same unit and were killed together on 12 October 1917. In the end the second attribution based on the name plate was withheld. In both cases the Australian Graves Service asked

for the other grave to be re-opened, but the request was refused. Private James McCulloch of the Canadian 72nd Battalion also had two graves, one at 37/A/2 and the other at 37/F/3. Both identifications were made from a disc with the same reference of 28.D.17.a.4.9. Today the 22-year-old of Scots origin is officially buried at 37/F/3. It is not known why the other grave was rejected.[42]

Even though the arrival of bodies had ended by April 1921, the ministerial decree No. 11751 that made this possible was signed only on 12 September that year. Finally the Belgian war graves authorities in Bruges were responsible on behalf of the Belgian state for dispossessing the owners of the land and turning ownership into perpetual concessions for the Imperial War Graves Commission. This involved 12 complete or partial plots of ground which belonged to Lucia Joos (Ieper), Emiel Wattrelot (Armentières), Maria Malfait (then in the cloister at Gits), Maria Macquart (Langemark) and Hendrik Markey

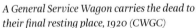

A General Service Wagon carries the dead to their final resting place, 1920 (CWGC)

(Passchendaele). By far the largest amount of dispossessed land came from the ruined farm of Karel Verfaillie, owned by Lucia Joos. It was situated on the north-west side of the cemetery and was therefore not available for rebuilding. Many things went wrong with rent payments and the dispossession procedure, mainly by the lack of funds from the department concerned. In 1922 the lands of Lucia Joos were bought by Jerome Van Eecke, who, on 30 May 1925, wrote to the office in Bruges asking why no measures had been taken to pay for his land. Only in 1928 were the changes adopted into the land register. The dispossessed pieces of land were reunited under the new lot number 373a with an area of 3 ha 49 a 71 ca.[43]

At the end of 1921, 11,871 war dead lay buried or remembered by name at Tyne Cot Cemetery. In the following years 90 more were added, mainly 'Special Memorials'. This makes Tyne Cot the Commonwealth's largest cemetery in the world. The second is Etaples with 11,557 graves and then Lyssenthoek in Flanders with 10,787. Because the largest number at Tyne Cot had died in 1917 and had only been recovered after the war, more than 70% of all bodies have not been fully identified. Around 1927 most cemeteries were closed which meant that no more remains could be buried there. Prior to the Second World War, new discoveries in the Zonnebeke-Passchendaele sector were sent to Bedford House Cemetery in Zillebeke, while until a few years ago they were almost exclusively buried at Cement House in Langemark. The latest trend for newly found remains is again to lay them at rest in the cemetery closest to the discovery.[44]

Concentration of small burial grounds

The remains sent to Tyne Cot Cemetery between June 1919 and April 1921 not only originated from widely dispersed field graves but often also from smaller burial sites. As a rule, cemeteries with fewer than 40 graves were not to be maintained. Sometimes cemeteries which were slightly larger could also be concentrated due to a difficult location. The original registers only record five burial sites by name that had been transferred to Tyne Cot although it is also mentioned that there had been more. We discovered at least eleven references to burial sites where more than 15 dead were exhumed and which therefore can be referred to as small cemeteries. The picture will only be complete when all burial return sheets have been amalgamated in a database and linked to the new survey of the current graves. But it already seems that in almost half of the cases these wartime burial grounds were limited to the victims of a particular action. This points towards burial by the units themselves rather than to open cemeteries. Only a few of them seem to have effectively had a name. Another question which can been raised is what number of dead and what geographical size constitutes a cemetery.

28.D.4.b.3.3: 17 (19) graves
28/B/21-22, 28/B/24, 30/C/21-24, 30/E/13-22

At this burial place between 's Graventafelstraat and the hamlet of Wallemolen there were solely Canadians interred from the 1st, 4th and 5th Canadian Mounted Rifles, all of whom died between 26 and 31 October, 1917. Graves 28/B/23 and 31/A/21 come from D.4.b.3.4, but it is more than likely that it was the same site.[45]

28.D.9.d.50.70: 40 (54) graves
12/D/22-24, 12/F/1-4, 12/F/6-10, 13/E/2, 13/E/5-7, 13/E/15, 13/E/20, 13/E/22-23, 13/E/26, 14/E/10, 14/H/1-2, 17/A/1-12, 18/B/3-4, 18/E/10-11

This burial site was located on the southern side of 's Graventafelstraat at about Berlin Farm. We counted 11 British, 11 Canadians and 18 New Zealanders, all of whom died in 1917 and of whom 21 were identified by name. Seven of the Canadians belonged to the Eaton's Motor Machine Gun Battery. At 28.D.9.d.50.50 were 14 graves: 12/F/5, 13/E/8, 13/E/9-14, 13/E/16-17, 13/E/21, 13/E/24-25, 18/B/5, 18/D/7.

Mortal remains are brought into the cemetery across a duckboard track, 1920 (CWGC)

A chaplain reads a prayer before the dead are buried in a narrow trench, 1920 (CWGC)

Ready for the final journey, 1920 (CWGC)

Given that they were for the most part integrated with those at D.9.d.50.70 on reburial, it is not impossible that this concerns the same burial site.[46]

28.D.9.d.9.9: Waterloo Farm Cemetery 21 graves
14/C/13, 14/C/19-20, 14/C/22, 14/C/24, 14/E/13, 14/E/16-17, 14/F/20-22, 19/G/9, 20/A/7-9, 21/G/6-11

The register mentions seven British, 10 Canadians and two New Zealanders from during and after the Battle of Passchendaele who were buried across from the Old Cheese Dairy. We found 14 British and seven Canadians of whom only six were identified.[47]

28.D.17.a.9.0: 25 graves
3/A/1/24, 23/G/2

This small burial site was just to the south of the railway cutting and not far from where the railway crosses the Passendalestraat. There were only Australians here of whom, after the war, 16 could still be identified. Graves 1-23 all resulted from the major attack of October 12, 1917, and were mostly of men from the 47th Battalion AIF. At 3/A/24 the burial return sheets show: Lieutenant Charles W.C. Bluett of the 9th Battalion, died November 3, 1917. Today Bluett rests at 4/C/21, for which no grave co-ordinate has been found. His military file states that he was buried at D.16.b.9.2, at the present cemetery, a fact which also coincides with the information gathered by the Australian Red Cross Society. "The Medical Officer Captain Rae and his assistant Private E.M. Kelly buried Lieutenant Bluett at Tyne Cottage, just behind the Aid Post. There is no registered cemetery at this place." Another document states that this occurred about 50 yards from the aid post where he died soon after his arrival. He was shot in the jaw, and witnesses did not give a uniform account on how long

left: *Levelling the battlefield before laying out Passchendaele New British Cemetery, 1920 (CWGC)*
right: *Clearing shells at Hooge Crater Cemetery, 1920 (CWGC)*

he stayed alive after receiving his wound. Today, grave 3/A/24 holds: 'A Soldier of the Great War, Known unto God'.[48]

28.D.19.a.10.10: 56 graves
5/F/4-5, 5/F/7, 5/G/21-24, 6/C/19, 6/E/2, 6/G/1-4, 7/C/1-3, 7/H/10-11, 7/H/12-16, 8/A/4-6, 8/A/22-24, 8/C/7-8, 8/C/10, 8/D/8-15, 9/A/22-24, 9/G/9, 9/G/20-21, 10/A/1-4, 10/C/17-19, 10/C/22, 10/E/22, 13/B/21

This burial site, with additions between 31 July and 31 October, was close to Pommern Redoubt in the Sint Julien district. We found 50 British, two Canadians and four New Zealanders, of whom 19 were fully identified and 37 partly identified or unknown. The additions were made from 31 July to 31 October, 1917.[49]

28.D.19.(?): Iberian South & Iberian Trench Cemetery: 30 graves
According to the register this relates to 30 British soldiers who fell between August 1917 and March 1918. Iberian Farm is situated to the north of Zonnebeek, thus again in the Sint Julien district. A search

of the burial return sheets gave absolutely no clue as to a small cemetery around the farm. On 12 April, 1921, the family of Freddy Cade (1/9th King's Liverpool Regiment, died 22 September, 1917) received information that his remains had been moved from a small burial site to Tyne Cot Cemetery. The exhumation occurred at 28.D.19.c.20.20, which is southwest of Iberian on the other side of Zonnebeke. In addition to Cade we found four graves with the same reference: 14/F/2, 17/C/3-4 and 17/C/7. Only two were identified and both of the men had died in August-September 1917. Freddy Cade worked in Leeds as a construction worker and in 1913 married Ann Jane Potter. They had two sons, Frederick and Jimmy, the latter of whom was killed in 1942 at El Alamein. The epitaph on Cade's grave 17/C/2 speaks volumes: 'Missed by those who loved him most'.[50]

28.D.21.a.30.45: Levi Cottage Cemetery: 21 graves
This burial site was situated along the Langemarkstraat opposite Maarlestraat. 10 British, eight Canadians and three Australians were buried here between September and November 1917.

left: Tyne Cot Cemetery with the north-west pillbox and a primitive morgue, viewed from a location somewhere in what is now the central axis. Note the ventilation holes, 1920 (CWGC)
right: View of the cemetery and the three eastern pillboxes, the one on the right is under plot 45, which is why the narrower plots 45 to 49 have not yet been laid out (CWGC)

A clear view of the boundaries of the original cemetery marked with pickets and barbed wire behind the central pillbox. The pillbox on the left is outside the cemetery (CWGC)

Four Canadians were identified at the time of their first interment but could not be found as such. They are remembered at the Duhallow Block. The site is mentioned in documents from 1920, but there is not a single reference to it in the burial return sheets. What happened here remains unclear.[51]

28.D22.d.25.25: Zonnebeke British Cemetery No. 2: 51 graves
44/B/28, 44/B/31-32, 44/B/35-39, 44/D/27-29, 44/D/32-33, 44/D/35-36, 44/D/38-39, 44/H/29-32, 54/F/16, 55/A/1, 55/A/4, 55/B/13-17, 56/A/15-16, 56/A/20, 57/A/16, 57/A/18, 57/A/44, 57/A/47, **Special Memorial 6-20**

Zonnebeke British Cemetery No. 2 contained 36 clearly marked individual burials, of which only seven were fully identified. Beneath the crosses lay 10 soldiers of the Buffs (Royal East Kent), 11 Royal Fusiliers, four Australians and 11 unknowns. The cemetery lay half way between Zonnebeke and Broodseinde. According to the register, it was started in April 1915, when the Germans buried 18 soldiers of the 2nd Buffs and 20 of the 3rd Royal Fusiliers on this spot. After the war, only 15 Royal Fusiliers could be traced back to this cemetery, although they could not be found as such. They received special memorials and it is almost certain that some of them received an unknown grave. According to a document dating back to 1925, something similar was intended for the 16 soldiers of the Buffs. However, this plan was abandoned as their names were already inscribed on the Menin Gate.

Around the same time in 1915, the Germans consolidated two other British cemeteries: Zonnebeke Cemeteries No. 1 and No. 3. After the war, both were transferred to Bedford House Cemetery. The register for Zonnebeke No. 1 showed 31 interments, of which 15 could not be found during the exhumations. All victims belonged to the 2nd East Surry Regiment and are remembered on a Special Memorial.

In his substantial collection, Wilfried Deraeve holds a unique picture of this spot, taken by the Germans after their successful breakthrough in April-May 1915.[52]

28.D.26.a.7.4: Kink Corner Cemetery: 11 (32) graves
57/D/22, 57/D/38-41, 57/D/43-44, 57/F/4, 57/F/29-31

This burial site was opposite the current Terca brickworks and, ac-

Freddy Cade (1884-1917), 1/9th King's Liverpool Regiment (Cade)

His surviving family: Freddy's wife, Ann Jane, with their sons Frederick and Jimmy (on her lap) (Cade)

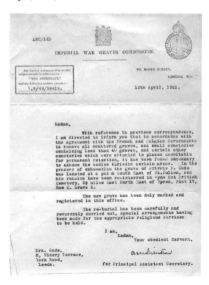

Moving the grave to Tyne Cot Cemetery, 12 April 1921 (Cade).

His grandsons Jim and Chris Cade at the grave, 22 September 2005 (Cade)

Zonnebeke British Cemetery Nr 1 (Deraeve)

cording to the register, contained the bodies of 14 British, nine Canadians and nine Australians. 11 graves were found: five were British and six Canadian. Only four of these were fully identified. They included three victims of the 124th Canadian Pioneer Battalion, who were killed by artillery fire on 18 October, 1917, while constructing a plank road along the main Zonnebeke road. Their names are Private James J. Dodd, Private Gilbert A. Evans and Private Alfred J. Michel. According to the unit's War Diary, there was also a fourth victim on that day together with 12 wounded of whom a fifth died as well.[53]

28.D.27.d.75.75: 16 (18) graves
55/B/22, 55/D/1-2, 56/D/16, 57/B/45, 57/D/4, 57/D/6, 57/D/16-17, 57/D/19, 57/A/40-43, 57/F/6-7

This small burial site, probably relating to the Second Battle of Ypres, was located on the corner of Grote Molenstraat and Citernestraat. Only one grave was identified, that of 20-year-old Private Ronald M. Sykes (57/D/17) of the 1st Cheshire Regiment. Of the 15 unidentified soldiers at least seven belonged to the same regiment. Two other

graves contained fallen from the King's Own and one grave a soldier from East Lancashire. At coordinates D.27.d.8.8. there are another two graves, 56/A/19 en 56/A/23, which more than probably were part of the same burial site.[54]

28.J.19.b.95.90: 20 graves
58/B/34, 58/B/37, 58/C/4-5, 58/C/7-16, 58/C/25, 58/F/32, 58/F/36, 58/F/41, 58/F/43, 58/F/47

All soldiers buried here fell on 20 September, 1917, during the heavy fighting in the park at Herenthage chateau ground. They belonged to the 10th Duke of Wellington's (West Riding Regiment) and were buried at the bend of the Zillebeekse Pappotstraat around Stirling Castle. Only six of the British casualties found here were known by name.[55]

left: *Entrance to the German cemetery at Oostnieuwkerke, ca. 1916 (Deraeve)*
right: *German cemetery at Staden, ca. 1916 (Deraeve)*

'Im Leben ein Feind, im Tode vereint'

During the war many British casualties, including those who died in German field hospitals, were buried in German cemeteries. They remained buried under the epitaph 'Im Leben ein Feind, im Tode vereint', until the beginning of 1921. It was then that the Exhumation Company's No. 1 Platoon began the process of moving them to specific British cemeteries. Some were moved directly to Tyne Cot Cemetery. Compiling a full list would be a long task, as several thousand coordinates would have to be looked at in order to ascertain whether there was a cemetery in such a place or not. Eight locations are specifically stated as being a German cemetery and in most cases we have been able to find some data on them.

28.J.36.a.8.5: Ehrenfriedhof No. 80 Kuiseyck: 63 graves
61/J/1-4, 61/K/1-24, 62/K/23, 63/J/9-21, 65/H/1-20

This cemetery was begun in October 1914 with various victims who fell in the First Battle of Ypres. It was the German cemetery from which the largest number of British were moved to Tyne Cot. In 1922, 138 British were moved to Zantvoorde British Cemetery and in 1932 two unidentified soldiers were moved to Sanctuary Wood. Hooge

Crater Cemetery is the final resting place of another two British soldiers who came from here. During the removal of the cemetery in November 1955, 393 unidentified Germans were moved to Langemark and 206 identified to Menin.[56]

20.W.9.b.65.95: Ehrenfriedhof Oostnieuwkerke: 24 graves
62/C/1-15, 63/C/1-9

The Tyne Cot register mentions only two burials which were disinterred here. However, the 'burial return sheets' refere to a total of 24. In the 1925-30 period the German cemetery beside Kouterweg was completely cleared and moved to De Ruiter in Roulers.[57]

20.P.23.b.7.6: Ehrenfriedhof No. 152 Staden: 24 graves
63/D/1-9, 66/D/1-15

There are 14 British and 10 Canadian soldiers at Tyne Cot Cemetery who were originally laid to rest in this cemetery. All of the Canadians died during the Second Battle of Ypres. The German cemetery was in the southwest of Staden village, with some 5,000 graves, was among the largest in the region.[58]

Memorial in the post-war 'Ehrenfriedhof Nr.29', De Ruyter (Deraeve)

right: Burial at the Colliemolenhoek, De Ruyter (Deraeve)

20.W.17.a.90.85: Ehrenfriedhof No. 29 De Ruyter: 8 graves
59/E/27-34

This was a German concentration cemetery on Ieperaardeweg, on the border between Roulers and Oostnieuwkerke. The spot was known as Colliemolenhoek, which is where the street runs to. Eight bodies were taken to Tyne Cot Cemetery from here.[59]

28.D.23.c.10.45: Ehrenfriedhof No. 103 Broodseinde: 1 grave.
Special Memorial 5

This was in use from May 1915, and was expanded as Broodseinde German Military Cemetery after the war. Here lay the original grave of Private Franklin Kelly, 1st Royal Welsh Fusiliers, who died on

19 October, 1914. His remains were never found again and he was therefore given a Special Memorial at the Duhallow Block, originally No. 56. Special Memorial No. 55 was established for a lost grave at Broodseinde German Military Cemetery. This was dedicated to Serjeant D.J. Healy of the same unit who died two days after Franklin and was buried by the Germans. His remains were finally found and he lies buried at Perth Cemetery (China Wall). The commemorative cross was removed.[60]

28.P.13.b.5.6: Ehrenfriedhof No. 109 Kortewilde: 1 grave
66/F/1

Lieutenant Campbell Lindsay-Smith was originally buried at

Zonnebeke Broodseinde Kriegerfriedhof

left: 'Ehrenfriedhof Nr 103' at Broodseinde between the wars (Deraeve)
right: Five airmen transferred from the German cemetery in the Praetbos at Vladslo (MMP)

Houthem in grave 337. He was attached to the 8th Gordon Highlanders, and died on 9 November, 1915.[61]

28.R.4.c.9.1: Ram Wood German Cemetery: 1 grave
59/F/14

Nothing is known about this burial site to the northeast of Menin on the road to Moorsele. Gunner Frank McIntosh of the Tank Corps, who died on 25 October, 1917, was moved from here. The original number of his grave was 914 D.[62]

20.N.30.d.00.80: Merckem Ford Military Cemetery: 2 graves
58/A/14-15

No thing of this cemetery is known to us. If the coordinates are correct it would have been on the north side of De Kippe – Merkem road. Whether this was a small German, French or Belgian burial site is not clear. In any case, the 20-year-old Captain Donald C. Rutter MC of the 43rd Squadron RFC, with beside him 'A Flight Sub-Lieutenant of the Great War' was exhumed here. Research shows that this must have been marksman/observer Lieutenant John B. Jackson. To-

day he is commemorated at the Arras Flying Services Memorial. His Sopwith 1 ½ Strutter was lost on 7 June, 1917, probably shot down by anti-aircraft fire. A file will be submitted to the CWGC for the identification of the grave of John B. Jackson.[63]

There are also three later exhumations at German cemeteries known to us at present:

21.S.b.6.2: Ehrenfriedhof Iseghem: 1 grave
59/C/12

This was an extension of the local cemetery on Roeselarestraat which came into use at the beginning of 1915 and held 3,102 graves after the war. On 9 June, 1924, the remains of Private Peter Pegg, 18th Canadian Battalion, who died on 19 November, 1917, were moved from here. He was re-interred at Tyne Cot Cemetery in the grave made vacant by the moving of Private Gordon B. Gavin to a grave near his brother's at Ypres Reservoir Cemetery. The number of British dead who originally had their graves at Isegem is not clear at present. In any event, there is an existing photo of the graves of two airmen

right: Soldiers from a Graves Registration Unit in an open Ford at Ypres, 1920 (CWGC).

from the 57th Squadron RFC who now lie at Harlebeke New British Cemetery.[64]

Ehrenfriedhof No. 153 Hooglede-West: 1 grave
58/A/28

This German cemetery opened in July 1917 and contained 1,117 graves including 16 British. On 24-25 June, 1924, the British burials were exhumed and the bodies taken to Harelbeke, with the exception of Second Lieutenant Charles A. Moody. Moody served with the 1st Squadron Royal Flying Corps and, for unknown reasons, was taken to Tyne Cot. On 21 August, 1917, he was flying in a patrol of six Nieuport 23 aircraft which was attacked by a Jasta 26 group. Moody's aircraft was shot down by the German Loerzer and the heavily wounded airman died later. In the 1930s all the German dead here were transferred to the still existing Hooglede cemetery, previously Hooglede-Ost.[65]

Ehrenfriedhof No. 7 Praetbos II: 5 graves
I/AA/18-22

Five British airmen were transferred in the 1920s from this well-known cemetery in Houtlandstraat, Vladslo, to Tyne Cot Cemetery. Lieutenant Cecil Barry and Second Lieutenant Frederick E.B. Falkiner of the 57th Squadron were in the same aircraft when, on 21 August 1917, they were shot down by the German ace Ernst Udet. They were buried at Vladslo at grave No. 339. Two other airmen were downed in October 1917 and a Serjeant from the 49th Squadron Royal Air Force got killed on 20 April, 1918. Vladslo itself was identified in the 1950s as one of the four German cemeteries to be kept. The number of graves rose from 3,233 to 25,644 today.[66]

Imperial War Graves Commission

Although the IWGC was established on 21 May 1917, the major responsibilities regarding war dead remained with the Directorate, and thus the army, until 1921. The Red Cross had set up a drawing office in the summer of 1918 to deal with the actual lay-out of the cemeteries and in May 1919 this was taken over by the IWGC. The design and maintenance of hundreds of cemeteries was now its main role. For this reason the Commission moved into a castle near St Omer, France, around which a former military hospital stood. By various means, but mostly via the army, materials were gathered so that, by way of example, a transport section with 150 vehicles and 250 bicycles could be formed in 1920. In Flanders the Commission used the same satellite base as the Exhumation Units, Remy Siding in Poperinge. In December 1922 the administrative base was moved to Ypres where it was housed firstly in several barracks on the Esplanadeplein and then, from November 1931 on, at its current location in Elverdingestraat.[67]

The first gardening groups were mobile ones and were often sent out for days with equipment, tents and provisions. In his analysis of the British presence in Ypres between both World Wars, Bert Hey-

vaert states there was only one gardener in 1919, but 85 in 1921 and a spectacular growth to 208 in 1924. Recruitment of new personnel was carried out at first among the former exhumation units. British veterans enjoyed an unvarying preference over the locally recruited staff, who nevertheless were much less expensive. In principle the actual building of cemeteries was contracted out and the staff were responsible only for the horticultural elements and the maintenance. But in many cases they were forced to level the ground and clean it before anything would grow. They also took care of drainage and the temporary enclosing of the cemeteries with barbed wire as well as functioning as the first guides. As many of the sites had reached their final status by 1925, staff numbers were again slimmed down to 86 in 1933. The situation in Ypres followed the general evolution in the rest of Flanders and northern France which saw a fall from 2,633 in 1922 to 667 in 1933.[68]

Initially the British were accommodated in former army barracks, but as the reconstruction took shape they rented rooms in civilian homes. Anyone who intended to stay here brought his family across or married a Belgian girl. An important factor was the devaluation of

the Belgian franc against the pound in 1926, which made the work very attractive. However well the British veterans were integrated in Ypres between both wars, there was a substantial British colony centered on St George's Memorial Church (1928) and the attached Eton Memorial School (1929). Chaplain George Robert Millner (born in 1890) was also chaplain for the Imperial War Graves Commission and was in Ypres from October 1924 until the beginning of 1939. The Memorial School was subsidized by the Commission because it considered that the children of its workforce should receive a British education. In September 1933 the school had three teachers, an assistant and 130 pupils. A special school bus picked the children up in Passchendaele and Zonnebeke. Because of the military backgrounds of most of its personnel the Commission also played an important role in the Ypres Branch of the British Legion. In 1925 Colonel H.T. Goodland was regional president and Lieutenant Colonel E.A.S. Gell one of the seven vice presidents. Members of the Commission were often the driving force behind initiatives to maintain British unity as much as possible. They had their own doctor and there was also an Ypres British Cricket Team with practice grounds near the Menin Road.[69]

left: Passchendaele New British Cemetery, duckboards can still be seen in the foreground, 1920 (CWGC)
right: Gardeners at work in Lyssenthoek, 1920 (CWGC)

In the period between the wars the IWGC also developed a good relationship with the German Volksbund Deutsche Kriegsgräberfürsorge. Fabian Ware devoted himself to the protection of peace in the name of the hundreds of thousands of British and German victims of the world war. An important development was the signing in Berlin (20 November 1935) of an agreement for the mutual respect of war graves. On 18 May 1940, Captain Reginald Haworth, director of the IWGC at Ypres from 1936 on, assembled more than 200 staff, women and children in the schoolyard for evacuation. At the time the Commission had 540 people in Flanders and northern France of whom 206 did not make it to Great Britain in time. Of those, in March 1942, 159 were interned, 36 were free (most by saying they were Irish) and 11 either dead or nothing was known about them. The British cemeteries fell rapidly into a state of neglect. The German cemeteries on the other hand were tidied up and much better maintained than they had been previously. Yet the Germans respected the agreement of 1935 and in a circular letter of 21 August 1941, the Kreiskommandantur Ypern ordered the Town Council to ensure minimal maintenance for the British cemeteries. Just as in the First World War, the now 73-year-old Fabian Ware was again Director of Graves Registration and Enquiries. He also remained head of the IWGC, through which everything was prepared in order to bury and remember the dead of the Second World War in the same manner accorded to those of the Great War. In March 1945 Captain Haworth of the IWGC was able to re-open his offices in Ypres.[70]

After the war, 152 staff members of the Commission did not return to the Continent at a time when a large number of graves had been added. The vacancies were filled by Second World War ex-servicemen, sons of the first generation of gardeners and now people recruited locally as well. In the 1960s the Commission changed its name from Imperial to Commonwealth War Graves Commission (CWGC). The head office in Maidenhead has a number of departments including Records, Works and Horticulture, which is the largest by far. In 2007 the CWGC has more than 1,300 staff for 23,264 cemeteries in 150 countries which together commemorate more than 1.6 million dead. Ypres is the headquarters of the Northern Europe Area, responsible for Belgium, the Netherlands, Germany, Poland and Scandinavia. Belgium itself has 138 staff. From 1926 on the financing of this massive operation was based on an Endowment Fund of five million pounds, the interest from which was intended to pay annual costs. The countries concerned had to add to this fund, including an 80% contribution from the United Kingdom. In 1937 the Commission had spent a total of 8.15 million pounds. Only in 1940 was the Fund complete, but this naturally enough did not take into account the large numbers of graves that would be added by the Second World War. Today the Commonwealth countries each pay an annual amount based on the number of their war graves maintained by the Commission: United Kingdom 78.43%, Canada 10.07%, Australia 6.05%, New Zealand 2.14%, South Africa 2.11% and India 1.20%. Ireland is the only nation involved which is not a member of the Commission. In 2006 a total of 42.6 million pounds was spent, equating to around 40 euro per war death.[71]

9 October 1917:

Harry and Ronald Moorhouse

King's Own Yorkshire Light Infantry

A poignant story from the Battle of Passchendaele is that of Lieutenant-Colonel Harry Moorhouse and his son Captain Ronald Wilkinson Moorhouse.

Harry Moorhouse, born in 1869, was a professional soldier, having joined the British army at the age of 22. He married Susanna Elizabeth Marsden and in 1895 they had a son, Ronald Wilkinson Moorhouse. Harry Moorhouse fought in South Africa during the Boer War between April 1901 and May 1902 and when the First World War broke out and mobilization started Harry was in a state of almost child-like excitement and could hardly wait to report for duty at the depot in Wakefield. He served with the 4th Battalion King's Own Yorkshire Light Infantry (KOYLI) from the beginning of the war and in September 1914 his son Ronald also received a commission as a Second Lieutenant with the 4th KOYLI.

France

The battalion landed in Boulogne on 12 April 1915 as part of the 49th Division. Both the Moorhouses, father and son, fought in the trenches on the Western front and had their share of wounds. On 28 August 1915 Harry, who was then still a Major, received a bullet through his right ankle. The medical officer managed to remove the bullet in a nearby dug-out and Harry was then transferred to a hospital, where it was decided to send him back to England. On 7 September 1915 he sailed from Calais to Dover on the Dieppe. His wounds were further cared for in an English hospital and he was given a few weeks convalescence leave. He returned to the front at the end of his leave and at the beginning of January 1916 he was awarded the Distinguished Service Order. In May 1916 the battalion commander, Lieutenant-Colonel Musgrove, was wounded and Harry Moorhouse was required to assume temporary command of the battalion. At the end of June 1916 he returned to his unit, but was wounded again a few days later. On 7 July 1916,

at around 4.00 a.m., at Thiepval during the first days of the Battle of the Somme, he received a bullet in his left shoulder and a piece of shrapnel in his upper-arm and *'in lightning not classified rockets they back fired before it started and burnt right hand rather severely.'* He remained at his post for another hour and a half, but *'was forced by loss of blood to seek the dressing station.'* He again sailed from Calais to England, this time on *De Stad Antwerpen* and was admitted to Leeds General Hospital where his wounds were treated. *'His general health is good'*, wrote his doctor, *'but he is weak from the loss of blood'*. Harry was again given a few weeks leave.

In the meantime, his son Ronald had been promoted to Temporary Lieutenant and later to Temporary Captain and now commanded a company in the battalion. On 10 April 1917 he was given command of a raid on enemy trenches in the Neuve Chapelle sector, involving four other officers and 91 men. *'The party blackened their faces and were fitted with body shields.'* They advanced towards the German front line under a protective barrage, but it turned out that the Germans had abandoned and all the machine guns had been removed. They immediately came under German artillery fire. *'The withdrawal was conducted with great precision, and great credit was given to Capt. Moorhouse, who was wounded, for the manner in which the raid was conducted from start to finish, though the results were not material.'* Moorhouse was slightly wounded. *'A small superficial wound under [right] eye'* put him on a hospital ship bound for England. He was admitted to the Queen Alexandria Military Hospital where he appeared before a Medical Board on 21 April. He was given three weeks convalescence leave, after which he returned to the front, where he was promoted to the rank of Captain on 4 July 1917.

top: Captain Ronald Moorhouse (Perry)
bottom: Lieutenant Colonel Harry Moorhouse (Perry)

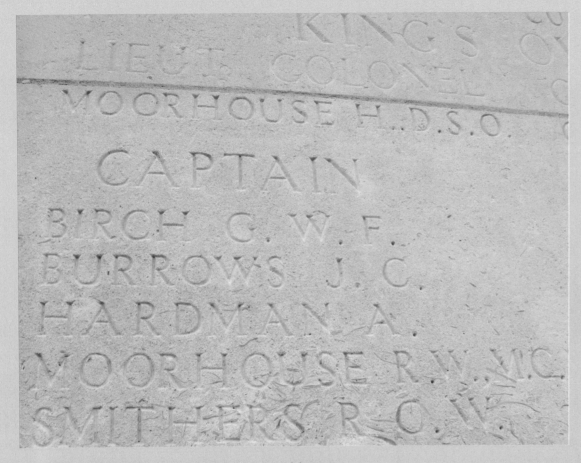

Father and son, both missing, together on the Tyne Cot Memorial (MMP)

Passchendaele

The 49th Division was due to go into action southwest of Passchendaele on 9 October 1917. In the meantime, Harry Moorhouse had assumed command of the 4th Battalion KOYLI and had been given the rank of Lieutenant-Colonel. The battalion was in reserve, but could be deployed at any moment during the attack. Their jumping off line lay between Berlin Wood and Fleet Cottage.

During the night of 8 to 9 October Harry led his men to the old German positions. In front of them men of the 5th Battalion KOYLI shuffled with difficulty over the narrow tracks which led to the front line. *'The night was intensely dark, the track was in bad repair, and progress was consequently slow.'* The signal for the attack was given just as they had reached their positions. The men of the attacking battalions immediately came under heavy fire and the 4th Battalion KOYLI was sent forward to reinforce them and they too had a hard time of it. The Ravebeek was an impenetrable morass, so the battalion had to take a detour around to the 's Graventafel-Mosselmarkt road which ran across the heights at Belle Vue. Captain Moorhouse led his company across the road to its first objective just in front of Kronprinz Farm. The Germans had a clear view of his company and *'the fire from Wolf Copse on the left and from Belle Vue on the top of the slope was devastating. Capt. R.W. Moorhouse was killed whilst gallantly leading his company. Half an hour later Lt.-Col. H. Moorhouse was killed by a bullet when leaving his headquarters (...).'* The attack came to a halt and further progress became impossible. The entire brigade fell back almost to their start position. In the evening, the New Zealanders relieved them and took over the front line. The 4th Battalion KOYLI had lost 191 men, including 43 who were missing presumed dead. The 48-year-old Lieutenant-Colonel Harry Moorhouse and his 23-year-old son Captain Ronald Wilkinson were among the dead. Their bodies were never recovered, and both men are remembered at the Tyne Cot Memorial.

3 Architecture

Herbert Baker (1862-1946), the architect of Tyne Cot Cemetery, ca. 1925 (CWGC).

< Building the Memorial to the Missing, in the background is the roof of the Dierick farm, on the site of the present visitors' centre, 1926 (Daniel)

Herbert Baker

Herbert Baker was born in 1862 at Cobham in Kent and studied at Tonbridge. He undertook his professional studies with his London cousin Arthur Baker and following this was chief assistant to Sir Ernest George, through whom he met Edwin Lutyens. In 1892 Baker left for South Africa where he became friends with the British statesman and mining magnate Cecil Rhodes. There he was able to rebuild Rhodes's burned out house 'de Grote Schuur', for which he took inspiration from the Dutch-origin Boers. His work impressed Rhodes so much that he was entrusted with major official projects. First, however, Rhodes financed a study trip for Baker to Italy and Greece because he believed that inspiration for the new South African architecture should come from the Classical era. By the time Baker returned Rhodes had died. Baker designed a large monument in honour of Rhodes, that was to prove the beginning of an impressive series of state projects, including Government House, the Union Buildings, the cathedral and station at Pretoria, Rhodes University College at Cape Town and many more. In 1912 Baker joined Edwin Lutyens as architect for the new government buildings in New Delhi (India). Both in South Africa and India he mixed classical architecture with typical elements of the country. This did not strike a chord with Lutyens, whose architecture was considerably more abstract and monumental. They both had a different temperament, a fact which on more than one occasion led to clashes.[72]

As early as the autumn of 1917 Baker was asked by Fabian Ware to be one of the principal architects for the design of the cemeteries. The others were Edwin Lutyens, with whom Baker would rather no longer work, Reginald Blomfield and later Charles Holden. Baker worked in France, with Tyne Cot Cemetery his only project in Flanders. His most important work includes the Memorial to the Indian Missing at Neuve Chapelle, the South African monument at Delville Wood and the Dud Corner Cemetery at Loos. He worked for the Commission until 31 March 1928. During that time he also designed war memorials for a variety of prestigious schools, of which the memorial at Winchester College is by far the most important. Later he designed India House, South Africa House and – not without some controversy – the new building of the Bank of England, all in London. In 1916 he was knighted and a year later was awarded the gold medal for architecture by the Royal Institute of British Architects. Sir Herbert Baker died on 4 February 1946.[73]

The four principal architects worked on a part-time basis for the War Graves Commission and received 600 pounds a year for this. In addition, some ten assistants, mostly military architects, were working full-time at Longuenesse and received 500 pounds. In practice many of the cemeteries were designed entirely by them. Baker drew or supervised the design of 113 cemeteries and memorials. One of his leading assistants, who also designed for Tyne Cot Cemetery, was Major John Reginald Truelove (1886-1942). Before the war he had worked for six years as an independent architect and then served as a captain with the 24th London Regiment until wounded, first in 1915 at Festubert and then in 1916 at Vimy. In 1919 he was appointed assistant resident architect. During the Second World War Truelove again worked for the War Department and designed anti-aircraft headquarters. The submission of a design was mostly the result of basic discussions between the principal and assistant architect, and the horticultural officer. Advice then had to be taken in London from

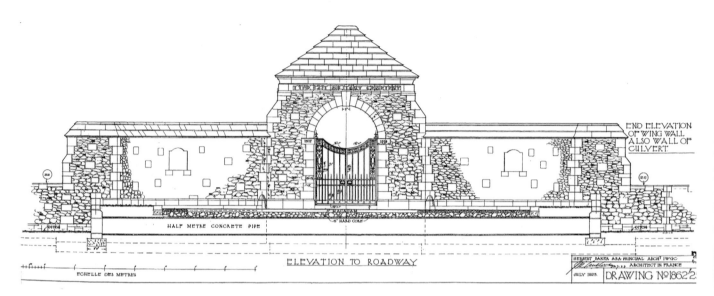

The monumental entrance gate (MMP)
left: Original plan of the entrance gate, drawn
by J.R. Truelove, July 1923 (CWGC)

the Director of Works on matters such as the garden design and the cost of the project. Final approval was given by Sir Frederic Kenyon, Director of the British Museum, who, as architectural supervisor, weighed up the design in accordance with the basic principles of the IWGC.[74]

Old English and Classical: A unique concept

We have seen that the introduction of the principal architects themselves to many cemetery projects was limited to formal approval of submitted designs. In the case of Tyne Cot Cemetery the general plan was designed by the assistant Reginald Truelove. This presumably occurred in 1919, because in April 1921 all human remains had already been placed in their present positions. The earliest existing plan, that of 23 March 1921, is in the Visitors' Centre at Tyne Cot. The south-eastern bunker was not preserved in this first plan, although the north-eastern one initially was as there were no talks at that stage of a Memorial to the Missing. The decision on this came only in mid-1922. The actual architectural design and attachments, which are today held at Maidenhead, date from 30 July 1923. These were also drawn by Major Truelove, but Baker's input was clearly much greater at this stage. In any event, photos confirm that building did

not start before the end of 1923. The architecture of Tyne Cot Cemetery is an exceptionally successful mix of the Classical with elements of Old English.[75]

Before Baker set to work on Tyne Cot he was asked among other things to design a memorial to the old boys of Winchester College who had died in the war. This was dedicated on 31 May 1924. Between the old buildings he set a type of cloister passage with, in the centre, a memorial and an entrance way inspired by those in the old English cemeteries of Hampshire. It was in these churchyards that he also learned the use of silex. Both elements return emphatically in his design for Tyne Cot Cemetery. The gate is closely related to that at the memorial in Winchester and also has a tented style of roof and bowed entrance with a wrought iron fence. In Winchester Baker also learned the Latin name of the city Venta Belgarum and it is not impossible that the architect had thoughts about linking this Belgian connection in England with the largest British cemetery in Belgium. His memorials almost always reveal something of the national romanticism of the country for which they are destined. He saw Tyne Cot Cemetery as an old English cemetery that was so beautiful that direct confrontation with the dead was tempered by the beauty

The entrance gate of Winchester College and
that of Tyne Cot Cemetery (Deseyne).

The two angels were finished in situ, ca. 1926 (CWGC)

itself. 'Our task was to beautify the hallowed resting-places of our dead, and, even when they slept on hard-won battleground, to glorify the victory rather than the sacrifices seemed to savour of that undue pride which the Greek called hubris.' With this outlook he was also against monuments that were too ambitious. 'My feelings, too, were against any general tendency to grandiose monumental architecture', he said, a statement which in the first place was meant for his long-standing colleague and competitor Lutyens. The Old English style must provide relatives of those fallen with the idea that their loved ones had, in one way or another, come home. The cemeteries designed by Herbert Baker are therefore the least abstract, the most sentimental and, for many visitors, the most stunning.[76]

In addition to national elements, the architect always found inspiration in classical architecture which, at Tyne Cot, is mostly to be seen in the Memorial to the Missing. This curving memorial is 230 metres long and represents the three different angles of the rear wall. We will expand on its content and symbolism in chapter six. At the centre of the memorial, two rows of six Tuscan pillars provide the entrance to a semi-circular paved inner court with eight wall panels bearing the

names of missing New Zealanders. At an equal distance from each side of the central opening is a round court with a colonnade of two four-pillar entrances. Each is of grass with the exception of the paved path that follows around the wall. This style causes one to think immediately of the Greek peristylium, an inner garden ringed with pillars, to which the Old English cloister corridors also owe something. These gave inspiration to Baker for the memorial in Winchester and for a great many more memorials. Circular and semi-circular elements are a clear constant in all his architecture. The two ends of the memorial wall each have a pavilion with a bowed opening borne by four heavy corner pillars. Each is crowned by a finely designed dome with a sculpture of a kneeling angel bearing a wreath. These two figures create an entirely different impression than, for example, the lions at the Ploegsteert Memorial or the Menin Gate in Ypres. They weigh around 3.5 tons and were made by the sculpture atelier of Ferdinand Victor Blundstone (born 1882). The wreaths were completed by Joseph Armitage on site at the beginning of May 1927, only weeks before the dedication. The impressive pavilions are closely related to another of Baker's important works, the memorial to the South Africans at Delville Wood.[77]

There is virtually nothing remaining in the CWGC archives at Maidenhead about the actual building of Tyne Cot Cemetery. The execution of the work was mostly put out to British contractors who then worked with local sub-contractors. There is, however, a little remaining about the materials used. The silex in the walls is combined everywhere with pieces of white stone (about one per 3 m²) and red brick (about one per m²). The wall construction itself is hollow allowing extension and contraction resulting from frost, with a foundation of dark bluestone from Normandy (Basse Normande). During the building works enormous quantities of silex arrived at the Zonnebeke station and were then loaded onto wagons by farmers and taken to the site. There the stone was split and placed with the level side facing outwards. 75 % of all pieces had to be larger than 15 cm. The covering stones on the wall were cut from Pierre Romaine de Lens, a silver-white chalk stone from the Nimes region in France which was also used for the pillars in the Memorial to the Missing. The stone steps were made of French white stone, mostly Villars

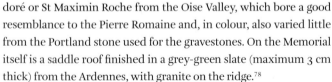

doré or St Maximin Roche from the Oise Valley, which bore a good resemblance to the Pierre Romaine and, in colour, also varied little from the Portland stone used for the gravestones. On the Memorial itself is a saddle roof finished in a grey-green slate (maximum 3 cm thick) from the Ardennes, with granite on the ridge.[78]

Cross of Sacrifice and Stone of Remembrance

A visitor to Tyne Cot Cemetery is led, as it were, to the centrally situated Cross of Sacrifice. This architectural element can be found at virtually all Commonwealth cemeteries. On the cross is a sword, blade down, as a symbol of sacrifice – the battle has been fought

and the dead are now mourned. Only much later, the cross was assigned a religious symbolism. The Cross of Sacrifice was designed by Reginald Blomfield (1856-1942) who, among other works, also did the Menin Gate, St George's Memorial Church and 120 cemeteries, including Lyssenthoek, Brandhoek and New Irish Farm. There are four variants of the cross between 4.5 and 9 metres high depending on the size of the cemetery and the location. They mostly stand on an eight-sided base and, in construction terms, are of two parts: the bottom piece, and the top piece with two arms. The placement of the Cross of Sacrifice at Tyne Cot Cemetery is one of the most unusual on the Western Front. Indeed, it was mounted on a type of

Original plans of the southern pavilion and the Cross of Sacrifice, drawn by J.R. Truelove, July 1923 (CWGC)

Pavilions of the South-African monument at Delville Wood and at Tyne Cot Cemetery (Deseyne)

pyramid structure above a German bunker which had been partly demolished for this purpose. It is often said that this was an idea of King George V, but in his memoires Baker wrote explicitly that the King had proposed only that the bunker be preserved within the cemetery. On the western side of the bunker a square section of 1.1 metres remains visible. There is a laurel wreath in bronze set on it and underneath the following words: 'THIS WAS THE TYNE COT BLOCKHOUSE CAPTURED BY THE 3RD AUSTRALIAN DIVISION 4TH OCTOBER 1917'. For a number of years the capture was incorrectly ascribed to the 2nd Australian Division. Both the steps and the cross itself are clad in the stone rather grandly named Pierre Ro-

maine de Lens. From the Cross there is a fine view of Ieper and the West Flanders range of hills.[79]

After the Cross of Sacrifice, the visitor is drawn further through the main axis of the cemetery by the Stone of Remembrance. This resembles a type of altar – and in large services is used as such – but is in fact a stone sarcophagus. De monolith weighs some 10 tons and offers an impression of the idea of eternity. It stands on a plinth with three steps and measures 3.66 x 0.84 x 1.07 metres at the base with a slight narrowing at the top. The stone is a typical creation of Edwin Lutyens (1869-1944) who often used elements from Greek antiquity,

Blomfield's Cross of Sacrifice at dusk (MMP)

Memorial plaque commemorating the capture of Tyne Cot by the 3rd Australian Division with remnant of the original pillbox under the 'Cross of Sacrifice' (MMP)

The Stone of Remembrance designed by Edwin Lutyens with text by Rudyard Kipling (MMP)

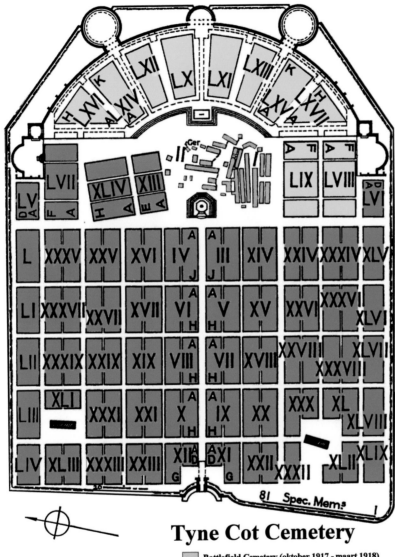

Tyne Cot Cemetery

Plan of Tyne Cot Cemetery (CWGC / MMP)

right: Design by Herbert Baker, 1923 (Wipers Times)

	Battlefield Cemetery (oktober 1917 - maart 1918)
	728 Labour Company (juni 1919 - september 1920)
	126 Labour Company (maart 1920 - december 1920)
	N° 1 Platoon Exhumation Company (januari - april 1921)

reducing these to their essence with stark lines and colossal dimensions as a consequence. Examples of this are the large Memorial to the Missing at Thiepval, the Cenotaph in London and, in more or less the same way, the 130 cemeteries he designed including Birr Crossroads, Hooge Crater and Sanctuary Wood in Zillebeke. The making of a Stone of Remembrance at that time cost 500 pounds, a sum which would represent 75,000 euro today. Lutyens refused to accept a smaller and cheaper version while Blomfield agreed to the different sizes of the Cross of Sacrifice. The Stone of Remembrance is therefore only placed in cemeteries of more than 400 graves. On both sides are the words 'THEIR NAME LIVETH FOR EVERMORE', chosen by Rudyard Kipling from Ecclesiastics, chapter 44. Verse 14 in fact reads: 'Their bodies are buried in peace, but their name liveth for evermore'. The first part was not acceptable to Hindus and Sikhs who do not bury their dead but cremate them.[80]

General overview

Rudyard Kipling (1865-1936) described the establishment of the cemeteries as 'the biggest single bit of work since any of the Pharaohs - and they only worked in their own country'. The high costs of establishing the first cemeteries caused the British Government to intervene and put a ceiling on spending. As a result of this, Stones of Remembrance, entrance buildings and remembrance pavilions were not placed at all sites. There was, however, no saving on elementary items and, for example, gravel was resolutely avoided in

Aerial photograph, ca. 1970 (MMP)

favour of natural stone. The good taste of design was never allowed to be squeezed. Finally, limitation of costs led to more discipline and uniformity, and less extravagance on the part of the architects. Through their successful combination of Classical architecture with frequent Old English elements, most British cemeteries have a sense of timelessness, in contrast with the French and Belgian cemeteries which are dated. 'There is an absence of spirit and feeling', wrote Luc Schepens about the Belgian cemeteries, 'because there is something lacking in the architecture... the bombastic gravestone is not sober enough to provide meaning nowadays'. The British architects also

paid great attention to the role of the cemeteries within the landscape. Thus the design of Tyne Cot Cemetery is entirely integrated within the slopes of the Passchendaele ridge. Because of this factor, no two cemeteries are identical. Today the CWGC endeavours to ensure that the immediate environments of the cemeteries as far as possible remain free of newly built edifices which have an impact on the perceptions of the visitor.[81]

Tyne Cot Cemetery covers 3.5 hectares and is designed around five bunkers of the Flandern I Stellung, of which three visibly modify the

left: View of the south side of baker Markey's house, now the 'Klaproos' Bed & Breakfast, 1926 (Daniel)
right: The central axis, seen from the Cross of Sacrifice, 1926 (Daniel)

architecture. The central bunker lies at an equal distance from the two foremost concrete constructions but the line is not parallel to the Tyne Cotstraat. Symmetry which is the most apparent characteristic of this site when you visit it, has not been carried through the entire plan. The entrance frontage follows the curve in the street but the northern and southern sides, which are parallel, are not at right angles to the street and are therefore not the same length. As a result, the western entrance wall is detached in the sense that it does follow the other lines, with the exception of the entrance building situated at the centre. This is where the main axis of the site begins. The central axis follows a grass path to the Cross of Sacrifice, the Stone of Remembrance and the New Zealand Memorial. The first part of the cemetery on each side of the main axis between the entrance and the cross, is divided into almost symmetrical rectangular grass plots to which the long sides run parallel. These plots are quite uniform and generally consist of eight rows of some 200 graves each.[82]

The Cross of Sacrifice is the central point of two concentric fragments of a circle. The smallest of these is built as steps leading up to the

Stone of Remembrance while the largest is the rear wall and Memorial to the Missing. Between the two, the graves have been arranged concentrically while between the sections there are seven rows radiating from the Cross to the rear wall. The three most important are the main axis leading to the NZ Memorial and the two paths to the rotundas at the northeast and southeast ends of the rear wall. The highest step of the concentric semi-circle around the Stone of Remembrance passes over a small north-south oriented wall which, on its western side, connects on the same level as the remembrance pavilions to the curved rear wall. At the same time this functions as the demarcation line for the upper section of the cemetery. Two other extensions leave from the Pavilions into the lower part of the cemetery and because of this the impression of the Memorial to the Missing is enhanced. The seven grass plots between the Cross of Sacrifice and the Stone of Remembrance all have different lay-outs while the eight plots against the back wall fan out with the Stone of Remembrance as the focal point.[83]

From the air, Tyne Cot Cemetery gives the impression of a large church with the graves as the pews, the Stone of Remembrance as the altar and the curved back wall as the choir. The Australians, for whom the cemetery is especially important, tend to recognize in this the rising sun of their country. And, according to Baker himself, there are similarities with classical amphitheatres – the cemetery has about the same diameter as the Coliseum in Rome. Whichever way the architecture is interpreted, it first and foremost honours the dead. Tubby Clayton of Talbot House wrote that Tyne Cot 'with this reverent feeling of the English churchyard, made a deeper impression on old soldiers, who visited it, than some of the more imposing architectural monuments'. On a visit to the cemetery a feeling of grief is overtaken by one of consolation, the idea that in death everything has come good.[84]

Horticulture

Walking through Tyne Cot, the visitor is immediately struck by the greenery, which is as important as the architecture itself. From the very first phase of design, the IWGC aimed at the perfect balance between each. For all major projects the IWGC sought the advice of the Royal Botanic Garden at Kew and particularly of its director, Arthur Hill. Even the choice of flowers, plants, shrubs and trees had to reflect the national romanticism. This led to the idea of an open English garden, the typical cottage garden which, at Tyne Cot, is even enhanced by the architecture. Flowers and plants add to the feeling of consolation rather than hinting at death itself. This is in sharp contrast to the German cemeteries where the feeling of death is omnipresent because of their abundance of oak trees and lack of flowers among other reasons.[85]

Each year the Tyne Cot gardeners replace a fifth of all the plants which means that the entire cemetery is renewed every five years without ever really being in a state of refurbishment. This work usually occurs between mid-October and the beginning of March. In the summer, gardeners are mainly occupied mowing the grass, trimming

left: View of the north side with the reconstructed Henri Deleu farm, known during the war as Hamburg Farm, 1926 (Daniel)

In full bloom, ca. 1965 (MMP)

George Waite in his last years at Tyne Cot, ca. 1970 (Saelens)

left: Edgar Blake on one of the first sit-down lawnmowers, ca. 1950 (Blake)
middle: Posing for a photograph: Ted Owen, ca 1950 (Owen)
right: Gardener George Duprés just before his death, 1958 (Duprés)

After the Second World War the gardeners wore a blue uniform resembling the army battledress. On the far right is the young Edgar Blake and in front of him (with moustache and beret) his father William, ca. 1950 (Blake)

the edges and spraying weeds. It is important to note the distinction between front and back borders, the planting in front of and behind the gravestones. These vary in width from 45 cm to 60 cm. At first sight the planting appears natural and spontaneous but on closer inspection reveals an apparently systematic approach. Roses and dots alternate between the graves. In front of the gravestones are so-called anti-splash plants, which are tall enough to prevent gravestones being spattered with mud but low enough to enable the epitaph to be read. In front of these are front plants which usually grow taller but are not so dense as to block sight of the gravestone. The flowers and plants were chosen so as to be in bloom with every season. Only five rows of gravestones with a broader pathway also have back borders. In 1964 almost all gravestones had back borders but by 1971 these had been reduced to every other row. Repeatedly there were demands to reduce the numbers even further. In many of those back borders stood tall and often bombastic hedge plants such as holly. The last of these were finally removed in the 1980s. Today's plants in the five remaining rows do not come much higher than the gravestones and give extra cachet to the cemetery.[86]

Bertram Rooke, who worked at Tyne Cot in the early 1950s, seen here in later life during maintenance work on the grass borders at Perth Cemetery (China Wall), ca. 1980 (Rooke).

Cutting up the roots of a tree behind Tyne Cot Cemetery (left to right: Peter Grant, Michel Dejonghe and Tom Beswick), ca. 1970 (Beswick)

The permanent team at Tyne Cot anno 2007 (from left to right: Koen Lobelle, Dirk Derycke, Stephane Mortier and John Gilliland (MMP)

Another characteristic element of the CWGC cemeteries is the perfectly maintained grass, mown every week to a height of 2 cm. This is usually done with a cylinder mower and at Tyne Cot means four men working an entire day. In dry periods a rotary tractor mower is employed allowing only one gardener to mow the entire cemetery in one and a half days. The machine is so cumbersome, however, that on a wet day it actually causes damage and therefore cannot always be used. Due to the rising number of visitors the grass in the middle path has been re-sown several times. For this reason the grass has recently been reinforced with a plastic netting underlay. In the spaces between the graves where there are no paths, stood conifer-style trees until the early 1990s, and between the entrance and the Cross of Sacrifice there were conically shaped box plants on each side. The removal of the holly, conifers and the box plants combined with control over the growth of plants has, over the last 15 years, greatly enhanced the simplicity and provides a much more evocative experience for the visitor.

Although Tyne Cot is a very large cemetery there are, in fact, not many trees. The most famous are the two times four Italian poplars close to the foremost bunkers. These trees were replaced once about 1960. The bunkers themselves were overgrown with ivy. In line with the Cross of Sacrifice stand six maples and along each of the two side walls are eight young oaks. As was the case with their predecessors, their growth is being hindered by the wind. On the outer side of both walls stood a thorny hedge until well into the 1920s. There are also ten funereally associated green yews in front of the steps leading to the semi-circular rear section, and smaller yellow yews near the New Zealand Memorial to the Missing. Originally there were more poplars behind the Memorial to the Missing and three cedars which cast shadow and are recently replanted.[87]

The Commonwealth cemeteries always look in prime condition. Badly maintained cemeteries give the impression that the past and the fallen are not important. It is for this reason that the maintenance standards applied today are as high as they were in the 1920s. This does not preclude searching for new techniques in order to reduce maintenance costs. The number of full-time gardeners at the

The Last Post sounded by the buglers of the Last Post Association during the visit of a delegation from South Africa, 1985 (Deforche)

cemetery has been reduced from 12 before the war to eight in the 1950s to four today: Stephane Mortier, Dirk Derycke, John Gilliland and Koen Lobelle. In 1994 the gardeners were provided with a new workshop behind the northern pavilion of the cemetery. In terms of organization Tyne Cot Cemetery is the major site of the Tyne Cot Group. There are two more staff stationed at Poelcapelle New British Cemetery while the six other gardeners in the group are mobile and perform maintenance at Passchendaele New British Cemetery, Dochy Farm, Dadizele, Harelbeke, Crest Farm and 17 more locations that even reach beyond Courtrai.[88]

Symbols of remembrance
Words count for little where emotionally laden memories relating to the fallen are concerned. Symbols are much less explicit and more recognizable. When individual memories are shared publicly we speak of remembrance. Here too, symbols or symbolic acts clearly indicate the importance of the past and its relevance for the future. These symbols and symbolic acts link memories with those who are being remembered, the present with the past, life with death. People

who visit Tyne Cot today are quickly confronted with various symbols of individual or collective memory. On a daily basis there are small or much larger acts of remembrance and from time to time official commemorations, which we will discuss in the final chapter.[89]

The best known symbol of remembrance for those who died at war is, of course, the poppy. Poppies have always been a symbol of a gentle death, which has to do with the blood-red colour of the flower and the fact that opium is harvested from it. The poppy flowers for a short time just like life itself, and grows best in untilled ground. On the battlefields of the First World War poppies were often the only flowers in an unendingly desolate landscape. The Canadian Army doctor John McCrae thought much the same way when he wrote his most famous poem in 1915: 'In Flanders Fields the poppies blow, between the crosses row on row'. This poem made the poppy into an important symbol of remembrance already during the war itself. The idea of producing artificial poppies came from within American veteran circles and the British Legion began production in 1921. Revenue from poppy sales helped to support needy veterans and the surviving families of those who died. The Poppy Appeal was such a huge success that a small factory was built in 1926 and the company still exists today in Richmond, Surrey. Right from the beginning the factory employed disabled servicemen. Today the factory has a staff of 42 of whom 70% are disabled. In 2006 the factory produced 36 million poppies for a total revenue of 24.7 million pounds, which still goes to the original charity. Scotland has its own Lady Haig Poppy Factory in Edinburgh where a further four million are produced annually. In the period around 11 November hundreds of thousands of Britons – from the newsreader at the BBC to the Prime Minister – wear the poppy as a symbol of remembrance.[90]

In addition to the individual poppies there are also wreaths and small crosses bearing the word 'Remembrance'. Wreaths of poppies have almost entirely replaced flowers at services. Many British schools and regimental associations lay a wreath at the Stone of Remembrance or the Cross of Sacrifice. The small crosses are more of an individual offering on which something is written or attached. Sometimes that can be a photo of the soldier or his children, some-

Written in a child's hands and left by the grave of a unknown soldier (MMP)

times a personal message to someone that the writer in fact never knew. At large international services poppies are still scattered, following the tradition of the British Legion Festival of Remembrance at the Royal Albert Hall, London, which began in 1927. In recent years use of the poppy has further expanded as a universal symbol of remembrance for all war dead, including those of the Second World War. Visiting the area, even numbers of Belgians and Dutch are wearing the poppy...[91]

Apart from poppies, other things are also brought to Tyne Cot Cemetery. Canadians mostly bring small white flags with a red maple leaf as their national symbol. For New Zealanders this is frequently an item such as a silver fern on a black stoneware backing. Scottish bring often a piece of stone from the birth region of the person they have come to remember. Folios with photos and normal flowers are to be seen at all times. When these are destroyed by the wind and the rain, or can no longer be read, they are discreetly removed by the gardeners. The Jewish death ritual is an entirely different thing. In the Old Testament the dead were covered with stones so they would not fall prey to wild animals. In this way they could lie undisturbed

Disabled employees at work in the 'Poppy factory' in Richmond (British Legion)

until the resurrection. There are therefore small stones on virtually all the Jewish graves at Tyne Cot – flowers are given only to the living. Anyone who does not bring a material item of remembrance is able to sign his or her name and write a comment in the Visitors' Book. This can be found in the special register box at the entrance to the cemetery.

In addition to material symbols there are also several recurring acts of remembrance such as one or two minutes of silence and the playing of the Last Post. Observing two minutes of silence first occurred on 11 November 1919, at precisely 11.00 hours. It has since become a fixed part of many remembrance services. The Last Post is an old bugle call used by the British Army to indicate the end of the day. Even during the First World War, and particularly afterwards, it was often played as a tribute to fallen comrades. Today the Last Post is, of course, primarily associated with the Menin Gate in Ypres where it is sounded every night at 8 pm. At Tyne Cot too you can hear the call regularly, certainly when visited by one of the many military groups. At Scottish remembrance services one will often hear the gripping lament 'Flowers of the Forest'.[92]

13 October 1917:
Phillip Schubert
34th Battalion AIF

Anton Schubert and Karoline Walk arrived in Australia in early March 1853. They had been married in October 1843 in Kafertal, Germany. Both came from farming families, but in rural Kafertal they had suffered a string of bad luck. The economic crisis of the 1840s had hit their family very hard and four of their children died when they were scarcely a year old. The Schuberts decided to take their three remaining children and risk the passage to Australia in order to start a new life. Two of them died during the voyage and when they finally got to New South Wales only their oldest child was still with them. Anton and Karoline went on to have four more children while in Australia. The oldest, Joseph, was born in Singleton in January 1855 and married Elizabeth Benton, the daughter of English emigrants in February 1884. They had thirteen children and their sixth child was Phillip Stanley Schubert, born in Singleton on 31 December 1892. As a boy, Phillip regularly helped on his parents' farm and vineyard. His father Joseph spoke English fluently, but could not disguise his German origins.

To war

Phillip eventually left the farm and found a job as a clerk with a railway company. The railways, like the coal mining industry, were new economic activities in the region and provided work for a large number of young men. Phillip moved to Scone, but did not forget his parents, brothers and sisters and took advantage of his working for the railway to send them regular parcels containing food and other items. Inspired by the enthusiasm of the volunteers in the recruiting campaign *The March of the Wallabies,* which also passed through Scone and Singleton, Schubert left his job with the railways on 7 January 1916 and reported to the recruiting office in West Maitland. His decision to join up was not taken overnight and he would almost certainly have consulted his family before doing so. He was, after all, of German origin and it was by no means impossible that there might be other members of the family fighting on the enemy side.

Sergeant Phillip Schubert (Schubert)

Soon afterwards, the 23-year-old Schubert was posted to D company of the 34th Battalion and was promoted to Sergeant, probably because of his previous military experience serving with the local militia. He underwent basic training at Albion Showground in West-Maitland and in early March 1916 the battalion moved to a new training camp in Rutherford. On 1 May 1916 the 34th Battalion boarded a train for Sydney, where they embarked on the Hororata the following day. After a brief stopover in Port Said on the Suez Canal, the men sailed for England aboard the Aragon. The battalion disembarked in Plymouth on 23 June and marched to Salisbury for further training. On arrival, Schubert immediately

Grave 27/D/9 in Tyne Cot Cemetery (MMP)

wrote a postcard home: *'Just a [postcard] to let you know I have arrived in England and am quite well. I will write a long letter to you as soon as I get settled. Give my love to all at home and kiss little Ettie [Ethel, his eight year old sister] for me from your loving son.'* In mid-December Schubert was admitted to hospital suffering from flu, but was fit again two weeks later. He wrote another card home at the beginning of January 1917: *'Just a [postcard] of myself & my mate to let you see that I am still alive and smiling. It must be because we think of home as we go about our daily work.'*

The front

His training continued and he was not able to join his unit until 2 September 1917, sailing from Southampton and arriving in Le Havre. His younger brother John Edward ('Ted') also wanted to join up, but Schubert did not want him to. In a letter home he warned him: *'Don't come over here as conditions are appalling and I will be most angry if you disregard this advice from your Brother – Don't do it, Don't join up!'* At the end of September the 34th Battalion, as part of the 3rd Australian Division was transferred to Belgium where they found themselves in the middle of the Battle of Passchendaele. On 12 October 1917 the battalion carried out a disastrous attack on Passchendaele itself. The battalion's jumping off line was what is now Tyne Cot Cemetery, and its final objective lay just beyond Passchendaele village. The attack quickly went awry and the Australians only managed to seize a small piece of ground. Losses were heavy, however. According to official sources, Sergeant Phillip Stanley Schubert was killed on 13 October 1917. The chaplain of the 34th Battalion, John Calder, wrote a letter to Schubert's mother informing her: *'So far as I can make out, he was killed instantaneously by a machine-gun bullet during the first or second day of the attack. As we had eventually to retire from the positions we captured on that occasion, it was impossible for me to bury his body, but that task would be reverently carried out by the Canadian troops who relieved us in that sector.'* In reality, Schubert was probably killed on 12 October, as there were no attacks on that part of the front on 13 October. It is, incidentally, not unusual to find that official sources give incorrect

dates, bearing in mind that attacks often disintegrated into complete chaos and the difficulties caused by subsequent reorganisation. The location at which Schubert's body was eventually found also suggests an incorrect date. In March 1920 his mortal remains were found on the site of Tyne Cot Cemetery and Schubert was reburied only a hundred metres from where he was found. His family certainly never forgot him. *'His mother was observed to cry for him on her 90th birthday when Phillip's name was mentioned. This occurred some forty two years after his death and his family was always emotional when discussing the tragedy of their great loss of a son and brother.'* She was never able to visit her son's grave. It was too far to travel and the journey was too expensive. Schubert's younger brother, who had also wanted to join up, gave one of his sons 'Phillip' as a second forename in memory of the brother who had been killed in the war. By an interesting coincidence Terry Phillip Schubert was born almost exactly 43 years to the day after his deceased uncle.

4 Graves and Memorial Stones

Stones

The standard commission headstone is a vertical, flat-faced stone with a slightly curved top. It is 81 cm high, 38 cm wide, 7.5 cm deep and is set on a concrete base. Most of the stones at Tyne Cot Cemetery are cut from white Portland stone quarried from Portland Island off the English coast. This is a fossil-bearing stone in which the remnants of sea shells can often be seen. In the beginning the texts and emblems were engraved entirely by hand but given the hundreds of thousands of gravestones required this was seen as a task without end. After various experiments a company in Lancashire finally designed a special machine which, in 1923, could engrave up to 4,000 stones a week at a cost of less than five pounds a piece. It soon became apparent that the gravestones were attractive to algae and mosses. In order to limit the amount of manual washing required, today's cemetery staff wash each stone with a special chemical mix once or twice a year. Stones with inscriptions which can no longer easily be read are restored in situ by a special team while those which are in a more serious condition are replaced. In the latter case – and also for new graves – botticino, a marble-like white stone from Brescia, in the north of Italy, is used. Botticino is smoother and more weather resistant than Portland stone and has virtually the same appearance. All stones are uniform in shape and placement without distinction in positioning or rank.[93]

Emblem / Nationality

Visitors walking around the graves will have their attention drawn immediately to the regimental emblems for the British (including Irish) units and the national symbols for the others; the maple leaf for Canada, the rising sun for Australia, the fern leaf for New Zealand,

Stones are mechanically cut into headstones, 1920 (CWGC)

Blocks of Portland stone at the Arrowsmith works, Stockwell, London, 1920 (CWGC)

left: finishing a Canadian stone, 1920 (CWGC)
right: Restored headstone, subsequently demolished (MMP)

(Special Memorial 2), Ludwick Zgrzyblowski from Poland (18/F/1) and Richard Verhaeghe, the only Belgian. The de Voogd family had moved to Australia, while the other three had emigrated to Canada. More about De Voogd and Verhaeghe can be read elsewhere in this book.[94]

Name

On the gravestones of the identified are engraved the initial(s) and the surname, seldom the full first name. In 14 cases we see 'served as'. This means that the person involved entered service under a different name because he was too young, for example, did not want to be found or had a past involving the courts. Serjeant James Proctor Brett (24/G/20) from Geraldine, New Zealand, died on 4 October 1917 during the large attack on 's Graventafel. He served with the 3rd Canterbury Regiment and gave his second first name, Proctor, as his surname. English-born Urban Parr (23/G/4) from New South Wales went into service on 29 March 1915 with the 12th Light Horse but deserted three months later on leaving Australia. On 6 January 1916, he again entered service under the name of William Barry with the 3rd Divisional Signal Company. On 12 October 1917, he got killed to the east of the present Tyne Cot Cemetery. His grave states 'Barry served as Parr', but his military files show that this, in fact, is the wrong way around.[95]

the springbok for South Africa and the rare caribou for Newfoundland. Since 1949, the latter has formed part of Canada and those in the register are no longer remembered as Newfoundlanders. In plot 53, three men are buried together from a total of 23 who are remembered as Newfoundlanders: Serjeant Samuel Murray (53/H/6), Private Thomas Bladgon (53/H/7) and Second Lieutenant Lionel T. Duley (53/H/8). They belonged to the 1st Royal Newfoundland Regiment and lost their lives on 29 and 30 September 1918, during the final offensive between Molenaarelst and Dadizele. Many of those who died then lost their lives near Keiberg. Occasionally we find names that seem out of place, such as Henry J. de Voogd from the Netherlands (25/G/18), Dominick Naplava from the Czech Republic

Three gravestones of Newfoundlanders, one of which is without a cross (53/H/6-8) (MMP)

Rank

The rank of a victim always precedes his name. Among those at Tyne Cot Cemetery is a Brigadier General, James F. Riddell (34/H/14), commanding officer of the 149th Northumberland Brigade. On 26 April 1915, he died after being shot in the head near St Julien, 150 metres south of Vanheule Farm. He was buried at Cambridge Road, half way between the railway line and the Zonnebeke-Ypres road. On his grave one can read: 'Killed leading his brigade but 5 days landed, soldier and great gentleman'. On each side lies an unknown officer, including a Northumberland Fusilier. Lieutenant-Colonel Stephen H. Dix (46/B/1) won the Military Cross as a captain in the Leinster Regiment and in August 1917 was given command of the amalgamated 12/13th Northumberland Fusiliers. On 4 October 1917, he was fatally wounded on the eastern side of Polygon Wood. There are seven more high-ranking officers: the majors Arnold K. Hosking (27/C/24), Horace S. Green (8/C/5), John B. Buchanan (54/E/16), Tom L. Bourdillon (58/E/44), Henry Leech (6/A/5), Frederick W.O. Maycock (64/C/2) and N.E.C. Norsworthy (59/B/24).[96]

Major Horace S. Green was a clerk with the British House of Commons and died on 20 September 1917, northeast of Keerselare as the much-liked commander of A Company, 2/7th London Regiment. After his unit was relieved, two volunteers returned to bury his body and place a wooden cross above his grave. A number of details about him were provided in two glass bottles. Post-war identification was made only on the basis of a simple 'disc'. An analysis of the identified graves also provides 22 captains, including the 18-year-old Canadian John M. Hensley (35/A/1). When he joined up on 16 October 1915, he gave his birth date as 2 January 1897, instead of 1899. A year later he was made a lieutenant and in 1917 a captain with the 85th Nova Scotia Highlanders. He died on 30 October 1917, under machine-gun fire close to the battalion memorial east of the Passchendaele-Broodseinde road. A soldier without rank was known in the infantry as Private (Pte), in the artillery as Gunner (Gnr), in the engineers as Sapper (Spr) and in the cavalry as Trooper (Tpr). Other designations which can be seen at regular intervals at Tyne Cot are Pioneer (an infantryman who did engineering work), Driver (a vehicle or wagon driver) and Rifleman (a member of the special Rifle Brigades, King's Royal Rifle Corps, etc.). A service number is always given for men and non-commissioned officers but never for officers.[97]

Urban Parr deserted and enlisted again under the name of William Barry. The names are the wrong way around on his gravestone (23/G/4) (MMP).

Major Horace Green was killed on 20 September 1917 commanding the 2/7th London Regiment at Wurst Farm (8/C/5) (MMP).

The Canadian John Hensley was killed as an 18-year-old captain with the 85th Nova Scotia Highlanders (35/A/1) (MMP)

Ages

Age is also given for a large number of the identified, but not for all by far. Until the end of 1921 this had to be paid for. After that it was free but then only at the request of the family. Brigadier General James F. Riddell (34/H/14) and the Australian John N. Crowley (19/D/1) are, at 52 years of age, the oldest. Private F. Bonfield (14/E/1) was 48 years and James J. Doyle (52/D/15) and Louis Thould (43/B/8) were both 47. John Crowley had been a journalist at Wyalong as well as a well-known sports shot. On 12 October 1917, he was hit in a grenade attack and, fatally wounded, left in a shell-hole not far from the Passchendaele-Broodseinde road. According to the official report he died shortly after, but the inscription on his grave reads: 'Though wounded in the morning, he fought till evening when he fell'. Crowley served with the 34th Battalion AIF and had three sons on the front. One of them, 18-year-old Reginald, served with the same unit and died at Villers-Bretonneux. John's brother Matthew lost his life at Gallipoli. Private Alexander Barter (59/C/6) and Private F.C. Sedge (54/F/6) were just 17 years old when they died. Barter was from Newfoundland and lost his life during the final offensive together with the previously mentioned Murray, Bladgon and Duley. Sedge was with the 1st Queen's Own and died on 26 October 1917, after heavy fighting around Polderhoek. He was buried east of Shrewsbury Forest. Twenty-eight graves state: 'Age 18'.[98]

Religious symbols

Almost all gravestones bear a religious symbol; a cross for Christians, a Star of David for Jews. In composition we can distinguish between the small Latin cross with the emblem above the text and cross, and the broad cross with the emblem in the cross and under the text. Contrary to what is generally believed, this has nothing to do with whether a person was Catholic or Protestant but with agreements between particular countries, regiments and the IWGC. Thus the graves of New Zealanders and Lancashire Fusiliers in most of the cases have a broad cross. A small cross was always placed on the graves of the partly identified and unidentified. At Tyne Cot Cemetery there are ten graves with a six-pointed Star of David and within it the words: 'TIHIE NICHMA TO TSROERA BITSROR HACHAÏM', which read from right to left and mean 'May his soul rest in peace'.

top: The 52-year-old John Crowley is the oldest of the war dead at Tyne Cot Cemetery. He was left mortally wounded in a shell hole on 12 October 1917 (19/D/1) (MMP)
right bottom: Airman Charles Moody was shot down at the age of 18 and was originally buried in Hooglede (58/A/28) (MMP)
left bottom: Alexander Barter from Newfoundland was only 17 (59/C/6) (MMP)

James Proctor Brett took his second name as his surname. He was killed at 's Graventafel (MMP)

These appear on the graves of privates Marcus L. Marks (Spec. Mem. 78), Jack Jacobs (6/B/2), L. Carp (19/H/2), Lewis Dacosta (47/B/11), B. Levy (24/E/16), William C. Meyer (41/A/21) and A. Taylor (25/G/17), Rifleman M.M. Green (40/G/11), Lance Corporal Stanley W. Harris (3/A/2) and Company Quartermaster Serjeant S. Schonewald (8/D/6). Only one Jewish grave also has an epitaph in Hebrew; that of Private Marcus L. Marks of the 1st Field Ambulance AAMC, fatally shot on 4 October 1917 near the Menin Road and remembered as 'special memorial' 78. Some 30 graves have no religious symbol, something that only occurred at the explicit request of the family or because, for example, the epitaph was too long.[99]

Military honours

In addition to the name of a victim, military honours are also engraved on a gravestone. The most frequent for officers are the MC (Military Cross) and the DSO (Distinguished Service Order) with the equivalents for the lower ranks being the MM (Military Medal) and the DCM (Distinguished Conduct Medal), possibly with Bars if more than one was awarded to an individual. In principle all honours awarded were published in the London Gazette, but not always with the citation or reason for the award. Civil honours such as the MBE (Member of the British Empire) are not given on the gravestone but sometimes appear in the register. Serjeant William Machray (14/E/4) of the 12th Royal Scots was awarded the DCM on 16 August 1917, but died two months later on 12 October north of the Stroombeek (St Julien). An officer wrote: 'He was an NCO we could depend on at all times for the fulfilment of his duties and orders, absolutely to the letter. In short, he was a fine man and a good soldier. Men such as he can little be spared at such a time as the present'. Among the many holders of the MC who are buried at Tyne Cot Cemetery we find Major Tom L. Bourdillon (58/E/44) of the 8th King's Royal Rifle Corps, who died on 24 August 1917 and was originally buried at Stirling Castle. On 14 November 1916, the London Gazette published the following citation concerning the award of the Military Cross to the then still temporary Lieutenant Bourdillon: 'For conspicuous gallantry in action. Although wounded, he led his Company with great courage and initiative, and organised the consolidation of the position gained.'[100]

top: Sergeant William Machray, Distinguished Conduct Medal, killed on 12 October 1917 (de Ruvigny)
bottom: Major Tom L. Bourdillon, Military Cross, killed on 24 August 1917 (Perry)

The highest British military honour is the Victoria Cross, established in 1856 by Queen Victoria and made of bronze from a Chinese Cannon captured at Sebastopol. Until now, 1,356 Victoria Crosses plus three bars have been awarded, including 634 during the First World War. On the gravestones of Victoria Cross winners the religious symbol is replaced by the honour itself and there are three of these to be found at Tyne Cot Cemetery: the Australians McGee (20/D/1) of the 40th Battalion and Jeffries (40/E/1) of the 34th Battalion AIF, and the Canadian Robertson (58/D/26) of the 27th Battalion CEF. Serjeant Lewis McGee and Captain Clarence S. Jeffries won their VCs in October 1917 with the capture of the machine-gun bunkers at Hamburg Farm (4 October) and Hillside Farm (12 October). Private J. Peter Robertson also received his VC posthumously for the capture of a machine-gun post on 6 November 1917, close to the village of Passchendaele. Their graves are the most frequently visited at Tyne Cot.[101]

Epitaphs

Towards the bottom of a gravestone an epitaph chosen by the family can frequently be found. After a great deal of discussion and change it was decided to charge the country concerned for the associated costs. In the UK, families were given the right to a text of four lines with a maximum of 66 letters including spaces. Anyone who wanted additional text had to pay the difference. Many of the epitaphs came from poems or the Bible, others were more personal messages of pride and solace such as 'in loving memory of my dear husband & our dear dada, our hero'. Some spoke of sacrifice, others of duty and in rare cases the validity of the war was questioned. In the latter case, the gravestone of 26-year-old Second Lieutenant Arthur C. Young (4/G/21) bears the following epitaph: 'Sacrificed to the fallacy that war can end war'. The inspiration for this possibly came from the well-known philosopher Bertrand Russell, a good friend of Arthur's father, publisher of the English-language 'Japan Chronicle' in Kobe. Arthur Young died on 16 August 1917, whilst serving with the 7th/8th Royal Irish Fusiliers between Pommern Castle and Somme in the St Julien area. On the gravestone of Private Henry Graham (46/A/12), who fell at Veldhoek on 11 November 1914, we can read: 'Also in memory of Willie & Bob, (brothers) killed in action.' This refers to Robert and William Graham who died on 17 and 23 April 1918 respectively and are commemorated on the Tyne Cot Memorial and the Memorial to the Missing at Pozières. The New Zealand Government did not allow epitaphs because it considered that no words could convey the grief and pride of the nation. Australian gravestones have more epitaphs than those of other nations.[102]

Partly identified and unidentified

In statistics relating to the various cemeteries, the CWGC makes a distinction between the identified and the unidentified. Frans Descamps further divided this latter group into partly identified and unidentified. The gravestones of the partly identified can show the nationality, sometimes the regimental emblem, the rank of the victim and in several cases even the date of death. The gravestones of the unidentified are limited to 'A Soldier of the Great War - Known unto God', words chosen by Rudyard Kipling. The word 'soldier' does not indicate rank, thus giving all an equal status.[103]

Special Memorials

In addition to gravestones for fully identified, partly identified and unidentified men, Tyne Cot also has a number of 'special memorials'. These relate to the presumed graves or memorial stones for graves which have been lost. The names on these gravestones are recorded on the stones only and thus not on the Memorial to the Missing. At the top are special inscriptions:

'*Believed to be*': These gravestones are those of Privates C.H. Corday (1/AA/6), A. Guest (62/H/8), L. Hanchett (18/A/4-5), A.E. Wheeler (18/D/10) and Captain J. Hislop (13/C/35). Hislop and Wheeler both died north of Frezenberg, Hislop on 31 July and Wheeler on 20 September 1917. Hislop was with the 6th Cameron Highlanders and Wheeler with the 2nd South African Infantry. Both units served within a Scottish division. The 'burial return sheets' do not mention this 'believed to be' formula and there is no indication of why it is presumed these are their graves.[104]

'*Believed to be buried in this cemetery*' or '*known to be buried in this cemetery*': Upon entering Tyne Cot Cemetery, there are 81 similar gravestones to be seen against the front wall on the right-hand side. These relate to identified human remains which were presumed or certain to have been brought to this cemetery but which, for one reason or another, do not have an identified grave. These soldiers are therefore commemorated here and are assumed to be buried somewhere in the cemetery as unidentified. In a note dated 19 November 1927, it is stated that this formula 'has occasionally been added to the records by this department where the evidence of burial in, or concentration to, the cemetery was not conclusive, but I believe that in the majority of cases it is the result of pressure from relatives'. One notable gravestone is that of the 33-year-old professional piper Henry Barrie (Spec. Mem. 60) who had also won various prizes as a dancer. He entered military service in 1900 and from 1909 served with the 1st Cameron Highlanders. On 5 November 1914, he was fatally shot at Veldhoek (Verbeek Farm).[105]

'*To the memory of*': These are gravestones for the missing who are not named on the Memorial to the Missing because they had an

Prophetic epitaph of Second Lieutenant Arthur C. Young, inspired by the words of the philosopher Bertrand Russell (4/G/21) (MMP)

A partial and unidentified grave 'Known unto God' (MMP)

Second Lieutenant Arthur C. Young

'believed to be buried' (13/C/35) (MMP)

Piper Henry Barry is 'believed to be buried on this cemetery' (Spec. Mem. 60) (MMP)

right: 'Duhallow block' for 20 men whose graves were lost in a cemetery that was subsequently transferred to Tyne Cot. 14 of the men are from the former Zonnebeke British Cemetery N°2 (MMP)

earlier grave or were commemorated at one of the cemeteries that were concentrated here and have now disappeared. They bear the inscription 'Their glory shall not be blotted out', chosen by Rudyard Kipling from Ecclesiastes (44:13) and were therefore known as 'Kipling memorials'. An upright pillar has been placed at one or more of these stones and is named 'Duhallow Block' after the first case of this at the Duhallow A.D.S. Cemetery in Ypres. On entering Tyne Cot Cemetery, there is a Duhallow Block to the left with 20 gravestones and the following words: 'TO THE MEMORY OF THESE 20 SOLDIERS OF THE BRITISH EMPIRE KILLED IN ACTION IN 1914, 1915 AND 1917 AND BURIED AT THE TIME IN BROODSEINDE WEST GERMAN CEMETERY, IN LEVI COTTAGE CEMETERY ZONNEBEKE

AND IN ZONNEBEKE BRITISH CEMETERY N°2 WHOSE GRAVES WERE DESTROYED IN LATER BATTLES - THEIR GLORY SHALL NOT BE BLOTTED OUT'. Among them are 15 men of the 3rd Royal Fusiliers (28th Division) who died between 13 and 15 April 1915, and were originally buried at the Zonnebeke British Cemetery No. 2 which was moved to here. Originally there were many more similar gravestones - we found six names with numbers between 55 and 61. Just one of these is commemorated today: Private Franklin Kelly (56). Serjeant D.J. Healy (55) appeared to be at Perth Cemetery (China Wall) and Gunner C. Winterbottom (57) at Duhallow A.D.S. Research into the latter showed that on 8 February 1921: '28.C.25. d.25.30: G.R.U. cross was found but no body'. The remains of Privates

Collective grave with 9 stones and 18 men, of whom only 1 has been identified (4/B/16-24) (MMP)

T. Hines (59), Christopher Cregan (60) and J. McNamara (61), serving with the 2nd Leinsters, were found together and are now buried at Birr Cross Roads Cemetery. Other special memorials no doubt disappeared with the establishment of the Memorial to the Missing because, according to documents from the Summer of 1925, 16 Buffs (East Kent Regiment) should also have received a permanent commemorative stone but their names were already inscribed on panels at the Menin Gate.[106]

In the early years following the war, Tyne Cot Cemetery also had a number of remembrance crosses placed for family members who had no grave at which to express their grief. When the large Memorial to the Missing was dedicated these were all removed. In various documents there are references to a similar cross for the 'Son of Mr. Hughes, Australian Minister'. No minister of that name could be found who had a son who died in the area.[107]

Collective grave of four artillerymen, 'bones found in sandbag' (28/H/18) (MMP)

Collective graves

However much the British looked in principle to bury their dead in individual graves, it still happened that bodies were buried together on the battlefield or when remains were difficult to separate. The most well-known collective grave is that of 27 men at the battlefield cemetery (2/A/3) who are buried beneath five gravestones for three identified, one for eight unknown Britons and one for four unknown Australians. The second largest is at plot 4 and has nine gravestones and 18 men, although it is not denoted in this way as the stones have separate numbers (4/B/16-24). At 4/B/20 Serjeant Proctor from Comber (County Down) is the only one identified. He took part with the 13th Royal Irish Rifles in the catastrophic attack of 16 August 1917, and probably died near Gallipoli Farm. The stones further mark an unidentified Irishman (4/B/23), possibly the nationality of all of those in that grave. In plot 1 (1/B/1) are three stones set against each other to mark the last resting place of soldiers Turner, Middleton and Greenwood from the 2/5th East Lancashire Regiment who died together on 3 December 1917. Finally there are two more stones (28/H/18) bearing the inscription 'believed to be', indicating the grave of four men from D Battery 232nd Brigade Royal Field Artillery. The names are in alphabetical order. According to the 'burial return sheets' their skeletons were found in a sandbag west of Van Meulen and close to 's Graventafelstraat.[108]

12 October 1917:

Private John de Voogd

51st Battalion AIF

Gold

In late December 1862 the 19-year-old Dutchman Henry de Voogd boarded the Dutch ship Jan Van Schaffelaar in Rotterdam and set sail for Australia. He had worked as a merchant seaman, but decided to try his luck Down Under. He established himself in Eaglehawk near Bendigo, Victoria, which at that time was in the grip of gold fever. A number of gold fields had been opened up and the young de Voogd found work as a gold miner. It was also in Eaglehawk that he married the 16-year-old Mary Ann Hamilton, with whom he was to have ten children, five boys and five girls. Their oldest son was Henry John de Voogd, who was born in Eaglehawk in July 1883. He attended the local school until the age of twelve and then followed in his father's footsteps as a miner. He excelled at rugby and played with the Eaglehawk Rangers. He also played a musical instrument, probably the clarinet, as did his father. By the turn of the 20th century the boom years of the gold mining industry in Bendigo were long passed and many families were plunged into poverty. Henry John decided it was time to move on and set out for Western Australia, where around 1893 several major new gold veins had been discovered, which in turn led to the creation of the town of Kalgoorlie. The gold fields were known as the Golden Mile, which is where Henry John went in the hope of striking it lucky.

To war

On 10 February 1916 de Voogd enlisted in the Australian army at Blackboy Hill, Western Australia. He was 32 years old but, still physically fit. He underwent basic instruction at a training camp in Blackboy Hill and shipped out on 17 April 1916 on H.M.A.T. Aeneas from Fremantle, Western Australia. The voyage took him to the Mediterranean where he transferred to the Franconia in Alexandria. He arrived in Plymouth, England, on 16 June 1916 and after a few days at Rollestone Camp he was sent to France in August

1916 and posted to the 51st Battalion, where his musical talents secured him a place in the battalion band. In early September 1916 he was wounded at Mouquet Farm during the Battle of the Somme when a bullet went through his wrist. The wound required further treatment and de Voogd was sent to a hospital in Birmingham, England via Rouen and Le Havre. He quickly recovered and in mid-November 1916 he was already able to return to his unit, travelling via Folkestone and Etaples. He was brought up before a court martial at the end of December in relation to an incident which occurred on 21 December of that year at the front in Longueval in which he had failed to obey an order given to him by a British officer. When the officer concerned ordered him to help some other men engaged in fatigue duties, de Voogd replied bluntly: *'I won't, I am already working on another job.'* De Voogd pleaded not guilty, but the court sentenced him to two years in a military prison with hard labour, although this was deferred a few days after the trial and de Voogd was able to return to his unit. On 19 February 1917 he was again admitted to hospital, this time due to illness, first in France and later in England. His stay in England lasted longer than expected, but he had no illusions about how long the war would last. From a camp in Windmill Hill he wrote a letter home on 9 September 1917: *'I am pleased to be able to say once more that I am in the best of health and in England. I had a bit of luck miss leaving on another trip to France. I was examined and in a draft to go back to the old Battalion, but they left four of us out. Some say that it was a Brigade order not to send any of the Staff, for the Band belongs to the Staff, so I was lucky being one. (...) I hope all the family are well and that I will see you all again. (when Fritz turns the game up) No sign yet of him feeling that way.'* Ten days later he received his embarkation orders and rejoined his unit in Flanders on 30 September 1917.

Henry John de Voogd in sporting attire (Pike)

A Dutch emigrant: Henry de Voogd (Pike)

Passchendaele

On 12 October 1917 the men of the 4th Australian Division went into action south of Passchendaele to protect the right flank of the 3rd Australian Division. On the evening of the same day the 51st Battalion was sent up the line to relieve the men who had taken part in the attack. C Company got lost and came under a heavy artillery fire and this was probably how Private Henry John de Voogd lost his life. No Red Cross file was opened on his case and the precise circumstances of his death are not known.

In early July 1920 his body was found some 200 metres north of the Zonnebeke-Broodseinde road and 200 metres west of the Broodseinde-Passchendaele road. De Voogd's mortal remains were transferred to Tyne Cot Cemetery and subsequently buried. A wooden cross was placed on the grave, but his surname was incorrectly spelt as: 'De Noogd'. In a letter to the army, his father complained that: *My friends spent three days trying to find the grave but were not successful, no wonder for they were looking for de Voogd and of course could not find that name.'* The grave-stone which stands at Tyne Cot Cemetery now bears his correct name, although it is unusual in that it lacks a cross.

Original wooden grave cross with incorrect name (Pike)

Grave 25/G/18 in Tyne Cot Cemetery, without a cross (MMP)

5 Analysis

Method

According to the CWGC's official register, 3,587 of the 11,957 graves at Tyne Cot Cemetery are identified. Various questions immediately come to mind, including the correct number of the dead, where all of these interments came from precisely and if truly nothing is known about the unidentified. The starting point for the additional investigation was a completely new register of all the gravestones. A voluntary museum worker, Frans Descamps, who is also deputy chairman of the Belgian Western Front Association, took on this massive task and between February and July 2005 compiled almost 12,000 index cards by hand. These were checked a second time in the August-September period. In order to work in a systematic and orderly way, all graves were considered as separate entities and then placed within the appropriate row. This meant that possible errors in the second count could easily be focused on a well-defined row. A distinction was also made between the not identified and the partly identified. As a result of this the new total casts a completely different light on the composition of the cemetery.

To process the cards, Commander Dany Titeca, together with the museum, designed a special database which is specifically aimed at reproducing the personal data of victims of the First World War. His wife, Jeannine Desender, entered all 12,000 index cards combined with the unique data from the 'burial return sheets'. This meant it was possible to check virtually every grave, where it originated from and on what basis it was or was not identified. In a second phase, all individual details of the identified were copied from the cemetery register. Several museum volunteers also researched the division or operational unit of all those identified. The current database will be extended in the future with details from service records. These are preserved for all Australian, Canadian and New Zealand other ranks and British officers. Most of the files of British soldiers below the rank of officer were lost in 1940, but 'Rolls of Honour' and the official 'Soldiers died in the Great War' enable various details to be reconstructed in these cases. It speaks for itself that war diaries, regimental histories and the like can be consulted too. Photos of more than 150 of those who died have also been found. The new database makes it possible to request data according to the original place the person was found, or by unit, within the data you select yourself. For example, anyone who previously requested a CWGC list of all Lancashire Fusiliers buried at Tyne Cot received 127 names. They will now find 153 names on that list because the partly identified will also be included. In combination with data on the original site of the grave this opens important perspectives for historical research in general and individual research in particular.

Figures

TYNE COT CEMETERY: TOTAL WAR DEAD (F. Descamps)

	Not Identified	Partly Identified	Identified	Memorial tablets	Total
UK Army	2.251	4.103	2.489	54	8.897
UK Navy	15	4	28	0	47
UK Air Force	16	1	10	0	27
Australia	563	670	124	15	1.372
Canada	412	363	180	31	986
Newfoundland	8	8	7	0	23
New Zealand	197	238	78	1	514
South Africa	24	43	20	0	87
B.W.I.	0	1	0	0	1
R.G.L.I.	1	2	0	0	3
Duitsers	1	3	0	0	4
Total	**3.488**	**5.436**	**2.936**	**101**	**11.961**

Notes:

(1) According to the CWGC, 11,957 of those who died have graves or are remembered on memorial stones. This makes a difference of just four with the total counted by Frans Descamps. There are, however, underlying differences concerning nationalities and the number of those identified. The new count confirms, in any event, that the original CWGC registration was exceptionally good.

(2) The un-identified from the UK have graves with the words 'A Soldier of the Great War - Known unto God'. This indicates that at the time of burial it could only be confirmed that this was a soldier from the British Empire. With an absence of distinguishing features and personal effects it could undoubtedly be the case that a large number of Canadians were interred as unidentified Britons. This situation also explains the high number of unidentified UK soldiers. This is less probable in the case of Australians as the latter had different clothing and footwear. The kit of New Zealanders was also comparable with that of the British.

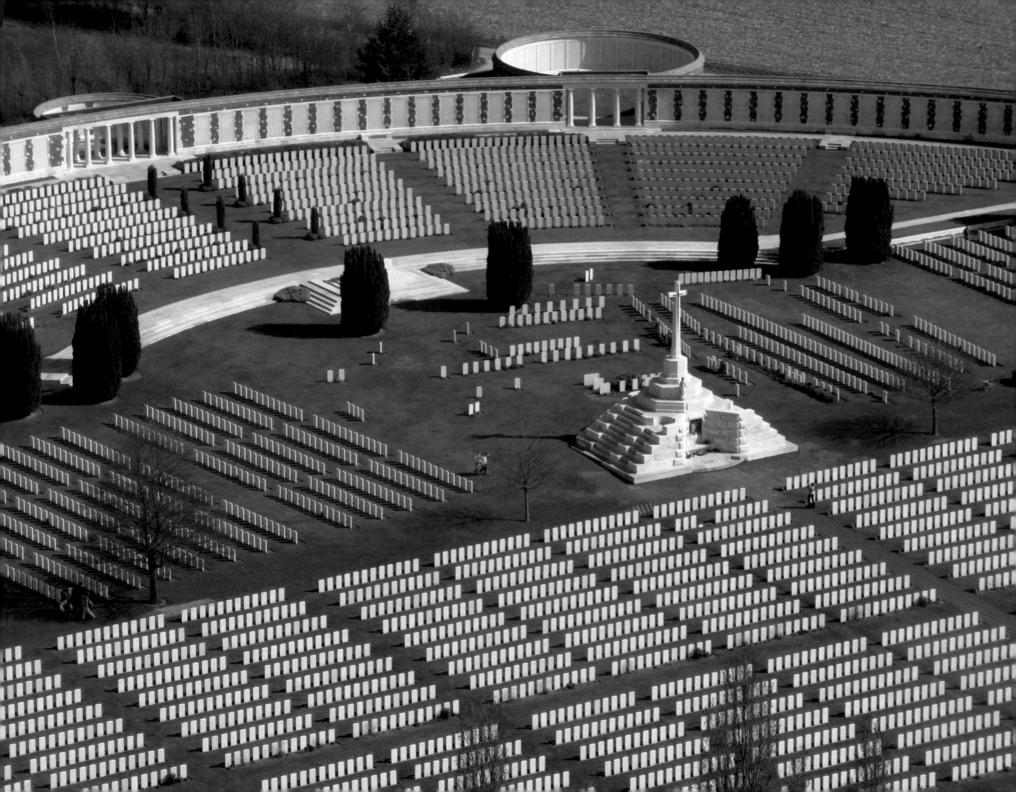

TYNE COT CEMETERY: WAR DEAD PER PLOT (F. Descamps)

Grave	1	2	3	4	5	6	7	8	9	10	11	12	13	14	15	16	1…
UK Army	119	72	196	211	185	185	187	185	188	184	106	105	172	166	162	147	13…
UK Navy	0	0	2	0	0		0	1	0	0	1	0	0	3	1	0	
UK Air Force	5	0	0	0	0		0	1	0	0	0	0	0	0	0	0	
Australia	8	15	23	2	0	2	0	1	0	0	6	6	1	0	2	34	1…
Canada	102	19	1	10	4	3	4	2	1	0	4	8	5	31	19	23	2…
New Foundland	0	0	0	0	0	0	0	0	0	0	0	0	0	0	0	0	
New Zealand	0	0	1	12	2	1	1	2	2	6	12	9	13	14	7	12	1…
South Africa	0	0	0	0	1	1	0	0	1	2	3	3	4	2	1	0	
B.W.I.	0	0	0	0	0	0	0	0	0	0	0	0	0	0	0	0	
R.G.L.I.	0	0	0	0	0	0	0	0	0	0	0	0	0	0	0	0	
Germans	0	4	0	0	0	0	0	0	0	0	0	0	0	0	0	0	
Total	234	110	223	235	192	192	192	192	192	192	132	131	195	216	192	216	19…

Grave	36	37	38	39	40	41	42	43	44	45	46	47	48	49	50	51	5…
UK Army	109	105	74	118	41	42	83	145	262	125	126	118	117	97	122	109	10…
UK Navy	1	1	3	1	0	0	0	0	1	0	0	0	0	0	0	0	0
UK Air Force	0	0	0	0	0	0	0	0	0	1	0	1	1	0	0	0	0
Australia	41	25	75	28	89	25	44	21	33	6	2	4	6	9	7	7	2…
Canada	33	54	25	34	23	4	3	0	3	2	0	4	4	4	15	6	…
New Foundland	0	6	1	1	0	0	0	0	0	0	0	0	0	0	0	0	0
New Zealand	8	1	13	10	3	0	2	2	10	8	0	0	0	0	2	6	9…
South Africa	0	0	0	0	0	1	0	0	3	0	0	1	0	2	0	0	8…
B.W.I.	0	0	0	0	0	0	0	0	0	0	0	0	0	0	0	0	0
R.G.L.I.	0	0	1	0	0	0	0	0	0	0	0	0	0	0	0	0	0
Germans	0	0	0	0	0	0	0	0	0	0	0	0	0	0	0	0	0
Total	192	192	192	192	156	72	132	168	312	142	128	128	128	112	146	128	12…

289

18	19	20	21	22	23	24	25	26	27	28	29	30	31	32	33	34	35
142	142	157	110	2	8	156	145	167	147	126	117	93	122	61	67	114	128
0	0	1	0	0	0	3	2	1	0	4	2	4	4	0	0	0	3
0	0	0	0	0	0	0	0	0	0	0	0	0	0	0	0	0	1
4	17	11	0	166	160	0	30	4	28	6	0	1	12	0	96	54	53
29	18	11	26	0	0	29	22	10	12	32	42	36	20	5	5	25	23
0	0	0	0	0	0	0	2	0	0	0	0	0	0	0	0	0	1
11	14	11	56	0	0	21	10	1	0	24	30	21	32	17	0	23	6
6	0	1	0	0	0	7	5	9	5	3	1	1	2	0	0	0	1
0	0	0	0	0	0	0	0	0	0	0	0	0	0	0	0	0	0
0	1	0	0	0	0	0	0	0	0	0	0	0	0	1	0	0	0
0	0	0	0	0	0	0	0	0	0	0	0	0	0	0	0	0	0
192	192	192	192	168	168	216	216	192	192	195	192	156	192	84	168	216	216

53	54	55	56	57	58	59	60	61	62	63	64	65	66	67	Kipling	Duhallow	Total
110	98	81	77	227	252	242	151	155	154	155	161	153	108	118	38	16	8897
1	1	3	0	3	0	0	0	0	0	0	0	0	0	0	0	0	47
1	0	0	0	0	3	7	1	0	2	2	0	0	0	0	0	0	27
6	4	2	8	28	13	12	22	14	11	11	8	15	14	13	15	0	1372
4	3	0	5	15	16	23	6	11	6	6	5	4	17	9	27	4	990
3	0	0	0	0	2	1	0	0	2	0	0	0	0	0	0	0	19
0	1	7	5	15	2	3	3	3	1	2	2	4	1	0	1	0	514
2	5	3	0	0	0	0	0	0	0	0	0	0	0	0	0	0	87
1	0	0	0	0	0	0	0	0	0	0	0	0	0	0	0	0	1
0	0	0	0	0	0	0	0	0	0	0	0	0	0	0	0	0	3
0	0	0	0	0	0	0	0	0	0	0	0	0	0	0	0	0	4
128	112	96	95	288	288	288	183	183	176	176	176	176	140	140	81	20	11961

30 October 1917:
Corporal Richard Verhaeghe
5th Canadian Mounted Rifles

The Verhaeghe family

On 26 April 1878 the 25-year-old labourer, Adolphus Fernandus Verhaeghe, went to the town hall of Zerkegem, near Jabbeke, to register the birth of his son, Richard Léon Verhaeghe, to whom his 21-year-old wife, Sidonia Alicia Van Steenkiste had given birth the day before. A year later the young family moved to Sint-Michiels, near Bruges, where their daughter, Nathalie, was born in late September 1880. They spent the next two years in Lille, France, probably looking for work. Luck was not on their side, however. Verhaeghe's daughter, Nathalie, died at the beginning of January 1883 a few days after the birth of his second son, Ferdinand. The couple had another daughter, Pharaïlde, who was born in September 1884, but died ten months later. Shaken by these cruel strokes of fate, the family moved again, this time to Ostend, where Adolf Verhaeghe, died in April 1898. A few months later his oldest son Richard married Augusta Verhaeghe, who bore him a daughter. His younger brother, Ferdinand, married Amandina Vanmaele at the end of October 1905.

To Canada

At some point between 1898 and 1913 Richard Verhaeghe emigrated to Canada, taking his family with him. The precise date is not known. The number of Belgians emigrating to Canada at that time was still relatively small, but growing every year. In 1900 only 132 Belgian nationals did so, while the figure for 1907 stands at 1,214. By 1913 this had risen to 2,651. Exactly why Verhaeghe chose to try his luck in Canada is not clear, but it may well have been due to poverty, unemployment or the promise of a better future. At the time there were large extensions of land to be had in Canada, but Verhaeghe was not interested in becoming a farmer and in 1913 he took a job as a clerk with the Street Railway. The family set up home in Saskatoon, a small town in central Saskatchewan, whose population was fast being swelled by the arrival of huge

numbers of European immigrants. While in Canada the Verhaeghe family had two more children.

From Sewell Camp to Mount Sorrel

In early August 1915 Verhaeghe left his job at the Street Railway and reported to the recruiting office at Sewell Camp, Manitoba, to enlist as a volunteer in the Canadian army. His home country was at war and his family in Flanders was suffering under the German occupation. He underwent basic instruction and was made a Sergeant, although he was later required to turn in his stripes when he embarked for England, where he landed in early December 1915. Verhaeghe belonged to the 9th Battalion Canadian Mounted Rifles, but at the end of January 1916 he was sent to the front with the 5th Battalion. On 2 June 1916 he found himself in Maple Copse, a small wood in the vicinity of Zillebeke, near Mount Sorrel, where his unit came under heavy artillery fire when the Germans began their offensive. The War Diary of the 5th Canadian Mounted Rifles records: *'A red letter day in the history of the Battalion, ever to be remembered by those who lived through it.'* The fighting only lasted a few days but the Canadians, who tried to recapture the terrain that had been lost by launching a counter-attack, suffered heavy losses. Battalion strength was halved, with 63 dead, 279 wounded and 51 missing. Richard Verhaeghe was one of those on the wounded list, having received a bullet wound to the eye. He was sent to hospital for convalescence, but was able to return to his unit a few weeks later.

The Somme

Verhaeghe spent another short spell in hospital in August 1916, this time due to illness, but in early October 1916 he was again with the Canadian Mounted Rifles in France, this time on the Somme. On 1 October the Canadian Mounted Rifles carried out an attack on the German-held Regina Trench, not far from Thiepval. The

Verhaeghe as a motorman on the Saskatoon Electric Street Car (Carline)

position could not be captured in its entirety and the Canadians were forced to fall back, but Verhaeghe, seeing that there were several wounded men who were too badly hit to withdraw, *'remained behind and dressed a number of wounded, in the open under heavy rifle fire and machine gun fire without regard for his own safety.'* In early November 1916 he was awarded the Military Medal for his bravery on that day and was promoted to the rank of Lance Corporal.

Passchendaele

Richard Verhaeghe came through a Canadian assault on Vimy Ridge in May 1917 unscathed and after ten days' leave returned to his unit in June 1917. The battalion spent the summer in the trenches in France, but was transferred to Flanders in late October, where they went into action at Bellevue Spur on 30 October. The obstacles facing the 5th Canadian Mounted Rifles were not only the well-organized German defences, but also the ground conditions at Woodlands Plantation, which had been shelled to smithereens by the intense artillery bombardment and had become impenetrable quagmire. In the early morning of 30 October the shattered remnants of the wood were to cause the Canadians serious problems. Various companies lost sight of each other and the attack progressed at a snail's pace due to the appalling state of the terrain. The Germans were able to withdraw to high ground from which they subjected the Canadians to merciless fire. Lance Corporal Richard Verhaeghe was among those killed.

In early March 1920 the body of a Canadian soldier was discovered in the west corner of Woodlands Plantation, which was subsequently identified as that of Richard Verhaeghe on the basis of his identity disc. His remains were then transferred to Tyne Cot Cemetery, where they were duly buried.

Richard's brother, Ferdinand, also emigrated to Canada and named one of his sons Richard, in honour of his dead brother. Ferdinand himself later returned to Ostend where his family still lives.

Corporal Richard Verhaeghe with sergeants stripes (Carline)

Richard Verhaeghe, the only Belgian in Tyne Cot Cemetery (MMP)

THOMAS B.
THOMSIT. F. G.
THOMSON A.
THORNE W. L.
TOYNBEE A. D.
TREDREA W. J.
TRUEBLOOD N.
TRUELOVE J.
TURNER E.
VICKERY F. B. B.
WALKER A. B. G.
WALKINSHAW D.
WARD W. H.
WEBB F.

6 Memorial to the Missing

A monument to those with no known grave

Immediately after the war it became clear there was a great desire that the missing should also be remembered. For those who survived it was important that considerable effort be put into this. 'They seem to be more worried about that than anything else,' Rudyard Kipling wrote in a letter to Fabian Ware on 22 February 1919. These people too needed something tangible in order to cope with the process of grieving. Kipling, whose own son was among the missing, was able to convince the IWGC to ask the public how this could best be done. The outcome was clear: The wish was for the missing to be commemorated as close as possible to the place they had fallen. An early Australian proposal that all the missing be given a (symbolic) individual gravestone was not financially viable. Another idea, this time from Sir Frederic Kenyon, to engrave the names of the missing on a wall at the nearest existing cemetery appeared difficult in a practical sense as no location could be assigned for many of the soldiers. Finally it was decided to build a large memorial to the missing on each sector of the front. In Ypres this would also serve as a national war memorial: the Menin Gate. Because no more than 60,000 names could be included, a second Memorial to the Missing was planned for Tyne Cot, the most important concentrated burial ground which also had a large number of the missing. After a lot of calculations it was decided in 1924 that the names of all those missing prior to 16 August 1917 (the Battle of Langemark) would be given a place at the Menin Gate. Those missing between Douve and Estaires-Fournes in northern France were to be commemorated on a third Memorial to the Missing at Ploegsteert. The missing from the overseas contingents would all be commemorated at the Menin Gate because, if the date rule was applied, there would be virtually no Australians

Text of the Memorial to the Missing, typewritten by Rudyard Kipling and signed as approved by Fabian Ware. A different text was used on the Menin Gate (CWGC).

< *'Somewhere in Flanders'* (MMP)

named on the Gate. New Zealand was not in accord with this decision and chose to have its memorials to the missing at the closest cemetery: Tyne Cot, Buttes New British and Messines Ridge. The only man missing from the Royal Newfoundland Regiment has his name on panel 161 at Tyne Cot ; Second Lieutenant Harold George Barrett.[109]

The procedure of deciding which name should appear on which panel of which memorial, numbering no fewer than 25 steps, was an extremely complicated process. Essentially it boiled down to comparing the official list of those who died ('Soldiers died in the Great War') with the IWGC index cards. People who were confirmed dead but who had no IWGC grave were defined as missing. From summaries of the divisional diaries it was then decided in which region a particular person was missing and therefore on which memorial he should be remembered. The information collected was, wherever possible, passed on to the relevant regiments and families for

Memorial card for Lieutenant Benard N. Cryer, who went missing after the capture of a pillbox, 400m from Clapham Junction, 15 September 1917 (MMP)

After his death the pillbox and the nearby farm were known as Cryer Farm. The farm has been open to visitors since 2002, provided an appointment is made at the Memorial Museum (Sheil)

completion and any necessary corrections. Finally the lists were compiled per memorial and then by panel for engraving. This massive task was mostly completed by 1926, and this in an age without computers. Almost immediately it was undermined by a number of errors: survivors who unexpectedly came across their own names, names that indeed had a marked grave and a large number who appeared on the wrong memorials. The latter was decided to be less important, leading to the fact that today rather a large number of names, mostly involving the London Regiment, are on the Menin Gate whereas they should have been at Tyne Cot. One example of this is Lieutenant Bernard N. Cryer of the 1/7th London Regiment who, on 15 September 1917 died during the capture of the Cryer Farm bunker, now restored by us, near the Menin Road. His name appears on the Menin Gate despite the fact that he died after 15 August 1917. In the years following the completion of the memorials, more names of those who had been forgotten, arose. Both the Menin Gate and Tyne Cot have addenda, in the case of Tyne Cot on panels 162 and 163. When newly discovered remains lead to identification or part identification of graves on an historical basis and this fact is confirmed, the name is immediately deleted from the register of the relevant Memorial to the Missing. On the monument itself this occurs by replacement of the appropriate panel. The Tyne Cot Memorial is thus a 'living memorial' on which the number of names is subject to change and can never be declared exact. It is best therefore to speak of 'almost 35,000'.[110]

In its annual report for 2005-2006, the CWGC stated that in Belgium there were 204,833 Commonwealth service men and women commemorated at 613 different sites of which 210 are the CWGC's own cemeteries. From an overall total of 1,695,174 war dead this makes Belgium the third largest such country after France and the UK. 102,497 of the victims have a known grave, 102,336 are missing. All of the missing are commemorated on one of the memorials to the missing, of which there are two more on the coast. 48,555 of the missing are interred as partly identified or unidentified. For every four Commonwealth dead there are two buried with an identified

Private Fred P. Young from Shepton, 8/Duke of Wellington's Regiment (MMP)

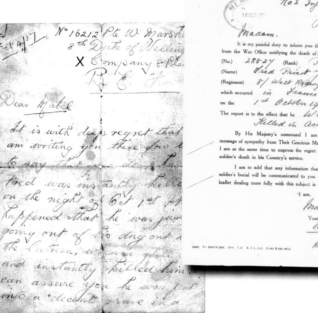

left: Letter to Young's widow, Mabel Lee, concerning his death on 1 October 1917 (MMP)

left top: Official notification of death sent on 18 October 1917 (MMP)

left bottom: After verification of the details in London, the identification discs were sent to the family (MMP)

right top: Standard bronze 'death plaque' with accompanying letter from King George V (MMP)

right bottom: The grave indicated at Rudolph Farm (Pilkem Ridge) was never found after the war and for this reason Fred Young is remembered on the Tyne Cot Memorial (MMP)

headstone, one with an unidentified headstone, who is commemorated on a memorial to the missing and one who is in fact still missing on the battlefield and only commemorated on a memorial.[111]

Interpretation

The 230-metre long Memorial to the Missing is built as an arc with three apses and two rotundas. When you face the memorial, the numbering runs from left to right, from north to south, for a total of 166 panels. In the centre the numbering is broken by the New Zealand Memorial to the Missing which itself has nine panels with the names of the 1,166 missing who fell in October 1917 near 's Graventafel. Between the elevated north and south apses are two pavilions. In the most northerly of these visitors are able to consult the registers of both memorials to the missing. The units of the British Expeditionary Force (BEF) are listed according to the British order of precedence; first the Navy followed by cavalry, artillery, engineers and infantry, and finally other corps and services. The cavalry and infantry regiments also have an order of precedence assigned by seniority and numbering. London Regiment battalions are listed by number. By unit, names are listed by rank and within each rank in alphabetical order. Those with the same surname are distinguished by initials and sometimes also by service number. On several panels names that have been added later follow on from the alphabetical list. Sometimes a pseudonym appears ('served as'). The three Victoria Cross holders are distinguished by the letters VC before the name while other military honours appear in abbreviated form after the initials. Panels 162 and 163 are addenda. Panels 164, 165 and 166 are not engraved. Along the length of the memorial wall are the words: '1914 - HERE ARE RECORDED THE NAMES OF BRITISH OFFICERS AND MEN OF THE ARMIES OF THE BRITISH EMPIRE WHO FELL IN YPRES SALIENT, BUT TO WHOM THE FORTUNE OF WAR DENIED THE KNOWN AND HONOURED BURIAL GIVEN TO THEIR COMRADES IN DEATH – 1918'.[112]

The central 'New Zealand Memorial to the Missing' with the names of 1,166 of missing servicemen(MMP)

MEMORIALS TO THE MISSING ON THE YPRES FRONT 2007 (CWGC)

	Menin Gate (all - NZ)	Tyne Cot (UK + NZ)	Ploegsteert (UK)	Messines Ridge (NZ)	Buttes New British (NZ)	Total
UK	40.243	33.707	11.357	0	0	85.307
Australië	6.195	0	0	0	0	6.195
Canada	6.932	1 (NF)	0	0	0	6.933
New Zealand	0	1.166	0	826	378	2.370
South Africa	560	0	13	0	0	573
India	414	0	0	0	0	414
R.G.L.I.	0	0	0	0	0	0
Total	54.344	34.874	11.370	826	378	101.792

TYNE COT & NEW ZEALAND MEMORIAL TO THE MISSING PER REGIMENT
According to the original register of 1927 (CWGC)

	Panel	Number
Army Cyclist Corps	154	7
Argyll and Sutherland Highlanders	141-143	342
Bedfordshire Regiment	48-50	278
Black Watch (Royal Highlanders)	94-96	287
Border Regiment	85-86	407
Buffs (East Kent Regiment)	17	143
Cambridgeshire Regiment	148	77
Cameron Highlanders	136-138	254
Cameronians (Scottish Rifles)	68-70	405
Channel Islands Militia	161	29
Cheshire Regiment	61-63	557
Cheshire Yeomanry	3	1
Coldstream Guards	9-10	118
Connaught Rangers	141	3
Devonshire Regiment	38-40	465
Dorsetshire Regiment	92	90
6/ (Inniskilling) Dragoons	3	1
Duke of Cornwall's Light Infantry	80-82	308
Duke of Wellington's	82-85	569
Durham Light Infantry	128-131	637
East Lancashire Regiment	77-79	325
East Surrey Regiment	79-80	321
East Yorkshire Regiment	47-48	252
Essex Regiment	98-99	182
General List *	161	5
Gloucestershire Regiment	72-75	642
Gordon Highlanders	135-136	363
Grenadier Guards	9	132
Guards Machine Gun Regiment	11	11
Hampshire Regiment	88-90	374
Hampshire Carabiniers	4	2
Herefordshire Regiment	154	27
Hertfordshire Regiment	153	48
Highland Light Infantry	131-132	363
Honourable Artillery Company	7	100

	Panel	Number
Household Battalion	3	114
Huntingdonshire Cyclist Battalion	154	1
Irish Guards	10-11	100
1/King Edward's Horse	3	1
King's (Liverpool Regiment)	31-34	721
King's Royal Rifle Corps	115-119	862
King's Shropshire Light Infantry	112-113	231
King's Own Royal Lancaster Regiment	18-19	258
King's Own Scottish Borderers	66-68	325
King's Own Yorkshire Light Infantry	108-111	776
Labour Corps	160	26
Lancashire Fusiliers	54-60	1.303
Lancashire Hussars	4	1
Leicestershire Regiment	50-51	381
Leicestershire Yeomanry	3	2
Leinster Regiment (Royal Canadians)	143	9
Lincolnshire Regiment	35-37	540
London Regiment	148-153	821
Loyal North Lancashire Regiment	102-104	447
Machine Gun Corps (Cavalry)	159	1
Machine Gun Corps (Infantry)	154-159	1.181
Manchester Regiment	120-124	919
Middlesex Regiment (Duke of Cambridge's Own)	113-115	555
Military Police Corps	161	2
Monmouthshire Regiment	147	6
Norfolk Regiment	34-35	255
Northamptonshire Regiment	104-105	106
Northern Cyclist Battalion	154	1
Northumberland Fusiliers	19-23	1.008
Northumberland Hussars	3	1
North Staffordshire Regiment (Prince of Wales's)	124-125	199
Notts & Derbyshire Regiment (Sherwood Foresters)	99-102	629
Oxfordshire & Buckinghamshire Light Infantry	96-98	544
Queen's (Royal West Surrey Regiment)	14-17	509
Rifle Brigade	145-147	606

Royal Army Chaplain's Department	160	5
Royal Army Medical Corps	160	104
Royal Army Ordnance Corps	161	3
Royal Army Service Corps	160	16
Royal Berkshire Regiment	105-106	322
Royal Dublin Fusiliers	144-145	196
Royal Engineers	8	209
Royal Horse & Royal Field Artillery	4-6	588
Royal Fusiliers (City of London Regiment)	28-30	540
Royal Garrison Artillery	6-7	119
Royal Inniskilling Fusiliers	70-72	465
Royal Irish Fusiliers (Princess Victoria's)	140-141	267
Royal Irish Regiment	51-52	23
Royal Irish Rifles	138-140	507
Royal Marines	1	208
Royal Munster Fusiliers	143-144	106
Royal Naval Volunteer Reserve	2-3	240
Royal Scots (Lothian Regiment)	11-14	752
Royal Scots Fusiliers	60-61	177
Royal Sussex Regiment	86-88	312
Royal Warwickshire Regiment	23-28	1.035
Royal Welch Fusiliers	63-65	350
Royal West Kent Regiment (Queen's Own)	106-108	396
Royal Wiltshire Yeomanry	3	1
Seaforth Highlanders	132-135	489
Scots Guards	10	68
Scottish Horse	4	1
Somerset Light Infantry (Prince Albert's)	41-42	299
South Lancashire Regiment	92-93	164
South Staffordshire Regiment	90-92	405
South Wales Borderers	65-66	269
Suffolk Regiment	40-41	193
Tank Corps	159-160	58
Welsh Guards	11	35
Welch Regiment	93-94	294

Westmorland and Cumberland Yeomanry	3	1
West Somerset Yeomanry	3	1
West Yorkshire Regiment (Prince of Wales's)	42-47	1.109
Wiltshire Regiment (Duke of Edinburgh's)	119-120	148
Worcestershire Regiment	75-77	557
York & Lancaster Regiment	125-128	616
Yorskshire Regiment	52-54	404
Royal Newfoundland Regiment	161	1
New Zealand Field Artillery	1 (NZ)	1
New Zealand Engineers	1 (NZ)	3
Auckland Infantry Regiment	1-2 (NZ)	175
Canterbury Infantry Regiment	2-3 (NZ)	215
Otago Infantry Regiment	3-4, 6 (NZ)	287
Wellington Infantry Regiment	6-7 (NZ)	178
New Zealand Rifle Brigade	7-9 (NZ)	270
New Zealand Machine Gun Battalion	9 (NZ)	36
New Zealand Medical Corps	9 (NZ)	13
New Zealand Army Chaplain	9 (NZ)	1

Total   **34.798**

9 October 1917:
Private Alfred Brown
2nd Royal Fusiliers

Private Alfred Brown (Sutcliffe)

The Somme

Alfred Heaton Brown was born on 14 August 1896 in Bury, Lancashire, a small town north of Manchester with a flourishing cotton industry. His father, William Robinson Brown, was a master clothier. The family, which included Alfred's mother Elizabeth Brown and his brother Henry, lived in North Shore Blackpool, some eighty kilometres away. Alfred Brown attended Arnold House School, although it is not known what trade he followed thereafter. He enlisted in the British army in September 1915, ending up in the Royal Fusiliers and was sent to the western front. He was wounded during the Battle of the Somme in September 1916 during the assault on Guillemont, *'where he was buried by one shell and unburied by another.'* After a spell in hospital and a short period of home leave, he returned to the front.

Passchendaele

On 9 October 1917 the 2nd Battalion Royal Fusiliers went into action south of the Ypres-Staden railway. In the pouring rain the men began an advance towards an objective which was at a distance of around 1 kilometre. There were various bunkers which had to be captured. The 1st Lancashire Fusiliers, who were advancing in front of the Royal Fusiliers, came under fire from Olga Farm, a strongly defended German position. The Royal Fusiliers came to their assistance and together they advanced from shell hole to shell hole. By 10.00 a.m. all their objectives had been secured. Brown was killed while taking one of the bunkers. The battalion chaplain wrote a brief letter giving his family the sad news and his parents received the official notification of his death a few days later. It was not until January 1918, however, that the family learnt the details of how their son had died. A comrade of Brown's, A. Spence, had found his body in No Man's Land. *'We went [in] the line on Nov 4th and got down into shell holes, there was quite a number of our boys lying about that had been killed in the push*

(...), on the second morning I crept out to get one of our boys I could see lying in no mans land and what a shock I got when I found it was Alfred, with a little difficulty I got him back and buried him at a place called Teadique Farm, Polecapelle [sic].' Teadique Farm is probably a misspelling of Tragique Farm. The soldier who found his body, also picked up Brown's wallet and later sent this to his family. *'I was so glad that I found Albert as I know you will feel more settled now you know he is buried alright.'* He also took both Brown's identity discs and sent these to the family, which meant that the body could not be identified. In August 1929 Brown's mother received notification that her son's name had been engraved on the Tyne Cot Memorial. His letters, identity discs, pocket book and medals are still treasured by his family.

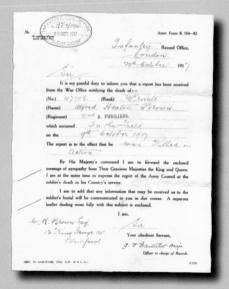

Official notification of death Private Brown (Sutcliffe)

France
6-1-18

Dear Mr & Mrs Brown

I know you will have been
worrying anxiously for a letter from
me since you received the news I
[…] it as been impossible to write
before now as I only got to know you
were back home again on Dec 23rd
and and we went into the line again
Xmas Eve and only came out
[…]erday so you will understand
it is I have been unable to
[…] you before now. I cannot
[…] how very sorry I am for
[…]ing Alfred, you can just
[…] shock I got when I went
[…] break and found it was
[…] chums. We went

top: *Letter with envelope from Spencer to Brown's mother, January 1918 (Sutcliffe)*
bottom: *Newspaper cutting with death notice and dentification disc (Sutcliffe)*

Envelope:
O.A.S.
Mr & Mrs Brown
Ivy Dene
13 King George Ave
North Shore
Blackpool
Eng

ARMY POST OFFICE
B
14 JA
18

Newspaper clipping:

[…]shire, suffering
from Myalgis De-
bility contracted
whilst in the
trenches in France.
Pte. Hornby en-
listed on the out-
break of war and
had been in the
firing line in
France for some
time past. He is
37 years of age,
and has a wife and one child who reside at
40, Harrison Street, Revoe.

Pte. Alfred H. Brown, a son of Mr.
W. R. Brown, of
"Ivy Dene," King
George Avenue,
North Shore,
Blackpool, has
been wounded.
He joined the
Royal Fusiliers
Public Schools
Battalion in Sep-
tember, 1915, and
has seen service
in Belgium and
France, was in at
the taking of
Guillemont, where
he was buried by
one shell and un-
buried by another. He was in hospital in
London a time, and is now on leave at
home. He was just 19 years old when he
joined.

Corpl. E. Davis, of the Grenadier
Guards, of North Warton-street, Lytham,
has been wounded by shrapnel in the thigh,
and is now in hospital in Warrington. He
was formerly a member of the Lytham
police force.

Quartermaster-Sergeant Ernest Oakley,
who is of Blackpool, has been promoted
to the rank of Sergeant-Major, carrying with
it warrant rank. Sergt. Major Oakley is

BLACKPOOL.
SUCCESS.
SPECIAL VISIT.
[…]AY October 23.
and Deaf Hear.
[…]hat Mr. Ison, oculist and
Eye and Ear Dispensary,
make a special visit to
Blackpool, on Monday,
[…] 12 to 6. Old Red
[…]y, on Monday, October
[…]o. Sufferers from fail-
[…] will do well to avail
[…]portunity of consulta-
[…] for all diseases of the
[…] operation. Those un-
[…]should write to Leeds
[…]estions to answer,
71, Great George-

King's Visit to
the 16th, have

week-end
[…]y." "It is
more fre-
[…]han on
[…] that
[…]that

suffering
shell shock, an[…]
at present in […]
Edmonton Militar[…]
Hospital, London.
He enlisted on the
outbreak of war,
and was drafted
out to France in
November, 1915.
He was buried
with seven others
on the explosion
of a shell, but only
he and another escaped.
was employed by Mr. L[…]

Pte. Basil Senior, o[…]
North Lancashire
Regiment, and who
is the son of Mrs.
F. A. Senior, 10,
Percy Street, South
Shore, has sent a
message to his
mother, saying
that he is a pris-
oner of war in
Germany. Private
Senior was previ-
ously reported
missing after an
attack on the
enemy on August
5, in which so
many local boys
were taken prisoners a[…]
men Camp, Westphalia.

Mrs. Cardwell, of 34[…]
has received a letter
Corporal A. Cardwell
pool Regiment, intim[…]
oner of war in Ger[…]
forces in November[…]
ploy of Poulton Po[…]
ported missing in m[…]

A COOL

7 An eternal vigil

The first pilgrimages (1919-1927)

The possibility of visiting a grave was for many family, friends and survivors an important part of the grieving process. The first pilgrimages started as early as the summer of 1919, about the same time that the return of civilian refugees began. By the end of 1921 the transport of human remains to Tyne Cot was as good as completed although the dead still lay beneath small wooden crosses and a start was yet to be made on the architectural lay-out. The pilgrimages too were subject to hardships: poor travel connections, barely passable roads and little accommodation to speak of. As early as August 1919 the YMCA improvised a hotel for 40 guests in a wooden building at Ypres. In December 1922 the IWGC was granted a concession to use several army barracks on the Esplanadeplein where information could be provided about the precise location of graves. Organisations such as the British Legion and the Ypres League organised a good number of pilgrimages by groups. Among other things, the British Legion offered a four-day trip for the all-in price of three pounds, a price which roughly equated to a week's pay for a labourer. For thousands of poorer people, however, this was still too much and led to charity trips being established. In 1923 more than 2,000 relatives of those who had died were able to make the trip free of charge through the St Barnabas Society.[113]

Of major importance was the pilgrimage made by King George V on 11 May 1922. For nine days 150 men and 10 wagons were set to work between Zonnebeke and Passchendaele to improve the neighbouring roads, a project for which the costs jumped to 30,000 Belgian francs. Around 11 am on May 11 a special train from Brussels arrived at Zeebrugge. Accompanying the King were, among others, his pri-

vate secretary Colonel Clive Wigram, Field Marshal Douglas Haig and Major General Fabian Ware. The King visited a small cemetery for British and German seamen and was also told about the attack on Zeebrugge on St George's Day, 23 April 1918. From there the party travelled by train and car to Tyne Cot Cemetery. The monarch showed a great deal of interest in the remaining German bunkers and even entered the central one. Here he made the suggestion – or declared himself in favour of the idea – that the Cross of Sacrifice should be erected above the concrete structure. He also paid tribute at the grave of the Australian VC Lewis McGee and inspected the former soldiers who were working at the cemetery for the IWGC.

left: The King's 'pilgrimage' to Tyne Cot Cemetery. From left to right: Major W.B. Binnie (Deputy Director of Works, IWGC); Captain John Reginald Truelove (Assistant Architect, IWGC); Major General Fabian Ware (IWGC); Colonel Clive Wigram (private secretary to King George); Field Marshal Sir Douglas Haig; Colonel H.T. Goodland (Deputy Controller, IWGC); King George V; T. Elvidge (Head Gardener at Tyne Cot)

right: on the pillbox, 11 May 1922 (CWGC)

From Tyne Cot the party left for Ypres, stopping off for a short visit at the British and French Potyze cemeteries. At the Ypres town cemetery he visited the grave of his cousin Prince Maurice von Battenberg. The mayor welcomed the visitors in the town square where they were also able to see the plans for the Menin Gate. At the almost completed Vlamertinge Military Cemetery the King met Rudyard Kipling and the Canadian High Commissioner. From there the party moved on to visit several cemeteries at Poperinge and then travelled to Vimy. A book of the 'King's Pilgrimage' was printed and more than 25,000 copies were sold to fund pilgrimages. The royal visit was an important catalyst and in the party's footsteps came not only thousands of veterans but tens of thousands of tourists all wanting to see the devastated area with their own eyes.[114]

top: Head Gardener Elvidge, King George V and Fabian Ware leaving the cemetery, 11 May 1922 (CWGC).

top left: the King inspects the workmen, 11 May 1922 (CWGC)

middle left: Major Binnie (formerly of the Black Watch and Deputy Director of Works, IWGC) explains the plans for Tyne Cot Cemetery at the central pillbox, 11 May 1922 (CWGC)

bottom left: The King's travel documents for his 'pilgrimage', May 1922 (CWGC)

Tourists inspect abandoned tanks, ca. 1919 (Deraeve)

Modest opening ceremony of Tyne Cot Cemetery just before the unveiling of the Stone of Remembrance. The flag on the far right is that of the Flemish veterans of Zonnebeke, 19 June 1927 (CWGC)

Ceremony, ca. 1930 (IFF)

Flourishing battlefield tourism (1927-1940)

By the time of the IWGC's 10th anniversary in 1927 most of the cemeteries on the front around Ypres had been completed. The highlight was the dedication of the Menin Gate on 24 July 1917, by Field Marshal Plumer. The dedication of Tyne Cot Cemetery on Sunday 19 June 1927, was completely overshadowed by this event, although the cemeteries themselves had not been officially opened. There were no exceptionally high-ranking guests at Tyne Cot and the emphasis was firmly on the ANZACs. The Cross of Sacrifice was dedicated by Sir Gilbert J.C. Dyett, founder of the still existing Australian Returned Services League, followed by the dedication of the New Zealand Memorial to the Missing. The religious ceremony was led by the Reverend F. Molyneux, former Chaplain of the New Zealand Division. Several speeches followed and the hymn 'O God, Our Help in Ages Past' was sung. After the blessing by Chaplain Millner of Ypres British sounded played the 'Last Post' and 'Reveille'. The service closed with playing of national anthems by the local Sint-Cecilia band from Zonnebeke and the laying of a large number of flowers. This was performed by delegations from the British Empire Service League, the British Legion and the Imperial War Graves Commission. Sir Gilbert J.C. Dyett (1891-1962) was a former captain in the 38th Battalion A.I.F., which was responsible for the capture of Tyne Cot on 4 October 1917. He was also involved in the founding of the still existing Passchendaele Barracks and the Military Memorial Museum at Bendigo (Victoria) Australia.[115]

In the 1920s and 1930s Tyne Cot was on the itinerary of most pilgrimages to the Western Front. Thousands of veterans and relatives of those who had died made the trip across to Flanders. The largest pilgrimage was that of the British Legion in August 1928 when the climax was a large service at the Menin Gate witnessed by 11,000 veterans and their families. But the stream of tourists coming to the region was even larger. Numerous guidebooks were published, all refering to Tyne Cot Cemetery. Hotels, restaurants and cafés

left: Wooden café hut opposite the entrance to Tyne Cot Cemetery. From left to right: Maurice Deleye, Donald Castelein, Albert Deleu, Celesta Soen, Lea Soen, unknown, Joseph Verstraete, Jules Castelein, Henri Van Walleghem, Achiel Versavel, Cyriel Castelein and (in the doorway) Irma Blanckaert, 1927-1940 (Deneut)

right: Old IWGC signpost to Tyne Cot Cemetery and the now disappeared German cemetery on the Keerselaarhoek (MMP)

flourished and war souvenirs were sold like ice cream. The line between pilgrimage, respectful tourism and full-out commercialism was sometimes difficult to distinguish. Various agencies offered to take photos of graves for a payment and the laying of wreaths was also a possibility. A number of individuals naturally saw fast money in the situation. The total number of visitors between the wars is difficult to estimate. An indication can perhaps be seen at the Menin Gate where in July and August 1928 at least 23,000 people signed the book. In 1937 there were more than 60,000 signatures, most of them in the summer months.[116]

One special story relates to Cyriel Castelein of Passchendaele. A soldier in the Belgian Army he was wounded and evacuated to a hospital in England. There he met the attractive Margaret Currie (1895-1965) and described himself as a big farmer with a lot of land. After the war she came to Passchendaele with him, but the opposite proved to be the case. Around 1927 the brewer Van Eecke opened a hut as a café on his land in front of Tyne Cot Cemetery, an establishment which 'Maggie' ran. There were stereoscopic viewers of a type still to be seen at Hill 62, English beer was dispensed and all types of souvenirs were for sale. A sole remaining photo reveals that Maggie came from Gateshead-on-Tyne where her brother Robert was mayor. On Sunday afternoons large numbers of people from Passchendaele walked

down to Tyne Cot to have a beer with Maggie. Irma Blanckaert from Zonnebeke worked there as a waitress. The IWGC workmen were also good clients although the Commission itself was a lot less enthusiastic. The inn closed when the Second World War began and, according to some sources, it was blown down by the wind. Maggie never returned to her family; she didn't dare tell them about the rich landowner she had married.[117]

In the years between the wars there were also a number of interesting people visiting Tyne Cot although it is difficult to provide an overview because no visitors' book remains. On 27 November 1930, the Prime Minister of Canada, Richard Bennett (1870-1947), visited, going on to Ypres and to the Canadian memorials at St-Julien and Passchendaele. During the Whitsunday holiday of 1931 a delegation of British MPs visited at the invitation of the IWGC. On the same Sunday German and British veterans met at Tyne Cot Cemetery for an emotional 'reunion'. They laid flowers and went together to the large German cemetery at Broodseinde in the spirit of brotherhood.[118]

In the shadow of a new war (1940-1964)

When the Second World War began the IWGC was forced to suspend its work in Flanders. We have already mentioned that the British

Royal visit: H.M. Elisabeth II and the Duke of Edinburgh being welcomed at entrance to Tyne Cot, 13 May 1966 (Deforche)

pletely over-shadowed by that of the Second. Only occasionally did close relatives of those who had died visit the former battlefields. In June 1956 the VCs Joseph (Joe) Maxwell and John (Jack) Hamilton visited the grave of Serjeant Lewis McGee. Hamilton, a Scot, won his Victoria Cross on 25 September 1917, at Polygon Wood. On Tuesday 14 May 1957, Prince Henry, Duke of Gloucester, visited Tyne Cot Cemetery in his role as President of the IWGC. He also went to Ypres where he visited the Ramparts Cemetery, St George's Memorial Church and the Menin Gate to attended the Last Post ceremony. The rest of the week was spent visiting newly laid cemeteries in the Netherlands and Germany. From the mid 1960s interest in the First World War rose again. The 50th anniversary of the outbreak of the war acted as the catalyst.[120]

Half a century later (1964-1968)

On Friday 13 May 1966, Queen Elizabeth II came to this part of Flanders on the final day of a state visit to Belgium. Shortly after 4 pm she arrived at Tyne Cot together with the Duke of Edinburgh and the Belgian King Boudewijn. For weeks, more than 50 people had worked to get everything in tip-top condition for the royal visit and there were also special security provisions in force. An unusually large crowd had gathered to catch a glimpse of their majesties and Passchendaele schoolchildren waved Belgian and British flags. The public was not allowed into the cemetery itself. The Queen met members of the CWGC staff and also laid a wreath at the Cross of Sacrifice. Mayor Vercruysse made a speech of welcome. At 4.20 pm the Royal party left for Talbot House at Poperinge, after which the visit ended at Ypres. On the way there was a short stop at the Canadian monument at St-Julien. The visit by the British Queen met with a great response both at home and abroad.[121]

cemeteries were very soon neglected, but that the Germans forced the local authorities to carry out minimal maintenance. In general the Germans showed respect for the British war dead, whom they honoured as worthy opponents. Among them were also various veterans from the First World War, including Adolph Hitler himself who twice visited the Menin Gate at Ypres. Nowhere were British cemeteries damaged and, with the exception of two monuments related to the first gas attack, all memorials were spared. After the war, however, all German cemeteries and memorials had to disappear, but the initiative for this came from the Belgians, not the British.[119]

After 1945 the grief associated with the First World War was com-

In 1967 the 50th commemorations of the Battle of Passchendaele took place with the British Ministry of Defence organising an international service at Tyne Cot Cemetery on 8 October. First there was a modest remembrance service at the Canadian monument at Crest Farm in the presence of the Canadian Ambassador and Major General Pearkes. Special guest at the main ceremony was Field Marshal Harold Alexander of Tunis, who represented the Queen, while General

Vaneenderbrugghe represented the Belgian Minister of Defence. The ambassadors and military attachés of Great Britain, Australia, New Zealand, Canada, India, Pakistan, South Africa and France were also present. Hundreds of veterans had made the journey, mostly with the British Legion, and there were some 10 regimental representatives, among them some from Commonwealth countries. The Lancashire Fusiliers, which has the largest number of names on the Tyne Cot Memorial to the Missing, provided the honour guard around the Cross of Sacrifice together with a French detachment and the Belgian 6th Lancers. The ecumenical service was taken by the Chaplain General to the Forces assisted by a Roman Catholic Chaplain. The imposing service lasted about one hour and was supported by the Band of the Royal Anglian Regiment. At the close of the service an aircraft from the Canadian Air Force dropped thousands of poppies over the cemetery. A large number of people attended the ceremony which was recorded by Belgian radio and television along with the BBC. Afterwards, the attention moved to Ypres for a service at St George's Memorial Church and a special Last Post ceremony at the Menin Gate. Field Marshal the Earl Alexander of Tunis (1891-1969) served with the Irish Guards in the First World War and during the Second World War was, among other things, senior officer in North Africa and Italy. Following a very distinguished military career he became Governor-General of Canada and Minister of Defence.[122]

Stagnation and slow growth (1968-1984)

The renewal of battlefield tourism in the 1960s stagnated once again in the 1970s. This was clear from the 60th commemorations of the Battle of Passchendaele. In addition, 1977 was the year of council mergers in Flanders, something that did not run altogether smoothly in Zonnebeke and Passchendaele. Ypres put everything into the 50th anniversary of the Menin Gate, an occasion which attracted a considerable number of prominent people. The ceremonies took place over the weekend of 3 and 4 September and on the Sunday afternoon a shuttle bus was provided to Tyne Cot Cemetery. At 4.30 pm there was a rather modest service there in the presence of various ambassadors, Lieutenant General Theysen (senior officer of Belgium's home forces), General Tuzo (second in command at SHAPE), Air Commodore Atkinson (NATO) and a Canadian admiral. The

top left: King Baudouin getting out of his official car, the public were not allowed into the cemetery, 13 May 1966 (Deforche)

bottom left: the Queen greeting CWGC employees, from left to right Omer Cruyt, Michel Dejonghe, Albert Declercq, Roger Noyez, Richard Lucas, George Waite, Tom Beswick and Peter Grant. The latter is talking to King Baudouin, 13 May 1966 (Deforche)

At the Stone of Remembrance, 13 May 1966 (SAI)

Cigar bands commemorating the royal visit, 1966 (Deforche)

top right: 50th anniversary of the Battle of Passchendaele: Field Marshal Alexander of Tunis reviews the Belgian 6th Lancers, 8 October 1967 (MMP)

bottom right: Alexander of Tunis lays a wreath on behalf of the Queen, 8 October 1967 (Deforche)

same year, on 22 May, German veterans from the XXII Reserve Korps came to Zonnebeke for the last time and were welcomed over again by Mayor Priem. In Zonnebeke they remembered 'Flandern-schlacht 1917' and also laid flowers at Tyne Cot. On 20 November, the South African Ambassador visited Zonnebeke and Tyne Cot Cemetery. From the beginning of the 1980s battlefield tourism was again increasing. An important factor in this was the opening of the new 'Ypres Salient Museum 1914-1918' in the Ypres Cloth Hall in 1984. On 6 June 1984, the Duke of Kent, President of the CWGC, paid an informal visit to Tyne Cot Cemetery where he met the staff.[123]

Renewed interest (1984-1992) [124]

The 70th anniversary of the Battle of Passchendaele in 1987 was the most important to date. The initiative was taken by the Zonnebeke council with Aleks Deseyne, as co-ordinator, the driving force. At Ypres request the link was again made with the 60th anniversary of the Menin Gate. On Sunday 12 July there was a small remembrance service at the Canadian Monument at Crest Farm. At 11 am the main service began at Tyne Cot Cemetery with two royal guests: the 86-year-old Princess Alice, Duchess of Gloucester and widow of the third son of King George V, and Crown Prince Filip of Belgium. Among the many military representatives was General Sir Martin Farndale, senior commander of the British Army in Germany. As in 1967, the ambassadors and military attachés of all the allied countries were present. This time the service was supported by the Band of the Royal Dragoon Guards. The British Chaplain General to the Forces took the ecumenical part of the ceremony assisted by the Bishop of Brugge, a Protestant pastor and a rabbi. At the end of the service a Seaking helicopter from Belgium's 40th Squadron scattered 10,000 poppies over the cemetery. At 1 pm there was a ceremony at the Menin Gate and at 6 pm a service in St George's Memorial Church. The impressive remembrance service was recorded by Belgium's BRT and the BBC. The previous day had seen the opening of a large overview exhibition entitled 'Passchendaele 1917' at the Passchendaele School, an exhibition which was to run throughout the summer. There were also special battlefield tours, postmarks, walks and the like. On 12 July 1987, Zonnebeke-Passchendaele was once again on the world map.

50th anniversary of the Battle of Passchendaele: The Mayor of Passchendaele, Felix Vercruysse, at the Stone of Remembrance, 8 October 1967 (Deforche)
At the end of the ceremony a Dakota belonging to the Canadian Air Force drops thousands of poppies over the cemetery. Below left the honour guard of the Lancashire Fusiliers, 8 October 1967 (MMP)

60th anniversary of the Battle of Passchendaele: Mayor Priem reviews the colours, 4 September 1977 (Deforche)
Dignitaries during the ecumenical service, among them (in the first row) General Tuzo and a Canadian admiral, 4 September 1977 (Deforche)

The 60th anniversary of the Battle of
Passchendaele: coinciding with the 50th
anniversary of the Menin Gate,
3-4 September 1977 (Deforche)

View of the modest ceremony with a Belgian honour guard in the
foreground, 4 September 1977 (Deforche)

left: The Duke of Kent, President of the CWGC, visiting employees at Tyne
Cot, from left to right: Bernard Vanlerberghe, Jozef Titeca (shaking hands),
Stephane Mortier, Omer Lakiere, Jules Kesteloot and Kenneth Lane,
6 June 1984 (Deforche)

Different ways of remembering (1992-2002)

In 1992 a new programme was put forward for the 75th anniversary of the Battle of Passchendaele. In co-operation with a local art centre an art exhibition named 'Re-member' was mounted with more than 60 modern artists represented. It was the beginning of a new trend in remembering the First World War, a trend which placed more emphasis on individual stories and the universal message of peace from all war. The same year saw the first peace concert take place in the church at Passchendaele. The service on 12 July 1992, at Tyne Cot Cemetery was in fact a step down from 1987. There was no Royal presence and no prominent guests, only Major-General Ververken representing the King of Belgium. The ecumenical service was led by the Chaplain General to the Forces assisted by Assistant Bishop Laridon, a Protestant pastor and a rabbi. What was notable was the presence of some 20 flags from the Royal British Legion. The service was supported by the Band of the Queen's Own Highlanders. There were also 13 veterans present, among them the 94-year-old Charlie Young who was the only one to have taken part in the Battle of Pass-chendaele. The oldest member of the group, Reginald Glenn (99), gave the exhortation. The end of the service was marked by a heavy downpour.

In the following years interest in the First World War grew strongly, among other reasons because the Great War had become a compulsory part of the British school curriculum and school trips to the battlefields were greatly stimulated by this. As a result it was decided in Zonnebeke to establish a permanent war museum on the upper storey of the chateau. Because the archaeological excavations of the Augustin abbey also needed a place, the choice finally fell on a regional museum ('Streekmuseum'), which was opened on 29 April 1989. Among the many notable visitors in the years following were 12 veterans and six war widows from far-off Australia for whom a brief service was held at Tyne Cot Cemetery on September 1, 1993. Two of the visitors were Robert M. Lewis and his grandson Gary who, as a member of the forces, carried the Australian flag. Robert Lewis was able to find the names of a number of friends and family.

The 70th anniversary of the Battle of Passchendaele: the Belgian Prince Philip and the 86-year-old Princess Alice, Duchess of Gloucester, 12 July 1987 (MMP)

top left: Prince Philip and Princess Alice laying wreaths, 12 July 1987 (MMP)
bottom left: Veterans follow the ceremony, 12 July 1987 (Deforche)

A Sea King helicopter drops poppies at the end of the ceremony. In the foreground, the band of the Royal Dragoon Guards, 12 July 2007 (Deforche)

Bugler of the Coldstream Guards, 12 July 1987 (Deforche).

In 1997 Zonnebeke and Ypres worked together to mark the 80th anniversary of the Battle of Passchendaele and the 70th anniversary of the Menin Gate. Two Royal guests, both attending for the second time, were present at the international service on Sunday 13 July: Crown Prince Filip of Belgium and the Duke of Kent. Other prominent people included the Flanders Minister-President Vandenbrande and Federal Minister of Justice Declerck. What was notable is that the German Ambassador was invited for the first time. Most public attention, however, was on the 20 First World War veterans: 15 from the World War One Veterans Association and five who had made the journey with the British historian Lyn Macdonald. Among the veterans were five who had effectively taken part in the Battle of Passchendaele: Jack Haynes (100), George Littlefaire (101), Ed Brown (101), Mike Lully (102) and Dick Trafford (98). The atmosphere became exceptionally emotional when one gave the exhortation, followed by a minute's silence and then an unexpected outbreak of applause from the more then 1,500 people present. The service began at 10 am and was led by the Bishop of Gibraltar, Ambrose Weeks, the Bishop of Brugge and Jewish and Protestant representatives. The service was supported by the Band of the Belgian Guides and the Band of the

Light Division. Just as in 1987 a helicopter from the 40th Squadron dropped poppies over the cemetery. At midday guests gathered at the Menin Gate. In Ypres the remembrance occasion was completely given over to the new In Flanders Fields Museum which opened in April 1998. A preview was given and a peace concert was performed in both Ypres and Passchendaele. On the Sunday afternoon the Duke of Kent paid a private visit to Talbot House in Poperinge.

In September 1995 a peace concert was given for the first time at Tyne Cot Cemetery. On 24 August 2002, a second such concert took place with a great deal of interest from a folk-music minded Flanders. A storm of criticism emanated from the UK about political messages and the commercial character of the concert. Under the Menin Gate similar incidents took place, including the performance of a controversial collection of poetry. The CWGC declared itself against all forms of political expression at the last resting place of those who had died. It is a vision which has been supported by the overwhelming majority of the British public. No topical mission, only respectful remembrance of the tens of thousands who lost their lives here in 1917. And so, on 27 March 2003, a group of activists was refused

left: The famous Australian veteran 'Ted'
Smout (1898-2004) at the Cross of Sacrifice,
1 September 1993 (Deforche).

right: Soldier Gary Lewis carries the flag
during a small ceremony for a few visiting ex-
combatants from Australia, among them his
grandfather, 1 September 1993 (Deforche)

permission to demonstrate at Tyne Cot against the Iraq war. On 8
November 2005, the CWGC also refused permission for a performance of the CD 'Seeds of Peace', which took eventually place at the
entrance to the cemetery. Because, just as the inverted sword on the
Cross of Sacrifice symbolises, the battle for those who rest here is
long over - 'for evermore'.

Since 1981, ANZAC Day has also been remembered on 25 April at
Zonnebeke-Passchendaele. The date is that of the Gallipoli landing
of the Australian and New Zealand Army Corps in 1915. The Australians are welcomed in Zonnebeke and the New Zealanders at
Messines, after which they join at the Menin Gate in Ypres. The Australian Ambassador is mostly accompanied by a special delegation
and in recent years by increasing numbers of young people. Flowers are laid at the town war memorial and at Tyne Cot Cemetery,
where an explanation is provided. A memorable moment occurred
on ANZAC Day 2003 when Danna Vale, Minister of Veteran Affairs,
had tears in her eyes during her speech because her great-uncle had

died here in 1917. To mark the opening of the new Memorial Museum Passchendaele 1917, an original trench map of the Zonnebeke-
Passchendaele area was presented on 25 April 2004.

left: 80th anniversary of the Battle of Passchendaele: the Duke of Kent, Prince Philip and Mayor Bourgois, 13 July 1997 (MMP)

Twenty veterans attended, five of whom took part in the Battle of Passchendaele, 13 July 1997 (MMP)

Honouring fallen comrades, 13 July 1997 (MMP)

Public interest, 13 July 1997 (MMP)

ANZAC Day 2003 in the presence of Danna Vale, Australian Minister for Veteran Affairs, flanked by Mayor Bourgois and Alderman Cardoen, 25 April 2003 (Deforche)

Lasting development (2002-)

In recent years visits to the old battlefields have grown still further. Some 330,000 visitors come to the former battlefields of Flanders annually and around half of these have Tyne Cot on their itinerary. This means that Tyne Cot is not only the largest Commonwealth war cemetery in the world, it is also the most visited on the Western Front. A survey carried out by Westtoer in 2006 showed that 33% of the visitors were Britons or originating from other Commonwealth countries. A striking figure is the rise in the number of Dutch visitors even though the Netherlands were not a party to the First World War. French and Germans are seldom seen here, indeed they rarely come to the region. More than 35% of the Britons are travelling in groups with most of these from schools.

The number of visits by prominent people and the number of services at Tyne Cot can no longer be counted. On Saturday 19 June 1999, a group of nine veterans from the World War One Veterans Association visited Zonnebeke and Tyne Cot Cemetery. The last Passchendaele veteran to visit the cemetery was Harry Patch on 22 September 2004. It was eighty-seven years to the day since he was wounded by a grenade attack at Eagle Trench to the north-east of Langemark. A Lewis Gunner with the 7th Duke of Cornwall's Light Infantry, he lost his three best friends. For Harry Patch 22 September remained Remembrance Day for all time. Another notable guest was Air Marshal Bruce Ferguson, Chief of the New Zealand Defence Force. On Friday 5 November 2004, he visited 's Graventafel, Polygon Wood, Messines, Ypres and then northern France where the remains of a New Zealander were disinterred for reburial in Wellington as their unknown soldier. On 16 December 2006, the Australian Minister of Defence, Dr Brendan Nelson, paid a private visit to Tyne Cot Cemetery. And on Saturday 14 March 2007, it was the turn of Prince Edward, youngest son of the Queen, during an unofficial visit as Colonel-in-Chief of the Saskatchewan Dragoons from Canada.

Besides the large-scale official visits, wreaths are laid on an almost daily basis by school groups, visiting military, associations and close relatives, all of them without a ceremonial element. On 1 August 2004, a beautiful service was organised by the Memorial Museum

top left: Prins Edward, the Queen's youngest son, and CWGC director Philip Noakes at the Tyne Cot visitors' Centre, 14 April 2007

top right: Cadet Ethan Fleming playing with the Hampshire & Isle of Wight Army Cadet Force Band in honour of his great-great-grandfather Albert Jenkins, who is buried at Tyne Cot, 1 August 2004 (Deforche)

bottom right: Air Marshal Bruce Ferguson, Chief of Staff of the New Zealand Defence Force, at the New Zealand Memorial to the Missing (centre) and Mayor Cardoen (left), 5 November 2004 (www.westhoek.be)

Passchendaele 1917 and Bartletts Battlefield Journeys. Cadet Ethan Fleming laid flowers on grave 64/E/8 where his great-great-grandfather Albert J. Atkins (3rd Queen's Regiment) is buried, while Joanne Coyle laid flowers for her missing great-uncle Hugh Cairns (16th Highland Light Infantry). Music for the ceremony was provided by the Hampshire & Isle of Wight Army Cadet Force Band. The group then went by foot to the Goudberg in Passchendaele where Hugh Cairns was among the missing on 2 December 1917. A hazel was planted and a small plaque unveiled in his memory. Joanne closed the occasion in a moving manner with a Scottish song from the area where Hugh had been born.

The increasing stream of visitors also brought with it an ever-growing number of problems. First there was the total lack of sanitary facilities and the chaotic traffic situation. Occasionally Tyne Cot made the news because a coach had sunk into the soft roadside and had to be towed out. On 11 November 2002, at 3.30 pm we counted no fewer than 14 coaches and 65 cars. In the cemetery itself there are particularly problems with grass on the middle path despite strengthening with plastic nets. The same year, 2002, brought the first fundamental considerations of a better way of opening up Tyne Cot Cemetery

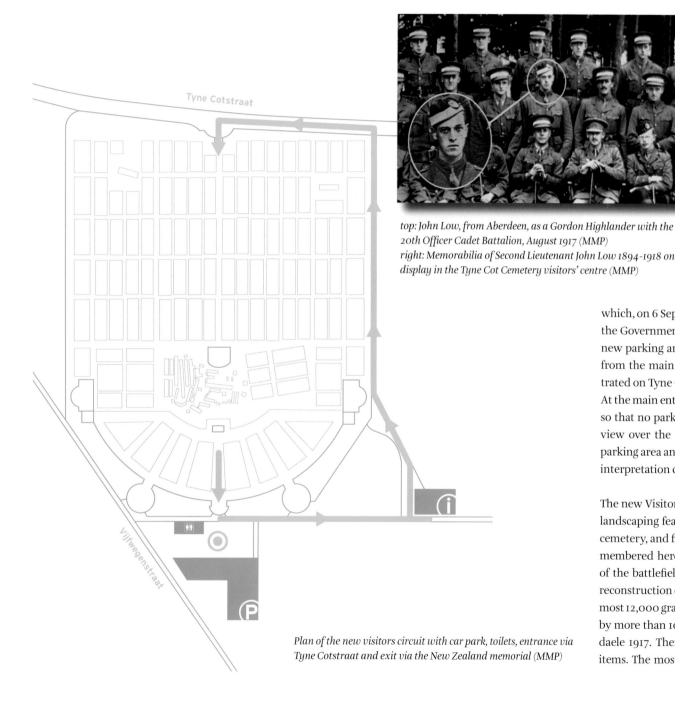

top: John Low, from Aberdeen, as a Gordon Highlander with the 20th Officer Cadet Battalion, August 1917 (MMP)
right: Memorabilia of Second Lieutenant John Low 1894-1918 on display in the Tyne Cot Cemetery visitors' centre (MMP)

Plan of the new visitors circuit with car park, toilets, entrance via Tyne Cotstraat and exit via the New Zealand memorial (MMP)

which, on 6 September 2002, had been protected as a monument by the Government of Flanders. As a solution to the traffic problems, a new parking area was opened behind the site. Since then all traffic from the main Passchendaele-Broodseinde road has been concentrated on Tyne Cotstraat and the specially widened Vijfwegenstraat. At the main entrance the road has been reduced to its original width so that no parking is available there and there is an uninterrupted view over the battlefield. A sanitary block is situated at the new parking area and, as an introduction to the cemetery, there is a small interpretation centre.

The new Visitors' Centre focuses on three themes: the planting and landscaping features of the site, the history and architecture of the cemetery, and finally those who lost their lives and are buried or remembered here. Two panoramic windows provide a unique view of the battlefield from Ypres to Passchendaele and alongside are a reconstruction drawing and a montage of historic air photos. The almost 12,000 graves and 35,000 names of the missing are symbolised by more than 100 of those who died, one for each day of Passchendaele 1917. There are also various related photos, documents and items. The most touching personal items are without doubt those of Second Lieutenant John Low from Aberdeen, who is remembered on the Tyne Cot Memorial. He served with the 13th King's Royal Rifle Corps and was listed missing on 10 January, 1918, at Zandvoorde. The centre houses his uniform jacket, binoculars, pocket book, medals and a 'Troddel' he had seized from a German subaltern. A number of his letters, including one written by his fiancée soon after his death, are poignant indeed. 'The thought that Jock died for his country is no comfort to me, his memory is all I have left to love,' she wrote. Those visitors who wish to read and view everything at the centre will need about 30 minutes. A 200-metre path from the Visitors' Centre means the cemetery is still entered through the main gate. The new exit is at the rear of the cemetery through the apse of the New Zealand Memorial to the Missing. This leads directly into the parking area.

The opening up of Tyne Cot Cemetery has cost almost 1,500,000 euro, funded by co-financing through the European Community, Tourism Flanders, the Province of West Flanders, Zonnebeke Council and the Depuydt-Camerlynck family who donated the land. The project falls within the framework of the provincial 'War and Peace in the Westhoek' which, since 2002, has endeavoured to link the various war sites and museums clearly and in the best way possible. The pre-opening of the site took place on 8 September 2006, in the presence of the Flemish Minister of Tourism Geert Bourgeois. On 12 July 2007, the Visitors' Centre will be officially opened by Queen Elizabeth II and King Albert II. Then various heads of state and government leaders will again pay their tributes for the 90th anniversary of the Battle of Passchendaele, now finally with an appropriate welcome infrastructure. Tyne Cot Cemetery: an eternal vigil !

The new visitors' centre at Tyne Cot Cemetery (MMP)

Harry Patch, the last surviving Passchendaele veteran at Tyne Cot Cemetery, 22 September 2004 (Fear)

9 October 1917:
Private Dixon Overfield
6th Yorkshire Regiment

Dixon Overfield (Wheeler)

Dixon Overfield was born in Hunmanby on the East Yorkshire coast on 10 October 1883, where he spent his childhood and early adult life. He was the fourth child of Alfred Overfield and Elizabeth Ann Dixon, who went on to have three more boys and three more girls by 1900. It was in his home town of Hunmanby that he met Margaret Louise Dale from Flixton whom he subsequently married in Folkton on a particularly inauspicious date: 4 August 1914. On their wedding day the bridal couple had walked past an open grave and superstitious members of the family claimed that this meant that their marriage was cursed, an augury which did not seem overly far-fetched when war was declared on their wedding day. The newly-weds set up house in Filey, where Dixon opened a grocer's shop. He was a very active member of several charitable associations, gave Sunday school lessons and was a prominent member of the local Methodist church. His wife, who was a talented pianist and organist, also brought a little extra money into the family by giving private music lessons and played the organ in their local church. Their only daughter, Madge Elizabeth, was born on 21 June 1915.

In 1916 Dixon Overfield and a friend of his by the name of Harold Crimlisk presented themselves as volunteers at the army recruiting office in Filey. They were originally posted to an artillery regiment, but were transferred to the infantry shortly thereafter, joining the Yorkshire Regiment, where they ended up in the 6th Battalion. Overfield wrote various letters home, both while in training camps in England and later from France. In March 1917 he told his family: *'I have not been in the trenches yet, but been where the enemy has been + seen what they have left, the sight I won't try to describe, but hope the struggle may soon be over, I fail to understand the way they farm in France, I've seen one small flock of sheep only, since I came out.'* Overfield's friend and comrade in arms Private Harold Crimlisk was killed on 27 September 1917. Crimlisk, who was only 20 when he was killed, was buried in Cement House Cemetery, after the war. Overfield did not long survive his friend. The 6th Battalion Yorkshire Regiment was part of the 11th Division, which was the division picked for the attack on Poelkapelle on 9 October. The Germans had been shelling the British position all night, *'but there was no actual enemy barrage as far as could be seen.'* As soon as the signal for the attack was given, the men clambered out of their positions and charged across No Man's Land. Overfield, who would have turned 34 the next day, was killed almost as soon as he went over the top. An officer wrote: *'they were going into action when a shell burst amongst Private Overfield and a number colleagues with disastrous effect.'* One of the men of Overfield's former unit, who visited the family after the war, said that the last time he saw him he was on the edge of a large shell hole. The attack on 9 October was a complete disaster across the entire front. The casualties suffered by the 6th Yorkshires came to seven officers and 228 men, of whom 43 were killed and 31 missing. Overfield's body was never found. He is remembered today both on the Menin Gate, and on the local war memorial in Filey. Sadly, his death was not the only calamity to befall the family. His widow, Margaret Louise Dale, died on 9 October 1924, exactly nine years to the day after Overfield's own death, leaving their daughter, Madge Elizabeth, an orphan at the age of only nine.

Overfield married Margaret Louise Dale on 4 August 1914 (Wheeler)

Overfield's only daughter, Madge Elizabeth (Wheeler)

Endnotes part 1

1. The Battle of Pilkem Ridge

[1] EDMONDS, J.E. *History of the Great War based on official documents by direction of the historical section of the commitee of imperial defence. Military Operations France and Belgium 1917 volume II 7th June - 10th November Messines and Third Ypres (Passchendaele)*, London, 1948, pp. 125-126.

[2] STEWART, J., BUCHAN, J. *The Fifteenth (Scottish) Division, 1914-1919*, Edinburgh/London, 1926, p. 156.

[3] STEWART, J., BUCHAN, J. *The Fifteenth (Scottish) Division, ...*, pp. 155-156.

[4] NA WO339/60237 *service record F.M. Hills., s.n., Tonbridge School and The Great War of 1914 to 1919. A Record of the Services of Tonbridgians in the Great War of 1914 to 1919*, Tonbridge, 1923, pp. 158-159.

[5] BORASTON, J.H., BAX, C.E.O. *The Eight Division, 1914-1918*, Uckfield, 1999, p. 128.

[6] BORASTON, J.H., BAX, C.E.O. *The Eight Division,...*, p. 128.

[7] s.n., *de Ruvigny's Roll of Honour, A biographical record of members of his majesty's Naval and Military Forces who fell in the Great War 1914-1918, Part Three*, s.n., s.d., p. 41., NA WO339/59388 *service record R.A. Budden*.

[8] BORASTON, J.H., BAX, C.E.O. *The Eight Division,...*, p. 129.

[9] BORASTON, J.H., BAX, C.E.O. *The Eight Division,...*, p. 130., SNELLING, S. *VC's of the First World War, Passchendaele 1917*, Thrupp, 2000, pp. 8-15.

[10] Regimental Archives Sherwood Foresters *The Sherwood Foresters Roll, Meadows, Ernest*

[11] Private archive Michael A. Cross, Witney, England, PA *file A.J. Cross.*

[12] COOPER WALKER, G.D. *The Book of The Seventh Service Battalion The Royal Inniskilling Fusiliers from Tipperary to Ypres*, Dublin, 1920, p. 110.

[13] FALLS, C. *The History of the first seven battalions The Royal Irish Rifles in the Great War Vol. II*, Aldershot, 1925, p. 102.

[14] SIMPSON, C.R. *The history of the Lincolnshire Regiment, 1914-1918, Compiled from War Diaries, Despatches, Officers' Notes and Other Sources* London, 1931, p. 252.

[15] FALLS, C. *The Life of a regiment, Volume IV, The Gordon Highlanders in the First World War 1914-1919* (Aberdeen, 1958), p. 153.

[16] FALLS, C. *The Life of a regiment, ...*, p. 153.

[17] s.n., *de Ruvigny's Roll of Honour...Part Three...*, p. 254., NA WO339/77674 service record A.C. Spark.

[18] NA WO95/1940 *War Diary 8th Battalion Seaforth Highlanders.* 29-30/07/1917 tot 3-4/08/1917.

[19] STEWART, J., BUCHAN, J. *The Fifteenth (Scottish) Division...*, p. 163.

[20] s.n., *de Ruvigny's Roll of Honour...Part Three...*, p 80.

[21] STEWART, J., BUCHAN, J. *The Fifteenth (Scottish) Division...*, p. 166.

[22] NA WO339/57214 *service record A.E. Keppel.*

2. Westhoek and the Battle of Langemark

[23] EWING, J. *The Royal Scots, 1914-1919*, Edinburgh, 1925, p. 452.

[24] CWGC *Burial Return Sheets Tyne Cot Cemetery*.

[25] STEWART, J., BUCHAN, J. *The Fifteenth (Scottish) Division...*, pp. 169-170.

[26] BORASTON, J.H., BAX, C.E.O. *The Eight Division,...*, pp. 135-136.

[27] BORASTON, J.H., BAX, C.E.O. *The Eight Division,...*, p. 140.

[28] FALLS, C. *The History of the first seven battalions,...*, p. 103.

[29] SIMPSON, C.R. *The history of the Lincolnshire Regiment,...*, p. 258.

[30] STEWART, J., BUCHAN, J. *The Fifteenth (Scottish) Division,...*, p. 177.

[31] BORASTON, J.H., BAX, C.E.O. *The Eight Division,...*, p. 140.

[32] IWM *London Papers of F.H.T. Tatham*.

[33] O'RAHILLLY, A. *Father William Doyle S.J., A Spiritual Study*, London, 1925, p. 542.

[34] PA *file A. Craig*.

[35] FALLS, C. *The History of the 36th (Ulster) Division*, Londen, 1922, p. 116.

[36] FALLS, C. *The History of the 36th (Ulster)...*, p. 116.

[37] NA WO95/2505 *War Diary 9th Bn Royal Irish Fusiliers*.

[38] Private collection A.Shaw.

[39] NA WO339/17419 *service record T.G. Shillington*.

[40] PA *file A.W. Church*.

[41] s.n., *de Ruvigny's Roll of Honour, A biographical record of members of his majesty's Naval and Military Forces who fell in the Great War 1914-1918, Part Five*, s.n., s.d., p. 19.

[42] NA WO 95/1977 *War Diary 8th Royal Inniskilling Fusiliers, 08/1917*.

[43] PA *file J.T. Robinson*.

[44] HENNESSY, T.F. *The Great War 1914-1918, Bank of Ireland Staff, Dublin, 1920, p. 9.*, NA WO95/1978 *War Diary 7/8th Battalion Royal Irish Fusiliers 08/1917*.

[45] NA, WO339/42575 *service record R.D.Miles*.

[46] GRAHAM, L. *Downside & the War 1914-1919*, London, 1925, p. 178., NA WO339/7746 *service record J.O.W. Shine*.

[47] O'RAHILLLY, A. *Father William Doyle...*, pp. 546, 554-555. Doyles service record gives 18 August, but this is probably the date on which Doyle's death was recorded. Some eye witnesses claim it was 17 August, others 16 August.

[48] FALLS, C. *The History of the 36th (Ulster)...*, p. 119.

[49] NA WO 95/1977 *War Diary 7th Royal Inniskilling Fusiliers, 08/1917*.

[50] NA CAB45/140 *Official History Drafts*.

3. Preparations for a new Offensive

[51] CONNERTY, I., GILBERT, M., et al *At the Going Down of the Sun, 365 Soldiers from the Great War* Tielt, 2001, p. 213.

[52] MACDONALD, L. *They Called it Passchendaele, The story of the Battle of Ypres and of the men who fought in it* London, 1993, p. 167.

[53] MACDONALD, L. *They Called it Passchendaele...*, p. 175-176.

[54] PA *file T.K. Keeley.*

[55] EDMONDS, J.E. *History of the Great War based on official documents by direction of the historical section of the committee of imperial defence. Military Operations France and Belgium 1917 volume II 7th June - 10th November Messines and Third Ypres (Passchendaele)*, London, 1948, p. 202.

[56] PA *file S. Henshaw.*

[57] s.n. *de Ruvigny's Roll of Honour, A biographical record of members of his majesty's Naval and Military Forces who fell in the Great War 1914-1918, Part Four* (s.n., s.d.), p. 35

[58] STEWART, J en BUCHAN, J. *The Fifteenth (Scottish) Division, 1914-1919* Edinburgh/London, 1926, p. 181.

[59] s.n., *George Heriot's School, Roll of Honour, 1914-1919* Edinburgh, 1921, p. 40.

[60] NA WO339/57888 *service record G.A.F. Renwick., s.n., George Heriot's School...*, p. 159.

[61] STEWART, J en BUCHAN, J. *The Fifteenth (Scottish) Division...*, pp. 181-182.

[62] STEWART, J en BUCHAN, J. *The Fifteenth (Scottish) Division...*, p. 195.

[63] s.n. *A Memorial record of Watsonians who served in the Great War 1914-1918*, Edinburgh, 1920, p. 293.

[64] NA WO95/1940 *War Diary 8th Battalion Seaforth Highlanders 08/1917.*

[65] PA *file J.T. Hiddleston., CWGC Burial Return Sheets Tyne Cot Cemetery*

[66] CWGC *Burial Return Sheets Tyne Cot Cemetery, s.n., de Ruvigny's Roll of Honour...Part Four ...*, p. 5.

[67] STEWART, J en BUCHAN, J. *The Fifteenth (Scottish) Division...*, pp. 182-183.

[68] s.n., *de Ruvigny's Roll of Honour...Part Three ...*, p. 237.

[69] WILLIAMS-ELLIS, C., WILLIAMS-ELLIS, A. *The Tank Corps*, s.l., 1919, p. 94.

[70] NA WO339/3558 *service record D.I. Murray-Menzies.*

[71] MACDONALD, L. *They Called it Passchendaele...*, p. 164.

[72] NA WO339/36515 *service record A.R. Lawrie.*

[73] MILES, W. *The Durham Forces in the Field 1914-1918, The Service Battalions of the Durham Light Infantry* Londen, 1922, p. 179.

[74] PA *file T. Livermore., CWGC Burial Return Sheets Tyne Cot Cemetery.*

[75] EDMONDS, J.E. *History of the Great War ...*, p. 205.

[76] EDMONDS, J.E. *History of the Great War ...*, p. 206-208.

[77] PA *file E.A. Bradford.*

[78] NA WO95/2649 *War Diary 210th Bde RFA 09/1917.*

[79] PA *file D. Entwistle.*

4. The Battle of the Menin Road

[80] GILLON, S. *The K.O.S.B. in the Great War* London, 1930, pp. 353-354.

[81] EWING, J. *The History of the 9th (Scottish) Division, 1914-1919*, London, 1921, p. 229.

[82] EWING, J. *The History of the 9th ...*, p. 231

[83] EWING, J. *The History of the 9th ...*, p. 232.

[84] GILLON, S. *The K.O.S.B. ...*, p. 354.

[85] s.n., *George Heriot's School, Roll of Honour, 1914-1919*, Edinburgh, 1921, p. 68.

[86] EWING, J. *The Royal Scots, 1914-1919* Edinburgh, 1925, p. 473.

[87] SNELLING, S. *VCs of the First World War, Passchendaele 1917*, Thrupp, 2000, pp. 118-119.

[88] s.n., *de Ruvigny's Roll of Honour, A biographical record of members of his majesty's Naval and Military Forces who fell in the Great War 1914-1918, Part Three*, s.n., s.d., p. 277.

[89] Private Joseph Lavelle, 9th Cameronians (Scottish Rifles) was killed on 26 September 1915 during the Battle of Loos. He is remembered on a Special Memorial in Cambrin Churchyard Extension.

[90] 'Second Son Lost', in: 'Burnley Express', 6/10/1917, Burnley Borough Council's Towneley Hall Museum.

[91] s.n., *de Ruvigny's Roll of Honour...Part Three...*, p. 81.

[92] s.n., *de Ruvigny's Roll of Honour...Part Four...*, p. 4.

[93] CLAYTON, J.T. *Craven's Part in the Great War*, Skipton, 1919, p. 279.

[94] CLAYTON, J.T. *Craven's Part ...*, p. 279.

[95] NA WO95/1780 *War Diary 1st South African Regiment*, 20-21/09/1917.

[96] NA WO95/1780 *War Diary 1st South African Regiment*, 20-21/09/1917.

[97] SNELLING, S. *VCs of the First World War...*, pp. 121-122.

[98] LAC, RG 38/84 *service record Philips John.*, 2nd (Special Service) Battalion, Royal Canadian Regiment of Infantry, http://www.warmuseum.ca/cwm/boer/infantryregiment_e.html, s.n., *de Ruvigny's Roll of Honour...Part Four...*, p. 156.

[99] EWING, J. *The History of the 9th ...*, p. 235.

[100] EWING, J. *The History of the 9th ...*, p. 229.

[101] s.n., *A Memorial record of Watsonians who served in the Great War 1914-1918* Edinburgh, 1920, p. 346.

[102] PA *file Harold Hedley Art*

[103] s.n., *George Heriot's School, Roll of Honour, 1914-1919* Edinburgh, 1921, p. 179.

[104] DAVIES, F. and MADDOCKS,G. *Bloody Red Tabs, General Officer Casualties of the Great War 1914-1918* London, 1995, p. 93., NA WO374/46954 *service record F. A. Maxwell.*, EDMONDS, J.E. *History of the Great War...*, p. 278.

[105] Lieutenant-Colonel Eustace Lockhart Maxwell, 11th King Edward's Own Lancers (Prolyn's Horse), was killed on 20 July 1916. He is remembered on the Neuve-Chapelle Memorial in France.

[106] GILLON, S. *The K.O.S.B. ...*, p. 355.

[107] EDMONDS, J.E. *History of the Great War...*, p. 267 and 279.

5. The Battle of Polygon Wood

[108] ELLIS, A.D. *The story of the Fifth Australian Division, Being an Authoritative Account of the Division's Doings in Egypt, France and Belgium* London, 1920, p. 239.

[109] HUTCHINSON, G.S. *The Thirty-Third Division in France and Flanders, 1915-1919* (Uckfield, s.d.), p. 68.

[110] NAA 3909771 *service record William Alfred Fitch.*

[111] NAA 3034649 *service record John Thomas Hamilton Aram.*

[112] CORFIELD, R.S. *Hold hard, Cobbers, Volume One 1912-1930. The story of the 57th and 60th and 57/60th Australian Infantry Battalion 1912-1990* Glenhuntly, 1992, pp. 99-101.

[113] AWM 2390308 *Red Cross file Edward John Ryan.*

[114] ELLIS, A.D. *The story of the Fifth...* p. 243.

[115] ELLIS, A.D. *The story of the Fifth...,* p. 246.

[116] AWM 2130104 *Red Cross file William Henry Pegrum.,* NAA 11266927 *service records Willam Henry Pegrum.*

[117] They were: Pte Geoffrey Gladstones, Pte Horace George Cornford and Sgt James George Eccleston. Gladstones was buried in Oxford Road Cemetery and the other two are remembered on the Menin Gate.

[118] NAA 3128320 *service record Harry Wallace Brokenshire.*

[119] NAA 8010735 *service record Albert George Pegram.,* PA file *Albert George Pegram.*

[120] AWM 2130505 *Red Cross file Ernest Michael Penny.*

[121] BEAN, C.E.W. *The Australian Imperial ...,* p. 814.

[122] NA WO95/3619 *War Diary 31st Battalion AIF.*

[123] NAA 8072249 *service record Reginald Rowland.*

[124] AWM Honours and Awards *Patrick Bugden.,* Cpl Alf Thompson, quoted in: SNELLING S. *VC's of the First World War, Passchendaele 1917* Thrupp, 2000, pp. 155-156.

[125] AWM 1270711 *Red Cross file James Wilfred Harrap.*

[126] AWM 841006 *Red Cross file William Reeves Crossman.*

[127] ELLIS, A.D. *The story of the Fifth...* p. 249.

[128] AWM 801203 *Red Cross file Ellis Eric Cork.,* NAA 3421142 *service record Ellis Eric Cork.*

[129] AUSTIN, R.J. *Black and Gold, The history of the 29th Battalion, 1915-1918* McCrae, 1997, pp. 87-89.

[130] *smallholder.*

[131] Private archive G. Rose, Ashburton, Australia., PA *file H. McDonald.,* NAA 1840914 *service record Hugh McDonald.*

[132] NAA 4749877 *service record Arthur Heard.,* AWM 1301010 *Red Cross file Arthur Heard.*

[133] ELLIS, A.D. *The story of the Fifth...* p. 251.

[134] BEAN, C.E.W. *The Australian Imperial ...,* p. 831.

[135] ELLIS, A.D. *The story of the Fifth...* p. 251.

[136] ELLIS, A.D. *The story of the Fifth...* p. 248.

329

6. The Battle of Broodseinde

[137] *Geschichte des infanterieregiments nr 369 (10de Ersatz Divisie)*, p. 67.

[138] EDMONDS, J.E. *History of the Great War based on official documents by direction of the historical section of the committee of imperial defence. Military Operations France and Belgium 1917 volume II 7th June - 10th November Messines and Third Ypres (Passchendaele)*, London, 1948, p. 305.

[139] *the Ruvigny's Roll of Honour 1914-1918, A Biographical record of members of his majesty's naval and military forces who fell in the Great War 1914-1918. Part Five*, s.l., s.d., p. 127.

[140] STEWART, H. *The New Zealand Division, 1916-1919. A Popular History Based on Official Records*, Auckland, 1921, p. 258.

[141] CENOTAPH, http://www.aucklandmuseum.com/ *Forde, N.A.*

[142] STEWART, H. *The New Zealand Division...*, p. 260.

[143] HARPER, G. *Massacre at Passchendaele, The New Zealand Story*, Auckland, 2000, p. 36.

[144] STEWART, H. *The New Zealand Division...*, p. 262.

[145] s.n. *the Ruvigny's Roll of Honour ...Part Three ...*, p. 195.

[146] BURTON, O.E. *The Auckland Regiment, being an account of the doings on Active Service of the First, Second and Third Battalions of the Auckland Regiment*, Auckland, 1922, pp. 174-175.

[147] CENOTAPH, http://www.aucklandmuseum.com/ *Warrington, Henry Frank.*

[148] CENOTAPH, http://www.aucklandmuseum.com/ *Arden, Nevill Henry.*

[149] BURTON, O.E. *The Auckland Regiment...*, p. 173-174.

[150] CENOTAPH, http://www.aucklandmuseum.com/ *Sherlock, Alfred Charles.*

[151] BURTON, O.E. *The Auckland Regiment...*, p. 174.

[152] CENOTAPH, http://www.aucklandmuseum.com/ *Evers-Swindell, Ernest Frederick.*, CUNNINGHAM, W.L., TREADWELL, C.A.L., HANNA, J.S. *The Wellington Regiment...*, p. 217.

[153] CUNNINGHAM, W.L., TREADWELL, C.A.L., HANNA, J.S. *The Wellington Regiment ...*, p. 217.

[154] CENOTAPH, http://www.aucklandmuseum.com/ *Tosswill, William Wyndham.*

[155] CWGC *Burial Return Sheets, Tyne Cot Cemetery.*

[156] Auckland Weekly News, 8 November 1917, p. 30, quoted in: CENOTAPH, http://www.aucklandmuseum. com/ *Spaccesi, Antoine.*

[157] Auckland Weekly News, 8 November 1917, p. 22, quoted in: CENOTAPH, http://www.aucklandmuseum. com/ *Webb, Thomas Charles.*

[158] BURTON, O.E. *The Auckland Regiment...*, p. 175.

[159] CUNNINGHAM, W.L., TREADWELL, C.A.L., HANNA, J.S. *The Wellington Regiment N.Z.E.F.* 1914-1919, Wellington, 1928, p. 218.

[160] CWGC *Burial Return Sheets, Tyne Cot Cemetery.*

[161] CWGC *Burial Return Sheets, Tyne Cot Cemetery.*

[162] CUNNINGHAM, W.L., TREADWELL, C.A.L., HANNA, J.S. *The Wellington Regiment...*, pp. 219-220.

[163] STEWART, H. *The New Zealand Division...*, p. 268.

[164] In Memoriam 1914-1918, Wanganui Collegiate School, quoted in: CENOTAPH, http://www.aucklandmuseum.com, Maunsell Percy Harold

[165] In Memoriam, 1914-1918, Wanganui Collegiate School, quoted in: CENOTAPH, http://www.aucklandmuseum.com/ *Maunsell, Percy Harold.* CWGC Burial Return Sheets, Tyne Cot Cemetery

[166] BURTON, O.E. *The Auckland Regiment...*, p. 177.

[167] C s.n. *the Ruvigny's Roll of Honour ...Part Five ...*, p. 5., WGC *Burial Return Sheets, Tyne Cot Cemetery.*

[168] BURTON, O.E. *The Auckland Regiment...*, p. 178.

[169] Private-archive Ms E. Langford, Ashburton, Canterbury.

[170] BURTON, O.E. *The Auckland Regiment...*, p. 178.

[171] STEWART, H. *The New Zealand Division...*, p. 272.

[172] CUNNINGHAM, W.L., TREADWELL, C.A.L., HANNA, J.S. *The Wellington Regiment...*, p. 222., CARBERY, A.D. *The New Zealand Medical Service in the Great War 1914-1918, Based on Official Documents*, Auckland, 1924, p. 332 and 340.

[173] s.n. *the Ruvigny's Roll of Honour ...Part Four...*, p. 88., 'Absolutely Game, Heroic Burnley New Zealander', in Burnley Express. 21/11/1917, Burnley Borough Council's Towneley Hall Museum.

[174] Company Sergeant Major Douglas Wallace Gallaher, 11th Battalion Australian Infantry, aged 32, killed on 3 June 1916. He was buried in Rue-Petillon Military Cemetery in Fleurbaix. He had also served in the Boer War.

[175] Private Henry Fletcher Gallaher, 51st Australian Infantry, killed on 24 April 1918. He is remembered on the Villers-Bretonneux Memorial.

[176] Private archive of the Collins-Morgan family, New Zealand.

[177] Clare Church, *New Zealand Graves at Brockenhurst*, quoted in: CENOTAPH, http://www.aucklandmuseum. com/ *Player, Ernest Nicholson.*

[178] STEWART, H. *The New Zealand Division...*, p. 271.

[179] EDMONDS, J.E. *History of the Great War ...*, p. 309 and NZ, p. 271.

[180] BURTON, O.E. *The Auckland Regiment...*, p. 178.

7. The Battle of Poelcapelle

[181] BEAN, C.E.W. *The Australian Imperial ...*, p. 883.

[182] EDMONDS, J.E. *History of the Great War based on official documents by direction of the historical section of the committee of imperial defence. Military Operations France and Belgium 1917 volume II 7th June - 10th November Messines and Third Ypres (Passchendaele)*, London, 1948, p. 323-330.

[183] This raid is described extensively in: SPAGNOLY, T., SMITH, T. *The Anatomy of a Raid, Australia at Celtic Wood, 9th October 1917* Barnsley, 1998, 130 p.

[184] BEAN, C.E.W. *The Australian Imperial ...*, p. 890.

[185] BEAN, C.E.W. *The Australian Imperial ...*, p. 892.

[186] MACKENZIE, K.W. *The Story of the Seventeenth Battalion A.I.F. in the Great War 1914-1918* Sydney, 1946, p. 207.

[187] NAA 3461484 *service record Allan Marmaduke Crawley.*

[188] MACKENZIE, K.W. *The Story of the Seventeenth ...*, p. 207.

[189] AWM 1650706 *Red Cross file John Maher Lyons*, AWM Honours and Awards *John Maher Lyons.*, NAA 8207479 service record *John Maher Lyons.*

[190] AWM 1230408 *Red Cross file George Thomas Guinea.*, NAA 4391809 *service record George Thomas Guinea.*, AWM Honours and Awards *George Thomas Guinea.*

[191] Corporal John Leslie Guinea was with the 39th Battalion of the 3rd Australian Division. He was killed when an artillery shell exploded next to him at Messines. He was buried at Bethleem Farm West Cemetery in Messines.

[192] MACKENZIE, K.W. *The Story of the Seventeenth ...*, p. 208.

[193] MACKENZIE, K.W. *The Story of the Seventeenth...*, p. 212.

[194] PA *file Edgar Athling Morris.*, NAA 7981813 *service record Edgar Athling Morris.*

[195] BEAN, C.E.W. *The Australian Imperial ...*, p. 896.

[196] NAA 1854396 *service record John Donald Campbell.*

[197] NA WO 95/3334 *War Diary 24th Battalion 10/1917.*

[198] BEAN, C.E.W. *The Australian Imperial...*, p. 896, Captain Williams and Lieutenant Nation were buried together on the same day on the battlefield near Daisy Wood. Their bodies were found in September 1920 and were reburied in Tyne Cot Cemetery. They are still buried next to each other. (XXXVIII.F.23-24.)

[199] NAA 8014787 *service record Reginald James Pickett.*

[200] AWM R 620706 *Red Cross file Frederick William Bulling.*, NAA 3165349 *service record Frederick William Bulling.*

[201] NAA 3097146 *service record George Ernest Bolton.*

[202] NAA 7377055 *James Horace Lane.*, AWM 1550214 *Red Cross file James Horace Lane.*

[203] Private Arthur Jabez Lane, 54th Battalion, killed on 15/05/1917. Lane was a 22-year-old steward. He is remembered on the Villers-Bretonneux Memorial.

[204] NA WO 95/3334 *War Diary 24th Battalion, 10/1917.*

[205] NA WO 95/3326 *War Diary 21th Battalion, 10/1917.*

[206] AWM Roll of Honour Cards *Arthur Douglas Hogan.*, NAA 5283830 *service record Arthur Douglas Hogan.*

[207] NA WO 95/3334 *War Diary 24th Battalion 10/1917.*

[208] NAA 8094641 *service record Herbert John Strong.*

[209] NAA 8361112 *service record Arthur George Walmsley.*, AWM 2840906 *Red Cross file Arthur George Walmsley.*

[210] AWM 3040209 *Red Cross file Edwin St Clair Yeoman.*, NAA 3454819 *service record Edwin St Clair Yeoman.*

[211] AWM 2860802 *Red Cross file George Goulburn Warren.*, NAA 8361979 *service record George Goulburn Warren.*

[212] NAA 4736333 *service record Russel Highfield Hawse.*

[213] Figures vary from source to source. These casualty figures are based on BEAN, C.E.W. The Australian Imperial..., p. 900.

8. The First Battle of Passchendaele

[214] Lieutenant Telford Graham Gilder was awarded the MC for his bravery on 12 October 1917. He survived the war.

[215] The names of three of them are known: Robert Wilson; Richard Clarence Gunter and Ernest Adolphus Calov. The latter had a brother, Frederick Leopold, who lost a leg at Polygon Wood on 26 September 1917. He died of his wounds the following day at CCS no. 2 (Lijssenthoek near Poperinghe.)

[216] William Henry Burt died of his wounds the following day at CCS no. 2 (Lijssenthoek) on 14 October 1917. He had been badly wounded in both legs.

[217] AWM 2990307 *Red Cross file Robert Wilson.*

[218] AWM 2450705 *Red Cross file Harold Thomas Sell.*

[219] NA WO95/3405 *War Diary 34th Battalion AIF 10/1917.*

[220] NA WO95/3408 *War Diary 35th Battalion AIF 10/1917*

[221] NAA 8212049 *service record Charles Teesdale Main.*

[222] GREEN, F.C. *The Fortieth, A Record of the 40th Battalion, A.I.F.* Hobart, 1922, pp. 86-87.

[223] PALAZO, A. *Defenders of Australia: the 3rd Australian Division, 1916-1991* Canberra, 2002, p. 39.

[224] NA WO95/3405 *War Diary 34th Battalion AIF 10/1917.*

[225] NA, WO95/3405 *War Diary 34th Battalion AIF 10/1917.*

[226] BEAN, C.E.W. *The Australian Imperial ...,* p. 912.

[227] 'Bei uns fliegen die vielsagenden roten und grünen Leuchtkugeln hoch, einerseits, um das Feuer unserer Artillerie ausbrüllen zu lassen, andererseits, als Zeichen erhöhter Bereitschaft: Stehe fest auf deinem Posten, auf den die Pflicht dich gestellt hat, warte und weiche nicht, von deiner Kampfbereitschaft, deiner scharfen Beobachtung hängt das Schicksal von Tausenden Kameraden ab!!', BRENDLER, W. *Kriegserlebnisse 1914 bis 1918 im Reserve-Infanterie-Regiment 233 (Regimentsgeschichte),* Thüringen, s.d., p. 216.

[228] NAA 8397508 *service record Joseph Varcoe.* The book, together with the other belongings, did not come into the possession of Varcoe's brother until September 1918.

[229] NA WO 95/3409 *War Diary of the 36th Battalion AIF 10/1917.*

[230] NAA 3152474 *service record Buchanan John Bruce.*

[231] BEAN, C.E.W. *The Australian Imperial ...,* p. 915.

[232] NA WO95/3405 *War Diary 34th Battalion AIF 10/1917.*

[233] Lieutenant Garrard commanded the group of men who attacked Augustus Wood from the rear on 12 October. They captured one pillbox and took twenty prisoners of war.

[234] SNELLING, S. *VCs ...,* pp. 170-171.

[235] CWGC *Burial return Sheets Tyne Cot Cemetery.*

[236] James Roadknight is remembered today on the Menin Gate. His brother Walter Roadknight, a lieutenant with the 37th Battalion, was severely wounded in an attack on German positions at the Somme on 11 August 1918. He died of his wounds the same day. He was buried in Daours Communal Cemetery Extension. He was 32.

[237] NAA 8034259 *service record James Roadknight.*

[238] BEAN, C.E.W. *The Australian Imperial ...,* p. 914.

[239] AWM 2580703 *Red Cross file Henry Southby.*

[240] NA WO95/3420 *War Diary 40th Battalion AIF 10/1917.*

[241] BEAN, C.E.W. *The Australian Imperial ...,* pp. 917-918.

[242] NA WO 95/338 *War Diary 9th Aust. Field Amb. 10/1917.*

[243] Major Gother Robert Carlisle Clark, a 42-year old medical officer with the 34th Battalion who was assigned to the 9th Field Ambulance. Clark is buried in Buttes New British Cemetery, Polygon Wood. He was a doctor before the war. The Red Cross files include the following entry concerning his death: '*He was lying in the trench instantaneously killed in the act of dressing a wounded man, and still held the dressing in his hand. He was not shattered or disfigured. His body was laid aside and covered, and his regiment immediately notified.* EDWARDS, J. *Never a backward step, A history of the First 33rd Battalion, AIF* Grafton, s.d., p. 56., CWGC *Burial return Sheets Tyne Cot Cemetery.*

[244] AWM 2850405 *Red Cross file Charles Joseph Walsh.*

[245] AWM Roll of Honour Cards *C.J. Walsh.*

[246] Not only did Hardy have a brother serving in the Australian army, but six of his cousins were also on active service. Two of them were killed.

[247] AWM Honours and Awards *Daniel Joseph Hardy.*

[248] AWM 1270203 *Red Cross file Daniel Joseph Hardy.* NAA 4968376 *service record Daniel Joseph Hardy.*

[249] CWGC *Burial return Sheets Tyne Cot Cemetery*

[250] AWM 1230511 *Red Cross file Albert Edward Gundrill.* NAA 4391969 *Albert Edward Gundrill.*

[251] Alfred John and Albert Edward Gundrill enlisted together in the Australian Imperial Force on 28 February 1916. Alfred John was not yet nineteen. Albert Edward was only 24.

[252] NAA 1842471 *service record John Henry McDonald.*

[253] AWM 2360408 *Red Cross file Hugh Madigan Ross.* NAA 8038325 *service record Hugh Madigan Ross.*

[254] AWM 760505 *Red Cross file Joseph Henry Cock.*

9. The Second Battle of Passchendaele(1)

[255] AWM 1360510 *Red Cross file Leonard Parkes Holroyd.*

[256] AWM 1151004 *Red Cross file Albert Roy Barton Gibbs.* NAA 4104611 *service record Albert Roy Barton Gibbs.*

[257] NA WO95/3352 *War Diary 3rd Australian Division 08/1917.*

[258] AWM 1520604 *Red Cross file Thomas William Kinneard.*

[259] Company Sergeant Major George Andrew Werner, from Tenterfield, NSW was awarded the Distinguished Conduct Medal at Passchendaele for bringing back wounded men and for reorganizing his unit. He received a serious stomach wound at Villers-Brettoneux on 30 March 1918. He died the following day in Rouen general hospital.

[260] Second Lieutenant Richard 'Dick' Blomfield won the Military Cross in Passchendaele for bringing back wounded men from No Man's Land. He was also severely wounded and lost an eye. He was no longer able to return to active service after his convalescence, but wrote an extensive set of memoirs about his time at the front.

[261] Officially, Captain Wilfred Frank Hinton died on 13 October 1917, but 12 October is a more likely date.

[262] This was Evan Bruce McKillop, who was also with the 33rd Battalion. He was wounded by gas in April 1918 and joined the *Grave Registrations Detachment* in April 1919, probably as a volunteer in the hope of finding the body of his brother. He only worked in France, however. In July 1919 he left Europe and went back to Australia. EDWARDS, J. *Never a backward step, A history of the First 33rd Battalion, AIF* Grafton, s.d., p. 56., CWGC *Burial return Sheets Tyne Cot Cemetery.*

[263] CWGC *Burial return Sheets Tyne Cot Cemetery.*

[264] LAC RG9/4893 *War Diary 7th Infantry Brigade, 10/1917.*

[265] LAC RG9/4899 *War Diary 9th Canadian Infantry Brigade, 10/1917.*

[266] LAC RG9/4947 *War Diary 4th Canadian Mounted Rifles Battalion, 10/1917.*

[267] LAC RG9/4947 *War Diary 4th Canadian Mounted Rifles Battalion, 10/1917.*

[268] LAC, RG 150/10563 *service record J.R. Woods.*

[269] s.d., *University of Manitoba Roll of Honour 1914-1918 Manitoba, 1923, pp. 17-26,* LAC, RG 150/2853 *service record J. Einarson.*

[270] JERROLD, D. *The Royal Naval Division,* London, 1923, p. 251.

[271] PA *file J.L. Reynoldson,with grateful thanks to C. Page.*

[272] PA *file J. G. Welsh.*

[273] TNMP Military Genealogy *Record John George Welsh.*

[274] JERROLD, D. *The Royal Naval ...,* p. 253.

[275] Private archive Mrs R. Broom, Chinnor.

[276] TNMP Military Genealogy *Record Frederick William Keen.* PA *file F.W. Keen.*

[277] TNMP Military Genealogy *Record Josiah Mitchell.*

[278] s.n., *Tonbridge School and The Great War of 1914 to 1919. A record of the services of Tonbridgians in the Great War of 1914 to 1919,* London and Tonbridge, 1923, pp. 21-22, TNMP Military Genealogy *Record Francis Cedric Balcombe.*

[279] TNMP Military Genealogy *Record John Thomas Hopkins.,* NA ADM. 159/147 *John Thomas Hopkins.*

[280] s.n., *de Ruvigny's Roll of Honour 1914-1918, A Biographical record of members of his majesty's naval and military forces who fell in the Great War 1914-1918. Part Four* (s.l., s.d.), p. 150, TNMP Military Genealogy *Record Fred Parkin.*

[281] LAC RG9/4947 *War Diary 4th Canadian Mounted Rifles Battalion, 10/1917.*

[282] TNMP Military Genealogy *Record Francis Leonard Hunter Jackson.,* CWGC *Burial Return Sheets, Tyne Cot Cemetery.*

[283] TNMP Military Genealogy *Record Harry Trollope.*

[284] 'Hier ist der Gegner tief eingebrochen, die Betonhäuser am l. Fl. der II./73 in Feindeshand.', VON SZCZEPANSKI, Mark. *Erinnerungsblätter aus der Geschichte des Füsilier-Regiments Generalmarschall Prinz Albrecht von Preussen (Hann.) Nr. 73 währens des Weltkrieges 1914-1918* Berlin, 1923, pp. 113-114.

[285] 'Der Feind war in die vordere Linie eingedrungen und hatte einen Höhenrücken genommen, von dem er den wichtigen Paddebachgrund, in dem der Kampftruppen-Kommandeur lag, unter Feuer nehmen konnte. Nachdem ich

10. The Second Battle of Passchendaele(2)

diese Veränderung der Lage mit einigen Rotstiftstrichen in meine Karte eingetragen hatte, setzte ich mit meinen Leuten zu neuem Dauerlauf durch den Schlamm an. (...) Überall stießen wir auf die Spuren des Todes; es war fast, als ob keine lebende Seele mehr in dieser Wüste zu finden wäre.' JUNGER, E. *In Stahlgewittern, Ein Kriegstagebuch*, Berlin, 1937, pp. 219-220.

[286] JERROLD, D. *The Royal Naval ...*, p. 255.

[287] *'Das fdl. Feuer habe nachgelassen, und ein neuer Angriff des Gegners sei wohl nich mehr zu erwarten.'*, VON SZC-ZEPANSKI, Mark. *Erinnerungsblätter aus der Geschichte ...*, p. 114.

[288] LAC RG9/4938 *War Diary 43rd Canadian Battalion*, 10/1917.

[289] LAC RG 150/3203 *service record Charles Barclay Forrest.*, s.n., *War Memorial of Huron County's heroes and heroines* Wingham, 1918, s.p.

[290] LAC, RG150/433 *service record J.H. Barker.*, s.n., *War Memorial of Huron County's ...*, p. 4.

[291] LAC RG9/4942 *War Diary 58th Canadian Battalion*, 10/1917.

[292] MOORE, H. K. (ed.) *Croydon and the Great War. The Official History of the War Work of the Borough and its Citizens from 1914 to 1919, together with the Croydon Roll of Honour*, Croydon, 1920, p. 379, LAC RG 150/8539 *service record C.W. Ruffell.*

[293] s.d., *University of Manitoba Roll of Honour 1914-1918, Manitoba*, 1923, pp. 17-26, LAC RG 150/8965 *service record Skinner Morden Earl.*, *Photo Collection Mordon Earl Skinner*, http://www.vac-acc.gc.ca/remembers/sub.cfm?source=collections/virtualmem/photos&casualty=1596041

[294] LAC RG9/4899 *War Diary 9th Canadian Infantry Brigade*, 10/1917.

[295] LAC RG 150/7627 *service E. W. G. Patten.*, SMITH, G.O.(ed) *University of Toronto Roll of Service 1914-1918*, Toronto, 1921, p. 109.

[296] LAC RG 150/3110 service record R.W. Fisher., 'Another happy young life is given for cause', in: *The Leader (Regina)*, 20/11/1917, s.p.

[297] LAC RG 150/1249 *service record Hugh Buie.*, s.n. de Ruvigny's Roll of Honour *...Part Five ...*, p. 25.

[298] LAC RG9/4947 *War Diary 4th Canadian Mounted Rifles Battalion*, 10/1917.

[299] LAC RG9/4899 *War Diary 9th Canadian Infantry Brigade*, 10/1917.

[300] LAC RG 150/9553 *service record W. Taylor.*, PA file W. Taylor.

[301] LAC RG9/4899 *War Diary 9th Canadian Infantry Brigade*, 10/1917.

[302] LAC RG 150/9371 *service record J.R. Strachan.*, s.n. de Ruvigny's Roll of Honour *...Part Three ...*, p. 259.

[303] The War Diaries of the individual batallions do not give much information regarding losses and even in the official history of the division the author is vague with regard to figures.

[304] JERROLD, D. *The Royal Naval ...,*, p. 257.

[305] LAC RG9/4949 *War Diary 5th Canadian Mounted Rifles Battalion*, 10/1917.

[306] EDMONDS, J.E. *History of the Great War. Military Operations France and Belgium 1917, Volume II, 7th June – 10th November, Messines and Third Ypres (Passchendaele)*, London, 1948, p. 353.

[307] LAC RG9/4949 *War Diary 5th Canadian Mounted Rifles Battalion*, 10/1917.

[308] LAC RG9/4949 *War Diary 5th Canadian Mounted Rifles Battalion*, 10/1917.

[309] HODDER-WILLIAMS, R. *Princess Patricia's Canadian Light Infantry 1914-1919, Volume I. Narrative* London, 1923, pp. 251-252.

[310] LAC RG9/4949 *War Diary 5th Canadian Mounted Rifles Battalion*, 10/1917.

[311] LAC RG9/4949 *War Diary 5th Canadian Mounted Rifles Battalion*, 10/1917.

[312] LAC RG9/4949 *War Diary 5th Canadian Mounted Rifles Battalion*, 10/1917.

[313] LAC RG9/4949 *War Diary 5th Canadian Mounted Rifles Battalion*, 10/1917.

[314] LAC RG9/4949 *War Diary 5th Canadian Mounted Rifles Battalion*, 10/1917.

[315] s.n., *Letters from the front, being a record of the part played by officers of the bank [Canadian Bank of Commerce] in the Great War 1914-1919, Vol. II*, Toronto, 1920, s.p., LAC RG 150/2073 *service record Cowie John.*

[316] s.n., *de Ruvigny's Roll of Honour ...Part Four ...*, p. 221.

[317] Major George Randolph Pearkes, from Watford, England, was awarded the Victoria Cross for his part in the Battle of Passchendaele on 30 and 31 October 1917. He had previously won the Military Cross at Regina Trench on the Somme and received the Distinguished Service Order in August 1918. He ended the war as a Lieutenant Colonel, but was to rise even further in the 1930s and 1940s. When he finally left the army with the rank of Major General in 1945 he went into politics, becoming Minister of Defence and later Lieutenant Governor of British Columbia. Pearkes died in May 1984 at the age of 96 and was given a state funeral. (SNELLING, S. *VCs of the First World War, Passchendaele 1917*, Stroud, 2000, pp. 259-265.

[318] LAC RG9/4949 *War Diary 5th Canadian Mounted Rifles Battalion*, 10/1917.

[319] LAC RG 150/1692 service record Choquette Harry.

[320] NA, WO95/2276 *War Diary 2nd Battalion Cheshire Regiment*, 05/1915., CWGC Burial Return Sheets, Tyne Cot British Cemetery.

[321] LAC RG9/4949 *War Diary 5th Canadian Mounted Rifles Battalion*, 10/1917.

[322] LAC RG9/4949 *War Diary 5th Canadian Mounted Rifles Battalion*, 10/1917.

[323] LAC RG 150/8751 *service record Seale Theodore William. 748658 Theodore William Seale*, http://117thbattalion.com/748658Seale.htm

[324] LAC RG9/4949 *War Diary 5th Canadian Mounted Rifles Battalion*, 10/1917., LAC RG 150/2712 *service record*

Duggan Kenneth Locke.

[325] LAC RG/4940 *War Diaries 49th Canadian Battalion 11/1917.*

[326] LAC RG/4940 *War Diaries 49th Canadian Battalion 11/1917.*

[327] s.n., *George Heriot's School Roll of Honour 1914-1918* (Edinburgh, 1921), p 47.

[328] LAC RG 150/190 *service record Angus Robert George.*

[329] William McCall MacMillan was listed as missing on 9 October 1916. He is remembered on the Vimy Memorial in France. s.n., *de Ruvigny's Roll of Honour ...,* p. 124.

[330] LAC RG 150/7115 *service record MacMillan Ian.*

[331] Private C.J. Kinross was awarded the Victoria Cross for taking a German pillbox near Furst Farm, killing six Germans single-handedly. He was seriously wounded but survived the war. He died in 1957. SNELLING, S. *VCs ...,* pp. 246-257.

[332] LAC RG 150/2443 *service record Dennis John Harold.,* LAC RG/4938 War Diary 42nd Canadian Battalion, 10/1917., CWGC *Burial Return Sheets, Tyne Cot British Cemetery.*

[333] *'Die Bataillone griffen an. In zwei Wellen ging es den ansteigenden Hang hinauf. Heftiges Streufeuer mittlerer Granaten brachte Verluste. So rasch als möglich wurde dieser Streifen überwunden. Bald war man im Trichterfeld. Zäher Schlamm hing zentnerschwer an den Stiefeln, es ging durch wassergefüllte Trichter über zersplitterte Baumstümpfe, ein mühseliger Weg. Die Höhe nördlich von Passchendaele deckte ein Wildes Feuer, Schutz auf Schutz barsten hier die Granaten in rasender Folge. Diesen Feuergürtel zu durchbrechen war unmöglich. (...) Als die Schützenlinien diese Höhe überschritten hatten, kamen sie in die Sicht des Gegners. Sofort fasste die englische Artillerie das neue Ziel und legte einen starken Feuervorhang auf den westlichen Hang.'* WEGENER, H. *Die Geschichte des 3. Ober-Elsässischen Infanterie-Regiments Nr. 172,* Zeulenroda, 1934, p. 205.

[334] PA *file C.F. Dick.,* s.n., *Letters from the front...,* s.p., LAC RG 150/2503 *service record Dick Christian Fraser.*

[335] LAC RG 150/9280 *service record Sterns Sydney Smith.*

[336] LAC RG 150/8122 *service record Raynes Walter Livingstone.*

[337] HODDER-WILLIAMS, R. *Princess Patricia's ...,* p. 257.

[338] LAC RG 150/6550 *service record Mutton, Arthur Roy.*

[339] See the following chapter for more information about Papineau, PA *file T.M. Papineau.*

[340] LAC RG 150/1111 *service record Broom Roy.*

[341] HODDER-WILLIAMS, R. *Princess Patricia's ...,* p. 263.

[342] PA *file H.F. Christie.*

[343] HODDER-WILLIAMS, R. *Princess Patricia's ...,* p. 263.

[344] PA *file W.H. Morris.,* LAC RG 150/6396 *service record Morris William Hugoe.*

[345] LAC RG9/4983 *War Diary 7th Canadian Machine Gun Company 10/1917.* Cpl T. Hampson, quoted in: SNELLING, S. *VCs ...,* p. 249-251.

[346] HODDER-WILLIAMS, R. *Princess Patricia's...,* p. 265.

[347] LAC RG9/4912 *War Diary Princess Patricia's Canadian Light Infantry, 11/1917.*

[348] NEWMAN, S.K. *With the Patricia's, In the Mud & Blood, Passchendaele October 1917,* Saanichton, 2005, p. 77.

[349] LAC RG 150/48 *service record Agar Harold Edward.*

[350] LAC RG9/4912 *War Diary Princess Patricia's Canadian Light Infantry, 11/1917.*

[351] LAC RG9/4912 *War Diary Princess Patricia's Canadian Light Infantry, 11/1917.,* s.n., *de Ruvigny's Roll of Honour...Part Three...,* p. 261.LAC RG 150/9410 *service record Sulivan Henry Ernest.*

[352] The 23-year-old Capt. Eugene Gilbert Sulivan of the 1st battalion East Surrey Regiment was killed on 8 May 1917 during the Battle of Arras and is buried in Orchard Dump Cemetery, Arleux-en-Gohelle.

[353] The 20-year-old 2/Lieut. Philip Hamilton Sulivan of B Company 2nd Battalion Royal Munster Fusiliers was killed on 27 August 1914 and is buried in Etreux British Cemetery.

[354] LAC RG 150/1701 *service record Christie Hugh Farquhar.*

[355] LAC RG 150/2321 *service record Davison James.*

[356] Sergeant Christie: Plot 8 Row B Grave 21, Private Davison Plot 8 Row B Grave 20

[357] *'Englische Sanitätsmannschaften suchten unter dem Schuts des roten Kreuzes das Feld nach Verwundeten ab. Bis zum Nachmittag waren sie damit beschäftigt, die schweren Verluste des Vortages zu bergen.'* WEGENER, H. *Die Geschichte ...,* pp. 207-208.

[358] LAC RG9/4912 *War Diary Princess Patricia's Canadian Light Infantry, 11/1917.*

[359] LAC RG9/4912 *War Diary Princess Patricia's Canadian Light Infantry, 11/1917.*

[360] NEWMAN, S.K. *With the Patricia's...,* pp. 75-77.

[361] LAC RG 150/8537 *service record Davison James.*

[362] PA *file H.E. Agar.*

[363] C LAC RG/1720 *service record Clare Lionel Victor.,* WGC *Burial Return Sheets, Tyne Cot British Cemetery.*

[364] *'Dem nach stärkster Artillerie-Vorbereitung und unter gewaltigem Menscheneinsatz unternommenen englischen Angriff war dank der zähen Verteidigung nur eine geringe Einbuchtung, nicht aber ein Durchbruch gelungen. Der 30 Oktober war ein glänzender Erfolg schwacher Truppen gegen eine Übermacht. Er wurde anerkannt durch eine lobende Anerkennung des Oberbefehlshabers der 4. Armee. Gros waren die Verluste der Engländer.'* EKEL, H. *Das K.B. Reserve-Infanterie-Regiment Nr. 10,* München, 1930, p. 107.

ii. The Second Battle of Passchendaele(3)

[365] *'Immer offensichtlicher ist zu Tage getreten, dass der Engländer beabsichtigt, Passchendaele und die Höhen östlich des Ortes um jeden Preis zu nehmen, um sich dan flankierend gegen die Stellungen im Houthulster-Walde wenden zu können. Ungezählte Div. unermesslich viel Art. und Nahkampfwaffen hat er eingesetzt.'* VON SCHÜSS UND HOCHBAUM *Das Grenadier-regiment König Friedrich Wilhelm II (1. Schles. Nr. 10)*, Berlin, 1910, p. 214.

[366] LAC RG9/4846 *War Diary 2nd Canadian Division General Staff*, 02/11/1917.

[367] LAC RG9/4890 *War Diary 6th Canadian Infantry Brigade, Headquarters*, 20/11/1917.

[368] LAC RG9/4937 *War Diary 31st Canadian Battalion* 11/1917.

[369] LAC RG9/4935 *War Diary 27th Canadian Battalion*, 11/1917.

[370] LAC RG9/4935 *War Diary, 28th Canadian Battalion*, 11/1917.

[371] LAC RG9/4890 *War Diary 6th Canadian Infantry Brigade, Headquarters*, 20/11/1917.

[372] LAC RG9/4935 *War Diary 28th Canadian Battalion*.

[373] LAC RG9/4935 *War Diary 27th Canadian Battalion*, 09/11/1917.

[374] LAC RG9/4890 *War Diary 6th Canadian Infantry Brigade, Headquarters*, 20/11/1917.

[375] LAC RG9/4890 *War Diary 6th Canadian Infantry Brigade, Headquarters*, 20/11/1917.

[376] LAC RG 150/3764 *service record Gray William Ralph*.

[377] LAC RG9/4935 *War Diary 28th Canadian Battalion*, 11/1917.

[378] LAC RG 150/10631 *service record Yates Thomas*.

[379] LAC RG9/4935 *War Diary 28th Canadian Battalion*, 11/1917.

[380] LAC RG 150/3974 *service record Hamill Arthur*.

[381] Private archives Guy St.-Denis.

[382] LAC RG9/4935 *War Diary 27th Canadian Battalion*, 09/11/1917.

[383] LAC RG9/4935 *War Diary, 28th Canadian Battalion*, 11/1917.

[384] LAC RG9/4937 *War Diary 31st Canadian Battalion* 19/11/1917.

[385] LAC RG9/4937 *War Diary 31st Canadian Battalion* 19/11/1917., LAC RG 150/7950 *service record Powis Gordon Douglas*.

[386] LAC RG9/4937 *War Diary 31st Canadian Battalion* 19/11/1917.

[387] LAC RG9/4890 *War Diary 6th Canadian Infantry Brigade, Headquarters*, 20/11/1917.

[388] *'Der Feind musste von seinen guten Beobachtungen aus den Angriff frühzeitig erkannt haben, und alles setzte er daran, ihn zu verhindern. Handelte es sich doch für ihn darum, die günstige taktische Lage für ein Vorgehen am nächsten Tage zu behalten. Er war ein Vortasten, Vorkriechen, ein Wanken und Stürzen im Dreck und Wasser, in Granathagel und Blut. Und von oben unaushörlicher Regen. Schwere englische Schiffsgeschütze setzen ein. Ein*

[388 cont.] *Volltreffer haut in die 12. Kompagnie. (...) Da, an der grossen Strasse nördlich Passchendale prallt der Angriff auf die englische Infanterie. Doch ehe es zur Entscheidung kommt, trifft der Befehl ein, das Vorgehen einzustellen. Die erreichte Linie, schwer und verlustreich genug erreicht, ist zu halten.'*, NOLLAN, H. *Geschichte des Königlich Preussischen 4. Niederschlesinchen Infanterie-Regiment Nr. 51*, Berlin, 1931, p. 207.

[389] ROBERTS, T.G. *Thirty Canadian VCs*, Skeffington, 1919, quoted in: SNELLING, S. *VCs of the First World War, Passchendaele 1917*, Stroud, 2000, p. 270 en 272-273., CWGC *Burial Return Sheets Tyne Cot Cemetery*.

[390] LAC RG 150/8878 *service record Shore Stanley Richard*.

[391] LAC RG9/4935 *War Diary 27th Canadian Battalion*, 09/11/1917.

[392] LAC RG9/4935 *War Diary, 28th Canadian Battalion*, 11/1917.

[393] LAC RG 150/789 *service record Blackwood James Alexander.*, LAC RG9/5028 *War Diary 5th Canadian Field Ambulance*, 11/1917.

[394] s.n., *de Ruvigny's Roll of Honour 1914-1918, A Biographical record of members of his majesty's naval and military forces who fell in the Great War 1914-1918. Part Four*, s.l., s.d., p. 15.

[395] Joseph Blackwood, a Corporal with the 2nd Irish Guards, joined up in May 1915. He died of wounds in a hospital in Le Tréport on 30 March 1918. s.n. *de Ruvigny's Roll of Honour ...Part Four ...*, p. 15.

[396] The War Diary of the 31st Battalion makes no mention of this.

[397] LAC RG9/4935 *War Diary 27th Canadian Battalion*, 09/11/1917., LAC RG9/4935 *War Diary 28th Canadian Battalion*, 11/1917.

[398] LAC RG 150/8428 *service record Rogers Frank*.

[399] LAC RG9/4935 *War Diary 27th Canadian Battalion*, 09/11/1917.

[400] LAC RG9/4935 *War Diary 28th Canadian Battalion*, 11/1917. The 31st Battalion also makes no mention of this.

[401] His brother William Duncan was killed on 22 August 1917 and was buried in Fosse No. 10 Communal Cemetery Extension in Sains-en-Gohelles. He had also attended George Heriot's School.

[402] s.n., *George Heriot's School Roll of Honour 1914-1918*, Edinburgh, 1921, p 79., LAC RG 150/2858 *service record Donaldson David.*, CWGC *Burial Return Sheets Tyne Cot Cemetery*.

[403] 'Former Canadian Northern Employees prove their heroism on battlefields of Europe', in: : *The Leader (Regina)*, 29/11/1917. 'Fine Sportsmen has given his all for his country', in: *The Leader (Regina)*, 26/11/1917., LAC RG 150/8044 *service record Quesnell Francis John.*, CWGC *Burial Return Sheets Tyne Cot Cemetery*.

[404] 'North Regina Boy killed in action', in: *The Leader (Regina)*, 24/11/1917., LAC RG 150/10355 *service record Wild Wilfrid*.

[405] LAC RG9/4937 *War Diary 31st Canadian Battalion* 11/1917.

12. The End of the Battle of Passchendaele

[406] He has a no known grave and is remembered today on the Loos Memorial.

[407] s.n., *Tonbridge School and the Great War of 1914- to 1919, A record of the services of Tonbridgians in the Great War of 1914 to 1918* (Tonbridge, 1923), p. 124. The CWGC has no data regarding him.

[408] s.n., *Tonbridge School ...*, p. 124., LAC RG 150/3340 *service record Hurley George Frederick.*

[409] These losses are very light compared with the casualty figures for the 3rd Australian Division, who lost 66% of its men on 12 October 1917.

[410] LAC RG9/5032 *War Diary 2nd Canadian CCS*, 11/1917.

[411] LAC RG9/4890 *War Diary 6th Canadian Infantry Brigade, Headquarters, 20/11/1917.*

[412] LAC RG9/4937 *War Diary 31st Canadian Battalion 17/11/1917.*

[413] LAC RG9/4890 *War Diary 6th Canadian Infantry Brigade, Headquarters, 8/11/1917.*

[414] LAC RG9/4910 *War Diary 2nd Canadian Infantry Brigade*, 11/1917.

[415] LAC RG 150/1358 *service record Byers John James.* It was also Sarah's granddaughter, Ms J. Drennan from Belfast, who passed on the information relating to John James Byers to the Passchendaele Archives. Sarah's house in Belfast was bombed in 1941. By that time all the family photograph albums and letters had been moved to the house of her sister Elisabeth and so survived the Second World War.

[416] LAC RG9/4918 *War Diary 8th Canadian Infantry Battalion*, 11/1917.

[417] LAC RG 150/3046 *service record Ferguson Herbert Stanley.*, s.n., *University of Manitoba Roll of Honour, 1914-1918*, s.l., 1923, pp. 17-26.

[418] s.n., *George Heriot's School Roll of Honour 1914-1919*, Edinburgh, 1921, p. 147., LAC RG 150/7327 service record Nicol James.

[419] LAC, RG9/4930 *War Diary 20th Canadian Battalion*, 11/1917.

[420] LAC, RG9/4918 *War Diary 8th Canadian Infantry Battalion*, 11/1917.

[421] LAC, RG9/4917 *War Diary 7th Canadian Infantry Battalion*, 16/11/1917.

[422] LAC, RG 150/2324 *service record Davidson, Lawrence Lavell.*

[423] s.n., *Letters from the front, being a record of the part played by officers of the bank [Canadian Bank of Commerce] in the Great War 1914-1919, Vol. II*, Toronto, 1920, s.p., LAC RG 150/8999 *service record Smillie Charles Blair.*

[424] s.n., *Letters from the front...*, s.p., LAC RG 150/2989 *service record Fane Robert Frank.*

[425] LAC RG9/4910 *War Diary 2nd Canadian Infantry Brigade*, 11/1917.

[426] s.n., *University of Edinburgh, Roll of Honour, 1914-1919* (Edinburgh, 1921), p. 113.

[427] s.n., *Tonbridge School and The Great War of 1914 to 1919. A record of the services of Tonbridgians in the Great War of 1914 to 1919* (London and Tonbridge, 1923), pp. 110-111.

[428] s.n. *de Ruvigny's Roll of Honour, A biographical record of members of his majesty's Naval and Military Forces who fell in the Great War 1914-1918, Part Five* (s.n., s.d.), p. 78.

[429] s.n. *de Ruvigny's Roll of Honour,...Part Five ...*, p. 29.

[430] s.n. *de Ruvigny's Roll of Honour,...Part Five ...*, p. 56

13. The war in the air 1917

[431] O'CONNER, M. *Battlegrounds Europe, Airfields and Airmen, Ypres* Barnsley, 2001, p. 18.

[432] STEEL, N., HART, P. *Tumult in the clouds, The British Experience of the War in the Air 1914-1918* London, 1997, p. 222.

[433] NA WO339/2643 *service record Hutchinson C. D.*

[434] STEEL, N., HART, P. *Tumult in the clouds...*, p. 98.

[435] HENSHAW, T. *The Sky Their Battlefield, Air Fighting and the Complete List of Allied Air Casualties from Enemy Action in the First War* London, 1995, p. 209., FRANK, N.L.R., BAILY, F.W., GUEST, R. *Above the Lines, The Aces and Fighter Units of the German Air Service, Naval Air Service and Flanders Marine Corps 1914-1918* London, 1993, pp. 169-170.

[436] *Leutnant* Max Ritter von Müller, from Bavaria, was one of the most famous German aces of the First World War, with no less than 36 official kills to his name. He was killed at Moorslede on 9 January 1918 when he was obliged to jump from his burning aircraft from a great height. He was then just 21 and was one of the most highly decorated German pilots.

[437] NA WO339/2643 *service record Hutchinson C. D.*

[438] Mudros: a port on the Greek island of Lemnos.

[439] Known today as Thessaloniki, a large Greek port and industrial city.

[440] Ernst Udet was the most highly decorated German pilot to survive the war. He committed suicide in 1941. FRANK, N.L.R., BAILY, F.W., GUEST, R. *Above the Line...*, pp. 219-221.

[441] HENSHAW, T. *The Sky Their Battlefield...*, p. 217. and FRANK, N.L.R., BAILY, F.W., GUEST, R. *Above the Lines...*, pp. 219-221. NA WO339/64391 service record Falkiner F.

[442] HENSHAW, T. *The Sky Their Battlefield...*, p. 224.

[443] *Leutnant* Joseph Veltjens also claimed a victory over a British reconnaissance plane on that day. This particular kill was over Boezinge, however.

[444] FRANK, N.L.R., BAILY, F.W., GUEST, R. *Above the Lines...*, pp. 71-72.

[445] NA WO339/97078 *service record Humphries L.*

[446] See the following chapter for more information about Lieutenant Rhys Davids.

[447] REVELL, A. *Brief Glory, The Life of Arthur Rhys Davids, DSO, MC and Bar,* London, 1984, p. 178.

[448] STEEL, N., HART, P. *Tumult in the clouds...*, p. 212.

[449] SHORES, C., FRANKS, N., GUEST R. *Above the trenches, A Complete Record of the fighter Aces and Units of the British Empire Air Forces 1915-1920,* London, 1996, p. 36

[450] HENSHAW, T. *The Sky Their Battlefield...*, p. 209, NA WO339/7605 service record Fleming W. A.

[451] BOWER, C. (ed.) *Royal Flying Corps Communiques 1917-1918,* London, 1998, pp. 114-116, Robert Sloley, http://www.theaerodrome.com/aces/safrica/sloley.php, Quoted in REVELL, A. *Brief Glory...*, p. 184.

[452] William Rooper, http://www.theaerodrome.com/aces/wales/rooper.php
Christopher Shores, Norman Franks and Russel Guest claim, however, that Rooper was shot down by Leutnant Helmut Dilthey. It is difficult to establish which source is the more reliable as both sources give a different type of aircraft. SHORES, C., FRANKS, N., GUEST R. *Above the trenches...*, p. 324.

[453] SHORES, C., FRANKS, N., GUEST R. *Above the trenches...*, p. 324.

[454] Noel Webb, http://www.theaerodrome.com/aces/england/webb.php , MC Bar Citation, Supplement to the London Gazette, 9 January 1918, quoted in: http://www.theaerodrome.com/aces/england/webb.php.

[455] NA WO339/105511 *service record Machaffie J.*

[456] O'CONNER, M. *Battlegrounds Europe...*, p. 30., NA WO339/105511 service record Machaffie J.

[457] NA WO339/107366 *service record Cowie G.*

[458] LAC RG9/4854 *War Diary 3rd Canadian Division, General Staff, 11/1917.*

[459] STEEL, N., HART, P. *Tumult in the clouds...*, p. 227.

[460] STEEL, N., HART, P. *Tumult in the clouds...*, p. 225.

[461] The Memorial Museum Passchendaele 1917 was not able to request Captain A. L. Macdonald's Service Record in time to meet publication deadlines.

[462] NA WO339/36187 *service record Wodehouse F. J. A.*, HENSHAW, T. *The Sky Their Battlefield...*, p. 218., FRANK, N.L.R., BAILY, F.W., GUEST, R. *Above the Lines...*, p. 186.

[463] FRANKS, N., GIBLIN, N., McCRERY, N. *Under the guns of the Red Baron. The Complete record of Von Richthofen's Victories and Victims Fully Illustrated* London, 1998, pp. 152-153. HENSHAW, T. *The Sky Their Battlefield...*, p. 213.

[464] Monsieur De Brabander was a well-known personality in Wielsbeke during the First World War. He was a witness to the plane crash and preserved the personal effects of the British airman.

[465] Second Lieutenant H.M.S. Skefftington, 33 years old, came from London.

[466] HILL, D. *For King's and Country, The story of seventy old boys of Macclesfield Grammar School who gave their lives in the Great War 1914-19,* Wandsworth, 2003, p. 66, HENSHAW, T. *The Sky Their Battlefield...*, p. 205., s.n., *de Ruvigny's Roll of Honour 1914-1918, A Biographical record of members of his majesty's naval and military forces who fell in the Great War 1914-1918. Volume Five* London, s.d., p. 142., NA WO339/25601 *service record Rickards H. W. B.*, NA WO339/68934 *service record Corbishley R.*

[467] HENSHAW, T. *The Sky Their Battlefield...*, p. 203.

[468] s.n. *de Ruvigny's Roll of Honour ...Part Four ...*, p. 146.

[469] John Ingram Mullaniff O'Beirne, Lieutenant, 25th Squadron, Arras Flying Services Memorial.

Endnotes part II

I. History of the site

[1] DE FLOU K. Woordenboek der Toponymie van Westelijk Vlaanderen: XIII, Brugge, 1932, p. 840.

[2] GAZ *Burgerlijke Stand Passendale*; GAZ *Lijst der Kiezers Passchedaele*, 1913-1914; MMP *Popp-kaart Passchedaele*, ca. 1840; MMP *Trench Map 28 NEI Zonnebeke 7A*, 8/9/1917; *Archief Kadaster Brugge Passendale*; VAN-LERBERGHE P. *Twee Eeuwen Passendaalse Landbouwers 1800-1996*, Passendale, p. 193-195; interviews Gerard DEBRUYNE, Rosa DEMEYERE, Andre DENEUT, Michel VANHEE, Roger VERBEKE.

[3] FERRARIS, *Kabinetskaart der Oostenrijke Nederlanden*, 1774; MMP *Popp-kaart Passchedaele*, ca. 1840; MMP *Trench Map Zonnebeke 7A*, 8/9/1917; interview Gerard DEBRUYNE.

[4] Thanks to Kristof, Rosa en Roland Blieck for help with the excavation.

[5] More about this subject in our study on the former Ypres-Roulers railway.

[6] BOSTYN F. *Beecham Dugout*, Zonnebeke, 1999, p. 52-59.

[7] NA WO95/2821 *War Diary 7th Field Company RE.*; BOSTYN F. *Beecham Dugout*, Zonnebeke, 1999, p. 76-80.

[8] NAA 7363114 *Service record Frederick N. Inglis*; various copies of maps; BOSTYN F. & DENDOOVEN D. *De Westhoek en het Stenen Erfgoed van de Eerste Wereldoorlog* in: Open Monumentendag, 2003, p. 2-3.

[9] NA WO95/2811 *War Diary 50th Division*, 2/1/1918; NA WO95/2414 *War Diary 212th Field Company*, 13-21/1/1918; interview Andre DENEUT.

[10] CWGC *Working Drawings of Tyne Cot Military Cemetery by J.R. Truelove*, 30/7/1923; TAYLOR F.W. & CUSACK T.A. *Nulli Secundus: A History of the Second Battalion A.I.F. 1914-1919*, Sydney, 1942, p. 267; *Tyne Cot Cemetery* in: The Ypres Times, 1923 (9), p. 263; NAC RG9/4939 *War Diary 46th Battalion*, 26/10/1917

[11] Interview Andre DENEUT.

[12] Interview Gerard DEBRUYNE; various copies of maps.

[13] NAC RG9/4939 *War Diary 44th Battalion*, 26-29/10/1917.

[14] IWM Q56239, Q56253; NA WO95/2417 *War Diary 33rd Machine Gun Battalion*, 13/3/1918.

[15] *Trench Map 28NEI Zonnebeke 9C*, 30/5/1918.

[16] COOMBS R. *Before Endeavours Fade*, London, 1994, p. 40; *Tyne Cot: Origin of the Name* op http://1914-1918.invisionzone.com/forums/index.php?showtopic=37396&

[17] More about the five airmen of Vladslo in '2.7. Im Leben ein Feind, im Tode vereint'.

[18] *Letters from the Front, being a Record of the Part played by Officers of the Canadian Bank of Commerce in the Great War: II*, Toronto, 1920, s.p.; NAC RG9/4931 *War Diary 21st Battalion*, 5/11/1917.

[19] BRANDES H. *Geschichte des Königlich Preussischen Infanterie-Regiments von Voigts-Rhetz (3. Hannoverisches) Nr. 79 im Weltkrieg 1914-1918*, Hildesheim, 1930, p. 425-438; NAC RG150/4154-61 *Service record Frederick Hatt*; NAC RG150/4154-70 *Service record Creighton W. Hatt*.

2. Commonwealth War Graves Commission

[20] DESEYNE, A. *Tyne Cot Cemetery: Een Eeuwige Dodenwake*, Zonnebeke, 1985, p. 6-7; information given by Paul REED.

[21] *Reports by the Joint War Committee of the British Red Cross Society and the Order of St. John of Jerusalem*, London, 1921 p. 319-321, 359-360; LONGWORTH PH. *The Unending Vigil: A History of the Commonwealth War Graves Commission 1917-1967*, London, 1967, p. 1-15.

[22] NAC RG9/4863 *War Diary 4th Canadian Division*, 26/10/1917; LONGWORTH PH. *The Unending Vigil: A History of the Commonwealth War Graves Commission 1917-1967*, London, 1967, p. 19, 22.

[23] MEIRE J. *De Stilte van de Salient: De Herinnering aan de Eerste Wereldoorlog rond Ieper*, Tielt, 2003, p. 142-144; typical for what relatives of a fallen serviceman received, is the Private Fred P. Young file, donated to the Memorial Museum

[24] LONGWORTH PH. *The Unending Vigil: A History of the Commonwealth War Graves Commission 1917-1967*, London, 1967, p. 16-17, 23-28, 76-77.

[25] LONGWORTH PH. *The Unending Vigil: A History of the Commonwealth War Graves Commission 1917-1967*, London, 1967, p. 58; various notes Franky BOSTYN.

[26] CHRISTIE N. *The Canadians at Ypres: April 22 to 26*, Winnipeg, 1996, p. 55-63; CWGC WG1294/3: *Part 2: Exhumations and Reburials: Revised Instructions for Reinterment*, 1921.

[27] CWGC *Burial Return Sheets Tyne Cot Cemetery*; information given by CWGC Records Officer Roy HEMINGTON.

[28] VANCOILLIE J. *De Duitse Begraafplaatsen in Zonnebeke en zijn Deelgemeenten* in: Zonneheem, 2002 (2), p. 6-7, 20-23; Royal Army Museum Brussels, copies from uncatalogued archives given by Rob TROUBLEYN.

[29] CWGC WG1294/3/2 *D.G.R.&E. ceasing work*, 1921; LONGWORTH PH. *The Unending Vigil: A History of the Commonwealth War Graves Commission 1917-1967*, London, 1967, p. 58-59.

[30] CWGC WG1294/1 *Part 1: Exhumation by IWGC, General File*, 1921-1922.

[31] BOSTYN F. *De IJzeren Oogst* in: Halfweg Menin Road en Ypernstrasse, Gheluvelt 1914-1918, Voormezele, 2002, p. 283-290; CWGC WG421 *Part 1:Exhumations and Reburial*, 1922-1926; H.B. *Two 'Lost' British War Cemeteries* in: The Ypres Times, 1928 (3), p. 70-71; CWGC WG1294/3 *Part 5:Exhumations and Reburial*, 1935-1936.

[32] PA *Dossier John R. Thomson*; BOSTYN F. *Missing in Flanders: Remains of five Australian WWI soldiers found near Westhoek (Zonnebeke-Belgium)* (final report in preparation).

[33] CWGC WG1294/3 *Part 3: Exhumations and Reburial*, 1921.

[34] CWGC *Tyne Cot Cemetery: John William Hinckesman*, 9/4/1992; HOLT T. & V. *My Boy Jack: The Search for Kipling's only Son*, London, 1998, passim.

[35] CWGC *Burial Return Sheets Tyne Cot Cemetery*; PA Dossier William R.S. Smith (with thanks to Clive Harris); HENSHAW, T. The Sky Their Battlefield, London, 1995, p. 241.

[36] CWGC WG1294/3 *Part 3:Part 3: Exhumations and Reburial*, 1921; MEIRE J. *De Stilte van de Salient: De Herinnering aan de Eerste Wereldoorlog rond Ieper*, Tielt, 2003, p. 147-152; CHRISTIE N. *The Canadians at Passchendaele*, Winnipeg, 1996, p. 66-68.

[37] AWM 1150104 Red Cross file James T.B. Gavin; *AWM 1150102* Red Cross file G. Gordon B. Gavin.

[38] MEIRE J. *De Stilte van de Salient: De Herinnering aan de Eerste Wereldoorlog rond Ieper*, Tielt, 2003, p. 148-149; with thanks to Commander TROUBLEYN of the Belgian War Graves.

[39] CWGC *Burial Return Sheets Tyne Cot Cemetery*.

[40] CWGC WG1294/3 *Part 5: Exhumations and Reburials*, 1935-1936; CURME PH. & MORGAN T. *Original Battlefield Crosses in the UK* on: http://www.hellfire-corner.demon.co.uk/crosses.htm

[41] CWGC *Burial Return Sheets Tyne Cot Cemetery*; MMP *Matthew H. Austin* (on display at Tyne Cot Visitors Centre); BOSTYN F. *Missing in Flanders: Remains of five Australian WWI soldiers found near Westhoek (Zonnebeke-Belgium)* (final report in preparation); MMP *Randal A. Casson* (on display at Tyne Cot Visitors Centre).

[42] CWGC *Burial Return Sheets Tyne Cot Cemetery*; CWGC WG1294/3 *Part 4: Exhumations and Reburials: Duplicated Graves*, 14/12/1921.

[43] MMP *Tyne Cot Cemetery: Correspondentie met het Gemeentebestuur van Passendale*, 1921-1927; Archief Kadaster Brugge *Passendale*.

[44] Information given by CWGC Records Officer Roy HEMINGTON.

[45] CWGC *Burial Return Sheets Tyne Cot Cemetery*.

[46] CWGC *Burial Return Sheets Tyne Cot Cemetery*.

[47] CWGC *Burial Return Sheets Tyne Cot Cemetery*; CWGC *Tyne Cot Cemetery Register: Introduction*.

[48] CWGC *Burial Return Sheets Tyne Cot Cemetery*; NAA 3093957 *Service record Charles W.C. Bluett*; AWM 430702 *Red Cross file Charles W.C. Bluett*.

[49] CWGC *Burial Return Sheets Tyne Cot Cemetery*.

[50] CWGC *Burial Return Sheets Tyne Cot Cemetery*; CWGC *Tyne Cot Cemetery Register: Introduction*; PA *Dossier Freddy Cade* (thanks to the Cade family and Marc Glorieux).

[51] CWGC *Burial Return Sheets Tyne Cot Cemetery*; CWGC *Tyne Cot Cemetery Register: Introduction*; CWGC *List of Cemeteries in France and Belgium*, London, 1921, p. 35.

[52] CWGC *Burial Return Sheets Tyne Cot Cemetery*; CWGC *Tyne Cot Cemetery Register: Introduction*; CWGC *Bedford House Cemetery Register: Introduction*.

[53] CWGC *Burial Return Sheets Tyne Cot Cemetery;* CWGC *Tyne Cot Cemetery Register: Introduction;* NAC *War Diary 124th Pioneer Battalion,* 18/10/1917.

[54] CWGC *Burial Return Sheets Tyne Cot Cemetery.*

[55] CWGC *Burial Return Sheets Tyne Cot Cemetery.*

[56] CWGC *Burial Return Sheets Tyne Cot Cemetery;* notes Raoul MASSCHELEIN.

[57] CWGC *Burial Return Sheets Tyne Cot Cemetery;* CWGC *Tyne Cot Cemetery Register: Introduction,* London, 1927; DENTURCK A. *Gedenkboek aan Oostnieuwkerke 1914-1918,* Oostnieuwkerke, 1984, p. 144.

[58] CWGC *Burial Return Sheets Tyne Cot Cemetery;* CWGC *Tyne Cot Cemetery Register: Introduction;* WACKENIER W. *Archeologie van Staal en Beton: Bunkers en minierte Unterstände uit de Eerste Wereldoorlog in Staden, Westrozebeke en Oostnieuwkerke,* Gent, 2004, p. 93 (unpublished dissertation).

[59] CWGC *Burial Return Sheets Tyne Cot Cemetery;* SOENENS J. e.a. *De Ruiter: Geschiedenis van een Wijk te Roeselare,* Roeselare, 1979, p. 196.

[60] CWGC *Burial Return Sheets Tyne Cot Cemetery;* VANCOILLIE J. *De Duitse Begraafplaatsen in Zonnebeke en zijn Deelgemeenten* in: Zonneheem, 2002 (2), p. 20-23.

[61] CWGC *Burial Return Sheets Tyne Cot Cemetery.*

[62] CWGC *Burial Return Sheets Tyne Cot Cemetery.*

[63] CWGC *Burial Return Sheets Tyne Cot Cemetery;* HENSHAW, T. *The Sky Their Battlefield,* London, 1995, p. 186.

[64] CWGC *Burial Return Sheets Tyne Cot Cemetery;* LERMYTE J.M. *Het Oorlogsdagboek van Dokter Jules Gits,* Koksijde, 2000, passim.

[65] CWGC *Burial Return Sheets Tyne Cot Cemetery;* VERHELST D. *Het Duits Militair Kerkhof 1914-1918 in Hooglede,* Kortrijk, 1996, p. 33-37; HENSHAW, T. *The Sky Their Battlefield,* London, 1995, p. 216.

[66] CWGC *Tyne Cot Cemetery Register: Introduction;* HENSHAW, T. *The Sky Their Battlefield,* London, 1995, p. 217.

[67] LONGWORTH PH. *The Unending Vigil: A History of the Commonwealth War Graves Commission 1917-1967,* London, 1967, p. 59-61.

[68] HEYVAERT B. *A Little Sprig of the Empire: De Britse Kolonie in Ieper 1919-1940,* Leuven, 2003, passim (unpublished dissertation); LONGWORTH PH. *The Unending Vigil: A History of the Commonwealth War Graves Commission 1917-1967,* London, 1967, p. 62-63, 131.

[69] HEYVAERT B. *A Little Sprig of the Empire: De Britse Kolonie in Ieper 1919-1940,* Leuven, 2003, passim (unpublished dissertation).

[70] LONGWORTH PH. *The Unending Vigil: A History of the Commonwealth War Graves Commission 1917-1967,* London, 1967, p. 156-171, 185-186.

[71] LONGWORTH PH. *The Unending Vigil: A History of the Commonwealth War Graves Commission 1917-1967,* London, 1967, p. 138-143; GIBSON T.A.E. & WARD G.K. *Courage Remembered,* London, 1989, p. 56-57; CWGC *Annual Report 2005-2006.*

3. Architecture

[72] BAKER H. *Architecture & Personalities*, London, 1944, passim.

[73] BAKER H. *Architecture & Personalities*, London, 1944, p. 88-106.

[74] CWGC WG568 *John Reginald Truelove*; HARRIS J. & STAMP G. *Silent Cities: An Exhibition of the Memorial and Cemetery Architecture of the Great War*, London, 1977, p. 25-26; LONGWORTH PH. *The Unending Vigil: A History of the Commonwealth War Graves Commission 1917-1967*, London, 1967, p. 64-65.

[75] MMP *Plan Tyne Cot Cemetery*, 23/3/1921 (on display at the Visitors' Centre, Tyne Cot Cemetery); CWGC *Working Drawings of Tyne Cot Military Cemetery by J.R. Truelove*, 30/7/1923.

[76] BAKER H. *Architecture & Personalities*, London, 1944, 91-99.

[77] VANDEMAELE G. *Britse Oorlogskerkhoven en Monumenten voor de Gesneuvelden van 1914-1918 in Noord-Frankrijk en West-Vlaanderen*, Gent, 1986, p. 115-116 (unpublished essay); CWGC WG584 F.V. Blundstone, 1926-1927; BENEZIT E. Dictionnaire Critique et Documentaire des Peintres, Sculpteurs, Dessinateurs et Graveurs: II, Paris, 1976, p. 96.

[78] CWGC *Working Drawings of Tyne Cot Military Cemetery by J.R. Truelove*, 30/7/1923; VANDEMAELE G. *Britse Oorlogskerkhoven en Monumenten voor de Gesneuvelden van 1914-1918 in Noord-Frankrijk en West-Vlaanderen*, Gent, 1986, p. 250 (unpublished essay).

[79] GIBSON T.A.E. & WARD G.K. *Courage Remembered*, London, 1989, p. 52-55; HARRIS J. & STAMP G. *Silent Cities: An Exhibition of the Memorial and Cemetery Architecture of the Great War*, London, 1977, p. 21-22.

[80] GIBSON T.A.E. & WARD G.K. *Courage Remembered*, London, 1989, p. 53-54; HARRIS J. & STAMP G. *Silent Cities: An Exhibition of the Memorial and Cemetery Architecture of the Great War*, London, 1977, p. 22.

[81] LONGWORTH PH. *The Unending Vigil: A History of the Commonwealth War Graves Commission 1917-1967*, London, 1967, p. 70; SCHEPENS L. *In Pace: Soldatenkerkhoven in Vlaanderen*, Tielt, 1974, p. 22, 82.

[82] VANDEMAELE G. *Britse Oorlogskerkhoven en Monumenten voor de Gesneuvelden van 1914-1918 in Noord-Frankrijk en West-Vlaanderen*, Gent, 1986, p. 113 (unpublished essay).

[83] VANDEMAELE G. *Britse Oorlogskerkhoven en Monumenten voor de Gesneuvelden van 1914-1918 in Noord-Frankrijk en West-Vlaanderen*, Gent, 1986, p. 114 (unpublished essay).

[84] BAKER H. *Architecture & Personalities*, London, 1944, p. 91-92.

[85] CWGC *Information Sheet: The Commission's Horticulture*.

[86] Interview CALLUM LEGGATT, CWGC senior head gardener; CWGC *Tyne Cot Cemetery: Extract from Tour Report by Director of Finance and Establishments in Northern Region*, 1/7/1964; CWGC *Tyne Cot Cemetery: Extract from Tour Report by the Chief Horticultural Officer in North West Europe Area*, 8/5/1971.

[87] Interview CALLUM LEGGATT, CWGC senior head gardener; CWGC *Tyne Cot Cemetery: Extract from Tour Report by the Chief Horticultural Officer Northern Region*, 6/5/1966.

[88] Interview CALLUM LEGGATT, CWGC senior head gardener.

[89] MEIRE J. *De Stilte van de Salient: De Herinnering aan de Eerste Wereldoorlog rond Ieper*, Tielt, 2003, p. 321-325.

[90] *The Poppy Factory* op: http://www.britishlegion.org.uk/derbyshire/Poppy-Factory-514030.shtml

[91] MEIRE J. *De Stilte van de Salient: De Herinnering aan de Eerste Wereldoorlog rond Ieper*, Tielt, 2003, p. 299-304, 338-340.

[92] DENDOOVEN D. *Ieper als Heilige Grond: Menenpoort & Last Post*, Koksijde, 2001, p. 132-134.

4. Graves and Memorial Stones   5. Analysis

[93] GIBSON T.A.E. & WARD G.K. *Courage Remembered,* London, 1989, p. 66-67, 70-71.

[94] CWGC *Burial Return Sheets Tyne Cot Cemetery.*

[95] CWGC *Burial Return Sheets Tyne Cot Cemetery;* NAA 8008454 *Service file Urban Parr.*

[96] CWGC *Burial Return Sheets Tyne Cot Cemetery;* KEECH, G. St Julien, London, 2001, p. 71-72, 78, 140.

[97] CWGC *Burial Return Sheets Tyne Cot Cemetery;* DIGBY PLANCK C. *History of the 7th (City of London) Battalion The London Regiment,* London, 1946, p. 167-175; *John Manuel Hensley* op: http://www.canadiangreatwarproject.com/searches/soldierDetail.asp?ID=27432

[98] *Graves of the Fallen* in: The Ypres Times, 1922 (2), p. 47; AWM 850205 *Red Cross file John N. Crowley;* CWGC *Burial Return Sheets Tyne Cot Cemetery.*

[99] GIBSON T.A.E. & WARD G.K. *Courage Remembered,* London, 1989, p. 67; VERBEKE R.V. *De Grafstenen voor Joden* in: Gidsenkroniek Westland, 2005 (3), p. 71-75.

[100] WILLIAMSON H. *The Collector and Researchers Guide to the Great War:* I, Harwich, 2003, passim; CWGC *Burial Return Sheets Tyne Cot Cemetery;* DE RUVIGNY *Roll of Honour: III,* London, s.l., p. 181; *Supplement to the London Gazette,* 14/11/1916.

[101] Snelling, S. *VCs of the First World War: Passchendaele 1917,* Stroud, 1998, p. passim.

[102] MEIRE J. *De Stilte van de Salient: De Herinnering aan de Eerste Wereldoorlog rond Ieper,* Tielt, 2003, p. 179-183; CWGC *Burial Return Sheets Tyne Cot Cemetery;* with thanks to Erwin UREEL for information on Arthur Young.

[103] LONGWORTH PH. *The Unending Vigil: A History of the Commonwealth War Graves Commission 1917-1967,* London, 1967, p. 43.

[104] GIBSON T.A.E. & WARD G.K. *Courage Remembered,* London, 1989, p. 69; CWGC *Burial Return Sheets Tyne Cot Cemetery.*

[105] CWGC WG1031 *Note on special headstones,* 19/11/1927.

[106] GIBSON T.A.E. & WARD G.K. *Courage Remembered,* London, 1989, p. 69; CWGC WG219/1 *Memorials to the Missing Tyne Cot & Menin Gate:* Report by Director of Records, 20/1/1921; CWGC WG219/2/1 *Part 3: Memorials to the Missing Tyne Cot & Menin Gate: Reports by Director of Records,* 1925.

[107] CWGC WG219/1 *Part 1:Memorial to the Missing Tyne Cot & Menin Gate: List of Memorials erected by Units,* s.d.

[108] GIBSON T.A.E. & WARD G.K. *Courage Remembered,* London, 1989, p. 69-70; CWGC *Burial Return Sheets Tyne Cot Cemetery.*

6. Memorial to the Missing

[109] DENDOOVEN D. *Ieper als Heilige Grond: Menenpoort & Last Post,* Koksijde, 2001, passim; CWGC WG219/2/1 *Part 1: Memorials to the Missing Tyne Cot & Menin Gate: Reports by Director of Records,* 1923-1924; CWGC WG219/2/1 *Part 2: Memorials to the Missing Tyne Cot & Menin Gate,* 1924.

[110] CWGC WG219/2/1 *Part 1 & 3: Memorials to the Missing Tyne Cot & Menin Gate: Reports by Director of Records,* 1923-1924; BOSTYN F. *Cryer Farm: Excavation and Restoration of a WWI German Dressing Station on the Ypres-Menin Road* in: Battlefields Review, 2005, p. 87-94.

[111] CWGC *Annual Report 2005-2006.*

[112] CWGC *Tyne Cot Memorial Register;* notes Frans DESCAMPS.

7. An eternal vigil

[113] MEIRE J. *De Stilte van de Salient: De Herinnering aan de Eerste Wereldoorlog rond Ieper,* Tielt, 2003, p. 195-206.

[114] FOX F. *The King's Pilgrimage,* London, 1922, passim; *Flanders Graves: The King's Visit* in: The Times, 12/5/1922; BECKLES-WILSON *The Ypres Army: The King reviews his lost Legions* in: The Ypres Times, 1922 (4), p. 87-89.

[115] *Passchendaele: Heldenhulde* in: Het Ypersche, 18/6/1927; *A Passchendaele Cemetery: Dedication Ceremony* in: The Times, 20/6/1927; *Sir Gilbert Joseph Cullen Dyett* op: http://www.adb.online.anu.edu.au/biogs/A080419b.htm

[116] DENDOOVEN D. *Ypres als Heilige Grond: Menenpoort & Last Post,* Koksijde, 2001, p. 86-90.

[117] Various accounts

[118] *Mr. Bennett's Tour: Visit to War Cemeteries* in: The Times, 27/11/1930; LINETON F.J. *Kamerad* in: The Ypres Times, 1932 (1), p. 19-21.

[119] No study has been made yet of how the relics of the First World War (cemeteries, memorials, ammunition,...) were dealt with in World War Two.

[120] AWM P01312.003 *Photograph of Joseph Maxwell and John Hamilton near the Grave of Sergeant Lewis McGee; Tour of War Cemeteries: Duke of Gloucester's Itinerary* in: The Times, 13/5/1957.

[121] VERSAVEL G. *Passendale 1914-1918,* Passendale, 1968, p. 149-150.

[122] VERSAVEL G. *Passendale 1914-1918,* Passendale, 1968, p. 155-162 ; NA WO32/21171 *50th Anniversary of the Battle of Passchendaele,* 1967.

[123] GAZ *Gulden Boek van de Gemeente Zonnebeke.*

[124] What follows from here is based on various brochures, press clippings and hand notes kept in the Memorial Museum Passchendaele 1917, in collection of Raoul BLANCKAERT-CARREIN (Passendale) and in the personal archive of Franky BOSTYN.

First published in Great Britain in 2007 by
Pen & Sword Military
An imprint of
Pen & Sword Books Ltd
47 Church Street
Barnsley
South Yorkshire
S70 2AS

ISBN 978 1 84415 693 1

A CIP catalogue record for this book is available from the British Library

Printed and bound in Slovenia
By DZS – Grafik, Ljubljana

Pen & Sword Books Ltd incorporates the Imprints of Pen & Sword Aviation, Pen & Sword Maritime,
Pen & Sword Military, Wharncliffe Local History, Pen & Sword Select, Pen & Sword Military Classics and Leo Cooper.

For a complete list of Pen & Sword titles please contact
PEN & SWORD BOOKS LIMITED
47 Church Street, Barnsley, South Yorkshire, S70 2AS, England
E-mail: enquiries@pen-and-sword.co.uk
Website: www.pen-and-sword.co.uk